AGAINST AND FOR CBT

TOWARDS A CONSTRUCTIVE DIALOGUE?

EDITED BY

RICHARD HOUSE

and

DEL LOEWENTHAL

PCCS BOOKS

Ross-on-Wye

First published in 2008

PCCS BOOKS Ltd
2 Cropper Row
Alton Road
Ross-on-Wye
Herefordshire
HR9 5LA
UK
Tel +44 (0)1989 763 900
www.pccs-books.co.uk

Against and For CBT: Towards a constructive dialogue?

A CIP catalogue record for this book is available from the British Library

ISBN 978 1 906254 10 0

Cover design by Old Dog Graphics
Printed by Athenaeum Press, Gateshead, UK

CONTENTS

CLINICAL PERSPECTIVES

EPISTEMOLOGICAL AND RESEARCH PERSPECTIVES

POLITICAL AND CULTURAL PERSPECTIVES

THE FOLLOWING ARE REPRODUCED WITH THE KIND PERMISSION OF THE PUBLISHERS:

AMERICAN PSYCHOLOGICAL ASSOCIATION:
Chapter 5, Woolfolk, R. and Richardson, F. (1984) 'Behavior therapy and the ideology of modernity', *American Psychologist*, 39 (7): 777–86.

TAYLOR AND FRANCIS, UK:
Chapter 2, Mansell, W. (2008) 'Commentary on contexts of CBT: a weak case against a straw man but a strong case for an informed debate about how to improve access to effective psychological therapies', *European Journal of Psychotherapy and Counselling*, 10 (3): 261–9.

Chapter 4, Hemmings, A. (2008) 'Critiques of CBT', *European Journal of Psychotherapy and Counselling*, 10 (3): 271–9.

Chapter 7, Lees, J. (2008) 'Cognitive behavioural therapy and evidence-based practice: past present and future', *European Journal of Psychotherapy and Counselling*, 10 (3): 187–96.

Chapter 8, Bracken, P. and Thomas, P. (1999) 'Cognitive therapy, Cartesianism and the moral order', *European Journal of Psychotherapy and Counselling*, 2 (3): 325–44.

Chapter 11, Winter, D. (2008) 'Cognitive behaviour therapy: from rationalism to constructivism?', *European Journal of Psychotherapy and Counselling*, 10 (3): 221–9.

Chapter 13, Strong, T., Lysack, M., and Sutherland, O. (2008)'Considering the dialogic potentials of cognitive therapy', *European Journal of Psychotherapy and Counselling*, 10 (3): 207–19.

Chapter 19, Guilfoyle, M. (2008) 'CBT's integration into societal networks of power', *European Journal of Psychotherapy and Counselling*, 10 (3):197–205.

Chapter 20, Proctor, G. (2008) 'CBT: the obscuring of power in the name of science', *European Journal of Psychotherapy and Counselling*, 10 (3): 231–45.

Chapter 21, Pilgrim, D. (2008) Reading 'Happiness: CBT and the Layard thesis', *European Journal of Psychotherapy and Counselling*, 10 (3): 247–60.

Chapter 22, Snell, R., (2007) Book review, *European Journal of Psychotherapy and Counselling*, 9 (2): 231–9.

TAYLOR AND FRANCIS, USA:
Chapter 15, Bryceland, C. and Stam, H. (2005) Empirical validation and professional codes of ethics: description or prescription?', *Journal of Constructivist Psychology*, 18: 131–55 .

WILEY:
Chapter 9, Milton, J. (2001) 'Psychoanalysis and cognitive behavioural therapy: rival paradigms or common ground?', *International Journal of Psychoanalysis*, 82: 431–47.

ACKNOWLEDGEMENTS

First and foremost we would like to thank our many contributors for their good humour, patience, and commitment in working with us to develop this book and bring it to fruition: namely (in alphabetical order): Arthur C. Bohart, Patrick Bracken, David Brazier, Christy Bryceland, Isabel Clarke, Michael Guilfoyle, Adrian Hemmings, John D. Kaye, Paul Kelly, John Lees, Mishka Lysack, Warren Mansell, Jane Milton, Paul Moloney, Fred Newman, Stephen Palmer, David Pilgrim, Gillian Proctor, Frank C. Richardson, Andrew Samuels, Robert Snell, Henderikus J. Stam, Tom Strong, Olga Sutherland, Philip Thomas, Keith Tudor, David A. Winter, and Robert L. Woolfolk.

Secondly, we would like to acknowledge the many rich and enabling conversations with staff and doctoral students of the Research Centre for Therapeutic Education, Roehampton University's weekly Thursday evening Post-existential practitioner programme – including Erik Abrams, Onel Brooks, Julia Cayne, Angela Gillard, Sue Stephenson, Di Thomas, and Val Todd; and particularly, at the book's inception, Robert Hart for his initial inspiration. We would also like to single out for particular mention Dennis Greenwood and Robert Snell for their generous help in reviewing an early draft, and Rhiannon Stamp for helping to keep the project on track; all, again, from the Research Centre for Therapeutic Education.

Finally, our warm thanks to Maggie Taylor-Sanders and Pete Sanders of PCCS Books, who have worked so understandingly and flexibly with us; and to Wendy Leung and Janet Remmington of Taylor and Francis, publishers of the *European Journal of Psychotherapy and Counselling* (in which the basis of several of the book's chapters first appeared) for their co-operation.

ABBREVIATIONS

ACT	Acceptance and Commitment Therapy
AI	Artificial intelligence
APA	American Psychological Association
BPS	British Psychological Society
CAT	Cognitive Analytic Therapy
CBT	Cognitive-behaviour therapy
	Cognitive-behavioural therapy
	Cognitive behaviour therapy
	Cognitive behavioural therapy
CCT	Client-centred therapy
CPA	Canadian Psychological Association
CT	Cognitive therapy
DBT	Dialectical Behaviour Therapy
DoH	Department of Health
EBM	Evidence-based medicine
EBMWG	Evidence Based Medical Working Group
EBP	Evidence-based practice
EST	Empirically Supported Treatments
ESVT	Empirically Supported/Validated Treatments
IAPT	Improved Access to Psychological Therapies
ICS	Interacting Cognitive Subsystems
MCBT	Mindfulness-based Cognitive-Behaviour Therapy
NHS	National Health Service
NI[H]CE	National Institute for Health and Clinical Excellence
PCSR	Psychotherapists and Counsellors for Social Responsibility
PCT	Person-centred therapy *or* personal construct therapy
TCC	*Les therapies cognitivo-comportementales*
TEACCH	Treatment and Education of Autistic and Related Communication- handicapped Children
UKCP	United Kingdom Council for Psychotherapy

FOREWORD

Andrew Samuels

In the past few years, there have been some robust and enlivening engagements in the psychotherapy world between those favouring a major shift in the balance of available therapeutic help towards CBT, and those, like myself, who have long championed the importance of pluralism and diversity in the field. I take it as axiomatic that competition and bargaining are in some sense unavoidable, and even valuable, in terms of competing approaches to psychotherapy, or any other praxis (my book *The Plural Psyche* was all about this). If such pluralism is cancelled out by professional putsch or Government fiat, then the contribution psychotherapy can make to social justice and social policy will be muted.

It is therefore hardly surprising that what I (and many others) have objected to is the expectation that we will take CBT's allegedly scientific status as incontrovertible, accepting implicitly that it need not be exposed to the kind of pluralistic competition to which all other therapy modalities are ongoingly and rightly subject.

One of the main strengths of this welcome new collection is that it provides us with many cogent and convincing arguments for, at the very least, questioning the epistemological underpinnings and the methodological validity of the 'evidence-based' ideology in which CBT and its supporters have become accustomed to basking. We have long needed a systematic and incisive taking-apart of the case for positivistic Randomalised Controlled Trial and related methodologies. For too long, these have been uncritically accepted as being the 'gold standard' by which therapeutic experience should be measured. This book presents compelling arguments for a more reflective and considered methodological exploration.

Nearly all therapists agree that the relationship formed with the client or clients is at the core of what they do. CBT has recently begun to take a more concerted, creative, and non-mechanistic interest in the therapeutic relationship, and some have spotted an opportunity for an alliance between CBT and other therapies therein. But there is still little in the CBT literature about the power dynamics of the therapy relationship. Moreoever, the crucial, often decisive part played by the therapist's subjectivity is dangerously under-recognized. In CBT, the therapist and patient/client tend to be seen as what the jargon calls 'unified subjects' – monolithic agents with all that we know about external and internal difference and diversity smoothed out. A number of the chapters in this book shine a very revealing light on these lacunae.

It is also refreshing that the book faces head on (e.g. in David Pilgrim's chapter) the linked political and ethical questions that arise when psychotherapy is given – and slavishly accepts – a social-engineering or economistic mission (getting clients back into the workforce, off benefits, and so on). Certainly, a close reading of this book will decisively undermine any remaining claim that the inexorable rise of an allegedly value-free CBT in modern Western societies has nothing to do with political and economic interests. I am reminded here of the mediaeval notion of *trahison des clercs*, resurrected in the 1920s to mean the betrayal of their ideals and calling on the part of intellectuals and professionals in search of material gain.

Of the many other critical themes highlighted and skilfully developed in the book, I would like to mention just two that have especial resonance with my own interests and practice. First, there is what I perceive to be the silence of CBT around questions of meaning and purpose that are absolutely central to the contemporary clinical project of psychotherapy. I do not think the situation is changed much when an attempt is made to bolt on a bit of meaning in the case of mindfulness-based cognitive therapy. It is sometimes difficult to imagine how on earth CBT's 'model of the person' and the kinds of spiritual practices entailed in mindfulness could conceivably sit together – and sceptics like myself can easily find ourselves wondering whether this reversal on the part of CBT is not in fact driven by insuperable problems within its mainstream application. Jung, following Heraclitus, wrote of *enantiodromia*, the way things swing to their opposite when they have become too one-sided to survive unaltered. Sometimes, this leads to fruitful fusion; sometimes, to an ersatz outcome; sometimes, to the secret dominance of one of the elements in the equation, appearances to the contrary notwithstanding. *Enantiodromia* always requires penetrating analysis.

Another – and somewhat predictable – concern is CBT's lack of any perspective on, or consideration of, the unconscious, especially the creative unconscious. This in turn touches upon quite fundamental questions about the possibilities and limitations of agency and autonomy. To address these questions, we need to locate CBT and its model of the person in terms of the evolving history of ideas. A claim is made for the success of conscious and realistic control of 'thought' at the very moment when the *Zeitgeist* is redolent with a ubiquitous sense of perpetual and unmanageable risk and the consequent inevitability of political failure. We should invoke the Trade Descriptions Act! This book provides the reader with ample food for thought in addressing these questions.

In closing, I want to say as a pluralist that I am delighted to know of another competing Foreword to my own from a major figure in the field, Stephen Palmer, who I believe is far more favourably disposed to CBT than myself. I also greatly welcome the three substantial chapters in this book that make a case for CBT. I believe there needs to be a great deal more of such engagement before we can begin to assess just what common ground, if any, the different therapy approaches are able to inhabit. But I welcome most of all this splendid new book in itself; it promises to open up a crucial and long-overdue dialogue, and introduce the associated 'battle for the soul' of therapy work itself. Battles over praxis naturally involve polemic, and here, once again, I turn to Heraclitus, who told us that Polemos (war, strife, conflict) is 'the Father of all and the King of all'. How this battle unfolds – including its possible truces, armistices, treaties, and subsequent alliances – is an essential prerequisite for our work reaching the kind of maturity to which we individually and collectively aspire.

FOREWORD

POLEMICS AND COGNITIVE BEHAVIOUR THERAPY

Stephen Palmer

As I write this foreword, I have mixed feelings. I've just read yet another somewhat negative article about cognitive behaviour therapy published today in a national UK newspaper (Leader, 2008). Four pages of print are given over to one person's perspective.

Whether cognitive behaviour therapy practitioners or researchers like it or not, their decades of hard work focusing on what helps people overcome depression and anxiety-related disorders as efficiently as possible has sometimes been perceived as a threat or challenge to other practitioners. Like any other therapeutic approach, there have often been negative views about cognitive therapy, rational emotive behaviour therapy, and now, more latterly, cognitive behaviour therapy; but I suspect what appears to have thrown this therapy into the limelight, or perhaps the lion's den, is the British Government's interest in evidence-based practice; more specifically, its funding of cognitive behaviour therapy training with its launch of the Improving Access to Psychological Therapies (IAPT) initiative; and the National Institute for Health and Clinical Excellence (NICE) recommendations for its use for depression and anxiety-related disorders. One other factor could be the impending Health Professions Council registration of psychotherapists and counsellors. It's a period of much change and development in the UK therapeutic world after years of relative stability, with counselling and psychotherapy being loosely regulated by professional bodies. It's no wonder that an effective therapy for particular disorders and problems can trigger so much angst, derision, and bad feelings. The question I asked myself when I started to read this book was, will it be any different to the harsh polemical views I've read previously?

Going back in time, in 1995 I cited a number of factors which could influence the potential increase in the use of cognitive behaviour approaches over the subsequent decade. I was convinced that the increased public awareness of the effectiveness of cognitive counselling for various specific problems, reiterated many times in the media, paralleling the increase in cognitive-behaviourally based self-help books, would bring the approach into public consciousness. The demand for research-based cost-effective counselling in medical and work settings was increasing, and cognitive behaviour therapy could easily be applied to these brief therapy settings. Finally, at that time cognitive therapists and counsellors could at last be accessed by members of the public on national registers such as that of the United Kingdom Council for Psychotherapy.

I concluded my section of the article by predicting that there would be

> 'a steady increase in the use of cognitive approaches in Britain over the coming years as it becomes more easily available, and the desire for brief and effective

> counselling continues to grow, fuelled by both the service providers and, more importantly, the consumer.'
>
> (Palmer and Szymanska, 1995: 306)

Over a decade later, I think that my limited powers of clairvoyancy were not far off the mark, although I did not envisage the Government of the day providing so much financial backing for the implementation of a national therapeutic training programme for health practitioners.

In this book, the various authors have provided their own interesting perspective and framework when discussing different aspects relating to the cognitive behaviour approach, and some have taken a broader perspective of psychotherapy, seeing it within the social, cultural, post-modernist, and political milieu. In places, the therapy described resembles what I know as cognitive behaviour therapy, and in other places it is not the therapy I recognize and practise. However, this challenge reminds us how our personal *Weltanschauung* may differ from other psychotherapist's views. It's an exciting aspect of this book.

In the future when we look back at this decade, cognitive behaviour therapy may be seen as one of the symbols of the current *Zeitgeist*. Yet the third wave of cognitive behaviour therapy seems to be preparing itself for the next *Zeitgeist*. As a therapeutic approach, like the English language it is constantly developing, acquiring and integrating new ideas, many underpinned by research, and adapting to the requirements of the day. Unlike some approaches, it is not moribund, nor held back by dogma. Its commonsense, pragmatic approach will continue to have wide appeal, regardless of how it is viewed within the counselling and psychotherapy professions.

REFERENCES

Leader, D. (2008) 'A quick fix for the soul', The *Guardian*, G2, 9 September: 6–9.

Palmer, S. and Szymanska, K. (1995) 'An introduction to cognitive therapy and counselling', *Counselling: Journal of the British Association for Counselling*, 6 (4): 302–6.

Chapter 1

INTRODUCTION

AN EXPLORATION OF THE CRITICISMS OF CBT

Richard House & Del Loewenthal

INTRODUCTION

In the United Kingdom at the start of the twenty-first century, critical reflection on the place of cognitive behaviour therapy (CBT) in current therapeutic practice, and in the prevalent cultural discourse around well-being and 'happiness' (Layard, 2005), has garnered substantial (and not always flattering) media attention (e.g. Hope, 2008). These developments have dominated the kinds of impromptu discussions in which therapists commonly engage with each other about 'developments in the field'. In other European countries, such as France (see Miller, 2006; Snell, Chapter 22, this volume), and even further afield, for example Australia (see Kaye, Chapter 14, this volume), there is also a developing critical discourse around CBT. Yet what is the precise nature of these criticisms; and are they any more than the defensive arguments of vested interest groups whose over-long held privileges are being threatened? Or even the envious attacks of the displaced and the superceded in therapy's 'free' market?

We are being somewhat provocative here, of course. Yet in our experience, CBT has certainly tended to become the unwilling target – a convenient kind of cultural whipping-post, even – upon which disgruntled therapists of each and every hue have tended to project their current dissatisfactions, whatever their origin; and we certainly do not excuse ourselves from having occasionally 'used' CBT in such a less-than-mature way.

In some senses we do believe CBT to have received an unfair press, and to date, there has been little systematic and concerted attempt within the specifically *academic* therapy literature to engage thoughtfully with the controversies around CBT. In this book, then, we aim to address this previous lack by initiating a robust yet (as we hope and intend) constructive dialogue about CBT's place on the modern therapy landscape and within the wider culture.

As co-editors of *Against and For CBT*, we of course have our own views about CBT, which are located toward the critical end of the debate – ranging between, on the one hand, the view that CBT as *one approach amongst many* within a rich plurality of different approaches is fine – particulary for those who cannot bear the thought of thoughts coming to them – though disastrous as *the* main approach for a whole society (DL); and on the other, to the fundamental questioning of the assumptive (modernist) world-view that underpins CBT's foundational theory and practice (RH). Yet, we would like to think that we are both also committed to embracing a questioning, deconstructive sensibility in our work – and not least toward our own cherished and taken-for-granted assumptions and prejudices; so in this book, we have actively welcomed an open and mutually respectful dialogue between some of CBT's most articulate critics, and several of CBT's many able theorists and practitioners. It will not serve either 'side' if each merely snipes at the other from deeply entrenched positions and defences, without each, at the very least, making a genuine effort to understand the other's position.

'NORMAL SCHISM' IN THE PSYCHOTHERAPY WORLD? ...

The psychotherapy world has historically been riven by schism and, at worst, scarcely containable internecine warfare (e.g. King and Steiner, 1992; see also Dryden and Feltham, 1992; Feltham, 1999) – and it seems to us that recent struggles in and around CBT are merely the latest manifestation of such conflicts. This leads us in turn to say a few words about our chosen book title. Some colleagues have expressed surprise at, *Against and For CBT*, in that it suggests 'sides' and schism, and is potentially divisive. Our own view is that for some years, there has indeed been an all-too-real, eminently tangible 'paradigm war' going on in the therapy field, and we certainly don't wish to hide behind any 'mom 'n apple pie' political correctness in somehow denying that reality, or pretending everything is fine and that 'we all love each other *really*'! For such a position would be to deny the very real conflicts over power, resources, and (professional) identity that many of our contributors illuminatingly write about in this book. Moreover, our question-mark ('?') in the book's subtitle is also telling – for we believe it to be very much an open question, given the scale of the vested interests and competitive resource-issues at stake in what is an environment of comparative scarcity, whether *any* such rapprochement and shared understanding will ultimately be possible. In our view, we would not be doing the field any service at all to pretend that real-world schism and bad feeling doesn't exist, when they quite demonstrably do.Take the highly topical issue of research, for example. CBT has recently and very rapidly become the battleground upon which a veritable 'paradigm war' (Kuhn, 1962) is playing itself out, between 'modernist' and 'post-modernist' views on what legitimate and appropriate research into the psychological therapies might look like. From our own quasi-post-modernist position(*-which-is-not-one*), for example, we believe that Randomized Controlled Trial (RCT) methodology is open to a range of compelling challenges which, in our view, have never been satisfactorily responded to – namely, that (cf. Bohart and House, Chapter 16, this volume):

- its statistical methodology hides, through the comparison of means, what actually happens *to individuals* in the trial – meaning, for example, that there may easily be some people in both groups who are worse off after 'treatment';
- RCT methodology therefore ignores the different responses of different individuals to the same treatment, so that, as Heron argues, it 'cannot help with the everyday question, "What is the treatment of choice for this individual patient?"' (1996: 198; cf. Hemmings, Chapter 4);
- it tends to ignore the powerful effect of mind on body, and the latent phenomenon of self-healing;
- RCT methodology simply assumes the validity of its univariate approach, which separates out the single treatment variable from all other influences to assess its causal impact (as

if real, lived life were like that); thus, for example, the interplay of differences in the extent and quality of therapist experience, the nature and extent of their supervision, etc., etc... are not 'variables' that are able to be fully considered;

- it objectifies suffering as a 'thingified' process, reifying 'external' causal influence and ignoring subjective illness categories experienced and made sense of by the patient/client, and ignoring the meaning or tacit intentionality of the illness;
- RCT methodology ignores the possibility that its so-called 'statements of fact' (including variable specification and measurement) may inevitably be theory- and value-laden, and can only be formulated *within a pre-existing (and self-fulfilling) set of theoretical assumptions*, which can then so easily become a circular proving of what was assumed to exist at the outset (cf. Parker et al., 1995);
- The populations studied through RCTs are different to the ones that present for therapy; and finally
- The methodology usually assumes fixed treatment goals, which are only applicable to some modalities.

Hemmings (Chapter 4) and others in this book add further to the fascinating debate about the place of RCT and other 'positivist' methodologies in psychotherapy research. This can be seen as part of a wider discussion which is only starting to re-emerge, on 'What is research?' (see, for example, Loewenthal and Winter, 2006; Loewenthal, 2007). We would tend to follow Lees's approach (Chapter 7) in advocating a paradigmatic meta-view that attempts to locate and account for our historically and culturally specific methodological procedures within the context of the evolution of consciousness (Crook, 1980; Tarnas, 1991), if we are to gain a reflexive purchase on those methods and, hopefully, deepen and widen them (see also House and Bohart, Chapter 17).

Research methodology is just one of the central themes with which the chapters in this book grapple, in attempting to identify and clarify the various points of difference that exist between CBT and its critics, and just what might be at stake in legislating or choosing between those different positions.

OPENING UP A DIALOGUE?

As a way into opening up a long overdue dialogue – which included a conference on CBT held at Roehampton University in November 2008 – we offer some contextualizing questions under several key headings – questions which are variously addressed in the following chapters. It is the full engagement with these questions which we regard as essential if we are to make collective progress beyond the rather unhelpfully polarized positions that the 'pro' and 'anti' CBT camps have commonly occupied to date. As we will see, there are also some significant reservations from within the CBT field itself, such as the claim that it was never intended as just a short-term approach; while on the other hand, it is claimed by some CBT proponents that developments within CBT have more than answered what are claimed by them to be increasingly caricatured and outdated concerns. We have therefore organized below what are some hopefully evocative and pertinent questions, from the following perspectives: Paradigmatic, Clinical, Epistemological and Research, and Political and Cultural.

PARADIGMATIC PERSPECTIVES

- Is it helpful to attempt to locate CBT within wider paradigmatic perspectives on 'modernity' and 'post-modernity'? (for example, à la Lees, Chapter 7; and Woolfolk and Richardson, Chapter 5, this volume).
- To what extent is it possible to get to the root of the foundational/metaphysical differences between the world-views of CBT and other therapy approaches? – and can we at least respectfully 'agree to differ' about those metaphysical assumptions, and then track through what the implications are for therapy practice that necessarily stem from those paradigmatic differences?
- To what degree, if at all, can 'modernist' CBT, on the one hand, and therapies influenced by post-modern thinking on the other, be commensurable and able to converse with one another? – and if a 'good-enough' degree of commensurability is not achievable, then *what is to be done*?

CLINICAL PERSPECTIVES

- First, as a relatively unified approach to therapy practice, to what extent is the category 'CBT' a coherent, valid catgory – or is there greater diversity *within* the category than its assumed unitary status implies?
- To what extent might critics of CBT be setting up a 'straw-man' category?
- What model of therapeutic change underpins CBT, and to what extent does that model of change differ from that of other modalities?
- What does it mean to say that CBT 'works' – and to the extent that it does, can we say how much this is down to *CBT-specific* characteristics, and how much down to the kinds of relational 'common factors' across *all* modalities that some researchers have identified (e.g. Hubble et al., 1999; van Kalmthout et al., 1985), or to its being a culturally sanctioned vehicle for healing in 'Late Modernity' (e.g. Frank and Frank, 1991)?

EPISTEMOLOGICAL AND RESEARCH PERSPECTIVES

- What counts as valid research in reaching a view about CBT's efficacy? And how do we legislate or discriminate between different research ontologies and methodologies?
- Can we reach some kind of agreed consensus across the field about what an appropriate methodology researching into therapy experience and efficacy might look like? And what are the implications if such a consensus proves to be impossible to reach?
- How can we appropriately include *clients' voices* in our discussions about CBT, and how it is experienced by clients?
- How do we satisfactorily approach any possible trade-off that might exist between effectiveness, cost, and diversity in therapy practice?

This latter question then leads naturally on to …

POLITICAL AND CULTURAL PERSPECTIVES

- To what extent, if at all, is it fair to cast CBT as a 'quick-fix' therapy approach which is being pushed for wider economic, Treasury-driven motivations (the so-called 'happiness' agenda – Layard, 2005; see Pilgrim, Chapter 21)?
- What is the balance of responsibility between policy-makers, the CBT field itself, and the 'modernist' *Zeitgeist* for the way in which CBT has increasingly been made into *the* prevailing therapy of 'choice' within modern Western societies?
- What understanding of power as a social and political process does CBT subscribe to, if any? And how does CBT respond to its critics around questions of power?
- Can and should the influence of economics and a political agenda be kept out of the consulting room? And what are the implications of this for practitioners, clients, and for society more generally?

These various questions only begin to scratch the surface of the issues thrown up by the CBT question – and a close reading of the following chapters will doubtless throw up a long list of further questions that should surely be exercising a critically minded psychotherapy world at this key moment in the evolution of the field.

THE BOOK'S CHAPTERS IN SUMMARY

Now to the book's chapters themselves. We will give somewhat greater descriptive attention to the three chapters written by authorities on and proponents of CBT, as they hold a minority (though highly significant) position in relation to the chapters in the book as a whole.

In the first of the three chapters from authors sympathetic to CBT, '*What is CBT really …?*', WARREN MANSELL argues that many of CBT's critics woefully misrepresent CBT as actually practised. Whilst usefully attempting to account for what is indeed a very common picture painted of CBT by its detractors, Mansell is nonetheless greatly impressed by the various book contributors' 'breadth of scope and vision achieved through considering the societal and philosophical context of psychotherapy'. For Mansell, CBT proposes that the most effective method of facilitating change is 'to help them [clients] to become aware of their conscious experience of meaning-making'.

In the course of his chapter, Mansell sets about debunking what he sees as some of the myths surrounding CBT. Thus, for example, he makes the point raised by other contributors, that whilst CBT is often perceived as 'a single, knowable entity', in reality this is not the case. Rather, CBT has developed 'through the reciprocal interplay of theory, research, and clinical observation'. Another example is that of the scientific rationale for CBT – with Mansell claiming that CBT's support stems from 'a convergent range of diverse methodologies', and not merely from randomized controlled trials, as is commonly claimed.

There have always been diverse influences on CBT, and in his Figure 2.1, Mansell provides us with a useful illustration of the historical and theoretical origins of CBT, illustrating both the diversity of origins of CBT, and also its diversity of contemporary directions. Far from being a 'stand-alone treatment', Mansell sees CBT as embedded in a wide system of knowledge and discourse: as he writes, psychological therapy in general is, for him, 'a way of thinking and relating to other people, and is not a stand-alone intervention'. Following a spirited challenge to what he sees as the CBT 'straw man' that its critics commonly set up, he questions in particular what he terms 'the authoritarian archetype' of CBT.

Mansell concludes that there is emerging agreement that CBT as currently practised will not exist in the future – for it is constantly changing in relation to new research. He maintains that this will necessitate 'shifts in the nature of CBT and related psychotherapies during this process, and the evolving solution will lie in identifying commonalities rather than differences across approaches, and placing them within a coherent and clear scientific framework.'

The second CBT 'response' sees Isabel Clarke, in her chapter '*The case for CBT: a practical perspective from the NHS front line*', addressing the broader arena of politics and power within which much of the debate in this book takes place, drawing upon her own fascinating practitioner perspective and experience to illuminate this context. *Inter alia*, Clarke offers a very persuasive case for the pursuit of so-called 'third-wave' approaches to CBT (with the latter, incidentally, receiving substantial attention throughout the book). A notable and particularly useful feature of the chapter is how Clarke describes her own particular journey into CBT practitionership.

The author emphasizes that there are many points made by the book's other contributors about the current status of CBT with which she can agree; but she offers an important perspective that is often missing in discussions around the power dimensions of CBT – namely, the question of the dynamic around specifically *health-service* politics, centring in turn on the question of how to control the medical establishment.

Clarke's experience of the impact of Layard on the ground is also described as 'overwhelmingly positive', in terms of 'shifting the emphasis of service provision away from the purely medical (i.e. medication and ECT) and in favour of talking therapy' – with Layard having successfully argued for a huge injection of resources into the talking therapies which no-one else before him had ever achieved. She also considers the concept of 'evidence base', acknowledging how it has been used in the NHS power struggle, and recognizing its deployment as polemic – and the shortcomings of some of the research on which, for instance, the NICE guidelines are based.

Clarke certainly sees elements of rigidity in more 'old-fashioned' CBT approaches, which focused upon 'dysfunctional thinking' and relied more heavily upon thought challenging; and she acknowledges that this can be a particular problem where the therapy is given by people with inadequate training and supervision. She recognizes the dangers where it is perceived that *anyone* can deliver CBT after a brief training and with no specialist supervision – as she points out, especially popular with cost-cutting NHS managers! At worst, the 'therapist' is trying to 'fix' people's thoughts in the same way that the doctor uses medication to 'fix' symptoms.

For Clarke, 'there are historical factors, independent of the merits of the case, that have led to the extremes of the present situation', and she certainly does not wish to defend 'a monolithic situation where CBT was the only therapy available'. She points out how a number of the book's chapters do cite the 'elasticity' of CBT, and the 'third wave' as an example of such flexibility.

Then, in the final of these CBT 'response' chapters, ADRIAN HEMMINGS engages in a carefully non-partisan way with the various critical chapters. In what is a notably non-defensive and penetrating discussion, Hemmings comments on the alleged technical nature of CBT, and the notion that collaboration in CBT praxis easily becomes a form of coercion and an expression of power. He also reflects upon CBT's relationship with powerful institutions, and looks carefully at the contested notion of 'evidence-based treatment', especially in relation to Randomized Controlled Trial (RCT) methodology in effectiveness research. Finally, Hemmings looks at some of the issues arising from the current social and political context in which CBT is embedded.

His overall discussion is couched within three overriding backdrop concerns: current research that examines so-called 'therapist effects'; the Improving Access to Psychological Therapies (IAPT) training; and, again, the assumption that CBT constitutes a single entity. He concludes that, in his view, CBT has a great deal to offer the psychotherapy community: 'it is popular with clients and many therapists alike, as well as having a focus on behaviour change, along with insight and awareness. It also has considerable efficacy research to support it.' However, he is at pains to emphasize that it is by no means the only game in town; and CBT theorists are urged not to ignore the research evidence on therapist effects on outcome – a point with which many of this book's contributors would no doubt concur. Moreover, any such identified effects should, according to Hemmings, not be 'reduced to simply delivering a set of techniques' – which he sees as being 'so against the spirit of enquiry and curiosity that is prevalent in so much of CBT theory'.

In the first of the critical chapters, in the initial section on 'Paradigmatic perspectives', we are delighted to be reproducing in this book what is a classic in the critical literature – namely, ROBERT L. WOOLFOLK and FRANK C. RICHARDSON'S 1984 paper '*Behaviour therapy and the ideology of modernity*', in which they analyse the moral and epistemological underpinnings of behaviour therapy from a socio-historical, hermeneutic perspective; and consider the implications of behaviour therapy's close associations with modern ideological positions, having shown them to be closely linked with the values and patterns of thought characteristic of modernity. A notable feature of this chapter is an extensive and illuminating 'revisiting' of the original paper by the authors in a substantial postscript, written specially for this volume – in which they provocatively, and perhaps not altogether unfairly, conclude that: 'Although the CBT of today differs in some ways from the behaviour therapy of the middle of the previous century [which they extensively critique earlier in their chapter – eds], it retains [behaviour therapy's] simple-minded sensibility, with all the advantages and disadvantages of a simplistic world-view'.

In his chapter '*CBT in historico-cultural perspective*', DAVID BRAZIER then panoramically explores how the foundational ideals of our culture fared through what he argues to be a gradual erosion of standards and mounting ruthlessness, posing what is a key question for modern culture – who is caring for our souls now, and how are they to do so? Brazier illustrates how, in the broad psychology field, the three basic ideals of humanistic psychology, psychoanalysis, and behaviourism are still clearly represented, yet now exhibit marked rivalry one with another, and a notable lack of integration. For Brazier, 'a turn toward the romantic side of our culture would be welcome', but 'real healing requires more' – and specifically, for him we need to seek a higher-level integration, such that the three dimensions of psychoanalysis, humanistic psychology, and cognitive-behaviourism are able to work together.

In the third of the chapters on paradigmatic perspectives, '*The essence of cognitive behaviour therapy: past, present, and future*', John Lees develops a fresh and novel 'evolution of consciousness' perspective on CBT, locating it historically within 'modernist' Enlightenment thinking – maintaining that 'our understanding of such developments can be transformed if we adopt a broader evolutionary perspective'. For Lees, there are many signs that human consciousness is evolving 'beyond materialistic instrumental rationality to more integral, more spiritual' states of consciousness (quoting Jenny Gidley); and experience is already beginning to be understood in more diverse and subtle ways.

In the final chapter in this section, '*Cognitive therapy, Cartesianism, and the moral order*', Patrick Bracken and Philip Thomas seek to demonstrate the particular culture-bound (Western) 'philosophy of mind' that is implicit within the cognitivist framework, and the ethical assumptions which accompany it. For them, CT's presentation as a 'scientific' enterprise, free of value orientations, means that many of its implications remain unarticulated – raising major problems for the 'exporting' of therapies based on cognitivism to other parts of the world. Bracken and Thomas also draw upon the work of the Foucauldian Nikolas Rose, and the work of the great philosophers Martin Heidegger and Ludwig Wittgenstein, to question whether 'the moral order predicated upon the philosophy of mind implicit in cognitivism is the sort of order to which we should aspire'.

In the first of the book's chapters on 'Clinical perspectives', '*Psychoanalysis and cognitive behaviour therapy: rival paradigms or common ground*', Jane Milton suggests that contemporary enthusiasm for cognitive behaviour therapy reflects our longing for swift, rational help for psychological suffering. The author suggests that, in comparison to a psychoanalytic model, a cognitive model certainly *appears* to be attractively and reassuringly commonsensical, but is far less complex and, arguably, less complete, compared with an approach which acknowledges and works with far more than what is consciously cognitive. Such limitations, Milton implies, necessarily limit CBT's potential explanatory and therapeutic power.

In his intriguingly titled chapter '*Person-centred therapy, a cognitive behaviour therapy*', Keith Tudor then questions, this time from a person-centred perspective, some of the politics surrounding CBT, including the trend toward short-termism. Tudor also examines some of the research evidence of CBT in comparison with other therapies and especially person-centred therapy (PCT); and, as a counterpoint to the apparent dominance of CBT in the psychology of cognition and behaviour, he elaborates the cognitive and behavioural aspects of PCT in a way that perhaps points a way toward at least some kind of rapprochement, and even commonality, between the two approaches.

In the third clinical-perspectives chapter, '*Cognitive behaviour therapy: from rationalism to constructivism?*', David A. Winter looks at CBT's evidence base, arguing that there are alternative constructions possible as to what constitutes valid evidence – and which in turn, at the very least, calls into question the treatment guidelines that have been adopted from what Winter sees as CBT's narrowly conceived evidence base. Winter concludes that although there is little doubt that cognitive behaviour approaches are effective with some problems, 'it can no longer be confidently asserted that these therapies are generally more effective than any other, or that their effects are due to their specific cognitive behaviour ingredients' (cf. Bohart and House, Chapter 16, this volume). He also suggests that the widely averred diversification of CB therapies might 'render them so indistinct that one might ask when is such a therapy no longer cognitive-behavioural'.

DEL LOEWENTHAL'S chapter *'Post-existentialism as a reaction to CBT?'* then seeks to describe a place for exploring notions of well-being at the start of the twenty-first century that is in contrast to the increasing cultural dominance of cognitive behaviour therapy, and to offer an alternative post-postmodern place where we might still be able to think about how alienated we are through valuing existential notions such as experience and meaning, whilst at the same time questioning other dimensions. For Loewenthal, in proposing post-existentialism in part as a reaction to CBT, he is not doubting that some clients will benefit more from CBT; and furthermore, nor that in terms of conventional costings, it can be more cost effective. But he is concerned about *any* therapy approach being a 'totalizing move'; and 'whilst there have been the dangers of this previously with both psychoanalysis and humanism, CBT (despite the unheard protestations of some of its adherents) appears particularly susceptible to being used in this way'. Certainly, what post-existential approaches and their forerunners have in common is 'a concern with the humanness of the human, which is different from a managerialism based on very narrow notions of so-called evidence with which CBT has come to fit so well'. We need to beware of 'making CBT culturally dominant in a way such that we can no longer recognize ourselves, and are too frightened at any possibility of doing so'.

In the final chapter on clinical perspectives, *'Dialogic Cognitive Therapy?'*, TOM STRONG, MISHKA LYSACK, AND OLGA SUTHERLAND then present some constructive dialogical and discursive ideas for fruitful ways in which CBT might be more productively conceptualized and developed in the future. They refer to 'the continued development and hybridization of CBT', elaborating on their term 'dialogical' practice, relating it to meaning-making, particularly in how therapist and client make sense of and respond to each other in the clinical situation. The authors go on to discuss how the relationships between cognition, discourse, and dialogue can generatively inform the practice of CBT. Far from being uncritical, however, they also set out their objections to 'reducing the practice of CBT to narrow cultural and therapeutic prescriptions', concluding that 'it is fundamentally important to locate the practice of CBT as a dialogic practice, as an activity that takes place in "streams" of respectful and generative dialogues'.

The next section, on 'Epistemological and research perspectives', begins with JOHN D. KAYE'S *'Thinking thoughtfully about cognitive behaviour therapy'*, in which the author sets out to critique some of the governing paradigm's limits and consequences, and to question the privileged status granted to CBT in modern culture and, increasingly, within clinical practice. In the process, Kaye considers so-called 'third-wave' innovations such as Mindfulness-based Cognitive Behaviour Therapy (MCBT) and Acceptance and Commitment Therapy (ACT). He concludes that those innovators within the broad CBT family who have had the courage to step outside of the original limited view of therapy, and the impoverished conceptualization of human ways of being imposed by traditional cognitive behaviour thinking, deserve great credit – for our clients 'deserve better than the rigid methodologies imposed by the unimaginative guardians of the original CBT faith'.

This chapter is followed by CHRISTY BRYCELAND AND HANK STAM'S *'CBT and empirically validated therapies: infiltrating codes of ethics'*, in which the authors address the role played by codes of ethics, and the way in which they are used to legitimize and support empirically validated therapies, arguing that it is to misuse codes of ethics 'to co-opt them into debates that are essentially professional and bureaucratic, but are not primarily about proper or ethical conduct'. Bryceland and Stam conclude that Empirically Supported Therapies (ESTs) may become confused with the ends of therapy, and that 'by finding their way into the language of ethics, [they] have already pushed the debate in a direction inimical to the aims of psychotherapy'. In their foreclosing of 'other' therapies, the very enterprise of therapy itself is thereby threatened 'by promising technique above what is, after all, a moral vocation'. Any consequent demise of non-CBT therapies, they maintain, 'would greatly restrict the discourse of therapy'.

Next, in their two co-written chapters titled '*Empirically supported/validated treatments as modernist ideology...*', ART BOHART AND RICHARD HOUSE offer a wide-ranging discussion of the findings and practices of psychotherapy research in relation to what they see as contesting (and possibly 'incommensurable') modernist (CBT) and more 'post-modern' paradigms, and their associated therapeutic approaches. Their first chapter looks closely at the famous 'Dodo bird' verdict and the question of manualization, and their second looks at the kinds of research issues that might prevail under an alternative paradigm that privileged (for example) the subtle and the intuitive over the overtly cognitive and control-orientated. Bohart and House argue, *inter alia*, that the advocates of empirically supported treatments fail to recognize the paradigm-bound and assumption-laden nature of their position, and so uncritically assimilate and deal with objections to their approach from within their own paradigmatic position, rather than at least attempting to step outside it.

In the final chapter on epistemological and research perspectives, '*Where is the magic in cognitive therapy? – a philo/psychological investigation*', FRED NEWMAN explores the connection between cognitive therapy and common sense, the relationship between common sense and science, and the interrelationships between the cognitive, the linguistic, and the post-modern turn. We are treated to an engagingly discursive philosophical *tour de force* that incorporates such philosophical giants as Quine, Davidson, Wittgenstein, Vygotsky, and Searle – and, of course, Fred Newman and Lois Holzman's own distinctive brand of 'social therapy'. As always with Newman's writings, the reader is in for a journey of many fascinating philosophical twists and turn – and not least, the post-modern one.

In what is the first chapter of the final section of this book, on 'Political and cultural perspectives', '*CBT's integration into societal networks of power*', MICHAEL GUILFOYLE writes from a deconstructionist, post-structuralist perspective in looking penetratingly and critically at CBT's involvement in the networks of power that constitute modern Western social formations. In his view, therapists 'must be mindful of being reduced to government agents, to agents of governance' – a quandary that CBT practitioners are now facing. For 'therapies that perform such a reproductive function are useful institutional partners', with all therapists risking 'becoming inadvertent agents of "social control", a position that we should surely resist'. Guilfoyle hopes that the CBT world will resist the tempting invitations to perform such a function – yet, he maintains, such resistance might 'involve undermining the very games of power to which CBT's technologies are so well suited'.

Next, in '*CBT: the obscuring of power in the name of science*', GILLIAN PROCTOR builds thoughtfully upon her previous important work on power, forcefully to argue that CBT practice is saturated with what are normally unarticulated and even contradictory conceptions of power which, at worst, can cultivate client compliance rather than autonomy. She suggests that the most important factor that may determine whether or not the client experiences a therapy relationship as successful or not is the dynamics of power in the therapy relationship. If, she cautions, therapists fail to think carefully about how to avoid domination during psychotherapy, then how can we expect clients to feel more in control through a therapy experience? Proctor concludes that there are few if any questionings of the assumptions of power within CBT theory and practice – and that CBT needs 'to look realistically and honestly at the dynamics of power in therapy relationships. For without such an inquiry, CBT therapists are in danger of obscuring their power, and of not taking an ethical stance to avoid domination and abuse'.

DAVID PILGRIM then offers a critical and wide-ranging review essay of Richard Layard's influential book *Happiness*, in his chapter '*Reading "Happiness": CBT and the Layard thesis*'. For Pilgrim, whilst Layard's *Happiness* proposes a persuasive case for 'upstream' causes of mental-health problems, including a critique of modern consumerism, he makes a much less persuasive argument 'for therapeutic social engineering in response to psychological casualties of these socio-economic forces'. Pilgrim looks closely at Layard's selective use of evidence and his 'naïve realism', the 'technical fix' offered by CBT and its implicit faith in psychiatric knowledge, and the various weaknesses of CBT. He argues strongly that child protection should also be incorporated into Layard's frame of reference, and invites us to think critically about the limits of forms of therapeutic social engineering: for 'instead of more CBT for the masses, we might imagine and seek to create other possibilities. These could include ordinary forms of social solidarity, mutual support for the survivors of childhood adversity, and [new, non-neo-liberal] political initiatives'.

Next comes ROBERT SNELL'S chapter 'L'Anti-Livre noir de la psychanalyse: *CBT in French/Lacanian perspective*', in which Snell considers the 'invasion' of France by Anglo-Saxon-dominated CBT, and the attack on the 'irony, scepticism, and disrespect, definitively anti-modern' nature of French psychoanalysis. A new marketing onslaught is outlined: viz. 'TCC', which is being presented to health administrators and insurance companies as 'a fully developed product, meeting European and international standards, and offering rapid and low-cost solutions to the majority of psychological problems'. In the process, Snell shows us, psychoanalysis in France 'finds itself under new and fierce attack'. In summarizing *L'Anti-Livre noir de la psychanalyse* so comprehensively, Snell illustrates how the struggle so eloquently dramatized in the book has a far wider relevance. Thus, there is a political and ideological battle going on in the UK, as in France and elsewhere; and 'psychotherapists of whatever persuasion, if they are concerned to oppose the technologizing of the human spirit, need to take its arguments very seriously indeed'.

In the final chapter of this section, '*Beck never lived in Birmingham: why cognitive behaviour therapy may be a less helpful treatment for psychological distress than is often supposed*', whilst acknowledging that recipients of CBT can often report that it is helpful, PAUL MOLONEY AND PAUL KELLY nonetheless question claims of CBT researchers that it is the most effective form of therapy. Instead, they suggest that the current popularity of CBT may at least equally reflect the needs and values of the mental-health professions, and of those political and social institutions that help to mould their aims and activities. Thus, for the vast majority of clients who are struggling with noxious environmental circumstances, the emphasis of CBT on alleviating distress through challenging thoughts may be profoundly misleading for client and therapist alike. On this view, to gaze into clients' 'cognitions' while largely ignoring their world, experience, and history 'may have the effect of suggesting that oppression doesn't matter; it's just the way in which you view it that counts'. Maloney and Kelly conclude that although there may be aspects of CBT that are helpful, 'the practice and theory of CBT can only be seen as effective if viewed from the standpoint of those in positions of socio-economic privilege'.

TOWARD A CONVERSATION, RATHER THAN NONE AT ALL?

What we hope the following chapters succeed in doing is opening up a long-overdue conversation about the place of CBT within the evolving field of psychotherapy and counselling. This is a conversation which, to date, has been conducted via disgruntled snatches and polemical broadsides rather than in anything like the kind of systematic and respectfully open way that would be needed for light and insight (rather than heat and prejudice) to be generated and reflectively thought about.

The kinds of questions raised in this book are ones which we *all* surely need to face and reflect upon, if the unpleasantness of current schisms in the field are to lose at least some of their divisiveness, and we hope this can take us toward the kind of engaged and constructive, mutually respectful dialogue, and tolerance of difference, that we believe are important values of the work we do in this peculiar activity of ours.

REFERENCES

Crook, J. (1980) *The Evolution of Human Consciousness*, Oxford: Oxford University Press.

Dryden, W. and Feltham, C. (eds) (1992) *Psychotherapy and Its Discontents*, Milton Keynes: Open University Presss.

Feltham, C. (ed.) (1999) *Controversies in Psychotherapy and Counselling*, London: Sage.

Frank, J. D. and Frank, J. B. (1991) *Persuasion and Healing: A Comparative Study of Psychotherapy*, 3rd edn., Baltimore: Johns Hopkins University Press.

Heron, J. (1996) *Co-operative Inquiry: Research into the Human Condition*, London: Sage.

Hope, J. (2008) 'Talk therapy for the depressed "could be wasting millions"', *Daily Mail*, 7 July: 25.

Hubble, M. A., Duncan, B. L., and Miller, S. D. (1999) *The Heart and Soul of Change: What Works in Therapy*, Washington, D.C.: American Psychological Association.

King, P. and Steiner, R. (eds) (1992) *The Freud–Klein Controversies, 1941–45*, London: Routledge.

Kuhn, T. S. (1962) *The Structure of Scientific Revolutions*, Chicago: Chicago University Press.

Layard, R. (2005) *Happiness: Lessons from a New Science*, London: Penguin Books.

Loewenthal, D. (2007) *Case Studies in Relational Research*, Basingstoke: Palgrave Macmillan.

Loewenthal, D. and Winter, D. (2006) *What is Psychotherapeutic Research?*, London: Karnac Books.

Miller, J.-A. (ed.) (2006) *L'Anti-Livre noir de la psychoanalyse*, Paris: Editions de Seuil.

Parker, I., Georgaca, E., Harper, D., and McLaughlin, T. (1995) *Deconstructing Psychopathology*, London: Sage.

Tarnas, R. (1991) *The Passion of the Western Mind: Understanding the Ideas That Have Shaped Our World View*, London: Pimlico.

van Kalmthout, M. A., Schaap, C., and Wojciechowski, F. L. (eds) (1985) *Common Factors in Psychotherapy*, Lisse, The Netherlands: Swets & Zeitlinger.

Woolfolk, R. L. and Richardson, F. C. (1984) 'Behavior therapy and the ideology of modernity', *American Psychologist*, 39 (7): 777–86; reproduced as Chapter 5, this volume.

CHAPTER 2

WHAT IS CBT *REALLY*, AND HOW CAN WE ENHANCE THE IMPACT OF EFFECTIVE PSYCHOTHERAPIES SUCH AS CBT?

WARREN MANSELL

At its core, CBT focuses on how we attend, interpret, reason, reflect, and make sense of inner and outer events. It is a journey into personal meaning-making at the edge of mind and objective experience. It emerged from ego-analytic psychotherapy in the 1950s and 1960s, routed itself in academic psychology, and began the slow process of scientific investigation during the 1970s (Padesky, 2004).

One way to clarify CBT is to emphasize its focus on conscious mental processes. While it acknowledges that unconscious processing clearly exists, it proposes that the most effective method of engaging with a client and facilitating change is to help them to become aware of their conscious experience of meaning-making. Beck (1976) contrasts cognitive therapy with psychoanalysis, which emphasizes the therapist's interpretations of the client's unconscious motivations; with early behaviour therapy, which takes the measurement of observable behaviour as the only source of valid data; and with neuropsychiatry, which locates the source of the client's problems within a disordered neurochemical process. According to Beck (1976), all three approaches ignore the validity of the client's own reports. CBT therapists have to listen very carefully to what clients are saying because this is the information they use and share with the client to try to understand their lives better, and to work with them on improving their lives in line with the clients' own goals.

Yet contemporary CBT is not quite the same as Beck's early cognitive therapy. CBT is often perceived as a single, knowable entity, but this is not the case. It evolves through the reciprocal interplay of theory, research, and clinical observation (Salkovskis, 2002). It is often claimed that the only scientific support for CBT is from randomized controlled trials, but again, this is not the case. The scientific support for CBT derives from a convergent range of diverse methodologies, including qualitative and quantitative case studies, case series, experimental manipulations, statistical modelling, diary studies, qualitative interviews, service-user reports, practice-based evaluations, and, last but not least, randomized controlled trials.

Figure 2.1 provides a simplified illustration of the historical and theoretical origins of CBT. This diagram illustrates both the diversity of origins of CBT, and the diversity of contemporary directions for CBT. It has always had diverse influences. There is an emerging consensus that we are in the process of a 'third wave' of CBT that builds upon the first (cognitive therapy and behavioural therapy) and second (CBT) waves. While the second (and some of the first) waves are clearly still present and practised daily, the third-wave approaches represent a range of advances in CBT that have incorporated diverse theoretical and philosophical

This chapter is an extended version of a paper published in the *European Journal of Psychotherapy and Counselling*, Volume 10 (3), 2008: 261–9.

Figure 1. A simplified diagram of the development of contemporary CBT. Unbroken lines represent strong influences; dotted lines represent mild influences. Theoretical influences are printed in italics. All other labels refer to forms of CBT.

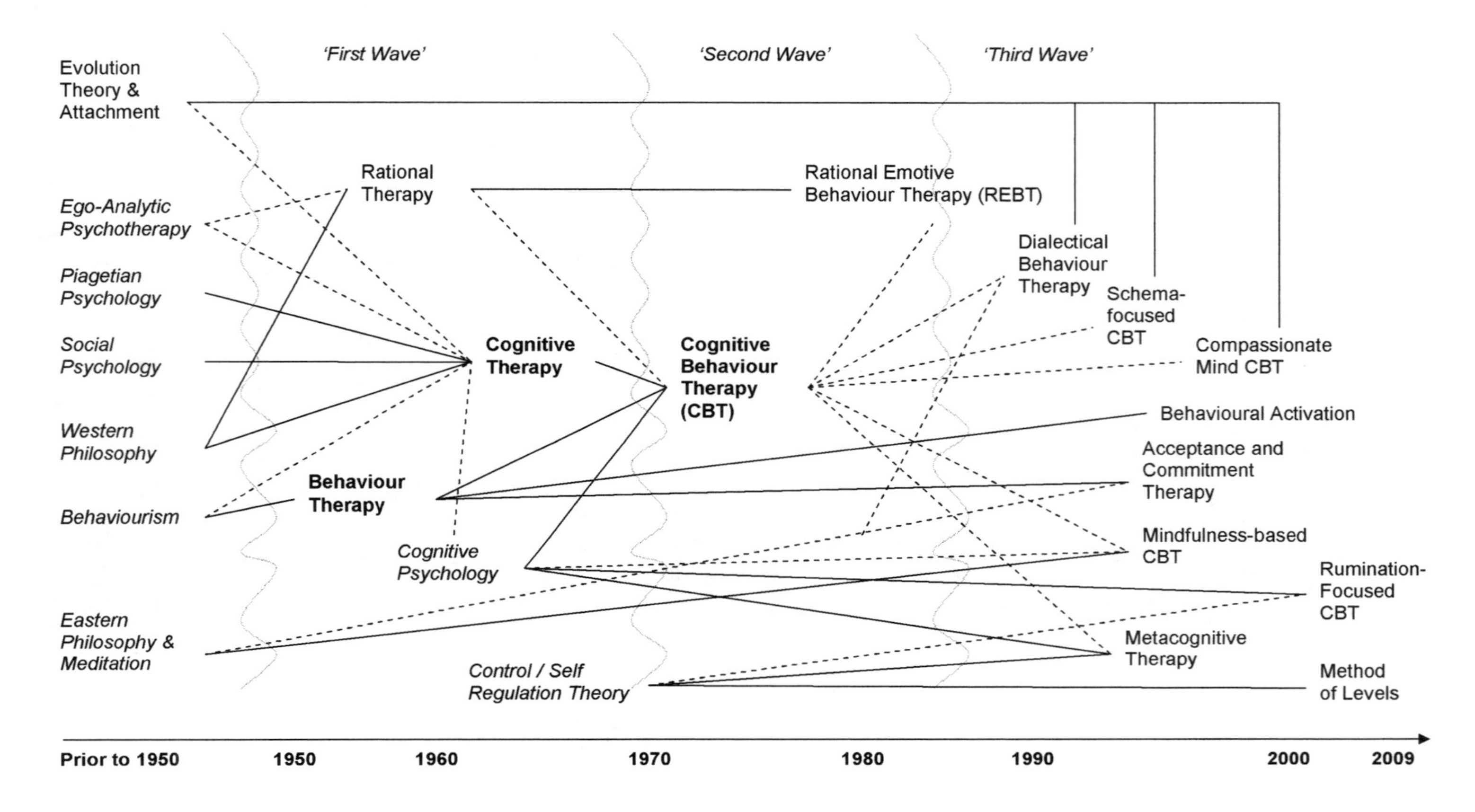

approaches. Clearly, CBT is not a stand-alone treatment, but is embedded within a wide system of knowledge and discourse. This is reflected in current definitions. At present, the UK CBT organization defines CBT as follows: 'The term "Cognitive behaviour Therapy" (CBT) is variously used to refer to behaviour therapy, cognitive therapy, and to therapy based on the pragmatic combination of principles of behavioural and cognitive theories" (BABCP, 2008).

Perhaps most importantly, how would you know that you were having a CBT session? Admittedly there are no absolute criteria, but in general you would expect:

1. to be working together, collaboratively, with the therapist in an equal power-sharing arrangement;
2. to be able to talk about your current problems and set your own goals for the therapy;
3. to be asked questions about your current and recent thoughts, feelings, memories, mental imagery, behaviours, environment, and social experiences;
4. to work together with the therapist to work out a map or 'formulation' for how these factors might combine negatively to contribute to problems, or positively to help you recover and improve your quality of life;
5. to test out new ways of thinking and behaving to see if they are helpful; and
6. to be able to manage independently or fully recover after the therapy, and be offered the opportunity to return for 'booster' sessions in the future.

In the following chapters of this book, you will read many critical chapters on CBT. When reading many of these chapters, I must admit that I shuddered at how many of them have misrepresented CBT. I therefore urge you to read the original sources explaining CBT, rather than taking at face value the accounts that are provided here. If at all possible, take the opportunity to see an experienced and well-trained CBT therapist at work, either live or on video. That's how you will know what it involves.

Despite my shock at how CBT was described in the following chapters, I do resonate with many of the reasoned concerns about where the field of psychological therapy is heading. I felt simultaneously frustrated by their inaccurate rendering of the therapy that I practise and research, and yet humbled and impressed by the breadth of scope and vision they achieved through considering the societal and philosophical context of psychotherapy. In fitting with these conflicted judgements, I would first like briefly to clarify the misrepresentation of CBT represented in *Against and For CBT*, and update the readers on the generally accepted view of the principles and context of CBT. Next, I will move on to tackle the more important question of how we are all to pursue both quality and quantity within the current expansion of evidence-based psychological therapies.

THE STRAW MAN AND THE AUTHORITARIAN ARCHETYPE OF CBT

Across the chapters as a whole, as I read further, I felt that I began to visualize an extreme characterization of CBT. The image generated in my mind by these chapters was of a CBT therapist who was controlling, over-rational, medicalizing, and only concerned with employing techniques and seeking evidence in the services of a power-hungry and oppressive Western state. My first thought was that this is a 'straw man', often employed to beef up an argument. Then I realized that this image resonated with a cultural myth within our society that was just as much of a Western social construction as the power structure that the chapters described. This person was the rigid, authoritarian, and punitive leader. I recognized this figure from a dozen Dickens stories, from Big Brother in George Orwell's *1984*, right up to 'The Man' in *School of Rock*, and a couple of po-faced penguins in *Happy Feet*. Then, I thought of those traits again to get a better picture – controlling, ruled by logic, a pawn of the state – and the image came to mind: it was the Enforcement Droid (ED-209) from *Robocop*. I could imagine his emotionless commands: 'You have 20 seconds to comply with cognitive restructuring!'. I am not surprised that these chapters had such a critical tone. Any self-respecting person would run for the door rather than spend more than a second with such a fear-provoking and uncompromising individual!

So I began to think – is this *really* the face of CBT? Or is it some pervasive Jungian archetype that is being mistaken for CBT? Alternatively, is it the critical inner mentality that we try to understand and challenge in CBT itself (Gilbert, 2005)? Suffice it to say, I do not recognize Enforcement Droids in any of my colleagues and friends who are CBT therapists, nor do I even tend to see any of these worrying properties in isolation. Why not? One possibility is that I do not mix with the kinds of CBT therapists who fit this description, yet they do exist. A second, overlapping, possibility is that there is a cultural view of CBT that spreads through the health services, academia, and the public independently of CBT therapists. A third possibility is that I have learned about CBT later than the authors of these critical chapters, and so I am unfamiliar with the early rigid origins of the approach that surely must have plagued the 1970s and 1980s. But this explanation does not fit with my reading of the primary sources of this period, which do not reflect this aversive image.

The explanation I favour is that the principles and practice of CBT guard against this grotesque abstraction, and in fact encourage the opposite traits of a CBT therapist: an approachable, emotionally attuned, empowering, real person who understands the reciprocal relationship between theory, research, and practice, and has only the concerns of the client at heart. For this reason, I particularly liked the chapter by Strong, Lysack, and Sutherland (Chapter 13) on the dialogic potentials of cognitive therapy. They point to the potential value of CBT as an empowering psychotherapy that provides open space for clients to develop personal meaning in their life, and share knowledge within a collaborative relationship.

It is important to acknowledge that the (mis)representation of CBT in the chapters varied widely from almost none to extreme. Rather than write any more on this issue, a reference and two tables will suffice. In describing the 'Myths about CBT', Paul Gilbert provides a succinct rebuttal of previous inaccurate representations of CBT that is available online (Gilbert, 2008). Here (in Table 2.1), I summarize several of the properties of CBT that were suggested in the chapters, and contrast them with the documented properties of CBT within the Cognitive Therapy Rating Scale (Young and Beck, 1980). This scale is currently accepted internationally as the means for assessing the competence of cognitive behaviour therapists (Kazantis, 2003). Thus, if the scale is being used as it was designed, then CBT therapists will emerge as truly collaborative, client-centred, formulation-led practitioners who facilitate clients' own alternative perspectives, and empower them to take

Table 2.1
Key suggested characteristics of CBT compared to the established characteristics and their systematic assessment during CBT training

Suggested characteristic of CBT	*Chapter author*	*Established feature of CBT*	*Indicator of a high level of therapist competence on the Cognitive Therapy Rating Scale (Young & Beck, 1980)*
Rationalist; cold and logical; the therapist models 'correct' thinking or guides to the 'right' solution	Winter, Proctor, Bracken & Thomas, some aspects of Strong et al.	Constructivist; clients consider multiple perspectives and are helped to form their own solutions	"The cognitive therapist often uses exploration and questioning to help patients see new perspectives." "Therapist was especially adept at using guided discovery during the session to explore problems and help patient draw his/her own conclusions." "The cognitive therapist should display optimal levels of warmth, concern, confidence, genuineness, and professionalism."
The therapist controls the session	Winter, Proctor, Kaye, Tudor	The balance of the control dynamic but generally equal or client-centred	"Collaboration seemed excellent; therapist encouraged patient as much as possible to take an active role during the session (e.g. by offering choices) so they could function as a 'team'."
Technique driven	Winter, Bohart & House some aspects of Milton	Formulation driven and particularly attuned to the interpersonal processes in the session. Techniques are used within this context.	"Therapist seemed to understand the patient's 'internal reality' thoroughly and was adept at communicating this understanding through appropriate verbal and non-verbal responses to the patient (e.g. the tone of the therapist's response conveyed a sympathetic understanding of the patient's 'message'). Excellent listening and empathic skills."

control of their own lives. This fits with the evidence. In a range of studies, CBT patients rate their therapists higher on various relationship variables (e.g. interpersonal skills, accurate empathy, support) than psychodynamic therapists, and their level of 'active listening' was equivalent to insight-oriented therapists (see Keijsers et al., 2000). CBT therapists are active, empathic people who enable clients to solve challenging life problems.

Table 2.2 summarizes the contexts of CBT that were suggested by some of the chapters. In each case, they are contrasted with perspectives from mainstream clinicians and researchers within the CBT field. Clearly, everyone does not speak with exactly the same voice, but these chapters would be deemed generally acceptable and consistent with CBT. Thus, it would seem quite possible to characterize CBT as a radical, innovative, socially aware, and scientifically grounded discipline of psychotherapy that questions received dogma about the nature of psychological distress, works to challenge rigid power arrangements within society, and yet takes a measured view of its strengths and limitations.

For the rest of this chapter, I would like to focus on the points of agreement I have with some of the book's contributors, and the important implications for the future of the psychological therapies.

TAKING STOCK OF THE BROADER PERSPECTIVE ON PSYCHOTHERAPY

Putting the chilling chimera of *CBT Enforcement Droid-209* to one side, the chapters in *Against and For CBT* have a refreshing interpersonal and societal angle on the process of training, practising, evaluating, and disseminating effective psychological therapies. They also address critical philosophical and scientific issues that may help us to understand where psychological therapy is heading. I will comment on a number of the key themes that are introduced within them.

INTERPERSONAL PROCESSES ARE IMPORTANT AND ARE CLOSELY RELATED TO INTRAPERSONAL (COGNITIVE) PROCESSES

Several of the chapters emphasize the importance of social context and interpersonal factors. The chapter by Strong et al. (Chapter 13) makes a strong case that our internal dialogue is shaped by our interactions with others. They are concerned that there may be a shift to seeing psychotherapy as focused on establishing objective truth and ignoring the reality of clients' lives that are potentially rich with social interaction. Bracken and Thomas (Chapter 8) are also very concerned that CBT ignores the social reality of people's lives in its focus on internal mental processes, as are Moloney and Kelly in Chapter 23. Similarly, in their Chapter 16, Arthur Bohart and Richard House note the importance of interpersonal processes in therapy – the moment-to-moment sensitivity during therapy, and the therapist's ability to respond in that moment; and in Chapter 10, Keith Tudor emphasizes the key importance of the 'other' in therapy and in everyday life, within a person-centred perspective.

Within CBT, therapist trainers also have a concern that CBT therapists maintain their attention to the social context, both within and outside the session. For this reason, within CBT, therapists are encouraged to help their clients challenge the pervasive cultural beliefs that are counterproductive for them (e.g. 'I must be thin'; 'I must earn lots of money'), and provide them with the opportunity, often through imagery work and role play, to explore and rehearse opportunities to assert themselves and achieve their goals in real life, often within harsh or poverty-stricken environments. CBT is not seen as a replacement for good public health schemes and social planning – it is merely what the health service provides to the individual to allow them to cope with their situation given the circumstances, along with any other necessary support from other organizations, and any more radical changes afoot within the culture.

In addition, a significant amount of the training process for CBT involves building up the interpersonal skills in therapists that are required to maintain a good collaborative relationship. From a theoretical perspective, the importance of interpersonal processes is also actively pursued (e.g. Gilbert and Leahy, 2007). It remains to be seen whether the new large-scale training schemes can maintain these essential features of CBT, but we have assurances that this will be the case (Holland, 2008).

CONTROLLED TRIALS ARE CONTEXTUALIZED AND OFFER ONLY ONE SOURCE OF SCIENTIFIC SUPPORT

It was encouraging to see that in his Chapter 7, John Lees immediately recognizes that CBT is in practice person-centred, and incorporates flexibility in response to client need. However, he is concerned that the decisions of how to decide on the investment in a particular psychological therapy is based almost entirely on the apparent evidence base, over and above the consideration of the context of how that evidence base is constructed and defined. He makes an excellent case that how we define evidence now is likely to change in the future, as the philosophy of our culture and our outlook change. Bohart and House make several similar points in their Chapters 16 and 17, and in their Chapter 15, Bryceland and Stam explore the ethical dimensions of the apparent overemphasis on evidence-based treatment.

Within CBT, we have many of the same concerns as Lees, Bohart and House, and Bryceland and Stam. It is possible to hide behind that shiny veneer of an evidence base without scrutinizing one's own practice and being a true science-practitioner. Yet without the dynamic interface of theory, research, and practice and the drive of innovation, CBT would not be as well developed as it is today (Salkovskis, 2002). There is a concern that CBT will become freeze-dried in a certain image in order to match the requirements of the health system as a whole, rather than to continue its propensity to evolve and adapt.

I chime with Bohart and House in stating that the best evidence for a therapy is contextual: within one's own practice with one's own patients (Mansell, in press; Margison et al., 2000; Miller et al., 2004). Therefore, a normal part of the development of a new form of CBT is to establish its effectiveness in a variety of practice settings (e.g. Gillespie et al., 2002). Within CBT, we need to monitor not just the apparent competence of therapists, and their grasp of the core theory underlying their work, but also their personal impact on the outcomes that matter to their clients. To do this, we need to continue to evaluate the therapy and to examine its correspondence with theory, rather than to assume its efficacy, and change it in an ongoing fashion. Thus, while it is appropriate to allow certain evidence-based psychotherapies, like CBT, to be accredited by the health system, we need space for innovators who adapt and devise their own approaches from a firm cultural and scientific foundation.

Table 2.2
Suggested contexts of CBT compared to the perspectives within the mainstream

Suggested context of CBT in chapter	*Reference*
Superficial relationship with cognitive theory	Pilgrim
Based on Cartesian dualism	Lees; Bracken & Thomas; Moloney & Kelly
Justification largely based on evidence from RCTs	Lees; Bohart & House; Bryceland & Stam
Pathologizes distress as a disease entity	Pilgrim; Bohart & House
Requires a diagnosis	Lees
Considers only outcomes based on symptoms of psychiatric illnesses; a form of psychiatric treatment	Lees; Pilgrim
Complicit with contemporary power arrangements	Guilfoyle; Bracken & Thomas; Kaye; Moloney & Kelly
Therapist has the power, and takes control of factors such as number of sessions	Winter; Proctor
Often ignores the role of interpersonal processes and the social context	Strong et al.; Tudor; Milton; Bracken & Thomas; Woolfolk & Richardson; Moloney & Kelly
CBT claims always to be superior in efficacy to other forms of psychological therapy	Guilfoyle; Bohart & House; Kaye; Moloney & Kelly
Does not typically involve bringing unconscious material into awareness and integrating life experiences	Milton

CBT literature

Alternative perspective on the context of CBT	*Examples of references*
Ongoing, reciprocal relationship with cognitive theory	Brewin (1988)
Based on a monistic, integrative model of human functioning	Beck, Emery, & Greenberg (1985); Gilbert (2002)
Justified and developed through reciprocal links between theory, research, and practice	Salkovskis (2002)
Based on a continuum model of psychological distress	Beck (1976); Morrison (2001); Mansell, Morrison, Reid, Lowens, & Tai (2007)
Does not require a diagnosis	Ellis (1962); Harvey, Watkins, Mansell, & Shafran (2004); Mansell (2008)
Considers impact on overall quality of life and seeks opinions from service-users as to appropriate outcome measures	Knight, Wykes, & Hayward (2006)
Radical, innovative, and questions and transforms existing power structures	Padesky (2004)
Therapist strives to balance power and help client determine key components of the therapy such as number, length, and frequency of sessions	Giesen-Bloo, J., van Dyck, R., Spinhoven, P., et al. (2006)
Interpersonal processes have a reciprocal relationship with intrapersonal processes; social context forms part of the cognitive formulation	Strong et al. (this volume); Gilbert (2005)
CBT has a substantially wider, more consistent evidence base than other therapies, but it is accepted that its relative efficacy varies across studies	Veale (2008)
Negative *automatic* thoughts occur fleetingly until brought into awareness; counterproductive avoidance strategies push distressing material outside awareness; cognitive formulation incorporates life experience including trauma	Beck (1976); Ehlers & Clark (2000)

PSYCHOLOGICAL THERAPY IS A WAY OF THINKING AND RELATING TO OTHER PEOPLE, AND IS NOT A STAND-ALONE INTERVENTION

David Pilgrim (Chapter 21), along with Moloney and Kelly (Chapter 23), are concerned that as a culture, we are cultivating a desire for happiness through consumerism but failing to address the real causes of distress. According to Pilgrim, while Layard has ostensibly attempted to counter this trend, the process has been compromised by a number of factors, including a limited understanding of social factors and an overemphasis on the medicalization of distress.

Within CBT, there are similar concerns. There is a concern that service users, managers, and health professionals will see CBT as a stand-alone treatment within a system that does not necessarily adhere to its principles. But this is not possible to sustain. The equal relationship that therapists and clients have in CBT impacts on the clients' expectations for how they relate to other health professionals, and the multidisciplinary working of the contemporary health system necessitates a negotiated debate about how to work with service users. On the positive side, it is possible that the increasing prevalence of psychological therapists in these teams will help facilitate an approach of collaboration and service-user choice that is beneficial to the systems themselves (Kinderman and Tai, 2007).

PSYCHOLOGICAL THERAPY NEEDS TO CHALLENGE EXISTING COUNTERPRODUCTIVE POWER STRUCTURES

A valuable point to take from Michael Guilfoyle's Chapter 19 is a concern that psychological therapy can become complicit with existing power structures in society that are themselves toxic to mental health. John Kaye takes a similar stance in Chapter 14, as do Paul Moloney and Paul Kelly (Chapter 23).

Within CBT, we are aware of this uneasy alliance. On the one hand, it is fruitful to think that CBT can help people to return to work, as that is what most of our clients wish to do. On the other hand, if this evidence were to be taken to justify the maintenance of an increasingly work-orientated society, then it would not fit with the aims of CBT, which is essentially to help facilitate our clients' quality of life, as they choose to define it.

Similarly, it can be very fruitful when CBT is promoted within psychiatry, to widen access to effective psychological therapy. Yet in contrast to most in psychiatry, the CBT therapist strives (unsuccessfully at times, of course!) to maintain an equal balance of power in the relationship, and to refute notions of being 'the expert' in the role. Enabling recovery during CBT often necessitates questioning assumptions that many in the psychiatric profession have about the lifelong nature of mental-health problems, and the dependence on medication as a treatment.

As a whole, it appears that people involved in CBT embrace the fact that the therapy has become recognized and recommended by key organizations, but most of us would not wish this at the cost of losing the central principles of the therapy, and its agenda for empowering all individuals to recover from mental-health problems through what they have learned during the therapy.

CONTROL, PURPOSE, MEANING, AND NEEDS

Perhaps the most valuable contributions from this book relate to theories of human functioning, and in particular how psychological therapy addresses the fact that human beings are purposeful agents who have their own needs, who want to be in control of their lives and imbue it with personal meaning. For example, in Chapter 20 Gillian Proctor emphasizes the importance of gaining a 'sense of control' in one's life. Where there are power imbalances within therapy, the client's sense of control is compromised.

There is an increasing interest in how to quantify and assess shifts in personal meaning and sense of purpose within CBT (Brown et al., 2008). In practice, the CBT therapist strives to maintain a collaborative relationship, to use the therapy in the service of the client's own needs (via a client-driven goal list and agenda at the start of each session), and to explore the development of meaning within thoughts, behaviours, emotion, and the social context. As CBT becomes more available and highly disseminated, it is important that new trainees can fully grasp the notion of collaborative goal setting – the standard, while not always achieved, is a true balance in power, where the clients can express themselves freely by stating their own goals for therapy, and take control of their lives outside the session. In the future, the equal balance of control aimed for within CBT is likely to expand to wider areas, such as patient choice over the number, frequency, and duration of sessions (Carey, 2005).

In Chapter 5, Woolfolk and Richardson take issue with the assumption that behaviour therapy (and presumably CBT), as it is currently *theorized*, can genuinely help individuals to consider and pursue their own goals. They cite at least two reasons – that the methods of helping clients elicit goals is not part of the theory or empirical evidence upon which behaviour therapy relies, and that a linear model of events predicting further events will not provide the appropriate approach for such an intervention. This is an important issue for psychological therapies: they need to use a theory that explains the whole process of therapy, not simply one component that is presumed to be core, such as 'distorted thinking' or 'unconscious conflict'. What is more, we need a theoretical approach that incorporates and explains the role of features such as how clients set goals, and how they derive and maintain purposeful values in their life.

In his Chapter 10, Keith Tudor articulates Carl Rogers' (1951) theory of personality and behaviour, which fulfils some of these requirements. Rogers (1951: 491) stated, 'Behaviour is basically the goal-directed attempt of the organism to satisfy its needs as experienced, in the field as perceived'. Tudor explains therefore that we may understand behaviour as the best a client can do in any given moment, given his perception of his inner and outer environment. Rogers articulated several important premises of this kind, yet he did not produce a working theory.

Interestingly, in 1973 Carl Rogers endorsed a theoretical framework that was highly consistent with his premises – *Behavior: The Control of Perception* (Powers, 1973): 'Here is a profound and original book with which every psychologist – indeed every behavioural scientist – should be acquainted', commented Rogers. The basic premiss of this book was the same as Rogers' – that behaviour is the control of perception. Yet Powers (1973), with a background in engineering, provided a sophisticated mechanistic framework for how human functioning is managed and orchestrated from this first principle through networks of hierarchical control systems. Computer simulations are available that provide some of the best evidence for its validity (Powers, 2008).

The theory described in Powers' (1973) book, Perceptual Control Theory (PCT), has had wide implications, and it would not be accurate to align it exclusively to either a person-centred approach or indeed any other therapeutic approach. Yet it has contributed to some of the most recent advances in CBT. For example, it has been used to reframe and extend existing CBT approaches (Mansell, 2005; Mansell et al., 2007), influenced new therapies through its influence on theories of self-regulation (Watkins, 2008), and had a direct impact in terms of a new form of cognitive therapy – Method of Levels (MOL; Carey, 2008). Nevertheless, in the broad family of CBT therapies, PCT-related innovations form just a small part of the eclectic mix.

PSYCHOTHERAPIES MUST BALANCE THE NEED TO EMBRACE DIVERSITY WITH THE NEED FOR PARSIMONY AND COHERENCE

In line with the kind of innovations stated above, David A. Winter's Chapter 11 draws appropriate attention to the shift from a rationalist to a constructive approach within CBT. Whatever the debate concerning the exact starting-point, degree, and timescale of this shift, it is surely to be welcomed and maintained. Winter also points to the high degree of diversity within contemporary CBT to include mindfulness, acceptance, and commitment therapies, and interpersonal approaches such as compassionate-mind based CBT. In Chapter 14, John Kaye also reviews these progressions in CBT, and is aware that CBT is not a homogeneous static entity. Paul Moloney and Paul Kelly (Chapter 23) acknowledge this diversity as well.

The heterogeneity of CBT is a two-edged sword. The open, scientific, and pragmatic approach of CBT therapists has perhaps encouraged this eclecticism, and it provides us with a wide range of different styles of CBT for new trainees to select. On the other hand, it does provide a strain on the boundaries of how CBT is defined, as David Winter suggests. One potential solution is for researchers involved in CBT and other psychotherapies to alter their research approach. Instead of using methodologies and statistics that engage a competitive mode of comparing therapies, we need to explore commonalities across different therapies, and then try to identify the mechanisms for change – cognitive, behavioural, emotional, interpersonal, or otherwise – that are tapped by different approaches (Mansell, in press). This concurs with Bohart and House's take on the importance of moment-to-moment sensitivity in therapy (Chapter 16), and Jane Milton's emphasis in Chapter 9 on evocation of affect and the development of personal coherence. Ultimately, we need a consensual theoretical framework that explains the importance of these core features of effective psychological therapy.

SUMMARY AND CONCLUSIONS

Although targeted at CBT, I would suggest that the key themes of these contributions provide important points for any widely accessible form of psychological therapy. Namely, an effective and acceptable psychotherapy:

1. needs to consider the person in their social context and their immediate interpersonal interactions because of the close relationship with inner mental processes;
2. must be based on more than the standardized evidence base, because it needs to match the needs of the clients to whom it is targeted when put into practice in a particular context;
3. is likely to be at odds with a purely medical model of mental 'illness', and so needs to develop ways to accommodate to, or transform, its health-service context;
4. needs consistently to monitor the process of control, sense of purpose, and the balance of power during therapy so that clients can gain a perception of control in their lives; and

5. needs a coherent theoretical model to guide its core principles that evolves in a dynamic way in response to new evidence or new ways of thinking about that evidence.

Taking the family of CBT therapies as a whole, I see that they are tackling the above issues directly, *in tandem* with the popularization and dissemination of the therapy. This process of evolution is likely to be a rocky one, as the desire for immediate accessibility is pitched against the need to adhere to these, and other, key principles. There is an emerging acceptance that CBT as it is currently practised will not exist in the future – it constantly changes depending on new research (Veale, 2008). There will need to be shifts in the nature of CBT and related psychotherapies during this process, and the evolving solution will lie in identifying commonalities rather than differences across approaches, and placing them within a coherent and clear scientific framework. In order to manage this, CBT clinicians and researchers will need to communicate and collaborate with a range of professions, including non-CBT psychotherapists, to form a coherent account of how to help to manage psychological distress and facilitate people's quality of life and well-being. This edited book can be one step on the way, if we agree to leave the straw (or metal?) man on the sidelines, and take psychotherapy forward together.

Acknowledgements
Thank you to Paul Gilbert, Roz Shafran, Tim Carey, David Veale, and Rod Holland for their helpful comments on an earlier version of this chapter.

REFERENCES

BABCP (2008) 'What is CBT?', retrieved on 7 August 2008 from: www.babcp.com

Beck, A. T. (1976) *Cognitive Therapy and the Emotional Disorders*, New York: Penguin.

Beck, A. T., Emery, G., and Greenberg, R. L. (1985) *Anxiety Disorders and Phobias: A Cognitive Perspective*, New York: Basic Books.

Brewin, C. R. (1988) *Cognitive Foundations of Clinical Psychology*, Hove, Sussex: LEA Associates.

Brown, G. P., Roach, A., Irving, L., and Joseph, K. (2008) 'Personal meaning: a neglected transdiagnostic construct', *International Journal of Cognitive Therapy*, 1: 223–36.

Carey, T. (2005) 'Can patients specify treatment parameters? A preliminary investigation', *Clinical Psychology and Psychotherapy*, 25: 326–35.

Carey, T. A. (2008) 'Perceptual control theory and the method of levels: further contributions to a transdiagnostic perspective', *International Journal of Cognitive Therapy*, 1: 237–55.

Ehlers, A. and Clark, D. M. (2000) 'A cognitive model of posttraumatic stress disorder', *Behaviour Research and Therapy*, 38: 319–45.

Ellis, A. (1962) *Reason and Emotion in Psychotherapy*, Secaucus, NJ: Citadel Press.

Giesen-Bloo, J., van Dyck, R., Spinhoven, P., van Tilburg, W., Dirksen, C., van Asselt, T., Nadort, M., and Arntz, A. (2006) 'Outpatient psychotherapy for borderline personality disorder: randomised trial of schema-focused therapy vs transference-focused psychotherapy', *Archives of General Psychiatry*, 63: 649–58.

Gilbert, P. (2002) 'Evolutionary approaches to psychotherapy and cognitive therapy', *Journal of Cognitive Psychotherapy*, 16: 263–94.

Gilbert, P. (2005) *Compassion: Conceptualisations, Research and Use in Psychotherapy*, Hove, Sussex: Routledge.

Gilbert. P. (2008) *Cognitive Behavioural Therapy: A Guide to Purchasers*, www.babcp.com/members/cbt_for_purchasers.htm

Gilbert, P. and Leahy, R. L. (2007) *The Therapeutic Relationship in the Cognitive Behavioural Psychotherapies*, Hove, Sussex: Routledge.

Gillespie, K., Duffy, M., Hackmann, A., and Clark, D. M. (2002) 'Community based cognitive therapy in the treatment of post-traumatic stress disorder following the Omagh bomb', *Behaviour Research and Therapy*, 40: 345–57.

Harvey, A. G., Watkins, E. R., Mansell, W., and Shafran, R. (2004) *Cognitive Behavioural Processes across Psychological Disorders: A Transdiagnostic Approach to Research and Treatment*, Oxford: Oxford University Press.

Holland, R. (2008) 'Accreditation standards "to be maintained"', *CBT Today*, 38: 3.

Kazantis, N. (2003) 'Therapist competence in cognitive-behavioural therapies: review of the contemporary empirical evidence', *Behaviour Change*, 20: 1–12.

Keijsers, G. P. J., Schaap, C. P. D. R., and Hoogduin, C. A. L. (2000) 'The impact of interpersonal patient and therapist behavior on outcome in cognitive-behavior therapy: a review of empirical studies', *Behavior Modification*, 24: 264–97.

Kinderman, P. and Tai, S. (2007) 'Clinical implications of a psychological model of mental disorder', *Behavioural and Cognitive Psychotherapy*, 35: 1–14.

Knight, M. T. D., Wykes, T., and Hayward, P. (2006) 'Group treatment of stigmatisation and self-esteem in schizophrenia: a waiting list trial of efficacy', *Behavioural and Cognitive Psychotherapy*, 35: 304–18.

Mansell, W. (2005) 'Control theory and psychopathology: an integrative approach', *Psychology and Psychotherapy: Theory, Research and Practice*, 78: 141–78.

Mansell, W. (2008) 'Keep it simple – the transdiagnostic approach to CBT', *International Journal of Cognitive Therapy*, 1: 179–80.

Mansell, W. (in press) 'The seven Cs of CBT: a consideration of the future challenges for cognitive behaviour therapy', *Behavioural and Cognitive Psychotherapy*, doi: 10.1017/S1352465808004700.

Mansell, W., Morrison, A.P., Reid, G., Lowens, I., and Tai, S. (2007) 'The interpretation of and responses to changes in internal states: an integrative cognitive model of mood swings and bipolar disorder', *Behavioural and Cognitive Psychotherapy*, 35: 515–40.

Margison, F. R., Barkham, M., Evans, C., McGrath, G., Clark, J. M., Audin, K., and Connell, J. (2000) 'Measurement and psychotherapy: evidence-based practice and practice-based evidence', *British Journal of Psychiatry*, 177: 123–30.

Miller, S. D., Duncan, B. L., and Hubble, M. A. (2004) 'Beyond integration: the triumph of outcome over process in clinical practice', *Psychotherapy in Australia*, 10: 2–19.

Morrison, A. P. (2001) 'The interpretation of intrusions in psychosis: an integrative cognitive approach to hallucinations and delusions', *Behavioural and Cognitive Psychotherapy*, 29: 257–76.

Padesky, C. A. (2004) 'Aaron T. Beck: mind, man, and mentor', in R. L. Leahy (ed.), *Contemporary Cognitive Therapy: Theory, Research and Practice*, New York: Guilford Press, pp. 3–26.

Powers, W. T. (1973/2005) *Behavior: The Control of Perception*, New Canaan, Conn.: Benchmark.

Powers, W. T. (2008) 'Workshop 1: an introduction to Perceptual Control Theory', in P. S. E. Farrell (ed.), *Control Systems Group: International Conference 2007 Proceedings*, www.psych-sci.manchester.ac.uk/aboutus/events/csgconference/

Rogers, C. (1951) *Client-centred Counselling*, London: Constable.

Salkovskis (2002) 'Empirically grounded clinical interventions: cognitive-behavioural therapy progresses through a multi-dimensional approach to clinical science', *Behavioural and Cognitive Psychotherapy*, 30: 3–10.

Veale, D. (2008) 'Psychotherapy in dissent', *Therapy Today*, February: 4–7.

Watkins, E. (2008) 'Constructive and unconstructive repetitive thought', *Psychological Bulletin*, 134: 163–206.

Young, J. E. and Beck, A. T. (1980) 'Cognitive Therapy Scale', University of Pennsylvania, Philadelphia: unpublished manuscript.

Chapter 3

THE CASE FOR CBT:
A PRACTICAL PERSPECTIVE FROM THE NHS FRONT LINE

Isabel Clarke

INTRODUCTION AND CONTEXT

In writing a response to the criticisms of CBT in this book, I will first address the broader arena of politics and power in which this debate takes place. I am in agreement with the editorial introduction and a number of the contributors in identifying issues of power and resources as a crucial factor in the current prominence of CBT, but will add my own perspective on this context. I will then explain why and how I ended up as a CBT as opposed to any other sort of therapist, before tackling the philosophical and scientific substrate of CBT which is a focus of a number of the chapters. I will not respond to the various points raised in all the chapters, but hope to cover a representative selection of the arguments.

A number of the contributors have noted that CBT is far from monolithic, and in what follows, I am probably only representing my own take on the modality, though I will make clear what this is, and how it fits into the wider picture. As a therapist accredited by the BABCP, and who has published CBT papers in peer-reviewed journals, and presented sypmposia and a workshop at BABCP conferences, I do not consider myself a complete outsider.

To begin with, there are many points made by both the editors and contributors about the current status of CBT with which I can agree. As someone who studied history before coming into psychology in mid life, I need no persuading that power and economics lie at the root of most movements in human affairs. As a fan of Gilbert's (1992) ecological view of human interactions (i.e. we are a bunch of primates vying for position in the hierarchy), I have no problem with seeing a very basic power dynamic and struggle for resources behind the language of 'evidence base'. However, I do take issue with Moloney and Kelly's exposition of this power dynamic (Chapter 23). They suggest that CBT has been seized upon as a means of maintaining the position of the ruling class by redefining discontent with social conditions as internal pathology. I am not denying that there is no element of that, especially in the Layard initiative (on which, more later); but having worked in or around the National Health Services (NHS) since the 1980s (first as a member of a Community Health Council and then as an employee), I can identify another and more immediately relevant power dynamic in the rise of CBT and evidence-based therapy: this is the dynamic around specifically health-service politics, which centres on the dilemma of how to control the medical establishment. What follows is very much a personal perspective from the shop floor.

Britain's National Health Service (NHS) was achieved through Bevan's Faustian pact with the doctors. The introduction of General Management in the 1980s was an attempt to temper the medical grip on the system. It was unsuccessful; managers found themselves managing everyone apart from the doctors. Evidence-based practice and the NICE guidelines are the next strategy for exerting some degree of political control over the medical juggernaut. Until recently, the therapeutic modality embraced by psychiatry was psychodynamic. The promotion of CBT was therefore part of this strategy, as well as being – as I will argue below – a more sensible therapy for your average NHS punter than, in particular, the psychoanalytic branch of the psychodynamic modality. Many of the contributors to this book represent other, humanistic, existentialist, and person-centred therapies that are neither psychodynamic nor CBT. I see them as incidental casualties in this particular battle – they have been caught in the cross-fire.

THE LAYARD DEBATE

The Layard debate, which provides a timely occasion for this volume, introduces a whole other dimension. I completely agree with Pilgrim (Chapter 21) and all other commentators who have pointed out that Layard's idea that CBT will turn everyone on incapacity benefit into a happy worker is implausible. However, my experience of the impact of Layard on the ground is overwhelmingly positive in the direction of shifting the emphasis of service provision away from the purely medical (i.e. medication and ECT) and in favour of talking therapy – and this impact is extended beyond the primary care, single-diagnosis interventions of the pilot projects, and into the serious mental-health area in which I work. Layard has successfully argued for a huge injection of resources into the talking therapies. No-one else has ever achieved that before, to my knowledge, despite the insistent request by service users that they want to be listened to, and to be given an opportunity to make sense of their situation. Service users often also appreciate being given tools to take responsibility for their own emotional well-being. I appreciate that some may say they should be listened to by people other than CBT therapists. From my perspective, the first priority is the provision of a therapy resource, and I am not sympathetic toward complications that might stall this (as I have seen happen in the past as a result of intermodality rivalries).

While welcoming the Layard initiative, I can only agree with the contention of Moloney and Kelly, Pilgrim (Chapters 23 and 21, respectively), and others that therapy cannot cure the ills of a sick society, or transform the situation of an individual ground down by poverty, injustice, and a degraded environment. On the other hand, as a therapist I feel a bit powerless to fix the social malaise of contemporary life, but I do know how to help the people who are struggling with an adverse social situation to go about it more effectively and stop shooting themselves in the foot. Often people do not wish to avail themselves of this help. Their choice can be to anaesthetize themselves with substances, remain in the parallel universe of psychosis, or choose one of the other escape routes devised by human ingenuity in the face of an intolerable reality. I can only respect their choice, while remaining aware that each of these solutions carries with it severe consequences for their quality of life. So I continue to offer a way out of these siren so-called 'symptoms' toward more effective engagement with the very real challenges faced by most of the people I see. In this respect, I am in complete agreement with Pilgrim (Chapter 21) where he argues against therapy delivery being linked to diagnostic category, as it is in the main Layard initiative, and for the importance of deconstructing 'diagnosis'. This is my agenda entirely, as I explain in a number of my previous writings (e.g. Clarke 2008a).

CHOICE OF THERAPY MODALITY

To return to the debate between modalities; the choice of which therapy in which to train will be influenced by a variety of factors, including individual inclination, chance encounter, and the state of the market. However arrived at, it is a major decision entailing a considerable investment in time, emotional energy, effort, and often money. As a psychologist, I am familiar with the confirmatory bias research; once someone has made a decision, they will register information that confirms that decision, and filter out or discount information that supports the rejected options. The greater the cost of the decision, the stronger is the confirmatory bias. Choice of therapeutic modality is a decision that cuts to the heart of an individual's sense of identity. It is only to be expected that such choices will be vigorously defended.

That is the individual perspective. In the wider social context, there are complex mechanisms that decide how resources should be distributed. In the case of private therapy, the market decides, but the market will be influenced by the wider rhetoric. The looming issue of compulsory accreditation will also reach into the private sector. In the UK, the NHS is the major player, and it is here that the battle for resources is most evident. When I started work in a hospital Department of Psychiatry as a newly qualified clinical psychologist in 1992, the weight of psychotherapy resources was concentrated in the psychodynamic department, and of the three psychologists, one was psychodynamic, and two were both Cognitive Analytic Therapy (CAT) and CBT trained. All the junior doctors took psychodynamic training cases, and the psychiatrists tended to see this as the modality of choice when referring. The shift in resources that has taken place over the whole country from mixed modalities with the weight of medical power supporting psychodynamics, toward an emphasis on CBT and other 'evidence-based therapies', has been mirrored in that department (where I no longer work). Such a shift in resources cannot be accomplished without pain. It is entirely understandable that the concept of 'evidence base' be viewed with suspicion as a means to accomplish a *coup d'état*, and its basis and details be questioned by those deposed by the said coup. The editorial introduction recognizes this argument when it refers to 'vested interest groups whose over-long held privileges are being threatened – or even the envious attacks of the displaced and the superseded in therapy's free market'.

A PERSONAL PERSPECTIVE

So where do I come from? What are my motives for nailing my colours to the CBT mast? A cursory glance at my background might suggest that it was a purely cynical choice on my part. C. G. Jung has always been one of my heroes, and I have read extensively in the psychoanalytic and psychodynamic literature. My road to clinical psychology was long and winding, taking me through a second degree with the Open University, extensive voluntary work with a mental-health theme, and finally arriving at clinical training in my mid-forties. The Samaritans, for whom I was a volunteer for nine years, gave me an essentially person-centred training. I value that induction into radical acceptance of the individual and their pain without flinching as a sure foundation for all my subsequent training. 'Relate' gave me an eclectic training, with a psychodynamic bias. During my three years of clinical psychology training, as well as learning CBT I spent one year under the supervision of a consultant psychotherapist learning to practise brief psychodynamic therapy, and started my CAT training, which I completed to practitioner level on qualification.

So with all those options to choose from, why CBT? Is it just because they have cornered the resources and I want a job? I see the real answer as residing with my primary motivation throughout those long years of career change and voluntary work that eventually allowed me to practise in the NHS with people with severe mental-health problems. It all took over 15 years. I would have arrived a whole lot sooner if I had opted for a counselling training and private practice.

My motivation was to understand, and to be able to make a difference for, people who had suffered severe breakdown, and were perhaps left with enduring problems. It started with the major depression of a good friend when we were all in our twenties; and my experience with following people into hospital after suicide attempts as a Samaritan strengthened my resolve. I did not like the way people were treated there. It did not seem to respect their humanity or their need to make sense of both their experiences and themselves. I wanted to work to change that. My primary loyalty has always been to those people, and it remains with them. My profession, which I greatly value, and the different therapy modalities, are for me just means to that end.

So again, why CBT? The other modalities in which I trained also had much to offer. As a newly trained clinical psychologist, I took the question of how best to help my chosen client group seriously, and in the early 1990s there was no pressure on me to opt for CBT. As the only clinician in my setting working with people who had acquired a diagnosis of psychosis, a new field for therapy at that time, I was resourced to attend any training or conference I could find. In this way, I surveyed the field and concluded that, when it came to psychosis, CBT offered the most collaborative, containing, and effective option. Furthermore, the CBT practitioners really were working with psychosis; often, when psychodynamic practitioners talked about psychosis, they were referring to transient psychotic states in people who were sufficiently 'together' to afford psychoanalysis several times a week.

Things changed, and I found myself working less with psychosis, and more with so-called 'personality disorders' (I prefer the term 'complex trauma'). Once again, I found the explicit and collaborative stance of CBT to be effective with people who were relatively fragmented, and to be respectful of the client group. The same is true of CAT, and it was purely local politics that caused me to leave CAT. The advent of Dialectical Behaviour Therapy (DBT) has alerted all of us in the field to the importance of introducing the individual to non-harmful ways of dealing with unbearable emotion before embarking on 'exploratory' or 'exposure' work to address the underlying trauma (Linehan, 1993a).

With the development of 'Third Wave', mindfulness-based CBT approaches such as Linhehan's DBT and Hayes' Acceptance and Commitment Therapy (he invented the term – see Hayes et al., 1999), I am even happier with this choice. These approaches get away from the thought-challenging aspect of CBT that worked for people with mild to moderate difficulties, but falters when faced with more intractable problems. Mindfulness seeks to alter the person's relationship to both thought and feeling, as opposed to seeking to alter feeling by altering thought. I have developed my own variant of the third-wave approach that is particularly suited to inpatient and crisis work, as that is the setting where I now work (Clarke and Wilson, 2008; Durrant et al., 2007).

EVIDENCE BASE

In explaining why I am a CBT therapist, I have concentrated on individual experience and failed to invoke the mantra of the 'evidence base'. Again, on this subject, I both have sympathy with many of the arguments put forward in the book, and will offer some defence of the concept. I have already indicated that I consider that the concept of 'evidence base' was used in the NHS power struggle, and recognize its deployment as polemic. On the other hand, in my wish to hand control to the service user, I have little sympathy with therapies that tend to promote dependency and be mysterious about their operation. If a therapist purports to have some effect on an individual, it should be possible to venture what this might be, and to check whether it is occurring in at least a majority of cases. I agree that randomized controlled trials translate poorly from the world of medication trials to therapy (cf. Bohart and House, Chapter 16). I can personally attest that they are a nightmare to conduct in routine clinical practice, and am suspicious of how representative some of the bigger trials are of such practice. It is always possible to pick holes in more rough and ready, 'before and after' measures, but I still think we owe it to our clients to use them, and to publish the results. That has been my practice whenever I have found myself developing the model in new directions (Bradbury and Clarke 2006; Durrant et al., 2007; Naeem et al., in revision).

UNDERLYING PHILOSOPHY AND SCIENCE

Perhaps the greatest weight of argument against CBT in this book concerns the philosophical basis of the modality (e.g. Bracken and Thomas, Brazier, Loewenthal, and others – Chapters 8, 6 and 12, respectively), and the psychology of its implied model of the person. A number of the contributors argue that CBT is a purely positivistic approach, which thereby excludes the subjective and relational. Woolfolk and Richardson (Chapter 5) make this point, accusing CBT of being mechanistic. Brazier (Chapter 6) sees CBT as the heir to a tradition starting at the end of the Middle Ages that replaced God with reason. Loewenthal (Chapter 12) compares CBT with existentialism thus – with existentialism confronting the pain of existence, whilst CBT, he argues, offers a way of escaping this reality.

There are two strands of argument that need distinguishing here. One concerns the positivistic values implicit in insisting on an evidence base, and the other is a comment on the character of CBT itself. I have covered the evidence-base issue above, so here I will concentrate on the underlying philosophy of CBT. First, as noted by many of the contributors, this is far from monolithic. A number of the book's chapters cite the 'elasticity' of CBT, and the 'third wave' as an example of this. The reliance on evaluation and evidence is integral to this. Any new element can become an accepted part of CBT, provided it is shown to be effective. Imagery, compassionate mind, and mindfulness are all examples of new approaches which have been introduced and evaluated over the last ten years. This factor does make it harder not to tilt at a 'straw man' as suggested by Warren Mansell's title (Chapter 2), but is also irritating to therapies whose techniques have been purloined in this way.

Strong, Lysack, and Sutherland (Chapter 13) note the limitations of a modality being purely intra-psychic, as opposed to inter-psychic, and it is undeniable that CBT concentrates on the individual. They also note the potential for moving toward a more dialogic view. The brief 'Making Friends with yourself' programme which we run in our hospital (Hill et al., 2008) would be an example of this. This programme exploits the internal dialogue by challenging self-critical cognitions through encouraging participants to treat themselves as they would a good friend, with the assistance of role play with fellow participants. This approach draws on the compassionate-mind techniques introduced by Gilbert and others (Gilbert, 2005). My hope is that such developments will serve to temper the possibly over-individualistic focus of classical CBT.

I am drawn to answer Loewenthal's comparison (Chapter 12) between CBT and existentialism (to the detriment of CBT), as I have always been attracted by the sense of freedom and moment of choice afforded by existentialism. That is precisely the place to which I seek to lead people in therapy – to a place where they can see clearly the vicious circles and redundant patterns of behaviour that keep them trapped, and can choose to walk free and make their own future; choice about both how they make sense of things and what they do. Management of state of arousal, so that the problematic affect need not hold sway, and clear-sighted mindful encounter with that affect, are integral to the process.

Loewenthal's charge that views CBT as a means of avoiding the real issues is a serious one, but one that I would suggest perpetuates a common misconception. In my former job, my psychodynamic colleagues would regularly refer people whom they had assessed as being avoidant of their feelings, and therefore unable to benefit from their therapy. The reality is that *all* therapy is at bottom about creating space to think about, and therefore be able to cope with, feelings. The fact that conventional CBT goes for the thought, the behaviour, or the state of physical arousal first as a means of reaching the feeling, as opposed to addressing the affect directly (as I learnt to do in order to practise brief psychodynamic therapy), is compatible with the feeling being the target. After all, the major diagnoses of depression and anxiety are simply another way of labelling troublesome emotions!

That is conventional CBT, but the third wave goes further in addressing emotion. Paradoxically, these approaches often market themselves as being behavioural rather than cognitive, but a cursory examination reveals them as being very different from the examples of behaviourist writing from the 1970s and 1980s cited by Woolfolk and Richardson (Chapter 5). DBT, for instance, identifies emotional dysregulation as lying at the heart of the presentation called 'Borderline Personality Disorder'. The therapy therefore teaches skills for the regulation and management of emotion. At first sight this sounds very mechanistic and 'untherapy-like'. I must confess that this was my suspicion when I first heard of it, but I have since become a complete convert.

On the 'skills teaching' issue, I would defend the approach on two counts. First, it really works. Secondly, time and again, service users find the idea of learning a skill, as opposed to being subjected to some mysterious therapy, really acceptable. To return to Loewenthal's argument, by encouraging direct engagement with painful emotions through mindful attention and acceptance, DBT and the other third-wave approaches at least cannot be accused of shirking affect.

On the other hand, I can recognize an element of rigidity in more 'old-fashioned' CBT approaches that target 'dysfunctional thinking' and rely more heavily on thought challenging. This is particularly a problem where the therapy is delivered by people with inadequate training and supervision. I recognize this as a real danger where there is a perception that anyone can deliver CBT after a brief training and with no specialist supervision; a view beloved of cost-cutting managers. At worst, the 'therapist' is trying to 'fix' people's thoughts in the same way that the doctor uses medication to 'fix' symptoms. This danger is an argument for good professional control, and the linking of training, practice, ongoing supervision, and continuous professional development in the delivery of therapy in the NHS.

THE MODEL OF THE PERSON IN CBT

A number of the contributors criticize the implied model of the human being and the operation of the human mind behind CBT. Moloney and Kelly (Chapter 23) point to the evidence for heuristic rather than logical reasoning dominating ordinary human thinking, stating: 'there is no "Cartesian Theatre" of the mind, in which our thoughts might be viewed and then manipulated' (p. 281). Bracken and Thomas (Chapter 8) state that CBT is based on a model where disorders of the mind are caused by 'dysfunctional beliefs', and associate this perspective with the Enlightenment. I will first consider the question of beliefs, and then look critically at the current theoretical basis for CBT, with emphasis on my own preferred perspective.

Beliefs, meaning, and the sense that people make of their situation do powerfully influence how they feel about it, and approaches based on re-appraising meaning undoubtedly work. As cognitive therapy became applied to more intractable conditions, they ceased to work as consistently. A gap opened up between the logical appraisal and emotional conviction, so that the individual might be able to agree with the reasonable explanation but still be governed by the emotional reaction. DBT characterizes this as the gap between 'Emotion Mind' and 'Reasonable Mind' (Linehan, 1993b). Teasdale and Barnard (1995) locate this gap deep in cognitive organization. Both Linehan and Teasdale have been at the forefront of the third wave movement in CBT. Both advocate mindfulness in order to bridge the gap.

Teasdale and Barnard have developed a solidly cognitive-science based exposition of cognitive architecture that they call 'Interacting Cognitive Subsystems' (ICS). If I could say that CBT as a whole had embraced this model, I would be able to refute the charge of philosophical and scientific incoherence with some confidence. When the model was first proposed, I was convinced that this was the way forward, and have based my own development of CBT firmly on this foundation (Clarke, 1999). By recognizing the modular nature of the brain, and the existence of not one, but two higher-order organizing systems, ICS neatly explains human fragility, the limitations of our grasp on 'reality', and the tenuous and illusory nature of our control of our situation and sense of self. This is not a model that produces a mechanistic, Cartesian take on the human being. Its subtleties offer a way of explaining spirituality and our persisting sense of the sacred, along with the 'otherness' of psychotic experience (Clarke, 2008b).

Unfortunately, the CBT community as a whole has not adopted ICS. Barnard argues eloquently (Barnard, 2004) that the diverse theoretical models promoted by different factions are partial and poorly supported by basic science, compared with ICS; and indeed, more and more papers have been appearing that base their argument on ICS (e.g. Duff and Kinderman, 2006; Lun, 2008). Perhaps this is another case of Gilbert's evolutionary argument, cited early on in this chapter; each CBT theory represents an element of identity for its author. Perhaps it is because the theory as originally presented is somewhat detailed and opaque which has the effect of masking its significance and explanatory power.

CONCLUSION

In conclusion, I would like to draw a distinction between three issues that can easily become confused in this important debate. One is the position of CBT in comparison or competition with other therapeutic modalities. The other is the spread of CBT as a means of making talking therapy more widely available, and therefore strengthening the position of therapy as a practical intervention for those in mental distress, and one that can stand up to the assumption in mental-health circles that medication is the first, and usually the only, remedy on offer. The third is the debate around evidence base.

To take the comparison argument first, I have already made clear my position that there are historical factors, independent of the merits of the case, that have led to the extremes of the present situation. Further, I would not defend a monolithic situation where CBT was the only therapy available. In fact, because of its increasing dominance, CBT has extended its range and adopted many of the principles associated with rival modalities, such as recognition of the role of transference and the unconscious (though for the most part without using those terms), and the significance of the therapeutic relationship. However, I would argue that, with its open, collaborative, and explicit way of operating, it is a therapy that is well suited to working with people with severe problems leading to a degree of fragmentation. I do not have sufficient breadth of experience and knowledge to state that it is the only one, but it has proved to work best to my satisfaction with this client group – and I have observed real dangers with some other approaches. For the wider client group, I would wish to see many modalities flourish.

On the 'availability of therapy' issue I have no doubts. I have seen inter-modality rivalry restrict the already miserable availability of therapy on the NHS, and I welcome the new climate in which talking therapy is seen as a right, and medication (or ECT) are no longer assumed to be the only options. There are certainly dangers with the current enthusiasm. It suits managers to regard CBT as a simple technical fix, for example, that can be applied by any of their existing staff with minimal training and no extra support or supervision. Qualified CBT therapists like myself try hard to stand up against this sort of travesty. It is too early to say where this particular struggle will end – probably in compromise.

Finally, to return to the question of evidence base. While fully acknowledging the shortcomings of some of the research on which, for instance, the NICE guidelines are based, I would take issue with those who argue that evidence has no place in the field of therapy. Routine evaluation and taking responsibility for the effects of our interventions is to respect those we treat. In the private sector, there is a free market. Within the NHS, because the therapy resource is so restricted, people tend to have to take what they are offered. If diligently collected feedback, supervision, and continuous professional development of practitioners ensure that this is of good quality, this often produces a better option than the vagaries of the market. Further, the principle of evaluation and development based on evidence has enshrined responsible creativity and flexibility within CBT. At the same time, the tally of evidence-based therapies increases all the time, as more research is conducted and published. This principle holds within itself the seeds of the end of the hegemony of CBT, but in a responsible manner, likely to benefit the end user.

REFERENCES

Barnard, P. J. (2004) 'Bridging between basic theory and clinical practice', *Behaviour Research and Therapy*, 42: 977–1000.

Bradbury, K. E. and Clarke, I. (2006) 'Cognitive behavioural therapy for anger management: effectiveness in adult mental health services', *Behavioural and Cognitive Psychotherapy*, 35: 201–8.

Clarke, I. (1999) 'Cognitive therapy and serious mental illness: an interacting Cognitive Subsystems approach', *Clinical Psychology and Psychotherapy*, 6: 375–83.

Clarke, I. (2008a) 'Pioneering a cross diagnostic approach, founded In cognitive science', in I. Clarke and H. Wilson (eds), *Cognitive Behaviour Therapy for Acute Inpatient Mental Health Units: Working with Clients, Staff and the Milieu*, London: Routledge.

Clarke, I. (2008b) *Madness, Mystery and the Survival of God*, Winchester: 'O' Books.

Clarke, I. and Wilson, H. (eds) (2008) *Cognitive Behaviour Therapy for Acute Inpatient Mental Health Units: Working with Clients, Staff and the Milieu*, London: Routledge.

Duff, S. and Kinderman, P. (2006) 'An Interacting Cognitive Subsystems approach to personality disorder', *Clinical Psychology and Psychotherapy*, 13: 233–45.

Durrant, C., Clarke, I., Tolland, A., and Wilson, H. (2007) 'Designing a CBT service for an acute in-patient setting: a pilot evaluation study', *Clinical Psychology and Psychotherapy*, 14: 117–25.

Gilbert, P. (1992) *Depression: The Evolution of Powerlessness*, Hove, UK and New York: Lawrence Erlbaum Associates; Guilford Press.

Gilbert, P. (ed.) (2005) *Compassion: Conceptualisations, Research and Use in Psychotherapy*, Hove: Routledge.

Hayes, S. Strosahl, K. D., and Wilson, K. G. (1999) *Acceptance and Commitment Therapy*, New York: Guilford Press.

Hill, G., Clarke, I., and Wilson, H. (2008) 'The "Making Friends with Yourself Group" and the "What is Real and What is Not Group', in I. Clarke and H. Wilson (eds), *Cognitive Behaviour Therapy for Acute Inpatient Mental Health Units: Working with Clients, Staff and the Milieu*, London: Routledge.

Linehan, M. (1993a) *Cognitive Behavioural Treatment of Borderline Personality Disorder*, New York: Guilford Press.

Linehan, M. (1993b) *Skills Training Manual for Treating Borderline Personality Disorder*, New York: Guilford Press.

Lun, L. M. W. (2008) 'A cognitive model of peritraumatic dissociation', *Psychology and Psychotherapy: Theory, Research and Practice*, 81: 297–307.

Naeem, F., Clarke, I., and Kingdon, D. (in revision) 'A randomized controlled trial of an anger management group program', *The Cognitive Behavior Therapist.*

Teasdale, J. D. and Barnard, P. J. (1995) *Affect, Cognition and Change: Remodelling Depressive Thought,* Hove: Lawrence Erlbaum Associates.

CHAPTER 4

A RESPONSE TO THE CHAPTERS IN *AGAINST AND FOR CBT*

ADRIAN HEMMINGS

INTRODUCTION

I have read the chapters in this book with interest, and have a number of comments to make on the specific criticisms of cognitive behaviour therapy (CBT) – namely, the technical nature of CBT, and the notion of collaboration becoming a form of coercion and an expression of power. I also reflect upon CBT's relationship with powerful institutions, as well as examining the notion of evidence-based treatment, particularly in the light of the Randomized Controlled Trials (RCTs) in effectiveness research. I also examine some of the issues arising from the current social and political context in which CBT lies. Before I do so, I wish to place these comments in the perspective of three main areas: current research that examines therapist effects; the Improving Access to Psychological Therapies (IAPT) training, perhaps more accurately described as IACBT…; and the notion of CBT being a single entity.

CURRENT RESEARCH AND THERAPIST EFFECTS

Let us look, first, at the current research. The initial thrust of psychotherapy research was centred on the question of 'does psychotherapy work?'. A considerable body of literature attested to the effectiveness of psychotherapy, culminating in a number of meta-analyses which have demonstrated effect sizes comparable to, and in some cases considerably better than, many medical and educational interventions (Lipsey and Wilson, 1993; Robinson et al., 1990; Shapiro and Shapiro, 1982; Wompold et al., 1997).

Since then, the research has changed to investigate the specific ingredient of the therapy that works and, in particular, whether there is a model of therapy that is superior to another. Here the famous Dodo bird effect (see Chapter 16, this volume) has been frustratingly consistent in showing that when one model of therapy is compared head to head with another, then there is little or no difference in outcome (Godley et al., 2004; Luborksy et al., 2002; McDonagh et al., 2005; Miller et al., 2008; Shapiro et al., 1994; Stiles et al., 2006). So when CBT has been compared with other forms of therapy, there has been little evidence that it is any less or more effective than any other model of therapy. In fact, meta-analyses of these comparative studies have shown that the model or technique used in the therapy only accounts for 8 per cent of the variance in the positive outcome (Wampold, 2001). Even in

---

This chapter is an extended version of a paper published in the *European Journal of Psychotherapy and Counselling,* Volume 10 (3), 2008: 271–9.

studies using a dismantling design, where specific ingredients that have been posited to be the main 'effective ingredient' have been taken out of the intervention, for instance exposure, still no difference in outcome has been found (Jacobson et al., 1996).

Psychotherapy research has now moved on to attempting to identify what it is that is effective in therapy, and in particular *who* it is that is effective in therapy. Therapist effects are increasingly becoming more evident, and when studies are comparing two forms of therapy delivered by the same therapists, then between-therapist effects are often considerably larger than between model effects (Elkin, 1999; Huppert et al., 2001; Kim et al., 2006; Okiishi et al., 2003). In other words, the title of Roth and Fonagy's next book should not be *What Works for Whom* (Roth and Fonagy, 2004), but perhaps *Who Works for Whom.* In relation to this chapter, the implication is clear; while there may be some specific criticisms of CBT as a model, equal concern should be about CBT carried out by an ineffective therapist, just as with any other model of treatment carried out by an ineffective therapist.

It is the training of therapists in the context of the IAPT that is my next contextual point. CBT focuses on the presenting problem, and positive outcome is couched in terms of symptom reduction. This makes CBT particularly amenable to current research methods which require specificity of treatment and specificity of presenting problem that is usually placed in a diagnostic category. This notion is explored very eloquently and in much more detail in the chapters by Bohart and House (Chapter 16) and Bryceland and Stam (Chapter 15) in this volume, in their critiques of Empirically Supported Treatments, or ESTs. ESTs are particularly prevalent in the United States,where much of the funding is provided by insurance companies where the dictum to the therapist is sometimes 'No EST – no payment'.

The basis of an EST is the splitting off of the technique used and the person that is delivering it. Perhaps because of this, it can collude with a fantasy that it is technique that is effective, in much the same way that a pill is effective. Carrying this fantasy further is the notion that by simply using a technique regardless of the people involved, is all that is required; and there is a consequent minimizing of the therapeutic relationship. This is in much the same way that a medication is delivered in the belief that it is separate from the practitioner and client. (Incidentally even this is being challenged by therapist-effect research, which has shown that the person prescribing the medication has a sometimes greater effect on outcome than the medication itself in working with people with depression – Mckay et al., 2006.) Taking this notion to its logical conclusion means that practitioners who deliver the technique simply need to learn how to deliver it with little acknowledgement of the relationship in which it is being used.

IMPROVING ACCESS TO PSYCHOLOGICAL THERAPIES (IAPT) TRAINING

This brings me to the current training of IAPT high- and low-intensity workers. Low-intensity workers will work with people with presenting problems of relatively low complexity, as defined by their GPs and a screening instrument which is usually the PHQ9 (Kroenke et al., 2001). Low-intensity workers will have 45 days of training in CBT skills and the stepped-care model. High-intensity workers, who will work with people with more complex needs, will have a year's training. My concern is that when a potentially potent CBT technique is used simply as a technique, without the sensitivity achieved by a more thorough training, it can prove to be destructive, and even dangerous. An example is the 'downward arrow technique', in which a client is invited to consider the implications of automatic thoughts. Using this technique with a person can rapidly move to fundamental core beliefs about him- or herself which, if not worked with in a safe, contained environment, could prove very distressing for the client, and indeed the inexperienced therapist. It is not the method of working that is inherently 'bad', but the way in which it can be practised.

My main concern is that while high- and low-intensity workers are currently being trained, there are approximately 26,000 therapists in the country who are already trained in other models, many of whom are employed as general-practice counsellors within the NHS. A large proportion of these counsellors will have to reapply unwillingly for their jobs in the form of high-intensity workers. Currently there seems to be little effort in working alongside these counsellors, and offering training that helps them to integrate CBT so that they can incorporate a cognitive behaviour approach into their practice. The effect of the idealizing of CBT, the employment of undertrained workers, and the undervaluing of other models is likely to be enormous. The disenfranchisement of so many practice counsellors is already leading to resignations and redundancies. These professionals have a wealth of experience in working with people and in the institutions of the NHS, as well as a depth of skills that have been built up over many years. The irony is that IAPT was set up initially to get people back to work who are on incapacity benefit, and to make unemployed those very people who could really help this happen would be little short of disastrous.

CBT AS A SINGLE ENTITY

Some of the criticisms in the book's chapters are levelled at CBT as if it were a monolithic entity. It is not. It is evolving, as David Winter and John Kaye describe in their chapters (respectively, Chapters 11 and 14). Current 'third wave' forms of CBT are rapidly integrating other theoretical models into their practice, such as Gestalt and object relations in schema therapy (Young et al., 2003), Buddhist mindfulness techniques in mindfulness CBT (Segal et al., 2002), Relational Frame Theory in ACT (Hayes and Spencer, 2005), and the dialogic approach so eloquently described by Strong, Lysack, and Sutherland in this volume's Chapter 13.

Grant et al. (2004: 243) describe CBT as occupying a continuum between two poles:

> 'One end represents an explicitly technique-focused style, where concern is given to standardised interventions based on experimental and randomised control research methods. At this end sits computerised CBT packages and highly structured manual intervention protocols that can be disseminated to a wide range of healthcare professionals at relatively low cost. Formulation based approaches are located at the other end of the continuum where the richness of individual experiences is celebrated and valued.'

They then go on to say that there is conflict in the CBT community between the 'technicalists' and the 'formulationists', particularly in relation to personal therapy. The 'technicalists' might disparage this notion as it is not evidence based, and 'might disparage the notion of personal therapy on the grounds that, unlike their clients they are on the other, non-disordered, side of the fence' (ibid.: 243).

Given this continuum, it is easy to see that the criticisms of mechanistic practice, positivist imperialism, rationalism, the use of simplistic diagnostic categorization, and the collusion with the medical model of mental 'health' can be levelled at the more 'technicalist' end of the spectrum. Having said this, it is easy simply to view 'technical' as 'bad', and more subtle 'formulations' as 'good'. In my view, there is a place for simple pragmatic and technical intervention for some people. It can be argued that not everyone needs complex input which, in some cases, can pull people into a system that is too complex and possibly self limiting. CBT practitioners at both ends of the spectrum tend to take people at face value, and do not automatically have an assumption that there is an underlying cause (which of course there might be), thus potentially avoiding what O'Hanlon et al. (1999) refer to as theory countertransference.

Simple information is sometimes sufficient, and I am reminded of the empowerment of information offered to someone who has panic attacks. Simple information on what happens in the body when in 'flight/fight' offers an alternative to a terrifying thought of 'I am going to die of a heart attack'. It is, of course, knowing how, when, and indeed if to share this information so that is not an imposed truth, that depends so much on the therapist, their training, experience, and the understanding of their relationship with the client. In the hands of an unsophisticated therapist, these techniques can be at best futile, at worst harmful; reinforcing fundamental notions of the client about him- or herself not feeling good enough. Once more we arrive at therapist effects.

THE RELATIONSHIP OF CBT WITH POWERFUL INSTITUTIONS – COLLABORATOR OR TROJAN HORSE?

Much is made in the chapters by Michael Guilfoyle (Chapter 19) and David Pilgrim (Chapter 21) of the relationship of the CBT practitioners with 'powerful institutions', such as the psychiatric community and medicine. The technicalist end of the CBT community spectrum has indeed taken the notion of diagnosis as reality, rather than perhaps a form of anxiety management for the practitioner. If we have a diagnosis, then we know what to do, and of course, something must be done. In some ways, I can see that the reification of what is essentially a process can have some benefits, such as 'naming the beast', universality, and hope (Yalom, 1995). However, the disadvantages (identification with the diagnosis, as in 'I am a depressive', externalization, reification, medicalization, passivity, inviting an external locus of control, collusion with pharmaceutical companies ...) seem to far outweigh the advantages; a discussion which is outside the remit of this chapter.

There seems to be a view in Guilfoyle's chapter that there has been an almost unethical collaboration with 'the enemy', and that the technicalist end of the CBT community has somehow sold its soul. I would suggest that this is not the case, and that they genuinely believe in these categorizations, and in the importance of the scientific method in establishing truth. In so doing, they have been taken seriously by the 'powerful institutions'. After all –

and this is one aspect of current practice that seems to be absent in the chapters in this book – the overwhelming alternative to psychological therapies is the use of medication for 'mental health' problems. Medication is by far the most common intervention, and up until the recent rise in interest in CBT, it was recommended as the first form of intervention – and is indeed the current mainstay in the General Practitioner's toolkit. It is really only since the interest in CBT that psychological therapies have been viewed as a realistic alternative for a large number of people with mild to moderate presenting difficulties. Because of this, psychological therapies will be available to many more patients, and will be accessed by other clinicians who are much more aware of alternatives to medication; and this will go some way toward redressing the imbalance between medication and psychological therapies.

David Brazier (Chapter 6) is right when he points out that CBT is very much a product of our time. Perhaps because of this, CBT theorists have matched the language that is understood by powerful institutions in the same way that an effective therapist uses the language of the client. What seems to have happened is that having been taken seriously, they have been invited into the fold. However, inside the Trojan horse there are also the formulationists, who are constantly reviewing and critiquing the model to a point where, as David Winter quite rightly says in his final paragraph (Chapter 11), 'one might ask when such a therapy is no longer cognitive-behavioural'. If this is the case, and I am aware of more than a little Pollyanna-ism, then this could have a profound effect for psychotherapy in general. Perhaps the psychotherapy community is reacting in a similar way to when threatened by Eysenck's (1952) broadside on psychotherapy.

The current infatuation with CBT, like most idealizations, is likely to fade when it is noticed that it is not the panacea for all ills. CBT can undoubtedly be used as a pragmatic and sophisticated form of therapy which many people find life changing. However, it has its limitations which, if allowed to, other forms of therapy can help to address. Indeed, useful alternatives are proposed in Del Loewenthal's and Keith Tudor's chapters in this book (respectively, Chapters 12 and 10). Perhaps this will be a little easier if, as a profession, we move away from potential paradigm zealotry to a more pan-theoretical model of therapy. This might be difficult, given the understandable potential envy in the church of the favoured son who is enjoying so much attention. However, if we can maintain a continued dialogue with the formulationist's wing of CBT, this could be a possibility. By doing this, we could, as a profession, examine how different paradigms of psychological therapy can integrate into a broader, more complex and viable alternative to medication rather than battling with ourselves. Yet all this appears to be relatively benign within the UK when compared to the French experience reviewed in Robert Snell's Chapter 22!

LIMITATIONS OF RCTS FOR EFFECTIVENESS RESEARCH

I agree with John Lees' criticisms (Chapter 7) of the notion of evidence-based treatment (EBTs; cf. Bohart and House's Chapter 16), particularly regarding their reliance on the Randomized Controlled Trial (RCT) in evidencing the effectiveness of psychological treatments. Whilst I can see a use for RCTs in efficacy trials, there are a number of difficulties in their use in effectiveness research (Hemmings, 2000).

RANDOMIZED CONTROLLED TRIALS (RCTS)

The RCT has come to represent the epitome of good scientific research. It was developed in medicine in order to evaluate physical treatments and was later adopted in psychiatry to test the efficacy of medication for certain psychiatric disorders. However, different commentators have identified several limitations to the use of RCTs in the study of effectiveness:

Representativeness: The controls required in an RCT, such as specificity of treatment using manuals and the inclusion of disorders which meet stringent research criteria, mean that the patients seen are simply not representative of normal clinical practice (Shapiro et al., 1995).

Feasibility: RCTs are expensive. They require large amounts of researcher time, and often large numbers of participants in order to achieve the necessary statistical power (Shapiro et al., 1995).

Informativeness: If these trials take place in such a rarefied environment of the efficacy study, how informative are they of real-life practice? (Shapiro et al., 1995). This is of particular concern in the current NICE guideline recommendations, which seem to rely almost entirely upon efficacy research on CBT.

Differing assumptions of the researcher and the model of therapy being used.

RCTs' attempt to measure 'technique': As I have described earlier, there is considerable emphasis on specificity of treatment, and technique and model account for small percentages of the variance associated with positive outcome.

Entry criteria for an RCT: The DSM IV is often used to classify the disorders being treated. There is considerable debate as to the usefulness of this form of classification (Morey, 1991; Rosenthal, 2008).

Dual diagnosis is also a problem. Personality disorders (Axis 2) are highly prevalent, and have a profound effect on treatment outcome (Das-Munshi et al., 2008; Sullivan et al., 1994).

Sample sizes are hardly ever enough to control for the confounding variables that are present in a clinically representative situation.

Randomization: While clients may be randomized, therapists almost never are, and given the increasing evidence that therapist variables are important (discussed earlier), this again introduces a confound.

Use of placebos and 'double blind' methods is the staple of pharmaceutical trials; and while placebos have been attempted in psychotherapy research, it is difficult to imagine therapists delivering a form of therapy that they do not know is sham.

Client dissatisfaction: Clients are active participants in therapy, and often choose to have a particular form of therapy. Not getting their preferred choice could introduce confounds.

Practitioner dissatisfaction: When a therapy is not blinded and therapists are delivering a form of therapy that they may not prefer, one might wonder about the effects on outcome.

So the RCT's journey from medicine to psychology has been fraught with difficulties. The RCT would appear to be the most useful when the disorder and intervention that are being studied are highly controlled and specific, i.e. during the efficacy stage. When the intervention is carried out in a more clinically realistic situation (i.e. effectiveness research), the usefulness of such a methodology is considerably reduced. Unfortunately, much of the evidence accepted in EBTs is from RCTs. One of the criticisms of CBT is that most of the evidence is based on efficacy research which is not based on real-world practice. Whilst there is considerable evidence that CBT is effective in the treatment of depression when the client has 'pure' depression, there is little evidence that CBT is effective in the real world of clinical practice. There are some exceptions to this (Wade et al., 1998), and attempts are being made to address this by the use of RCTs. It will be interesting to note how this practice-based evidence is managed and disseminated.

POWER BETWEEN THERAPIST AND CLIENT

Gillian Proctor's excellent analysis of the dangers of the potential abuse of power by the therapist over the client in CBT (Chapter 20) is a cogent reminder to practitioners. Her arguments are highly relevant, and are of particular concern when CBT is 'delivered' from the technicalist end of the spectrum. Where I part company with Proctor is in the notion that this is largely a problem within CBT. I would argue that these power dynamics are played out in other forms of therapy, from psychodynamic models where patient resistance is overtly interpreted, to a less overt acceptance of a power imbalance in person-centred therapy. The use and abuse of power within the helping professions has an extensive literature (Guggenbühl-Craig, 1971). Within CBT, the notion of *collaboration* is an overt attempt to recognize this imbalance, and the standard mantra of many CBT therapists is 'I have expertise in the model of CBT but I do not have expertise in you – only you have that'. Take, for example, the use of behavioural experiments. It is recognized that if these are imposed on the client as a form of 'homework', then this becomes part of the therapist's agenda and not the client's. If this is the case, then it is possible that the client will use his or her power in a passive way in order to confirm their world-view, or frustrate the therapist. Once again, I would argue that CBT done badly can have all the power dynamics described, but done well by a competent therapist, these are reduced.

Paul Moloney and Paul Kelly's intriguingly titled chapter (Chapter 23) makes the very relevant contextual point that CBT happens within a social environment. The larger system needs to be addressed, and here we move into the realms of social policy. I agree with this argument, but would point out that *any* form of psychosocial intervention needs to bear this in mind – this criticism cannot be laid solely at the feet of CBT. The development of the 'five areas' approach does at least go some way toward recognizing this problem (Wright et al., 2002).

CONCLUSION

CBT has a wealth to offer the psychotherapy community; it is popular with clients and many therapists alike, as well as having a focus on behaviour change, along with insight and awareness. It also has considerable efficacy research to support it. It is not, however, the only therapy in town. It is important that, in their attempt to be recognized as scientists, CBT theorists do not ignore the research evidence on therapist effects on outcome. It is also important that these effects are recognized in the training of new CBT therapists, and that they are not reduced to simply delivering a set of techniques which seems so against the spirit of enquiry and curiosity that is prevalent in so much of CBT theory.

REFERENCES

Das-Munshi, J., Goldberg, D., Bebbington, P., Bhugra, D., Brugha, T., Dewey, M. E., Jenkins, R., Stewart, R., and Prince, M. (2008) 'The public health significance of mixed anxiety and depressive disorder: beyond current classification', *British Journal of Psychiatry, 192:* 171–7.

Elkin, I. (1999) 'A major dilemma in psychotherapy outcome research: disentangling therapists from therapies', *Clinical Psychology: Science and Practice*, 6: 10–32.

Eysenck, H. (1952) 'The effects of psychotherapy: an evaluation', *Journal of Consulting and Clinical Psychology*, 60: 659–63.

Godley, S. H., Jones, N., Funk, R., Ives, M., and Passetti, L. (2004) 'Comparing outcomes of best-practice and research-based outpatient treatment protocols for adolescents', *Journal of Psychoactive Drugs*, 36 (1): 35–48.

Grant, A., Mills, J., Mulhern, R., and Short, N. (2004) *Cognitive Behavioural Therapy in Mental Health Care*, London: Sage

Guggenbühl-Craig, A. (1971) *Power in the Helping Professions*, Dallas: Spring Publications.

Hayes, S. C. and Spencer, S. (2005) *Get Out of Your Mind and into Your Life: The New Acceptance and Commitment Therapy*, Oakland, Calif.: New Harbinger Publications.

Hemmings, A. (2000) 'Evidence-based practice or practice based evidence?', *British Journal of Guidance and Counselling*, 28 (2): 233–52.

Huppert, J. D., Bufka, L. F., and Barlow, D. H. and others (2001) 'Therapists, therapist variables, and cognitive-behavioral therapy outcomes in a multicenter trial for panic disorder', *Journal of Consulting and Clinical Psychology*, 69: 747–55.

Jacobson, N. S., Dobson, K. S., Truax, P. A., Addis, M. E., Koerner, K., Gollan, J. K., Gortner, E., and Prince, S. E. (1996) 'A component analysis of cognitive-behavioral treatment for depression', *Journal of Consulting and Clinical Psychology*, 64: 295–304.

Kim, D. M., Wampold, B. E., and Bolt, D. M. (2006) 'Therapist effects and treatment effects in psychotherapy: analysis of the National Institute of Mental Health Treatment of Depression Collaborative Research Program', *Psychotherapy Research*, 16 (2): 161–72.

Kroenke, K., Spitzer, R. L., and Williams, J. B. (2001) 'The PHQ-9: validity of a brief depression severity measure', *Journal of General Internal Medicine, 16* (9): 606–13.

Lipsey, M. W., and Wilson, D. B. (1993) 'The efficacy of psychological, behavioral, and educational, and behavioral treatment: confirmation from meta-analysis', *American Psychologist*, 48 (12): 1181–209.

Luborsky, L., Rosenthal, R., Diguer, L., and others (2002) 'The dodo bird verdict is alive and well – mostly', *Journal of Psychotherapy Integration*, 12 (1): 32–57.

McDonagh, A., Friedman, M., McHugo, G., Ford, J., Sengupta, A., Mueser, K., and others (2005) 'Randomized trial of cognitive-behavioral therapy for chronic posttraumatic stress disorder in adult female survivors of childhood sexual abuse', *Journal of Consulting and Clinical Psychology*, 73 (3): 515–24.

McKay, K. M., Imel, Z. E., and Wampold, B. E. (2006) ' Psychiatrist effects in the pharmacological treatment of depression', *Journal of Affective Disorders*, 92 (2–3): 287–90.

Miller, S. D., Wampold, B. E., and Varhely, K. (2008) 'Direct comparisons of treatment modalities for youth disorders: a meta-analysis', *Psychotherapy Research*, 18 (1): 5–14.

Morey, L. C. (1991) *The Personality Assessment Inventory Professional Manual*, Odessa, Fla.: Psychological Assessment Resources.

O'Hanlon, W., O'Hanlon, S., and Bertolino, B. (1999) *Evolving Possibilities: Selected Papers of Bill O'Hanlon*, New York: Psychology Press.

Okiishi, J., Lambert, M. J., Nielsen, S. L., and others (2003) 'Waiting for supershrink: an empirical analysis of therapist effects', *Clinical Psychology and Psychotherapy*, 10: 361–73.

Robinson, L. A., Berman, J. S., and Neimeyer, R. A. (1990) 'Psychotherapy for treatment of depression: a comprehensive review of controlled outcome research', *Psychological Bulletin*, 108: 30–49.

Rosenthal, S. (2008) *Class, Health and Health Care*, Victoria, BC: Trafford Publishing.

Roth, A. and Fonagy, P. (2004) *What Works for Whom?* (2nd edn), London: Guilford Press.

Segal, Z. V., Williams, J. M., and Teasdale, J. D. (2002) *Mindfulness-Based Cognitive Therapy for Depression*, London: Guilford Press.

Shapiro, D. A. and Shapiro, D. (1982) 'Meta-analysis of comparative therapy outcome studies: a replication and refinement', *Psychological Bulletin*, 92: 581–604.

Shapiro, D. A., Barkham, M., Rees, A., Hardy, G. E., Reynolds, S., and Startup, M. (1994) 'Effects of treatment duration and severity of depression on the effectiveness of cognitive behavioural and psychodynamic-interpersonal psychotherapy', *Journal of Consulting and Clinical Psychology*, 62, 522–34.

Shapiro, D. A., Barkham, M., Rees, A., Hardy, G. E., Reynolds, S., and Startup, M. (1995) 'Decisions decisions decisions: determining the effects of treatment and duration on the outcome of psychotherapy for depression', in M. Aveline and D. Shapiro (eds), *Research Foundations for Psychotherapy Practice*, Chichester: Wiley.

Stiles, W. B., Barkham, M., Twigg, E., Mellor-Clark, J., and Cooper, M. (2006) 'Effectiveness of cognitive-behavioural, personcentred and psychodynamic therapies as practiced in UK national health service settings', *Psychological Medicine*, 26: 555–6.

Sullivan, P. F., Joyce, P. R., and Mulder, R. T. (1994) 'Borderline personality disorder in major depression', *Journal of Nervous and Mental Disease*, 182: 177–8.

Wade, W. A., Treat, T. T., and Stuart, G. L. (1998) 'Transporting an empirically supported treatment for panic disorder to a service clinic setting: a benchmarking strategy', *Journal of Consulting and Clinical Psychology*, 66: 231–9.

Wampold, B. (2001) *The Great Psychotherapy Debate*, New York: Lawrence Erlbaum.

Wampold, B. E., Mondin, G. W., Moody, M., and others (1997) 'A meta-analysis of outcome studies comparing bona fide psychotherapies: empirically, "All must have prizes"', *Psychological Bulletin*, 122: 203–15.

Wright, B., Williams, C., and Garland A. (2002) 'Using the Five Areas cognitive-behavioural

therapy model with psychiatric patients', *Advances in Psychiatric Treatment*, 8 (4): 307–15.
Yalom, I. (1995) *The Theory and Practice of Group Psychotherapy*, 4th edn, New York: Basic Books.
Young, J. E., Klosko, J. S., and Weishaar, M. (2003) *Schema Therapy: A Practitioner's Guide*, New York: Guilford Publications.

Chapter 5

BEHAVIOUR THERAPY AND THE IDEOLOGY OF MODERNITY

Robert L. Woolfolk & Frank C. Richardson

INTRODUCTION

In this chapter a critique of behaviour therapy is presented. The moral and epistemological underpinnings of behaviour therapy are analysed from a socio-historical, hermeneutic perspective. The *Weltanschauung* of behaviour therapy is shown to be closely linked with the values and patterns of thought characteristic of modernity. The implications of behaviour therapy's close association with modern ideological positions are discussed in the chapter.

A lucid and highly regarded textbook on behaviour therapy offered the following definition:

> 'As an applied science, behavior therapy is simply a collection of principles and techniques about how to change behavior; it says nothing about who should modify what behavior, why, or when' (Wilson and O'Leary, 1980: 285). Though behaviour therapy has been given many other definitions (Bandura, 1969; Wolpe, 1973), virtually all have conceived of it as a neutral structure, a body of "objective knowledge" verified by experimental test. Behaviour therapy's self-image is that of an applied science, devoid of any inherent prescriptive thrust or implicit system of values, the essence of which can be accounted for without reference to any cultural or historical context. Work in the philosophy and history of science, however, has undermined seriously the view of science on which behaviour therapy's self-image is based. Attempts to equate scientific knowledge with that which is empirically verifiable or to identify scientific progress with some inflexible standard of verification have proven lacking (Bartley, 1962; Burtt, 1964; Weimer, 1979). The form and content of scientific knowledge are strongly influenced by socio-political factors as well as those related to the attitudes and sensibilities of the community of scientists (Feyerabend, 1975; Kuhn, 1970a, 1970b; Polanyi, 1966). Because their subject matter bears so directly on, and is influenced by, the human self-image, the social sciences and systems of psychotherapy are even more limited in their ability to remain independent of cultural influence (Buss, 1975; London, 1964; Lowe, 1976; Sampson, 1978, 1981).

The original version of this chapter first appeared in the *American Psychologist*, 39 (7), 1984, pp. 777–86.

The notion that all knowledge arises out of a social context and that, hence, a complete account of any system of thought must encompass its cultural and ideological foundations has its roots in the philosophies of Hegel and Marx, and has found a strong expression in recent times in three related intellectual movements: the sociology of knowledge, critical theory, and hermeneutic philosophy. Our analysis of behaviour therapy draws on all three of these sources. The sociology of knowledge (Berger and Luckman, 1966; Mannheim, 1936; Scheler, 1960) takes the perspective that knowledge is one among the many and various products of culture. Thinkers in this tradition seek to elucidate the relationship between the nature of a given society and the *Weltanschauungen* to which it gives rise, as well as the processes by which definitions of 'reality' are socially constructed. Critical theory (Habermas, 1972, 1973; Horkheimer, 1972) has been engaged in the critique of contemporary patterns of intellectual activity and of modern social institutions.

One of the main concerns of thinkers in this tradition has been to trace the connection between intellectual and social forms of fragmentation and alienation in modern society, on the one hand, and on the other hand, the increasing rationalization (in the Weberian sense) of the relations of social life in a technically managed society. The interpretive or hermeneutic approach to the study of human society and action (Gadamer, 1975; Ricoeur, 1981; Taylor, 1971) holds that any scientific account of human activity is, of necessity, epistemologically embedded within a world of intersubjective cultural meanings that are constitutive of the conceptual categories within which the science operates. From this perspective, no social science can ever truly stand outside or transcend the social practices and institutions that have served to constitute it in the first place.

From the perspectives of the sociology of knowledge, critical theory, and hermeneutics, behaviour therapy is a more interesting and complex phenomenon than it purports to be. In addition to being a scientific account of the alteration of emotional and behavioral problems, behaviour therapy is also an intellectual movement, a set of social practices, and a system of thought. In each of these guises, it contains not only theoretical and technological aspects but also a prescriptive, ideological component: a favoured mode of thinking and implicit criteria for making judgements that guide behaviour therapists in their activities, and also represent a vision of reality underlying those activities that justify and support them. Our approach to behaviour therapy will not be to examine it as a body of techniques and a supporting theory to be compared on the dimensions of technical efficacy or theoretical elegance with some other therapeutic school such as psychoanalysis. Indeed, to do so would leave unexamined those tacit, epistemological biases and value commitments that must be encompassed by any fundamental critique.

Rather, we shall show how behaviour therapy is implicitly predicated on modern epistemological and ethical assumptions. We shall also demonstrate how its scientific-technological sensibility is reflected in both its immense and estimable achievements as well as in what appear to be very serious limitations in its capacity to address some aspects of the human situation that are basic to the conduct of psychotherapy in the contemporary world. Our explication of the ideological underpinnings of behaviour therapy is closely related to an analysis of modernity and modern modes of thought.

MODERNITY

Modernity refers to the total condition of culture in those societies that have been transformed by science and the application of scientific technology. What is involved in modernization is a 'total' transformation of a traditional or pre-modern society into the types of technology and associated social organization that characterize the 'advanced', economically prosperous, and relatively politically stable nations of the Western world. (Moore, 1963: 89)

Along with the application of scientific technology to the means of production within a society come inevitable changes in the world-view of its people (Berger, 1977). This modernization of the consciousness of pre-modern cultures is a reliable, patterned phenomenon that has been occurring in Western societies since the advent of the Industrial Revolution (Nelson, 1981). Such changes of outlook begin in the intellectual elites and extend to the population at large, as education, the absorption of individuals into modern, technocratically managed institutions, and the proliferation of media become more widespread (Parsons, 1971).

The world-view of modernity is dominated by science and scientific technology and the modes of thought peculiar to them (Gehlen, 1980). It is rooted in the ideal of progress, a faith in the power of human abilities to be equal to any problem, the quest for certitude, and a devaluation of the traditional past (Shils, 1981). The cognitive style of modern consciousness tends toward the pragmatic and the rational. The focus of evaluation shifts from the ends of activity to means and their efficiency, as technique and technical considerations achieve paramount importance. Utility emerges as a generally agreed-upon value (Ellul, 1964). The aims of prediction and control, and a style of planning and decision making in which emotional and aesthetic considerations are subservient to the rational and pragmatic, are the essential features of modern organizational direction, whether those organizations be communist bureaucracies or capitalist industrial corporations (Berger et al., 1973). Science becomes the ultimate source of knowledge and the model for all forms of intellectual activity (Hayek, 1952; Winner, 1977).

Modernization, whether it be of society or of methods of psychotherapy, always cuts two ways. Within society, the same forces that boldly advance human freedom and opportunity also erode those traditional belief systems that confer meaning upon experience and do damage to those social institutions that sustain emotional security, thus creating the heretofore novel human predicaments of loss of meaning, isolation, and alienation (Baumer, 1977). There is a 'dark side' to modernity chronicled thoroughly by sociologists from Weber to Berger: the 'disenchantment' of the world, the loss of community, the end of a self-evident moral structure and of a meaningful relationship between individual and cosmos. The 'modern consciousness' of the industrialized West is a world-view beset with dilemmas and malaises not found in primitive and traditional views of reality (Levi-Strauss, 1966). So, too, the world-view of behaviour therapy, even in its most complex and sophisticated contemporary variations – for example, cognitive behaviour therapy – partakes so fully of the modern perspective on life and living that it is consequently subject to both the advantages and disadvantages of the modern outlook. In this respect, behaviour therapy is not unique amongst systems of therapy, many of which have 'modern' thrusts (Bergin, 1980), but is rather a purer and more extreme embodiment of the chief strains of modernity.

THE BEHAVIOURAL *WELTANSCHAUUNG*

Behaviour therapy is a quintessential modern set of activities: the application of a scientifically derived technology to the alteration of behaviour. It is, in addition, a system of thought that adopts a radically scientific and technological perspective on human contact and on the enterprise of behaviour change. Behaviour therapy, in its theory and clinical practice, exemplifies both modern modes of thinking and the values of the modern technological society. The close affinity of the *Weltanschauung* of behaviour therapy and that of modernity can be seen clearly by examining the presence in behaviour therapy of four distinct but interrelated aspects of modernity: technicism, rationality, amorality, and humanism.

TECHNICISM

Although virtually every other system of therapy is partially composed of therapeutic activities that could be properly regarded as techniques, none has sought so self-consciously to function as pure 'psychotechnology' as has behaviour therapy. None has sought to characterize itself almost entirely in terms of relationships between sets of explicit therapeutic aims and specific methods thought reliably to achieve those aims as 'an empirically based technology of behavior change' (Kazdin and Wilson, 1978: 178). Most other systems carry what is, from a technological vantage point, some excess baggage: (a) methods of treatment that lack power, directness, and immediacy; (b) a theory of human functioning that contains rather obvious prescriptive components and, hence, a moral thrust; or (c) a prizing of certain forms of understanding or experiencing simply for their own sake, apart from any measurable, correlated changes in behaviour that might ensue.

From its inception, behaviour therapy adopted that most modern of sensibilities that has been variously termed the *technological attitude* (Berger and Kellner, 1981), or *technocratic consciousness* (Gouldner, 1976). From the very beginning, behaviour therapy avoided the sins of inactivity characteristic of the early insight therapies and placed its emphasis on the refinement of technique and on the achievement of measurable results (Kazdin, 1978). Perhaps the most distinctive feature of behaviour therapy's reformulation of psychotherapy theory and practice was its pragmatic temper, its insistence on the demonstrable utility of therapeutic activity, and its attempt to characterize that activity as a body of techniques with specific effects.

The goal of technology is the predictable, rational direction or control of events (Winner, 1977). Not surprisingly, the concept of control is crucial to behaviour therapy and permeates its literature. Krasner (1962) wrote that the fundamental aim of behaviour therapy research was that of devising 'techniques of behavior control' (p. 103). In their classic book, Goldfried and Davison (1976 : 9) state, 'To begin with, the very fact that the client has sought help is an open admission that he has been unable to adequately control certain aspects of his own life'. Similarly, Lazarus (1976) identified the 'control' of unpleasant emotions as an important goal of multimodal behavior therapy. Those methods involving the self-administration of behavioural procedures, termed *self-control,* further attest to the technological attitude of the behaviour therapist. Here the therapist seeks to train the client to manipulate both self and environment so as systematically to regulate affect, cognition, and behavior. Clients are taught, in essence, how to engineer their own actions and feelings by the use of specific techniques. Krasner (1982) has suggested that all behaviour therapy procedures might be properly viewed as methods of self-control.

The technological orientation of behaviour therapy has without question enabled it to supply useful methodological and theoretical correctives to the field of psychotherapy, and has greatly expanded the range of available therapeutic procedures. Successful technologies, however, carry with them a number of potential drawbacks. One unhappy effect of the proliferation of technology and technological thinking within contemporary society has been to drive out other forms of thinking, often resulting in a triumph of form over content, means over ends, methodology over theory (Barrett, 1978; Stanley, 1978). The ascendance of methodological and technical concerns can divert our attention from those troublesome questions that address the value of the goals achieved by the technology, or that ask upon what basis such goals are to be determined.

RATIONALITY

Max Weber (1958) spoke of the pre-modern world appearing as an 'enchanted garden' to its inhabitants. He observed that, in contrast, 'the fate of our times is characterized by rationalization and intellectualization and, above all, by the "disenchantment of the world" (p. 155). In a similar vein, Habermas (1973) has written that modern technological society prizes rationality above all other values:

> 'Because this value [rationality] can be legitimized by pointing to the process of scientific investigation and its technical application, and does not have to be justified in terms of pure commitment alone, it has a preferential status as against all other values.'
>
> (pp. 270–1)

Rationality can be thought of as the cognitive framework within which all forms of modern technological activity are constituted. It involves 'the imposition of strict means – end criteria ... the exclusion of all that is purely traditional, charismatic, or ritualistic, all, in short, that is not directly related to the means necessary to efficient realization of a given end' (Nisbet, 1976: 111).

Those patterns of thought and action that accompany the application of technology are in close harmony with the values linked to the Apollonian sensibility (Berger et al., 1973; Gehlen, 1980). The Apollonian – Dionysian continuum was first introduced by Nietzsche (1956), and was subsequently employed as a tool of cultural analysis by anthropologists (e.g. Benedict, 1934). The Apollonian emphasizes balance, restraint, order, reason, and sobriety. The Dionysian, on the other hand, values extremism, intensity of experience, spontaneity, emotionality, and passion.

The attitude of behaviour therapy toward emotion bespeaks its valuing of the rational, its Apollonian sensibility. The behaviour therapist does not 'work with' affect in any manner analogous to that of more traditional psychotherapy (Messer and Winokur, 1980). Helping clients 'get in touch with', develop, or explore feelings is not a high priority in behaviour therapy. Even in those instances in which emotion is purposefully aroused, such as in flooding or implosive therapy, the aim is the extinction rather than the exploration or cultivation of emotional responsiveness or sensitivity (Wilson and Evans, 1977). Mahoney (1980) suggested that then-current cognitive behaviour therapists took an overly narrow view of emotion, and has written critically of their 'strong and pervasive assumption' that feelings are phenomena to be 'averted, regulated, or otherwise controlled' (p. 167).

The behaviour therapy of the 1980s clearly emphasized rationality and logic over intuitive and emotional functions, perhaps to an even greater degree than in its precognitive days (Messer and Winokur, 1984). The cognitive revolution in behaviour therapy (Mahoney and Arnkoff, 1978; Meichenbaum, 1977) saw the rapid assimilation of therapies that stress reason, 'logical' thinking, and rational problem-solving. Among these consequent therapeutic inductees were rational-emotive therapy (Ellis and Grieger, 1977), cognitive therapy (Beck, 1976), and problem-solving therapy (D'Zurilla and Goldfried, 1971).

Many of the methods of behaviour therapy require of patients a rather advanced level of maturity, rationality, or ego strength, call it what you will. The ability of clients to achieve clarity about what they want, to trust and collaborate with the therapist, and then to act rationally upon the basis of that information – all of this is presupposed by behavioural interventions, especially those procedures labelled *instigation therapy* by Kanfer and Phillips (1966), which involve implementation of specific suggestions by the clients in their daily environments. Gurman and Knudson (1978) have suggested that in behavioural marital therapy it is assumed (often incorrectly) that the spouses are two 'rational' adults 'in large part, directly open to the therapist's suggestions and counsel on how to achieve behavioral change . . . in their own rational self-interest' (p. 125). Yet numerous clients seemingly do not enter therapy able to function at such mature levels. In fact, deficits in 'maturity' may be the chief problem. In some clients the capacities to act rationally on their own behalfs must first be developed. How best to do so is a question to which many systems of psychotherapy have proposed many different answers, all of which involve clinical and theoretical incorporation of the irrational, emotion-driven aspects of life. Both the limited power of the 'reason-based' methods of cognitive behaviour therapy to modify irrational feelings and actions, and the shortcomings of the theories of emotion upon which such methods are predicated, have been underscored by a number of eminent behaviour therapists (Bandura, 1977; Rachman, 1981). In developing its own answer to the dilemmas posed by the resistance, lack of motivation, and seeming self-destructiveness manifested by many clients in therapy, modern behaviour therapy will probably need to achieve some improved formulation of the capricious and evanescent realm of affect (Pervin, 1981). Here it may find its Apollonian sensibility to be a hindrance.

AMORALITY

Amorality, when described as a dimension of modern consciousness, refers to the modern separation of fact and value and the removal of 'the good' from the objective order of things (Smith, 1982). This aspect of modernity is related to secularization, the ascendance of science, and the proliferation of technical reason (Habermas, 1973). Within a technological society, the real, objective external reality of the world is constituted exclusively by empirically derived 'facts'. Morality comes to be viewed as subjective and relative (Adams, 1975; MacIntyre, 1981). Consistent with this axiological stance of modernity, behaviour therapists have tended to be ethical sceptics and relativists (Erwin, 1978; Kitchener, 1980). Behaviour therapy has also sought a clear demarcation between the realms of fact and value, and has attempted to include within its purview only those propositions that could be verified by empirical test. When contrasted with the theoretical foundations of other approaches, the clinical theory that underlies behaviour therapy is less normative. Two related developments in the history of behaviour therapy help to explain this lack of evaluative content.

The goals of traditional psychotherapy were provided in large measure by theories of personality that supplied some definition of what people ought to be and a picture of optimal human functioning. Numerous commentators have demonstrated the evaluative character of traditional personology (Hogan, 1975; Rieff, 1966; Sampson, 1977), revealing such constructs as 'sublimation', 'social interest', and 'self-actualization' to be moral terms operating in disguise, and serving a clear prescriptive function within their respective approaches.

But the kind of personality theory that infused earlier systems of psychotherapy with prescriptive thrust was antithetical to the behavioural approach. In its first years, behaviour therapy favoured explanations of behavioural dysfunction derived from conditioning theory, and emphasized the external, observable determinants of behaviour. Mischel's (1968) critique of classical personology and psychodiagnosis was widely read, and was so frequently cited by behaviour therapists that it came to be regarded as a basic text in the field. Behaviour therapy rejected trait-based conceptions of human behaviour (Craighead et al., 1981) in favour of a complex 'cognitive social learning theory' (Bandura, 1977; Mischel, 1973) that is neutral with respect to what would constitute a personal ideal or ideal person.

The inherent ethical thrust of behaviour therapy's clinical theory was also limited by what has frequently been cited as a defining characteristic of the approach (Kazdin, 1978) – that is, its opposition to the medical or disease model of psychological dysfunction. Here again, behaviour therapy divested itself of a system of global, evaluative labels that defines what kinds of persons are in need of therapeutic attention, and in what direction their behaviour ought to be changed. The amorality of behavioural clinical theory is entirely consistent with the proclivities of behaviour therapy toward objectivity and facticity. This kind of amorality, however, can serve a higher metamorality. The aspiration to a value-free clinical theory, one that minimally constrains possible therapeutic directions, is entirely consistent with the modern 'formal' virtues of freedom, tolerance, and equality (Stanley, 1978) and with an ideology that emphasizes democratic humanism.

HUMANISM

One of the odd ironies that emerged from the early literature critical of behavioural approaches (e.g. Wheelis, 1973) was the suggestion that behaviour therapy is antithetical to humanistic viewpoints. In the 1980s there were at least two versions of humanism reflected in contemporary psychology. The humanistic psychology of Rogers, Perls, and Maslow espoused a kind of 'romantic' humanism in its emphasis upon cultivation of the passions, aesthetic and emotional sensitivity, and creativity. Behaviour therapy, on the other hand, was imbued with a 'classical' humanism. In fact, no other system of psychotherapy can lay such a direct and legitimate claim to the humanistic tradition of the Enlightenment. This is the tradition that, without reservation, commits its allegiance to the primacy of science and reason in intellectual affairs, opposes all irrational authority and arbitrary privilege, and dedicates itself to the active enhancement of human liberty (Brinton, 1963). 1980s humanistic psychology, with its emphasis on feeling and spontaneity, was certainly antagonistic to the rationality of behaviour therapy, just as the Romantic movement of the nineteenth century was opposed to the Enlightenment's subordination of other human capacities to the dictates of reason. Both behaviour therapy and humanistic psychology, however, reflect what is common to all forms of humanism: a dedication to the promotion of human freedom and happiness (Lamont, 1982).

The early years of behaviour therapy are appropriately viewed as a kind of psychotherapeutic reformation. The flavour of this reformation is found in such classic works as Bandura's (1969) *Principles of Behavior Modification,* Ullmann and Krasner's (1965) *Case Studies in Behavior Modification,* and Lazarus's (1971) *Behavior Therapy and Beyond.* Behaviour therapy was a vigorous, polemical reform movement that sought to hold the feet of dogmatic therapeutic creeds to the fire of empirical test, to challenge irrational authority, and to unleash human capacities for exploration, achievement, and self-determination. Early behaviour therapy supplied powerful theoretical and methodological correctives to the field of psychotherapy by its introduction of alternative models of human functioning, and its insistence upon rigorous evaluation of therapeutic methods.

But behaviour therapy also provided an ethical as well as a scientific corrective to the field of psychotherapy. It was a social movement with an ideological agenda. The ethical motives of its founders, when inferred from their writings, seem clear:

> 'A behavioral approach to the formulation and treatment of people called abnormal ... can only end in the realm called humanism ... It is to be hoped that giving up concepts of demons and diseases leads to more accurate observation and more effective responses. The object is to give people not charity but dignity, not tolerance but respect. To the extent that a person can do this, he is a little closer to the realities of his existence, a little freer of his intellectual limitations, a little more a human being.'
>
> (Ullmann and Krasner, 1969: 599)

Even so rigorous and precise a thinker as Bandura, who was always careful to separate the realms of fact and value, showed in himself a bit of the reformer when he spoke out against the potential abuses of traditional psychotherapy:

> 'More serious from an ethical standpoint is the unilateral redefinition of goals by which psychotherapists often impose insight objectives (which mainly involve subtle belief conversions) upon persons desiring changes in their behavioral functioning . . . behavioral approaches hold much greater promise than traditional methods for the advancement of self-determination and the fulfillment of human capabilities.'
>
> (Bandura, 1969: 112)

The ethical spirit of behaviour therapy was iconoclastic, egalitarian, and radically pragmatic. These values functioned as an antithesis to the pronounced strain of scholasticism, indifference to scientific self-scrutiny, and conformity that, at that time, ran through medical psychiatry, much of psychoanalysis, and the mental-health movement in general (Franks and Rosenbaum, 1983; Szasz, 1978).

Early behavioural models were advanced in the spirit of reform, within that philosophical context that presupposes that science and hence human abilities are capable of transforming the human situation. Time has left largely unaltered both the humanistic purposes and the faith in science that were characteristic of the first days of behaviour therapy. In his presidential address to the Association for Advancement of Behavior Therapy, David Barlow (1980) stated:

> 'If nothing else behavior therapy is a true, humanistic approach to behavioral and emotional problems . . . [and] at the core of the philosophy of humanism is a supreme faith in human reason and the methods of science to confront and solve the many problems that humans face and to rearrange the world so that human life will prosper.'
>
> (p. 316)

PSYCHOTHERAPY AS TECHNOLOGY: LIMITATIONS AND ANOMALIES

VALUES AND PSYCHOTECHNOLOGY

Wilson and O'Leary (1980) provided a concise and illustrative statement on the place of values within the behavioural approach: 'Selecting effective techniques with which to change behavior is an empirical question in which the therapist is presumably an expert; choosing therapeutic objectives is a matter of value judgement and ought to be determined primarily by the client' (p. 285). The position on values stated here is not unique to these authors but is also found in Bandura (1969) and other major sources on behaviour therapy. When this position is pressed to its logical limits, however, certain anomalies emerge.

According to the behavioral view, the therapist ascertains the client's goals and then facilitates the realization of those objectives. Of course, the therapist and client must engage in some kind of communication for the therapeutic aims to emerge. But if behaviour therapy is, as it claims to be, 'nothing more than an applied science', several questions come to mind. Are there scientifically documented techniques of goal assessment? If not, then what procedures are being employed by the behaviour therapist in this sphere of activity? Is the behavioural clinician then thought to be operating outside the bounds of science? What about the statement that the therapeutic objectives ought to be determined by the client? Is this statement itself considered a value judgement or a proposition of science? Suppose the client wants the therapist to choose the objectives. What then? Because it is necessary for the behaviour therapist to get involved in some way in a discussion of objectives with the client, if this dialogue does not derive from controlled laboratory studies, then this important part of behaviour therapy is without empirical basis. We have in the behavioural literature thousands of studies of therapeutic technique and a growing literature on behavioural assessment but certainly up to the mid-1980s, virtually no attention to what therapists are doing when they assist the client in specifying exactly what it is that the client wants to achieve in therapy.

It is, in fact, inconceivable that a programme of laboratory research could dictate a total course of action for the therapist. The propositions of science take the logical form of material implication: If A, then B. In its most elegant and useful configuration, science is made up of testable, falsifiable propositions that specify *predictive* relationships among variables or events (Popper, 1962). Research can tell us only *which* techniques will achieve *what* therapeutic objectives or the achievement of *which* objectives is related to *what* life outcomes. But knowledge of this kind is insufficient to account for the conduct of behaviour therapy. The structure of scientific knowledge is such that it describes contingent relations among phenomena. Science can tell us only what events will follow other events. Hence, research can never generate the goals of therapy. Yet the therapist cannot act in the absence of a clear sense of which therapeutic objectives or what life outcomes to promote. The therapist requires a starting point, some basis upon which to make the first move, some rule that channels his or her attention and behaviour. These primary directives of any system of psychotherapy derive fundamentally not from research but from an ethical ideal, some vision of what is good and proper in human affairs. Any system of thought, when it enters the realm of application, requires bases for the decisions and choices necessary to that application and, therefore, some value position. Hence, behaviour therapy must necessarily contain propositions that do not derive from empirical research. The fundamental premiss of clinical behaviour therapy is that the client shall decide the goals of therapy. This directive, upon which clinical behaviour therapy is predicated, is not a scientific proposition but an ethical axiom, one that is related closely to its modern democratic, humanistic ideological underpinnings described earlier.

We must, however, question a viewpoint that requires that clinical activity be so subservient to the avowed preferences of the client. Perhaps the first years of behaviour therapy, with their redoubtable successes, led early practitioners astray and convinced them wrongly that all human difficulties can be treated as straightforwardly as simple phobias, given a proper behavioural assessment. Yet clients do not always know what they want, much less what ails them, in the initial stages of therapy. Presenting complaints often are only tangentially related to the client's fundamental problems (Woolfolk and Lazarus, 1979). Along with various critics of behaviour therapy (Gurman and Knudson, 1978; Messer and Winokur, 1980), we see in the behavioural literature an unfortunate tendency to take client behaviour dogmatically at face value, as though to do anything else would constitute an implicit endorsement of the kinds of psychoanalytic mystification that assumes nothing the client says is ever what it seems to be on the surface.

What we find missing in contemporary behaviour therapy is not only the absence of any locus of evaluation external to the therapeutic direction prescribed by the client, but also a failure to allow for any basis for such an evaluation. It has been apparent to poets, philosophers, and psychotherapists throughout the ages that an individual's aims in life are often functionally related to that individual's suffering. Inappropriate goals, fantastic goals, or conflict amongst goals are at the root of many problems of living. The great difficulty for behaviour therapists is in remaining faithful to their system while simultaneously managing to encompass client aims within a therapeutic dialectic, to challenge the client's goals, or to view certain of the objectives that people bring into therapy as manifestations or outright causes of their difficulties. Thus, behaviour therapy contains few concepts that allow the therapist to take any perspective on the client external to the client's frame of reference. Freud, at least, could within his system unabashedly advocate the ability to love and the ability to work as universal criteria of competence in living. The behaviour therapist has no analogous pronouncement to make. In the absence of such normative concepts as health and sickness, growth and stagnation, which in other systems transcend the preferences of the individual, the behaviour therapist has fewer categories with which to evaluate client behaviour. Thus, without an independent, therapeutic compass of this sort the behaviour therapist is always thrown back upon the preferences of the individual. One might, in fact, argue that this is a principal ideological vector of behaviour therapy: to dispense with perspectives that limit the rights of individuals to pursue self-chosen goals in the most expedient manner science can produce.

MEANING AND PURPOSE

Throughout its short history, behaviour therapy not only has aspired to the ideals of science but also has sought to exclude from its province all that was not or could not be science. Hence, it falls prey to the difficulties that the modern scientific-technological perspective has in encompassing some essential aspects of the contemporary human dilemma. Behaviour therapy seems especially limited in addressing those concerns and discontents that have come to be seen by sociologists and philosophers as inevitable accompaniments of modernity. A chief discontent relates to what is lost in the transition from pre-modern forms of social organization to modern society.

With the advent of modernity, those institutions that once provided a sense of meaningful identity and belonging – the church, the community, and the family – were weakened and the ties of individuals to them were diminished (Berger and Kellner, 1981). Such entities as religion, art, and ethics, once possessed of an authority equal or superior to that of science, have become debased epistemological currencies. They have lost their status as constituents of an objective external reality, been made relative, and been reduced to subjective elements in the inner lives of individuals (Heller, 1959). The loss of community, the failure of modern institutions to provide durable social support for so many, the relativization of standards of conduct, and the inability of modern consciousness to fashion some intersubjective consensus on metaphysical questions have led to considerable psychosocial stress (Garfield, 1979) and philosophical disorientation (Smith, 1982).

Modernity has accomplished many far-reaching transformations, but it has not fundamentally changed the finitude, fragility, and mortality of the human condition. What it has accomplished is seriously to weaken those definitions of reality that previously made the human condition easier to bear (Berger et al., 1973: 185).

As Frankl (1969) and numerous philosophers from Kierkegaard (1962) to Sartre (1956) have attested, there are inherent difficulties in any attempt to fashion a meaningful understanding of existence in terms of the moral and epistemological categories provided by scientific culture. Nor is a 'sense of meaning' a philosophical frill, an intellectual luxury with import only for those consumed by too much zeal for understanding the ultimate nature of things. Concluding his analysis of an impressive epidemiological data base, Antonovsky (1979) argued that some aspects of physical health and the maintenance of tolerable levels of psychological stress depend upon what he termed a *sense of coherence.* As Antonovsky defined it, a sense of coherence requires that one's coping activities occur within a personally meaningful context of community, tradition, or cosmos that both sets a limit to personal control and makes 'affectively comprehensible' the many uncontrollable and tragic aspects of human life. In related research that has confirmed the wisdom of sociologists and existential psychologists, Kobasa and her colleagues (Kobasa, 1979; Kobasa et al., 1981, 1982) have shown that the capacity to tolerate life stress is greatly impaired by alienation, lack of purpose, and the absence of commitment. Behaviour therapy has a difficult time conceptualizing and doing justice to questions of meaning and purpose. As we have seen, science and the technology that flows from it are capable of generating means for the achievement of preordained ends, but not the ends themselves. This is because the structure of knowledge within behaviour therapy allows it to illuminate only the relationship between means and ends. It cannot adumbrate the wisdom, appropriateness, or desirability of ends except in relation to some standard (some other end) that is generated independently of orthodox behaviour therapy procedure. Behaviour therapy, as it is presently constituted, is unable to further the search for meaning because success in this endeavour necessitates the discovery or creation of the goals and standards that supply purpose and meaning – the determination of what is worth doing at all rather than the most effective means of doing it.

As one might imagine, behaviour therapists have written sparingly on this topic of 'existential questions'. Kanfer and Saslow (1969) have essentially advocated an abdication by behaviour therapy of responsibility for addressing issues involving 'dissatisfactions with or uncertainties' about 'self-attitudes, or a loss of meaning or purpose' and a reliance upon 'clergymen, teachers, counsellors, work supervisors, even neighbors and friends' (p. 429). Ullmann and Krasner (1975) have quite correctly pointed out that some self-reports of *angst* mask more conventional clinical problems amenable to straightforward behavioural intervention. But not all existential quandaries can be explained away. And those that cannot do not admit of technical answers. About all behaviour therapy can offer here is some technique to control the emotional and behavioural impact of an absence of meaning. And although such palliatives have their place, one doubts that the simple elimination or control of the negative affect and cognitions emanating from our modern existential predicament is either an effective or a worthy solution. Among behavioural clinicians, Goldfried and Davison (1976) manifest the clearest understanding of this point and characterize the handling of existential concerns as a major shortcoming of behaviour therapy.

CODA: AN UNCRITICAL POSTSCRIPT

The aim of this writing has been critical. We have sought to uncover the ideological foundations of behaviour therapy and subject them to critical scrutiny. We see in this work neither an endorsement nor a repudiation of behaviour therapy, but rather a delineation of the distinctive features of its assumptive world as they emerge through the critical process. We have found problems with the approach that seem inextricably bound up with essential features of modern consciousness and contemporary Western culture. As we have mentioned earlier, behaviour therapy is not alone amongst systems of psychotherapy in reflecting modern ideological positions. Behaviour therapy is, perhaps, simply the most literal translation into therapy practice of certain facets of modernity. A comparative study of contemporary therapeutic ideologies is, however, a topic for another writing. We are satisfied here to take one step toward developing a model of inquiry for understanding the embeddedness of systems of psychotherapy within history and culture.

A hermeneutic analysis of psychotherapy allows us to take an alternative, somewhat more distal perspective – one not so thoroughly informed by the same assumptions as the object of scrutiny. Knowledge so derived is of both intrinsic interest and practical import. It is vital that we frame our understanding of psychotherapy in social and historical terms because the relation between psychotherapy and culture is one of reciprocal influence. Systems of psychotherapy not only reflect culture but shape culture as well. If modern men and women are indeed self-defining animals, as Charles Taylor (1975) has suggested, then the values and human image implicit in psychotherapies come to be consequential components in that process of self-definition.

REFERENCES

Adams, E. M. (1975) *Philosophy and the Modern Mind: A Philosophical Critique of Modern Western Civilization*, Chapel Hill: University of North Carolina Press.

Antonovsky, A. (1979) *Health, Stress, and Coping*, San Francisco: Jossey-Bass.

Bandura, A. (1969) *Principles of Behavior Modification*, New York: Holt, Rinehart, & Winston.

Bandura, A. (1977) *Social Learning Theory*, Englewood Cliffs, NJ: Prentice-Hall.

Barlow, D. (1980) 'Behavior therapy: the next decade', *Behavior Therapy*, 11: 315–28.

Barrett, W. (1978) *The Illusion of Technique*, Garden City, NY: Anchor Press/Doubleday.

Bartley, W. W. (1962) *The Retreat to Commitment*, New York: A. A. Knopf.

Baumer, F. L. (1977) *Modem European Thought: Continuity and Change in Ideas 1600–1950*, New York: Macmillan.

Beck, A. T. (1976) *Cognitive Therapy and the Emotional Disorders*, New York: International Universities Press.

Benedict, R. (1934) *Patterns of Culture*, Boston: Houghton Mifflin.

Berger, P. L. (1977) *Facing up to Modernity*, New York: Basic Books.

Berger, P. L. and Kellner, H. (1981) *Sociology Reinterpreted*, Garden City, NY: Anchor Press/Doubleday.

Berger, P. L. and Luckman, T. (1966) *The Social Construction of Reality*, Garden City, NY: Doubleday.

Berger, P. L., Berger, B., and Kellner, H. (1973) *The Homeless Mind*, New York: Random House.

Bergin, A. E. (1980) 'Psychotherapy and religious values', *Journal of Consulting and Clinical Psychology*, 48: 95–105.

Brinton, C. (1963) *The Shaping of Modern Thought*, Englewood Cliffs, NJ: Prentice-Hall.

Burtt, E. A. (1964) *The Metaphysical Foundations of Modern Science*, London: Routledge & Kegan Paul.

Buss, A. R. (1975) 'The emerging field of the sociology of psychological knowledge', *American Psychologist*, 30: 988–1002.

Craighead, W. E., Kazdin, A. E., and Mahoney, M. J. (1981) *Behavior Modification: Principles, Issues, and Applications*, Boston: Houghton Mifflin.

D'Zurilla, T. J. and Goldfried, M. R. (1971) 'Problem solving and behavior modification', *Journal of Abnormal Psychology*, 78: 107–26.

Ellis, A. and Grieger, R. (eds) (1977) *Handbook of Rational-emotive Therapy*, New York: Springer.

Ellul, J. (1964) *The Technological Society*, New York: Random House.

Erwin, E. (1978) *Behavior Therapy: Scientific, Philosophical, and Moral Foundations*, Cambridge:

Cambridge University Press.
Feyerabend, P. (1975) *Against Method : Toward an Anarchist Theory of Knowledge*, London: New Left Books.
Frankl, V. E. (1969) *The Will to Meaning*, New York: New American Library.
Franks, C. M. and Rosenbaum, M. (1983) 'Behavior therapy: overview and personal reflections', in M. Rosenbaum, C. M. Franks, and Y. Jaffe (eds), *Perspectives on Behavior Therapy in the Eighties*, New York: Springer.
Gadamer, H. (1975) *Truth and Method*, New York: Crossroad.
Garfield, C. A. (ed.) (1979) *Stress and Survival: The Emotional Realities of Life-threatening Illness*, St. Louis: C. V. Mosby.
Gehlen, A. (1980) *Man in the Age of Technology*, New York: Columbia University Press.
Goldfried, M. R. and Davison, G. C. (1976) *Clinical Behavior Therapy*, New York: Holt, Rinehart, & Winston.
Gouldner, A. W. (1976) *The Dialectic of Ideology and Technology*, New York: Seabury Press.
Gurman, A. S. and Knudson, R. M. (1978) 'Behavioral marriage therapy: I. A psychodynamic–systems analysis and critique'. *Family Process*, 17: 121–38.
Habermas, J. (1972) *Knowlege and Human Interests*, Boston: Beacon Press.
Habermas, J. (1973) *Theory and Practice*, Boston: Beacon Press.
Hayek, F. A. (1952) *The Counter-revolution of Science*, Glencoe, Ill.: Free Press.
Heller, E. (1959) *The Disinherited Mind*, New York: Meridian.
Hogan, R. (1975) 'Theoretical egocentrism and the problem of compliance', *American Psychologist*, 30, 533–40.
Horkheimer, M. (1972) *Critical Theory*, New York: The Seabury Press.
Kanfer, F. H. and Phillips, J. S. (1966) 'Behavior therapy: panacea for all ills or a passing fancy ?, *Archives of General Psychiatry*, 15, 114–28.
Kanfer, F. H, & Saslow, G. (1969) 'Behavioral diagnosis', in C. M. Franks (ed.), *Behavior Therapy: Appraisal and Status*, New York: McGraw-Hill.
Kazdin, A. E. (1978) *History of Behavior Modification: Experimental Foundations of Contemporary Research*, Baltimore: University Park Press.
Kazdin, A. E. and Wilson, G. T. (1978) *Evaluation of Behavior Therapy: Issues, Evidence, and Research Strategies*, Cambridge, Mass.: Ballinger.
Kierkegaard, S. (1962) *The Present Age*, New York: Harper & Row.
Kitchener, R. F. (1980) 'Ethical relativism and behavior therapy', *Journal of Consulting and Clinical Psychology*, 48: 1–7.
Kobasa, S. C. (1979) 'Stressful life events, personality and health: an inquiry into hardiness', *Journal of Personality and Social Psychology*, 37: 1–11.
Kobasa, S. C., Maddi, S. R., and Courington, S. (1981) 'Personality and constitution as mediators in the stress–illness relationship', *Journal of Health and Social Behavior*, 22: 368–78.
Kobasa, S. C., Maddi, S. R., and Puccetti, M. C. (1982) 'Personality and exercise as buffers in the stress-illness relationship', *Journal of Behavioral Medicine*, 5: 391–404.
Krasner, L. (1962) 'The therapist's contribution', in H. H. Strupp and L. Luborsky (eds), *Research in Psychotherapy: Vol. 2*, Washington, D.C.: American Psychological Association.
Krasner, L. (1982) 'Behavior therapy: on roots, contexts, and growth', in G. T. Wilson and C. M. Franks (eds), *Contemporary Behavior Therapy*, New York: Guilford Press.
Kuhn, T. S. (1970a) 'Reflections on my critics', in I. Lakatos and A. Musgrove (eds), *Criticism and the Growth of Knowledge*, Cambridge: Cambridge University Press.

Kuhn, T. S. (1970b) *The Structure of Scientific Revolutions* (2nd edn), Chicago: University of Chicago Press.
Lamont, C. (1982) *The Philosophy of Humanism*, New York: Frederick Ungar.
Lazarus, A. A. (1971) *Behavior Therapy and Beyond*, New York: McGraw-Hill.
Lazarus, A. A. (1976) *Multimodal Behavior Therapy*, New York: Springer.
Levi-Strauss, C. (1966) *The Savage Mind*, Chicago: University of Chicago Press.
London, P. (1964) *The Modes and Morals of Psychotherapy*, New York: Holt, Rinehart, & Winston.
Lowe, C. M. (1976) *Value Orientations in Counseling and Psychotherapy: The Meanings of Mental Health* (2nd edn), Cranston, R.I.: Carroll Press.
MacIntyre, A. (1981) *After Virtue: A Study in Moral Theory*, Notre Dame, Ind.: University of Notre Dame Press.
Mahoney, M. J. (1980) 'Psychotherapy and the structure of personal revolutions', in M. J. Mahoney (ed.), *Psychotherapy Process*, New York: Plenum.
Mahoney, M. J. and Arnkoff, D. B. (1978) 'Cognitive and self-control therapies', in S. L. Garfield and A. E. Bergin (eds), *Handbook of Psychotherapy and Behavior Change* (2nd edn), New York: Wiley.
Mannheim, K. (1936) *Ideology and Utopia*, New York: Harcourt, Brace, & World.
Meichenbaum, D. H. (1977) *Cognitive Behavior Modification: An Integralive Approach*, New York: Plenum.
Messer, S. B. and Winokur, M. (1980) 'Some limits to the integration of psychoanalytic and behavior therapy', *American Psychologist*, 35: 818–27.
Messer, S. B. and Winokur, M. (1984) 'Ways of knowing and visions of reality in psychoanalytic and behavior therapy', in H. Arkowitz and S. B. Messer (eds), *Psychoanalytic Therapy and Behavior Therapy: Is Integration Possible?*, New York: Plenum.
Mischel, W. (1968) *Personality and Assessment*, New York: Wiley.
Mischel, W. (1973) 'Toward a cognitive social learning reconceptualization of personality', *Psychological Review*, 80: 252–83.
Moore, W. E. (1963) *Social Change*, Englewood Cliffs, NJ: Prentice-Hall.
Nelson, B. (1981) *On the Roads to Modernity* (ed. T. E. Huff), Totowa, NJ: Rowman and Littlefield.
Nietzsche, F. (1956) *The Birth of Tragedy and the Genealogy of Morals*, Garden City, NY: Doubleday/Anchor.
Nisbet, R. (1976) *Sociology as an Art Form*, London: Oxford University Press.
Parsons, T. (1971) *The System of Modern Societies*, Englewood Cliffs, NJ: Prentice-Hall.
Pervin, L. A. (1981) 'Conceptual and applied limitations of behavior therapy: a dynamic systems perspective', paper presented at the meeting of the Association for Advancement of Behavior Therapy, Toronto, Canada, November.
Polanyi, M. (1966) *The Tacit Dimension*, Garden City, NY: Doubleday.
Popper, K. R. (1962) *The Logic of Scientific Discovery*, London: Hutchinson.
Rachman, S. (1981) 'The primacy of affect: some theoretical implications', *Behaviour Research and Therapy*, 19: 279–90.
Ricoeur, P. (1981) *Hermeneutics and the Human Sciences* (ed. J. B. Thompson), Cambridge: Cambridge University Press.
Rieff, P. (1966) *The Triumph of the Therapeutic*, New York: Harper & Row.
Sampson, E. E. (1977) 'Psychology and the American ideal', *Journal of Personality and Social Psychology*, 35: 767–82.
Sampson, E. E. (1978) 'Scientific paradigms and social values: wanted – a scientific revolution', *Journal of Personality and Social Psychology*, 36: 1332–43.

Sampson, E. E. (1981) 'Cognitive psychology as ideology', *American Psychologist*, 36: 730–43.
Sartre, J. (1956) *Being and Nothingness*, New York: Philosophical Library.
Scheler, M. (1960) *Die Wissenformen und die Gesellschaft*, Bern: Francke.
Shils, E. A. (1981) *Tradition*, Chicago: University of Chicago Press.
Smith, H. (1982) *Beyond the Post-modern Mind*, New York: Crossroad.
Stanley, M. (1978) *The Technological Conscience: Survival and Dignity in an Age of Expertise*, New York: Free Press.
Szasz, T. (1978) *The Myth of Psychotherapy*, New York: Anchor.
Taylor, C. (1971) 'Interpretation and the sciences of man', *Review of Metaphysics*, 25: 3–51.
Taylor, C. (1975) *Hegel*, Cambridge: Cambridge University Press.
Ullmann, L. P. and Krasner, L. (eds) (1965) *Case Studies in Behavior Modification*, New York: Holt.
Ullmann, L. P. and Krasner, L. (1969) *A Psychological Approach to Abnormal Behavior*, Englewood Cliffs, NJ: Prentice-Hall (2nd edn, 1975).
Weber, M. (1958) *From Max Weber: Essays in Sociology* (eds H. H. Gerth and C. W. Mills), New York: Oxford University Press.
Weimer, W. B. (1979) *Notes on the Methodology of Scientific Research*, Hillsdale, NJ: Erlbaum.
Wheelis, A. (1973) *How People Change*, New York: Harper & Row.
Wilson, G. T. and Evans, I. (1977) 'The therapist–client relationship in behavior therapy', in A. S. Gurman and A. M. Razin (eds), *The Therapist's Contribution to Effective Psychotherapy: An Empirical Approach*, New York: Pergamon Press.
Wilson, G. T. and O'Leary, K. D. (1980) *Principles of Behavior Therapy*, Englewood Cliffs, NJ: Prentice-Hall.
Winner, L. (1977) *Autonomous Technology: Technics-out-of-control as a Theme in Political Thought'* Cambridge, Mass.: MIT Press.
Wolpe, J. (1973) *The Practice of Behavior Therapy* (2nd edn), New York: Pergamon Press.
Woolfolk, R. L. and Lazarus, A. A. (1979) 'Between laboratory and clinic: paving the two-way street', *Cognitive Therapy and Research*, 3: 239–44.

CODA, 2008: CBT REVISITED ...

A paper upon which the article, 'Behavior therapy and the ideology of modernity' (Woolfolk and Richardson, 1984, reproduced above) was based was presented at the annual meeting of the Association for the Advancement of Behavior Therapy in the autumn of 1982. In the piece, we presented a critique of the behaviour therapy of the early 1980s, examining its sociocultural context and revealing its philosophical underpinnings. Much change has occurred in the culture of the mental-health professions during the period in which behaviour therapy evolved into cognitive behaviour therapy (CBT); and the target of our critique is in many ways different from the behaviour therapy of the mid-twentieth century.

The predecessors of the current CBT establishment, the early behaviour therapists, were committed to empirical testing of therapeutic interventions. They saw themselves as scientists, not artists; less as health-care providers or healers, and more as behavioural engineers or as educators. In its first years, behaviour therapy was theory-driven, committed to testing explanations of maladaptive behaviour that were derived from conditioning theory, and to a doctrinaire emphasis upon outcomes that were objective and observable. Mischel's (1968) critique of classical personology and psychodiagnosis was widely read and so frequently cited by behaviour therapists that it came to be regarded as a basic text in the field. Behaviour therapy rejected person-centred, trait-based conceptions of human psychology in favour of a complex 'social learning theory' (Bandura, 1977) that was idiographic in sensibility and focused on discrete behaviour in particular contexts. Rejection of the medical or disease model of psychopathology, including traditional psychiatric diagnostic categories, was so central to behaviour therapy that it was frequently cited as a defining characteristic of the approach (Kazdin, 1978). Behaviour therapists contrasted their system with the more manifestly value-laden therapies of psychoanalysis and humanistic psychotherapy, presenting it as a value-free psychotechnology.

How did the pioneer researchers of the early days of behaviour therapy become members of the scientific health-care establishment and bed-fellows with the pharmaceutical industry and various other advocates of evidence-based medicine? How did they come to abjure their commitments to observable behavioural outcome measures to embrace DSM and ICD diagnoses which are, in practice, little more than assessor-guided patient self-reports, i.e. based on data derived from structured clinical interviews? No one can say with certainty how the behaviour therapy movement evolved into an advocacy group for today's diagnosis-driven, empirically supported treatments, but the factors involved represent a complicated sociocultural evolution.

First, there was common cause with those psychiatrists who authored DSM-III. The biological revolution in psychiatry did what research on psychotherapy could never have done, put a stake in the heart of psychoanalysis. The enemy of my enemy is my friend. Most biological psychiatrists had little use for Freud; those who did put their loyalties aside in pursuit of the holy grail of a psychiatry that would resemble somatic medicine. The new DSM, stripped of its psychoanalytic theoretical underpinnings (and almost all theory of any kind), was substantially more palatable to behaviour therapists than were the two earlier versions of the document. But neither DSM-III nor any of its successors takes a behavioural, situationist, or idiographic approach to psychopathology. Behaviour therapy's original metatheoretical commitment to the potentially infinite variety and ultimate uniqueness of each individual patient's learning history was replaced with the medicalized, Procrustean categorical nosology of the DSMs and ICDs.

Biological psychiatry researchers, apparently, also found a way to live with CBT. It really wasn't that difficult, once DSM-III became orthodoxy. The methods of cognitive behaviour therapy were conceived as psychotechnology, standardized in manuals, and in their method of administration could be viewed as analogous to drug treatment and, therefore, amenable to inclusion in randomized controlled trials (RCTs). As the biopsychiatry revolution unfolded, and the pharmaceutical industry earned billions and invested billions more in developing and testing psychotropic drugs, RCTs, the state of the art for FDA approval for many decades, also became the gold standard for evaluating the efficacy of psychotherapy. The US National Institute of Health funded numerous RCTs evaluating psychosocial treatments for psychopathology, sometimes in tandem with pharmacological interventions. Standardized CBT techniques easily fit into the methodological mould of the RCT, and were readily assimilated into the culture of contemporary biomedical research and evidence-based medicine. All was copasetic.

Of course, along the way something was lost. The atheoretical stance of each DSM, along with the emergence of the 'horserace' or 'Coke versus Pepsi' comparative outcome study, produced another change in the culture of therapy efficacy studies. These studies became increasingly unmoored from theoretical formulations about the nature of psychopathology and from hypotheses about the fundamental mechanisms of therapeutic change. Pretensions to the status of applied science were widespread, but CBT research had, in fact, devolved into something that, although still empirical, was not science. Psychotherapy efficacy research had morphed into something much more straightforward and compatible with the industrial culture that it seemed inevitably to emulate. It had become little more than product testing.

Ensuing events justified the concerns of those who perceived an intellectual poverty and a failure of theoretical advance at the heart of the CBT establishment. Things were also a bit discouraging on the practical front. There was a lack of clear-cut winners in the various therapy derbies, as well as much evidence for the importance of 'common factors' and investigator allegiance effects. That very redoubtable medical-style research that had yielded various life-saving medicines seemed, in this case, to result mostly in review after review filled with meta-analyses signifying nothing, save that almost all psychotherapy produces some benefit for patients.

There is a place in psychotherapy research for something like simple product testing, just to get a pragmatic read on the impact of interventions. But this kind of activity can hardly be the mainstay of our efforts at intellectual advance, given that we are relatively ignorant about the active ingredients of our interventions as well as the mechanisms through which they produce their effects. The absence of viable theory, the lack of compelling research findings, and the role that extra-scientific sociocultural forces play in the process, invite us to do just what contributors to this book encourage – namely, try to identify and rethink the conceptual and sociocultural underpinnings of our work, and of the larger enterprises and institutions of which that work is a part. One way to proceed in this rethinking is to attempt to come to grips with the sociohistorical context in which psychotherapy occurs, and with the various disguised ideologies that may underlie it (Richardson et al., 1999; Woolfolk, 1998; Woolfolk and Murphy, 2004; see also Brazier and Lees, Chapters 7 and 7 respectively, this volume).

By the 1990s, some within the CBT movement had raised objections to the emphasis in CBT on modifying and manipulating cognition and behaviour and a view of the passions as entities to be regulated and controlled. The so-called 'third wave' of behaviour therapy (Hayes et al., 1999; Linehan, 1993) and its articulation of rationales for Buddhist-like attitudes of acceptance toward aversive emotional experiences are quite compatible with the pleading that we made years ago for behaviour therapists to question their view of psychotherapy as pure technique, to discard their Appollonian rationalistic sensibilities, and to understand that, frequently, one's experience should not be so much a target for modification as a process to be observed, savoured, or endured. Some years ago, in similar fashion, we called for behaviour therapists to seek and adopt in their work a richer appreciation of life, the kind that is found in the humanities. In our view, human flourishing is not equivalent to, nor inevitably results from, the elimination of diagnosable mental disorder.

So today CBT is no longer a renegade, revolutionary movement. It has traded its commitments to ruthless empiricism and anti-medicalization for a comfortable place inside the big tent of the medical-industrial complex. Today's CBT is highly compatible with the contemporary *Zeitgeist.* Neuroscience, behavioural genetics, cognitive science, the medicalization of problems of living, and 'happiness economics' are all highly consonant with the technicism, rationality, mechanism, philosophical materialism, and alleged value neutrality of CBT, features that we identified many years ago. We have several kinds of concerns with the scientism that underlies CBT, biological psychiatry, cognitive neuroscience, and related endeavours. The first of these might be termed practical, and is related to a marketing mentality that has developed within CBT circles.

Although CBT has achieved a kind of cultural ascendancy, especially within the UK, the evidence for the superiority of CBT over other approaches to psychotherapy seems scanty, at best, as several contributors to this volume argue. CBT's coup has been achieved, not by a disinterested review of evidence but by the result of factors that can be more appropriately characterized as political or sociological. As the American Civil War general Nathan Bedford Forest might have put it, at the dawn of the new era of evidence-based medicine, CBT arrived first, and was armed with the most data. Though we ourselves have been contributors to the CBT literature and believe that many CBT techniques, e.g. exposure therapy for phobic behaviour, are sound and very clinically valuable, we believe that CBT has been oversold to the public, and that claims of its efficacy have been widely overstated. There is a strong analogy with the history of second-generation anti-depressants, where, after 25 years of ballyhoo, expectations are finally coming into accord with reality, a less optimistic reality than was promised by early proselytizing and drug-company marketing.

Another related problem having to do with CBT's rapid rise, and its rather impudent disdain for other pre-existing forms of therapy, is that we may be witnessing the erosion of the psychotherapeutic know-how and the clinical wisdom accumulated over the last century. Virtually all of the CBT founders and pioneers (e.g. Ellis, Beck, Lazarus) were initially trained in the methods and stylistics of some form of traditional psychotherapy. We were fortunate to know those founders personally, and to observe their clinical work. Such folk took for granted basic competency in forming and maintaining salutary therapeutic relationships. They tended to function as teachers, as problem-solvers who manifested a profound appreciation for the uniqueness of each individual they treated. They brought compassion, humour, artistry, and wisdom derived from life experience into the therapeutic arena.

As training in CBT has come to be removed further and further from the influence of those tacit principles and human qualities of the founders of CBT, there has been (in our humble personal opinions) a decline in, and a disdain for, the kind of judgement that results from viewing patients as extremely complex purposive creatures rather than as repositories of mental disorders. The transformation of psychotherapy from therapeutic dialogue to application of quasi-medical technology, either through the process of trainee selection or due to the effects of the training itself, has produced a generation of therapists who prefer to paint by the numbers, and who search for simple problems that can putatively be remedied by the straightforward application of explicit techniques. Fortunately, such therapists, so ruthlessly disciplined by their scientistic orthodoxies, are unlikely to be prey to such follies as past-life regression or the recovery of repressed memories. But to many nuances of the therapeutic situation they are too often tone-deaf; in their ministrations they too often are a bit ham-handed.

Alfred North Whitehead famously attributed philosophical disagreements between himself and Bertrand Russell to the inevitable conflict between a 'simple-minded' intellect (Russell's) and a 'muddle-headed' approach to thought (his own). Somewhat analogously, the evolution of psychotherapy from the old-time religion of psychoanalysis to the Brave New World of CBT suggests a traversing of the distance between the Scylla of the muddle-headed to the Charyabdis of the simple-minded. Much of our critique of the 1980s suggested that early behaviour therapists made the error of over-simplifying the world, partially as a result of the laudable effort to avoid the intellectual perils of psychoanalysis and similar forms of thought. Although the CBT of today differs in some ways from the behaviour therapy of the middle of the previous century, it retains its simple-minded sensibility, with all the advantages and disadvantages of a simplistic world-view.

'CODA 2008' REFERENCES

Bandura, A. (1977) *Social Learning Theory*, Englewood Cliffs, NJ: Prentice-Hall.

Hayes, S. C., Strosahl, K. D., and Wilson K. G. (1999) *Acceptance and Commitment Therapy: An Experiential Approach to Behavior Change*, New York: Guilford.

Kazdin, A. E. (1978) *History of Behavior Modification: Experimental Foundations of Contemporary Research*, Baltimore: University Park Press.

Linehan, M. M. (1993) *Cognitive-behavioral Treatment of Borderline Personality Disorder*, New York: Guilford.

Mischel, W. (1968) *Personality and Assessment*, New York: Wiley.

Richardson, F., Fowers, B., and Guignon, C. (1999) *Re-envisioning Psychology: Moral Dimensions of Theory and Practice*, San Francisco: Jossey-Bass.

Woolfolk, R. L. (1998) *The Cure of Souls: Science, Values, and Psychotherapy*, San Francisco: Jossey-Bass.

Woolfolk, R. L. and Murphy, D. (2004) 'Axiological foundations of psychotherapy', *Journal of Psychotherapy Integration*, 14: 168–91.

Woolfolk, R. L. and Richardson, F. C. (1984) 'Behavior therapy and the ideology of modernity', *American Psychologist*, 39: 777–86; reprinted in Miller, D. B. (ed.) (1993) *The Restoration of Dialogue: Readings in the Philosophy of Clinical Psychology*, Washington, D.C.: American Psychological Association; and in this volume.

CHAPTER 6

CBT IN HISTORICO-CULTURAL PERSPECTIVE

DAVID BRAZIER

Once all Europe, more or less, had one God. That God's gospel had spread across the whole continent, largely by persuasion. The impetus of conversion had been accelerated by the moral force of martyrdom – the evident willingness of adherents to die for their cause without aggressing against others. The doctrine of turning the other cheek had a compelling moral power, demonstrating on the one hand an unconditionality of love, faith, and acceptance, and on the other a spirit of duty and self-sacrifice triumphing over sinful nature. These two formed, as it were, the yin and yang of the Christian way. Together, they made a dynamic revolutionary force, but it is difficult to stand on two legs without constant forward momentum. To build a civilization, a third prop is required. This third leg came from the classical world that Christianity displaced yet incorporated.

The triumph of the new religion was consolidated when its leading theorists showed skill in appropriating prime elements of pagan philosophy – Augustine incorporating Plato, Thomas Aquinas, Aristotle, and all and sundry borrowing from the Stoics. In the Middle Ages, further learning was incorporated from India via the Islamic world, and algebra and algorithm became two of the very few Arabic words to find a way into the English language. Christianity catered for the heart and for the shadow sides of human nature, but it had to import from elsewhere a repertoire for catering for the head. Here, therefore, we find the origins of a metaphysic of science and materialism that the early Christian thinkers integrated with varying degrees of success into the dominant theistic paradigm. Thus, Europe acquired a culture in which three ideals held sway, the two wings of the Christian formula being supplemented by the precursors of natural science. Here were planted the seeds of later crises that still reverberate.

Our culture's value system thus rests upon a tripod of supporting pillars: faith, duty, and empiricism, or, alternatively, love, guilt, and rationalism. We could also call these traditions the Romantic, the Conservative, and the Puritan or Utilitarian. The medieval period knit them into a single fabric.

Time passed, and some of the original ideals became tarnished. The gospel originally spread by peaceful means came to be defended by martial ones. The turning of the cheek was displaced by the inquisition and the stake. The Albigensian 'heretics', who arguably embodied many of the original ideals better than their persecutors, were nonetheless exterminated in the name of the all-merciful God. The cruel exigencies of power and state did not completely obliterate the original ideals, but moral decay sapped the foundations. Eventually it was the practice of indulgences, of selling salvation for money, that provoked the great schism, led by Luther, that would expose the fundamentally weakened condition of Christendom.

Nonetheless, the real damage was not immediately fully apparent. People quarrelled, but they quarrelled about the nature and wishes of the God whose ultimate position, as yet, still seemed unassailable. Great thinkers like Descartes and Newton believed themselves to be exploring and revealing the creations of the God, and thereby further glorifying his holy name. They little realised their work would later be looked back upon as the beginning of secular philosophy. In the Age of Reason, initially, Reason was thought of as that of God in everyman. Reason was the crowning glory that God had bestowed on humans as his ultimate mark of favour. Reason and soul were almost synonymous; they were what distinguished us from the beasts.

By a slow insidious process, however, Reason itself gradually became God, displacing the former God; and since Reason was housed in the human breast, man himself started to take on the divine mantle. Humankind dispensed God's functions – justice, healing, favour, education, punishment, pardon, and, eventually, even the healing of souls. However, culture does not change abruptly. Even in the post-theistic age, the same fundamental ideals continued to hold sway, often under new names.

In the Age of Reason, Kant took up the cause of duty, appealing now not to God, but to a 'categorical imperative'; Hegel built upon the Romantic heritage with its roots in faith and love, and foresaw a dialectic of spirit carrying us ever upward; while Bentham hoisted the banner of utility. The same strands were being carried forward under new insignia. Arguably they were trading upon, and perhaps running down, the capital built up during the theistic age. Certainly it appears that they were rationalizing and seeking a ground other than God for the ideals that had long held sway. First there was the hope, expressed by Rousseau's company, that Reason itself could provide a sound Godless foundation. This hope proved illusory. Reason proved capable of rationalizing anything. The French Revolution provoked hope, then revulsion, as the blood flowed. Without any metaphysic as an anchor, the ship of civilization was adrift in a manner that seemed alternately exciting and alarming, but the philosophies that arose to steady it were by now totally novel. They owed their popularity and acceptance to the fact that they were familiar currency with a new stamp.

Reaching the twentieth century, we see these processes gone further, but still in continuity with the old pattern. The momentum of cruelty had by now built up into a massive tide evident in two of the most destructive wars in human history and a multitude of lesser ones. In the 'post-war' period, there was never a year in which there was not serious warfare going on somewhere, and some of those wars, like the Iraq–Iran conflict, caused casualties running to millions of dead, not to mention the maimed, displaced, and bereaved. As the century drew to a close, we saw the emergence of 'ethnic cleansing' and genocide, and the greatest tide of displaced people that the world has seen in supposedly peaceful times. As the new century opens, we even see torture coming back into the political agenda of the supposedly most civilized countries.

How have the foundational ideals of our culture fared through this gradual erosion of standards and mounting ruthlessness? Who is caring for our souls now, and how are they to do so? In the psychology field, the three basic ideals are still clearly represented, now rivalrous with each other and unintegrated. Carrying forward the romantic tradition of unconditional positive regard, universal empathy, and faith in limitless human potential, we have the humanistic-psychology movement and its various off-shoots, including transpersonal psychology. The banner of duty and sinful nature is now carried by the diversity of psychoanalytic schools, each discerning our perversities and pointing out our duty. Utilitarian ideals gave us, first, behaviourism – an extreme of puritan minimalism in which nothing that happened 'inside' the person was to be given any consideration at all, and then broadened into a range of 'cognitive' or 'rational' approaches. Proponents of the behavioural approaches saw anything else as unscientific. The most extreme Pavlovian form of this approach found favour in the Soviet domain, which is not surprising since the whole Soviet phenomenon can be seen as having been an experiment in making Puritan Utilitarianism the guiding principle of a whole society.

While the Soviet experiment continued, behaviourism remained relatively eclipsed in the West by the representatives of the other two legs of our cultural tripod. With the experiment in scientific society going on elsewhere, the romantic and conservative tendencies could prosper. Humanistic psychology burgeoned, and psychoanalysis flourished not just as therapies, but as widespread cultural influences affecting every avenue of life. For a time, it seemed as though the Romantic movement would triumph over all as the 'Permissive Society' seemed to be overturning centuries of tradition, and even that bastion, the Catholic Church, had its 'Vatican II'. Then, as the costs of permissiveness surfaced, there was a swing 'back to basics' and a reinstatement of conservative duties. Throughout this time, 'scientific' behaviourism remained only a significant undertone.

With the fall of the Soviet system, however, the dynamics have changed. The third leg of the tripod is no longer associated with the enemy, and in a mere decade or two, the greater part of the measures that 'the Free World' was taught to regard as anathema in the Soviet way of doing things has become business as normal in our own backyard. We now imprison 'suspects' without trial more or less indefinitely, without compunction; we have surveillance of public spaces, comprehensive secret-police activity, severe restrictions on migration, and torture and brainwashing establishments that form a veritable gulag radiating out from a bay on the island of Cuba, that somehow seems not to fall under the jurisdiction of any civilized court of law. Nice people with the correct ethnic credentials are kept innocent and immune from all this. Momentarily, the state apparatus now centred on Washington, with its subsidiaries in London, Paris, and Berlin, is formidable. Never before has such a preponderance of military power on this planet resided within one chain of command. Even the immediate successors to Genghis Khan were never so dominant.

In this climate, it is not surprising that the utilitarian, 'scientific' branch of psychology has suddenly found favour. Non-directiveness is out. It is now legitimate and desirable to tell people how they should think and to re-programme them. If they are sad it is because they have unrealistic thoughts. If they cannot work, they need to be cognitively restructured. This is in their own best interests, and in any case, where is the evidence that any other approach can achieve patient conformity to desired targets so systematically? Cognitive behaviour therapy is inevitably the treatment of choice when the state sees its duty is to ensure public 'happiness' by the most utilitarian and scientific approaches available. Puritan, utilitarian rationalism now has its day.

The operatives of the system are not of malign intent. Most sincerely wish only to relieve the suffering of their patients by approved and proven means. They may get caught up in professional rivalries or institutional politics from time to time, but that is endemic in the system, and it is the system that we are commenting upon here rather than the individuals occupying the various niches within it, each doing their best to survive, prosper, and help others within the frame available from their spot on the social landscape.

In the present cultural climate, one has to reckon with the spirit of the times but not be seduced into thinking that 'twill ever be so. When we take a step back and try to get a longer-term historical perspective, it is possible to see this as simply the latest phase in a game that has been running for a very long time. It is like the weaving of a three-strand plait. As the plait extends, each strand takes its turn to go over the other two. In due course we shall see a cultural reaction and a change of fashion. The present bubble will burst, just as it has done time and again in the past. We have had Brave New Worlds – in which scientific mind-control aims to solve all human ills – in quantity, every time the rationalist aspect of our civilization becomes dominant; but the heart and the shadow of human nature cannot abide them for long, so this tide too will turn. When it does, people will think something unprecedented has occurred, and all of history is being overthrown; but in all probability, it will simply be that it is the turn of one of the other two strands to take precedence. An age of hope will dawn. The spirit of love and faith will rise again. After all, it is the Romantic's turn next, but a real discontinuity in the bigger project is unlikely.

What we need to be more deeply concerned about is the fact that the extension of this threefold plait has not diminished the longer-term trend of mounting cruelty. Planet Earth is getting full. If we cannot find a way of living together in greater harmony, then nature will assuredly solve the problem by exacting a substantial cull of our numbers. The real challenge to psychology lies not in the domain of how many patients suffering from such and such a defined depressive syndrome or such and such an anxiety category can be made to sustain more than *x* per cent improvement on tabulated performance indicators for more than two years; it lies in the area of what can actually change our inhumanity to one another on a societal and global scale. As long as we are all accomplices to acts of gross iniquity carried out on our behalf by officials employed by executives that we have elected for the purpose, we are not going to throw off our basic delusions, nor be healed of our collective sickness; and it is that collective sickness that exacts the greatest toll, and it is to that collective sickness that the roots of so much individual anguish should really be traced. It is the society that is sick, and that needs spiritual care.

Psychologies come and go. Professional rivalries are perennial. The game is, however, powered by larger forces. For the moment we are in an ephemeral mini Age of Reason, and we must all reckon with it. Even the Romantics must make what they do look 'scientific' and conduct 'research' to demonstrate the effectiveness of such contrivances as 'mindfulness-based stress reduction' or advance their cause under such banners as 'emotional intelligence' or 'optimism training'. Analysts must come up with 'treatment protocols' and 'replicable procedures' in order to stay in the game. Much of this is either cynical window-dressing or a Trojan Horse style strategy to sneak what one really wants, and believes in, into the citadels of utilitarian dogmatism. Most of it fails. Many are, therefore, content for the present to remain in the wilderness, gathering spiritual strength or forbearing their winter of discontent.

It is important, however, not to waste wilderness years. When the tide turns, there will be a need for creativity – but creativity can already be going on. In the psychological world, the conservative tendency has unfortunately got exceedingly bogged down, stifling itself in a pursuit of respectability, regulation, institutes, complaints procedures, and professionalism. The utilitarian rationalists are dominant and cock-a-hoop, but, in the nature of things, their reign will not last indefinitely. It is, therefore, vitally important that the carriers of what I have here called 'the romantic tendency' now be preparing themselves for the opportunity when it comes; but it is also important that we all gain some sense of perspective. When a movement loses favour, it has to return to its roots, and the roots of the romantic are in the spiritual. It is not surprising, therefore, that one of the few areas where creativity is going on in the psychotherapy world at present is on the psychology–pirituality interface. The spiritual, or perhaps we should say inter-spiritual, domain of our culture is vibrant, despite the problems of the institutional churches. God is stirring in his tomb. Interest in the spiritual dimension of therapy and the psychological dimension of pastoral care is currently a fertile field.

Spirituality must have in view not merely the salvation of the individual, but the raising of the whole human race to new levels of harmony, insight, peace, and co-operation. This grander agenda should arrest our attention. It is on our ability to address it that we will be judged when the hour comes. Those who have espoused human potentiality, self-actualization, personal growth, and so forth in the past must now learn to strive for goals of wider scope than the kind of super-individualism that once inspired us briefly, but then turned sour as it fell to the ridicule of the 'me generation'. We must now expand our minds to contemplate the state of the human spirit as we collectively degenerate into an Orwellian nightmare, and what could lift us out of it into a contemporary equivalent of 'love thy neighbour as thyself and the Lord with all thy soul and strength and might'. Yet even beyond such a humanistic grail, we must now think on the whole ecological scale. Not only is it too narrow to think of the individual, it is too narrow to think only of the species. The vision we need must turn back a tidal wave that is already threateningly close to our shore.

A turn toward the romantic side of our culture would be welcome, no doubt, but real healing requires more. Somehow the plait has become too unravelled. We need to seek a higher-level integration so that the three dimensions can work together. Should we not be addressing the real problems facing our times and deriving our work with individuals from that greater perspective, rather than either being sucked into the ubiquitous gulag of 'spin' and mind manipulation on the one hand, or narrowly focusing upon symptom-specific local remedies on the other? The individual in treatment needs to know that the treatment that he or she receives is a subset of a philosophy that is wholesome for humankind.

Let us by all means remember better times, when human potential was not a dirty term; but let us also learn from our failure to address the really big issue, which is the long-term ascendancy of cruelty in a world where every century sees a larger proportion of the human race destroyed by violent means than the century before, and where the advance of technology that could make life easy inexorably seems to make it more brutal, and the wealth divide more extreme. The question for psychology, as for several other human-science disciplines today, is not which school of practice shall prevail in public institutions and in the treatment of individual casualties, but where we will find a genuinely integrative approach that can harmonize the three dimensions of our culture, and enable us to live at peace with each other and with the planet.

CHAPTER 7

COGNITIVE BEHAVIOUR THERAPY AND EVIDENCE-BASED PRACTICE:

PAST, PRESENT, AND FUTURE

JOHN LEES

INTRODUCTION

In this chapter I look at the fact that cognitive behaviour therapy and evidence-based practice are currently favoured by the British Government and health-care authorities, and that this is a cause for anxiety and concern amongst some therapists. I argue for developing an approach to current debates about these approaches to clinical practice in the counselling and psychotherapy profession based on the principles of the evolution of consciousness. In particular, I take the view that our understanding of such developments can be transformed if we adopt a broader evolutionary perspective.

Cognitive behaviour therapy (henceforth CBT) has recently featured prominently in counselling and psychotherapy discourses by virtue of the fact that it has been put forward as the most efficacious method of treatment for some presenting problems, thereby giving it priority over other therapy approaches. One reason for this growing interest in CBT in recent years stems, in my view, from the move toward standardized treatments in this profession; in particular, the notion of evidence-based practice (EBP). In this chapter, therefore, I will discuss the current ascendancy of CBT and EBP and will explore some of their common characteristics. I will focus in particular on their underlying ontological and epistemological assumptions, their evolution and development, and the principles underpinning their methodology.

In relation to CBT I will look at its 'pure' underlying principles, as opposed to its 'applied' form: in a Platonic sense, I will be examining its basic guiding Idea. Two potential problems in my approach will also be mentioned. First, CBT practitioners often deviate from the pure form. They may adopt a 'person-centred' orientation, exercise a certain degree of flexibility in response to client need, and encourage 'client ownership of discovery over dramatic therapeutic interventions' (Salkovskis, 1996: 538). Secondly, concentrating on its pure form can easily involve adopting a caricatured view of what actually happens in practice – for instance, seeing it as a process of applying pre-defined techniques and procedures by an expert and detached scientist-practitioner.

My rationale for concentrating on the underlying philosophical principles of CBT and EBP and a broader evolutionary perspective arises out of my view, along with the late Petruska

---

An earlier version of this chapter appeared in the *European Journal of Psychotherapy and Counselling*, 10 (3), 2008, pp. 187–96.

Clarkson, that the therapy profession has reached a sufficient degree of maturity to be able to begin to reflect on itself in order to 'consider meta-theoretical issues' (Clarkson, 2000: 308). It has reached a stage in its development where it has the potential to develop 'an openness to explore the philosophical assumptions, value commitments and ideological bases of even our firmest "scientific" findings' (ibid.). In order to do this I will, first of all, establish the historical framework for looking at CBT and EBT – in particular the notion of the evolution of consciousness emphasized, for instance, in the work of Rudolf Steiner. Building on this temporal and evolutionary perspective I will then look anew at the meaning and significance of their ascendancy at this particular moment in time; and, in conclusion, I will broaden my perspective to include the future as well as the past and present.

THE HISTORICAL FRAMEWORK

The development of CBT – and, indeed, other therapies – is usually viewed within a short time-scale of a hundred years or so since the origins of depth psychology; that is to say, as having developed since the work of Freud toward the end of the nineteenth century. In fact, CBT has been viewed as being a reaction to the work of Freud and psychoanalysis generally. Joseph (2001: 88), for instance, sees behavioural therapy as a reaction to psychoanalysis, and refers to Eysenck's (1952) seminal critique of therapy, especially of psychoanalysis, based on his meta-analysis of therapeutic outcomes, as an important stimulus to developing behavioural psychology as a therapy. Furthermore, such pioneers of cognitive therapy as Aaron Beck and Albert Ellis both had personal experience of psychoanalysis and had found it wanting, thereby stimulating them to develop their own therapeutic approaches based on what they saw as more rational, efficacious, and researchable methods of treatment (see, for instance, Salkovskis, 1996: 535).

However, some advocates of cognitive therapy take a longer-term view of its origins. Ross (1999) and Ellis (Shostrom, 1965) see it as containing elements of the Graeco-Roman philosophy of Stoicism, in as much as it resembled the Stoic insight that 'people are not emotionally disturbed so much by events, as by their beliefs about them' (Ross, 1999: 75). I will also take a longer-term view of the origins of CBT, and will thus develop my argument on the basis of a broad historical perspective. However, my approach is different to that of Ross and Ellis: they simply compare cognitive therapy with a particular way of thinking in Ancient Greece. In contrast, I will adopt a shorter time-scale – namely, the last four hundred years or so; but more importantly, its development will be viewed in the light of the evolution of consciousness, as mentioned earlier. In particular, it will be argued that CBT is a product of the development of Enlightenment science since the beginning of the seventeenth century.

EBP is generally viewed as having developed over a shorter period of time than CBT. It was first introduced into clinical discourse in 1992 by the Evidence Based Medical Working Group (EBMWG). They referred to a 'new paradigm', and encouraged clinicians to use the research literature 'more effectively' in order to apply research findings to their everyday clinical practice as a result of analysing and critically appraising those aspects of the methods and results sections of research studies which are relevant to the clinical problem and then using any relevant findings to help to address the clinical problem. It is thus viewed as being both a pragmatic and a relatively new movement. But I will again adopt a different perspective, arguing that, as is the case with CBT, it is useful to view it from the perspective of a broader time-scale, once again beginning with the origins of contemporary science at the beginning of the seventeenth century; and, as in the case of CBT, it will be examined from the viewpoint of the evolution of consciousness.

Looking at these two approaches to clinical practice from a narrow historical point of view may give the impression that their current dominance in healthcare practice will result in those practitioners who work with other approaches to clinical practice eventually being overwhelmed and swept away – at least in the NHS. For instance, as early as the mid-1990s, the EBP movement was already beginning to have an impact on healthcare policy, and was tending to favour CBT clinical methods over and above other therapies. In 1996, the National Health Service (NHS) in Britain reviewed psychological therapies, and recommended that they should be evidence-based, also remarking that CBT had a significant advantage over other approaches, particularly with regard to those problems which feature prominently in most counselling services – namely, depression and anxiety – because of its efficacy-research orientated nature (Parry, 2004).

Then, in 2005, the National Institute for Clinical Excellence (NICE), the British Government's advisory body on health care, explicitly stated that cognitive behaviour therapy is the most efficacious treatment for anxiety and depression (Bower, 2005). It recommended that mild depression can be treated with counselling, but that the only variants of the talking therapies which are suitable for more severe depression are CBT, interpersonal therapy, and couple-focused therapy, thereby eliminating the work of the vast majority of therapy practitioners from the picture (Hughes, 2005). In the case of anxiety, the situation is even more depressing for those therapists who do not work with CBT methods. Here, it is just CBT, pharmacology, or self-help which are recommended (Lawrence, 2005). More recently the Government-funded Improved Access to Psychological Therapies (IAPT) movement recommends the use of CBT.

Overall, then, these developments have provoked a considerable amount of debate, and even anxiety, amongst practitioners. As Peter Fonagy said at a recent conference: 'I've never seen so much anxiety associated with receiving £170 million!'. At the same conference, he 'identified four areas of anxiety: research, NICE, IAPT, and CBT' (Conference report, 2007).

The picture begins to change, however, if we adopt the notion of the evolution of consciousness based on the work of Rudolf Steiner. Steiner speaks about this in many places (for instance, Steiner, 1904, 1909, 1911, 1923), expressing the essence of his view in the following way:

> 'The present age is however one that is peculiarly prejudiced in its thought about the evolution of man and of mankind. It is commonly believed that, as regards his life of soul and spirit, man has always been essentially the same as he is to-day throughout the whole of the time that we call history .... [I]n forming such a conception, we do not take the trouble to observe the important differences that exist in the soul-constitution of a man of the present-time, as compared even with that of a relatively not very far distant past .... [and then] .... if we go over to the ancient Oriental world ... there is a disposition of soul utterly different from that of the man of to-day.'
>
> (Steiner, 1923: 7–8)

In this statement Steiner is referring to the fact that human beings experience qualitatively different states of consciousness at different times in history. Indeed, the activities arising out of Steiner's work adopt these principles in a practical way. For instance, Steiner (Waldorf) schools adopt the view that the growth of the child emulates the evolution of consciousness. Thus, when the child is experiencing a state of consciousness which resembles that of Ancient India, the Steiner curriculum suggests that the children are taught about the myths, stories, and events of Ancient India. I thus agree with Welburn that Steiner's thought, and the practical applications arising out of it, comprise a 'most thorough-going response' to 'the possibilities of an evolutionary kind of thinking'; and, in terms of professional life, this viewpoint has the potential to inform the way we think about different theories and paradigms by virtue of the fact that it enables us to look at them in a new light; to view them in the light of 'the growing, changing being of Man' (Welburn, 2004: 48). In other words, we can approach our understanding of the world – and the theories and paradigms that are generated at any one moment in time – from the perspective of the ongoing changes in human consciousness.

Steiner's approach to the evolution of consciousness can be linked to a typically Central European thinking which was developed by Romantic and idealistic philosophers in the eighteenth and nineteenth centuries, who took the view that there are radical differences between the way we view the world in different historical periods (Gidley, 2007: 118). The sort of knowledge we generated in the past was not the same as it is today, and will be different again in the future. Consequently we begin to see current developments in therapy practice, including the current privileging of CBT and EBP, as historical moments corresponding to humanity's stage of development, and its current possibilities of knowledge generation and their practical application. Once we begin to see them in this way we realize that, in due course, they will be superseded by other ways of thinking.

In the next section the origins of CBT and EBP will be viewed within the perspective of the evolution of consciousness. My aim in doing this is to deepen our understanding of these two ways of thinking, cast some light on the reasons for their popularity, and look at both the usefulness and dangers of their underlying approach to clinical practice. I will argue that by understanding them in the light of this broader historical perspective, we will be more able to assess their place within current healthcare discourse in a balanced and informed way.

FROM THE PAST TO THE PRESENT

In looking at CBT and EBP from an historical perspective, as discussed earlier I take the view that they are both quintessential products of scientific Enlightenment thinking – in particular, that they are characterized by two key aspects of the scientific method: namely, the experimental model and rationality. One of the first people to espouse the use of the experimental method in research was Sir Francis Bacon in the sixteenth century. As Davy (1985) has remarked, his ideas 'define and describe the modern scientific method – and above all, emphasize the importance of impartial observation and experiment' (ibid.: 36). The notion of rationalistic epistemology, moreover, which complements the experimental method, was developed by such people as his contemporary, René Descartes, who has been referred to as 'the father of modern philosophy'

(Ferré, 1998: 1), but could equally be called the 'father of modern epistemology'. Descartes was not an experimenter, but he was aware of the development of the experimental method, and provided the philosophical and theoretical basis for it: 'he was always more concerned with general principles of method than with the detailed work of observation' (Lindsay, 1912: xi).

Descartes' work, above all else, incorporated two principles which dominate our way of thinking about the world today. First, he postulated that our capacity to know about the world is enhanced if it is based on mathematical reasoning, and that in order to acquire knowledge about the world, we need to use 'the clear vision of the intellect'. He consequently argued for a theory of knowledge which is based on logic and reason (Lynch, 1996), or what he called 'intuition' (Lindsay, 1912: xiv). Secondly, Descartes developed the notion of the split between mind and body, self and world – so-called Cartesian dualism; that is to say, he took the view that we can only know the world if we disconnect and detach ourselves from it. In summary, in order to know the world, we need to exercise our capacity for logical thinking within the framework of a strict method which distances us from our experience: 'Method is needed so to arrange the objects of our inquiry that we may be able thus to intuit them' (ibid.: xv).

There is no doubt that these Enlightenment principles – experimentalism, logic, dualism, and detachment – dominate our consciousness, and thus our relationship to the world today. Furthermore, along with Steiner I take the view that this has been necessary in order to contribute to the development of our individuality and our capacity for self-consciousness. However, like Steiner I also believe that we are now developing new possibilities in our consciousness. Indeed I have argued elsewhere that much of the thinking in the psychotherapeutic professions over the last hundred years has been attempting to break away from these basic Enlightenment principles (Lees, 2008). For example, many variants of psychotherapeutic thinking encourage us to overcome dualistic states of mind by focusing on the fact that there are moments in our experience when we are in non-dualistic (or monistic) states of mind; that is to say, when we make a strong connection with other people as a result of our capacity for empathy, or as a result of the experience of countertransference phenomena.

Steiner alludes to these new possibilities of consciousness in his fundamental book *The Philosophy of Freedom* (Steiner, 1894) when he refers to our sense that we are both 'estranged' from the world and 'within' it: 'Here we are no longer merely *I*; here is something which is more than *I*' (ibid.: 26). We can refer to this new state of consciousness as a form of dynamic dualism (or dynamic monism) in which we are constantly moving between dualistic states of mind – when we feel separated from each other and the world – and monistic states of mind, when we feel linked and interconnected with the world and with each other. The important issue, therefore, is whether psychotherapy responds to these new possibilities arising out of the evolution of consciousness, or reinforces the dualism of the Enlightenment. In my view, CBT and EBP, if applied in a pure way, tend to do the latter. The reinforcement of Enlightenment thinking in CBT and EBP can also be demonstrated by using, following Steiner, the metaphor of a building (1914: 67). There are two aspects to this.

First, they both adopt a clear experimental methodology which involves defining the field within which the therapy is going to take place, and which is also based on the epistemological principles which I have outlined. In the case of CBT, this may involve using a descriptive diagnostic tool such as DSM-IV, or an evaluation tool such as Beck's depression inventory. This may require identifying an ailment (such as depression) on the basis of a clear definition, measuring its severity by using, say, the Beck inventory and establishing the boundaries of the clinical field by eliminating other variables using the same principles as the experimental method. By evaluating the problem in this way, the therapist clarifies the task in hand and what needs to be done in a logical systematic manner, just as a builder identifies what needs to be done in regard to constructing a building.

The therapist then devises appropriate interventions to address the problem which has been defined and delineated. In terms of the building metaphor, s/he tries to determine how the construction is to be undertaken. This in turn will involve choosing appropriate materials, and adopting an appropriate building technique, just as a therapist operationalizes these principles by adopting a particular technique for addressing the problem which has been defined. Overall, the problem is diagnosed, the treatment applied, and the progress evaluated in a systematic way using logic and reason. This contrasts to the new possibilities of consciousness – what I have referred to as dynamic dualism – where actions tend to be more intuitive, and based on the needs of each individual situation (cf. House and Bohart's Chapter 17, this volume).

Secondly, as well as adopting clearly defined methods, a building also adopts a plan based on a particular ontological and epistemological position (post-modernist, modernist, or whatever). Similarly, CBT and EBP follow a definite 'plan' based on a particular philosophy, and, like a building, the plan incorporates a particular philosophical outlook or belief – in this case, as discussed, a belief in Cartesian dualism, the reliability of logical thought processes, and a clearly defined experimental method, whether this is at first obvious or not.

Their underlying beliefs also incorporate a high degree of scepticism and doubt about the emerging possibilities of human consciousness, including a reliance upon direct experience and the use of our sensing, feeling, and intuiting capacities in our therapeutic work; whereas the techniques of the psychodynamic and humanistic schools incorporate these qualities. As such, CBT and EBP incorporate the Cartesian notion of 'radical doubt' (Ferré, 1998: 1). But whereas Descartes' doubt was orientated toward medieval Christian views, they doubt the possibilities of consciousness open to us today – the use of our direct sensory experience of the world, and working with interconnectedness and intersubjectivity gained as a result of the development of non-dualistic monistic states of mind.

EBP is, in a sense, the quintessence of the above principles – experimentalism, systematization, and applying specific techniques – and the underlying belief in dualism, logic, and doubt in intuitive capacities. It also illustrates the historical Enlightenment basis of this approach and these principles very well. Even though its 'founders' view it as a relatively 'new paradigm for medical practice' which was discovered in 1992, from an historical perspective this is not actually the case. The basic principles of EBP – based on the notion of meta-analysis of research into clinical outcomes and then applying such research findings in practice – were actually 'invented' by Bacon in a visionary imagination called *New Atlantis: A Work Unfinished*, which he wrote just prior to his death in 1626. This fragment, in my view, incorporated the principles of EBP in a precise way. Bacon spoke of how, in the mythical Salomon's House, people were allotted various tasks. For instance, it was the job of the 'compilers' to look 'into the experiments of their fellows, and cast about how to draw out of them things of use and practice for man's life'. So they were, in the language of EBP, concerned with gathering the findings of research studies and putting them together in such a way as to be useful for practical life, such as in clinical practice. It is interesting to think that these notions were first created out of Bacon's visionary consciousness almost 400 years ago, and not just discovered for the first time in 1992. So it is not as new as it seems to be and, of course, does not explicitly recognize the new possibilities of clinical practice such as using countertransference and other intersubjective practices which have been emerging as a result of the changes in consciousness during the twentieth and twenty-first centuries.

As demonstrated throughout this volume, the dominant scientific-rationalistic Baconian–Cartesian paradigm which underpins CBT and EBP has been challenged by many ways of thinking over the ages, including Romanticism, critical theory, new-paradigm science, human-inquiry research, post-modernism and linguistics, and, as I have discussed, the thinking and practice of psychotherapy itself. However, it remains remarkably resilient and untouched by these critiques – in spite of the fact that the possibilities inherent in our consciousness are moving on. Consequently, it still remains the dominant paradigm within the healthcare professions and within society at large, including within our educational systems. However, it is my view that it can now be superseded by the new possibilities inherent in our consciousness. In short, in order to work through the many crises facing human beings and the planet in general, we need to develop ways of being, and create institutions, that help us to establish a different relationship with the world around, and thereby overcome the malign effects of dualistic states of mind (such as our individual potential for destructiveness, the exploitation of the environment, increased destructiveness, and social disintegration). In the final section of this chapter, I will look at the future; namely the question of where we go from here.

THE FUTURE

Whilst taking the view that CBT and EBT are products of contemporary Western scientific thinking and so, to some degree, are inevitable developments in our current age, the essential issue is how we can move on from this way of thinking. The first step is to realize that they are ways of viewing the human being which have been socially constructed in the past. The danger is then that they will become problematic if their hegemony is perpetuated beyond its time. Such a state of affairs would contribute to cramping our development, moulding us in a limited way, and perpetuating the destructive effects of scientism. In fact I am reminded of Erich Fromm's prophetic notion that:

> 'In the nineteenth century the problem was that *God is dead*; in the twentieth century the problem is that *man is dead*. In the nineteenth century inhumanity meant cruelty; in the twentieth century it means schizoid self-alienation. The danger of the past was that men became slaves. The danger of the future is that men may become robots.'
>
> (Fromm, 1956: 360, emphases in original)

This is similar to Steiner's notion of the 'abolition of the soul'. Steiner cites materialistic theories of history and certain aspects of the modern scientific outlook as reasons for this:

> 'This outlook – I am speaking not of the positive achievements of the scientific "Weltanschuauung" – which accepts only the reality of the corporeal and regards everything pertaining to the soul as an epiphenomenon, a superstructure on what is corporeal .... is the direct consequence [of previous historical developments].'
>
> (Steiner, 1917: 28)

In other words, logical systematized – one could say mathematical – thinking has many advantages but also carries many dangers. It can seriously inhibit, and even blunt, our human potential.

Fortunately, there are many other developments today which do not fit into such a narrow scientific paradigm, and which are trying to move beyond it. I have already mentioned some of them – Romanticism, critical theory, new-paradigm science, human-inquiry research, post-modernism, linguistics, and therapy. In the present time, we could now also add phenomenology, the transpersonal movement, environmentalism, feminism, the development of therapies arising out of the needs of minority and marginalized groups, the growth of alternative therapies, and Steiner's anthroposophy and many other spiritual movements. The present post-modern age seems to me to be ripe for building on these developments, and for developing a humane approach to science as a whole, and to therapy in particular, born out of our changing consciousness. There are many signs that 'human consciousness is evolving beyond materialistic instrumental rationality to more integral, more spiritual' states of consciousness (Gidley, 2007: 118); and the way in which we are beginning to understand our experience is becoming more diverse and subtle. We are beginning to value 'complex, dialectical, non-dualistic stances' (ibid.: 121). In a broader sense we are living in an age when there is a movement 'toward the potential integration of post-formal notions of cognition with love, reverence and spiritual development' (ibid.: 122).

The future of the therapy profession, and indeed of the human race, will, in my view, be dependent on whether we can respond to the new possibilities of our consciousness whilst recognizing the limitations of, but always looking for new ways of working with, the thinking which we have inherited from the past.

REFERENCES

Bower, P. (2005) 'Counselling for depression: the evidence for', *Healthcare Counselling and Psychotherapy Journal*, 5(2): 16–17.

Clarkson, P. (2000) 'Eclectic, integrative and integrating psychotherapy, or beyond schoolism', in S. Palmer and R. Woolfe (eds), *Integrative and Eclectic Counselling and Psychotherapy*, London: Sage.

Conference report (2007) 'Psychological therapies in the NHS – a landmark conference', *Therapy Today*, 18 (10): 8–9.

Davy, J. (1985) *Hope, Evolution, Change*, Stroud: Hawthorn Press.

Evidence-Based Medical Working Group (1992) 'Evidence-based medicine: a new approach to teaching the practice of medicine', *Journal of the American Medical Association (JAMA)*, 268: 2420–5.

Eysenck, H. (1952) 'The effects of psychotherapy: an evaluation', *Journal of Consulting Psychology*, 16: 319–24.

Ferré, F. (1998) *Knowing and Value*, New York: State University of New York Press.

Fromm, E. (1956) *The Sane Society*, London: Routledge & Kegan Paul (orig. 1963).

Gidley, J. M. (2007) 'Educational imperatives in the evolution of consciousness: the integral visions of Rudolf Steiner and Ken Wilber', *International Journal of Children's Spirituality*, 12 (2): 117–35.

Hughes, I. (2005) 'NICE in practice: some thoughts on delivering the new guideline on depression', *Counselling and Psychotherapy Journal*, 16 (3): 8–11.

Joseph, S. (2001) *Psychopathology and Therapeutic Approaches*, Basingstoke: Palgrave.

Lawrence S. (2005) 'Anxiety guidelines: why counselling doesn't get a look in', *Counselling and Psychotherapy Journal*, 16 (2): 34–7.

Lees, J. (2008) 'The epistemological basis and scope of psychotherapy research', unpublished paper.

Lindsay, A. D. (1912) 'Introduction', in R. Descartes, *A Discourse on Method*, London: Dent.

Lynch, G. (1996) 'What is truth? A philosophical introduction to counselling research', *Counselling*, 7 (2): 144–9.

Parry, G. (2004) 'Why should counsellors care about research?', *Counselling and Psychotherapy Journal*, 15 (6): 20–1.

Ross, P. (1999) 'Focusing the work: a cognitive-behavioural approach', in J. Lees and A. Vaspe (eds), *Clinical Counselling in Further and Higher Education*, London: Routledge.

Salkovskis, P. M. (1996) 'Cognitive therapy and Aaron Beck', in P. M. Salkovskis (ed.), *Frontiers of Cognitive Therapy*, New York: The Guilford Press.

Shostrom, E. (ed.) (1965) *Three Approaches to Psychotherapy*, Orange, Calif.: Psychological Films.

Steiner, R. (1894) *The Philosophy of Freedom*, London: Rudolf Steiner Press (1992).

Steiner, R. (1904) *Cosmic Memory*, San Francisco: Harper and Row Publishers (1981).

Steiner, R. (1909) *Occult Science*, London: Rudolf Steiner Press (1963).

Steiner, R. (1911) *Occult History*, London: Rudolf Steiner Press (1982).

Steiner, R. (1914) *The Riddles of Philosophy*, Spring Valley: Anthroposophic Press (1973).

Steiner, R. (1917) *Building Stones Towards an Understanding of the Mystery of Golgotha*, London: Rudolf Steiner Press (1972).

Steiner, R. (1923) *World History in the light of Anthroposophy*, London: Rudolf Steiner Press (1977).

Welburn, A. (2004) *Rudolf Steiner's Philosophy*, Edinburgh: Floris Books.

Chapter 8

COGNITIVE THERAPY, CARTESIANISM, AND THE MORAL ORDER

Patrick Bracken & Philip Thomas

INTRODUCTION

Over the last 30–40 years, cognitive therapy (hereafter, CT) has emerged as a popular intervention for a range of psychiatric problems, including anxiety, depression, obsessive compulsive disorder, and post-traumatic conditions as well as the symptoms of psychosis. Its political profile has risen following publication of Layard's report (2004), arguing on economic grounds that the British Government should make a substantial investment in therapists trained in CT to reduce the numbers of people unable to work because of depression. As a therapy it appears 'clear' in its concepts, efficient and effective, and it is relatively easy to learn. Its popularity – understandable in a culture placing a high priority on efficiency – may also have something to do with its capacity to define its operations, and purportedly to measure and quantify its benefits 'scientifically'. In this respect it differs from other forms of psychotherapy. However, like any form of therapy, CT makes certain assumptions about the nature of the self and its relationships to others, and to the world in general. Aaron Beck, one of its originators, writes that CT techniques 'are utilized within the framework of the cognitive model of psychopathology, and we do not believe that the therapy can be applied effectively without knowledge of the theory' (Beck et al., 1979: 4).

CT, therefore, is just one element in a particular approach to psychology and psychopathology. It is premissed upon the 'cognitive model' of mind, and disorders of mind are understood to be caused by 'dysfunctional beliefs' and 'faulty information processing' – involving a very particular philosophy of mind underlying which, in turn, are metaphysical and epistemological orientations. The model is not therefore 'value-neutral', but involves a specific orientation toward the problems of suffering and healing. Beneath its scientific self-understanding, there is thus a *moral agenda* inherent in the cognitive framework, which we wish to 'unearth' in this chapter.

Our position is not that CT, and cognitive models of mind and mental disorder, are fallacious. We maintain that the discourse of cognitivism works only on the back of highly challengeable assumptions. We will examine the philosophy of mind which underlies cognitivism, and demonstrate its origins in the philosophy of René Descartes. Philosopher Charles Taylor's work is then utilized to reveal some of the ethical assumptions hidden within this discourse, and we point to some clinical implications stemming from our analysis.

An earlier version of the chapter appeared in the *European Journal of Psychotherapy, Counselling and Health*, 2 (3), 1999: 325–44.

WHAT IS THE COGNITIVIST APPROACH TO MIND AND ITS DISORDERS?

Cognitivism assumes an underlying structure to mentation, based on the biological organization of the brain, but with a separate non-biological set of concepts being required fully to grasp it. In this framework it is logical to treat the brain and the mind as separate realms, so the project of cognitivism concerns an exploration of the structures and the underlying basic elements of the mind. A fundamental assumption is that the elements of psychological life can be characterized in causal terms, so that hypotheses can be generated which can then be used to predict behaviour under different circumstances. As Harré and Gillett (1994: 14) point out, the information-processing model offered the possibility of psychology becoming fully scientific, in the realist sense, with its theories comprising hypotheses about information-processing mechanisms. Behaviour-describing predictions could be deduced from these hypotheses, with speech, emotional display, the evincing of attitudes, problem solving, and so on all being in principle comprehensible.

As cognitivism gained influence, more areas of psychology adopted this framework, including Piagetian developmental psychology, social psychology, and Kelly's Personal Construct Theory (Kelly, 1955), as formulations based on unconscious drives and traits faded. Chomsky's (1959) critique of Skinner's behavioural account of language led ultimately to the new field of psycholinguistics, mapping grammar directly on to the mind, presaging in turn Artificial Intelligence (AI) models of mind. Though formulated in different terminologies, the basic proposition remains the same, with the concept of unconscious 'schemas' being especially popular: 'All knowledge and experience is packaged in schemas. Schemas are the ghost in the machine, the intelligence that guides information as it flows through the mind' (Goleman, 1985: 75).

In our own field of clinical psychiatry, the notion that human beings operate with unconscious models or schemas has been variously utilized, but it was in relation to 'depression' that CT first achieved prominence, and through which we can really grasp the significance of schemas. Beck's theory of depression has influenced thought in many areas, including the treatment of voices (e.g. Chadwick and Birchwood, 1994). Beck's model proposes that faulty or dysfunctional assumptions are laid down as cognitive schemata in childhood. These are subsequently activated by critical incidents in adulthood, and a meshing between the particular incident and the dysfunctional assumptions brings about a complex of 'negative automatic thoughts'. Beck proposes that these distorted, negative, dysfunctional, and unhelpful thoughts underlie the clinical state of depression. He writes:

> 'In brief, the theory postulates that the depressed or depression-prone individual has certain idiosyncratic patterns (schemas) which may become activated whether by specific stresses impinging on specific vulnerabilities, or by overwhelming nonspecific stresses. When the cognitive patterns are activated, they tend to dominate the individual's thinking and to produce the affective and motivational phenomena associated with depression.'
>
> (Beck, 1972: 129–30)

Thus, on this view depression is not simply an affective disturbance but rather involves a specific disorder of thinking, of cognition, with the patient's cognitions being out of step with the surrounding culture in a distorted way, and requiring a special form of psychotherapeutic intervention.

In contrast to dynamic approaches, CT does not involve any significant exploration of the past, focusing instead on the 'here and now'. It does not theorize about the therapeutic relationship in terms of unconscious forces, or transference and countertransference. It involves the therapist 'training' the patient to examine his/her thoughts in a systematic, logical, rational, and 'non-distorted' way. The patient, in turn, is involved in 'homework' and 'exercises' between sessions. The therapist's job is thus to help patients confront their cognitive distortions by motivating them to do their homework. CT believes at root in the importance and benefits of systematic reflection upon the contents of consciousness. By turning 'inwards', the patient is urged to bring reason to bear upon the internal workings of the mind. However, this 'turning inwards' remains unproblematized, as does the position of the therapist, judging which beliefs are realistic and which distorted.

Beck emphasizes the importance of the patient learning how to 'self-question' effectively:

> '... the patient begins to incorporate many of the therapeutic techniques of the therapist. For example, patients frequently find themselves spontaneously assuming the role of the therapist in questioning some of their conclusions or predictions ... Such self-questioning plays a major role in the generalization of cognitive techniques from the interview to external situations.'
>
> (Beck et al., 1979: 4–5)

In other words, the patient begins to think like the therapist and incorporates the therapist's view of what is reasonable, logical, and sensible. We noted earlier that CT is not independent of the 'cognitive theory of mind'. Therefore, the therapist is effectively training the patient to accept this particular model of mind. This in turn raises a number of fundamental ethical issues, which necessitates some understanding of the historical and cultural origins of cognitivism.

THE EMERGENCE OF THE COGNITIVIST FRAMEWORK

Cognitive approaches embody the central assumptions of what has been called the 'Enlightenment project'. Although a complex multi-faceted cultural process, the European Enlightenment privileged the importance of reason in human affairs. Finding a path to true knowledge and certainty became the major concern of many Enlightenment thinkers, and epistemology became the central concern of philosophy. A guiding theme was the quest to replace religious revelation and ancient pronouncements with reason and science as the path to truth.

The Enlightenment involved a dramatic reorientation of intellectual life, a movement from 'darkness' to 'light'. Modern man was to look to the future, rather than the past, and to find in his own reason the path to this future. Philosophy was to have a vital role, for it was through a critical philosophy that both the potential and the limits of reason could be defined.

Reason would therefore have to give up its preoccupation with what had already been said, and handed down in tradition. Kant expresses this forcefully in his declaration that:

> 'Enlightenment is man's emergence from his self-incurred immaturity. Immaturity is the inability to use one's understanding without the guidance of another. This immaturity is called "self-incurred" if its cause is not lack of understanding but lack of resolution and courage to use it without the guidance of another. The motto of Enlightenment is therefore: Sapere aude! Have courage to use your own understanding!'
>
> (Kant, 1992: 305)

The other major theme emerging from the European Enlightenment concerned the human self and its depths. European thinkers became preoccupied with the 'inner voice' and the structures of subjectivity. In Kant's philosophy, structures of subjectivity become almost the entire subject matter of philosophy. This turning inwards can be seen in the phenomenology of Edmund Husserl, and of course, in the psychoanalysis of Freud.

Foucault (1967) has pointed out that the disciplines of psychology and psychiatry became possible only in a cultural framework substantially influenced by these Enlightenment and post-Enlightenment preoccupations. These disciplines represented a search for causal, scientific accounts of the mind and its disorders. They needed theories of the self and behaviour which would explain human actions and so allow for rational technical interventions to be made. As Jerome Levin writes:

> 'In premodern conceptualizations, the self... [derived] its stability from its relationship with God, but now something else was required as a cement. The old verities were no longer certain, and the unity of the self, itself, was now problematical.'
>
> (Levin, 1992: 16)

While the search for true knowledge and certainty dominated philosophy up to the nineteenth century, views differed as to how this quest should be pursued. Empiricists like Hobbes, Locke, and Hume thought that the senses and empirical observation were the only path to certainty. Rationalist philosophers like Descartes, Spinoza and Leibniz, by contrast, proposed that reason and reflection were the source of true knowledge. Empiricist philosophy of science, dominant in the nineteenth and first half of the twentieth centuries, emphasized the primary importance of perception, observation, and data gathering, albeit acknowledging the essential role of reason in the form of induction and deduction. Behaviourism, in many ways a direct descendant of this empiricist tradition, relegated mental processes to a minor role in influencing human action. It refused to engage with the 'inner voice', the internal aspects of mind, and in its most radical form completely denied the existence of mental states. The advent of cognitive models and therapies challenged this view, and represented a fundamental shift in psychology toward an acceptance not only of the mind's existence, but also of the central premises of rationalism: the primacy of thought over sensation and the experiential world. In the cognitivist framework, then, inner mental processes come to have a central and dominant role in directing human action.

There are many reasons for the emergence of the 'cognitive revolution' in psychology (Harré and Gillett, 1994), including mounting dissatisfaction with behaviourism's limitations, and the emergence of the computer as a Western cultural icon. It has recently become popular not only to think of the mind as being like a computer, but to propose that it *is* in some sense a computer (Churchland and Sejnowski, 1992). As psychology became concerned to explain the mind in terms of causal mechanisms, it found a natural ally in various versions of rule-following formulae which were to be found in the developing world of AI. In fact, the assumptions underlying AI and cognitivist psychology are essentially the same. If it is possible, in principle, to account for different aspects of human thought and behaviour in terms of rule-following formulae, then it should also be possible in principle to build machines that operate on the basis of these formulae, replicating human intelligence and behaviour. Both developments assume that the human mind works in the same way that computers do.

WHAT PHILOSOPHY OF MIND IS INVOLVED IN COGNITIVISM?

Theoretical and practical developments in AI and cognitive psychology have gained substantial support from contemporary developments in philosophy of mind. Philosophers like Jerry Fodor argue for a computational view of thought, a fairly dominant position in current philosophy of mind (Crane, 1995). By the mid-1990s, Lyons (1995: lviii) could write that functionalism, as this philosophy had come to be called, had become 'something approaching an orthodoxy over the last ten years'.

Functionalists draw on the dualism implicit in the computer model to argue the case for a separate mental realm. Just as computer software cannot be fully accounted for by reference to hardware alone, so too mental states cannot be reductively explained through an account of brain states alone. Mentation has its own elements and structures which cannot be explained in the language of physics, chemistry, and neurophysiology. In his book *Mind, Language and Reality*, philosopher Hilary Putnam outlines the basic case of functionalism:

> 'According to functionalism, the behaviour of, say, a computing machine is not explained by the physics and chemistry of the computing machine. It is explained by the machine's program. Of course, that program is realized in a particular physics and chemistry, and could, perhaps, be deduced from that physics and chemistry. But that does not make the program a physical or chemical property of the machine: it is an abstract property of the machine. Similarly, I believe that the psychological properties of human beings are not physical and chemical properties of human beings, although they may be realized by physical and chemical properties of human beings.'
>
> (Putnam, 1975: xiii)

In addition to its assertion of mind–brain dualism, functionalism also makes assertions about the nature of thinking. In this view, representational mental states, such as beliefs, desires, memories, and aspirations are related to one another in a computational way. They are processed in a rule-governed way, as are the representational states of a computer. Fodor calls this the 'Representational Theory of Mind'. He writes: 'At the heart of this theory is the postulation of a language of thought: an infinite set of "mental representations" which function both as the immediate objects of propositional attitudes and as the domains of mental processes.' (Fodor, 1995: 258) He goes on to spell out what the notion of 'propositional attitude' means for him:

> 'To believe that such and such is to have a mental symbol that means such and such tokened in your head in a certain way; it's to have such a token "in your belief box" ... Correspondingly, to hope that such and such is to have a token of that same mental symbol tokened in your head, but in a different way; it's to have it tokened "in your hope box."'
>
> (ibid.)

Furthermore this theory of mind involves the claim that 'Mental processes are causal sequences of tokenings of mental representations' (ibid.).

In this framework, it makes perfect sense to explore the mind by using physical-scientific methods. With the elements of mind causally connected, hypothesis development and testing can occur, just as in physics or biology. Functionalism as a theory of mind incorporates assumptions which have a long heritage in Western philosophy; and with many stemming from the work of Descartes, and some derived from the philosophy of empiricists like Locke, functionalism has become subsumed under the heading of 'Cartesianism' (Dreyfus, 1991). Functionalism, as proposed by Fodor and others, then, essentially amounts to a form of Cartesianism which makes use of the computer metaphor.

A fundamental tenet of Cartesianism is the idea of a separate mental realm, or mind, within which the outside world is somehow represented, and with such representations being interrelated in a formally describable and analysable way. The central philosophical problem for Descartes was the question of certainty: how can we be certain that our internal representations provide an accurate account of the external world? He proposed a method of systematic reflection upon the contents of the mind, thereby separating what was clear and accurate from what was uncertain and vague. By way of systematically doubting everything which was unclear, he argued that we could reflexively reach a situation of certainty, which for him was guaranteed by God. Certainty was reached by turning away from the world and looking inwards to examine our own thoughts in isolation, without reference to what they represented in the outside world. While God was the ultimate guarantor of truth and certainty, his presence was not essential for Descartes' confidence in our ability to look inwards, clarify our thoughts, and separate the clear from the unclear. As long as we adhere to the representational theory of thought, then, even in the absence of a divine guarantor of truth, systematic reflexivity will render us better able to account for our thoughts. A central tenet of Cartesianism is, therefore, a belief in the importance of reflexive clarity, and thus our ability to define and map the ways in which our internal representations are ordered and related.

In addition, Cartesianism operates on a fundamental distinction between the 'inner' world of the mind and the 'outer' world with which it is in contact. Thought becomes the inner functioning of a 'thinking substance' or subject (subjectum). This subject is in contact with an outside world, and has knowledge of it through sensation and through the representations it has of it. Thus the mind stands outside of the world and has a relation to it. Mind becomes something conceivable apart from and separate to this relation.

It is this separation, elaborated in terms of the inner and the outer, which gives sense to the representational theory of mind and thought. It also provides the source for the project of phenomenology, at least as developed by Husserl and his followers. Husserl's orientation towards the Cartesian project is overtly positive (the title of one of his major works is *Cartesian Meditations*). His fundamental method of enquiry, which he called 'phenomenological reduction', involved setting aside, or 'bracketing', the existence of an outside world in order to focus in a clear and unbiased way upon the phenomena of consciousness and experience. His aim was to reach what he called the 'transcendental standpoint', to be achieved by a series of 'reductions' which were operations performed upon everyday experience to isolate the 'pure' consciousness which is obscured as long as it is not separated from the natural world. Like Descartes, Husserl was attempting to elaborate a method of investigation into the experiential world which was reliable and foundational. Sass writes:

> 'Like Descartes' method of doubt, Husserl's approach can be called a kind of "foundationalism": an attempt to discover a realm of indubitable and transparent meanings or experiential entities that can provide a firm basis on which to build valid knowledge about human existence.'
>
> (Sass, 1989: 443)

Cartesianism therefore provides an account of the self and thought which has been articulated in different ways through different philosophies. In many ways it has come to be taken as 'common sense', and through functionalism and phenomenology has come to be an orthodoxy in modern psychology and psychiatry. With reference to the latter, the Cartesian perspective involves a number of orientating assumptions, summarized here thus:

1. an endorsement of 'methodological individualism' and a belief in the possibility and importance of detached reflection upon the contents of mind;
2. an acceptance that the mind is something internal and separate to the world which is external to it;
3. a belief in the causal nature of psychological events and a reliance upon positivism to guide research and theory formation.

Many cognitivists insist that their understanding of the mind involves a rejection of Descartes' ontological dualism. Mind is a material, not a spiritual, entity. In a Cartesian idiom, it manifests the property of 'extension', it can be measured. By asserting the computational nature of mind and by using the computer analogy, they feel confident that they have overcome the major difficulties involved in Cartesian dualism. We have no difficulty with the idea that cognitivism involves a materialist understanding of human reality. However, it should be clear from the previous discussion that this move does not free cognitivism from the other assumptions of the Cartesian understanding of mind. In particular, the three assumptions listed above are all central to the cognitivist framework.

CARTESIANISM AND THE MORAL ORDER

Although this approach to mind has become something of an orthodoxy, the moral framework which it assumes has remained hidden. When this is revealed, the limitations of the cognitivist paradigm come clearly to light. In a series of influential writings, philosopher Charles Taylor has argued strongly that modern notions of self, individuality, and agency are historically contingent – thereby problematizing what routinely seem like self-evident facts in Western modernity. It is indeed difficult for us even to imagine other ways of thinking about our selves beyond the ways given to us by this culture. In his book *Sources of the Self: The Making of the Modern Identity*, for example, Taylor traces the origins of our modem notions about self, tracing the particular sense of a moral order established around this notion of the self. Modern ideas about good and bad, right and wrong are often predicated upon a certain concept of the individual self, and how this self is related to the wider order of the natural world and the universe at large. Taylor explores what he calls the 'background picture' lying behind our moral and spiritual intuitions – or our 'moral ontology' (Taylor, 1989: 8).

Taylor's investigation of the moral ontology of modernity leads directly to modern notions of human agency, and how these in turn are influenced by modern ideas about the mind and epistemology. He argues that a Cartesian approach to mind and the self, what he calls the 'epistemological tradition', is inextricably bound up with modern ideas about morality and spirituality. He uses this connection to explain the ease with which computer models of thinking have become established in Western societies. The concept of AI is closely allied to a philosophy of functionalism. Empirically, such models have had only limited success: AI has not lived up to its original aspirations and is, at least in its traditional form (described by John Haugeland as Good Old-Fashioned AI – GOFAI), an example of what Imré Lakatos called a 'degenerating research program' (Dreyfus, 1994). However, the computer model of thought is still widely accepted, and functionalism remains one of the dominant positions in modern philosophy of mind. It has already been noted that cognitivism is of growing importance in psychology and psychiatry. This contradiction leads Taylor to assert that:

> 'the great difficulties that the computer simulations have encountered ... don't seem to have dimmed the enthusiasm of real believers in the model. It is as though they had been vouchsafed some revelation a priori that it must all be done by formal calculi. Now this revelation, I submit, comes from the depth of our modern culture and the epistemological model anchored in it, whose strength is based not just on its affinity to mechanistic science but also on its congruence to the powerful ideal of reflexive, self-given certainty. For this has to be understood as something like a moral ideal.'
>
> (Taylor, 1997: 6)

In other words, our acceptance of cognitivism, and of computer models of mind and thinking, cannot be explained by the empirical success of these approaches alone. Instead, it appears to be driven by other cultural aspirations and ideals as well. Taylor's moral ideal relates to our cultural concern with autonomy and freedom. In the modern sense, a free agent is one who is able to rely on his/her own judgements, who can gaze in at his/her own needs and desires, and who can seek fulfilment of the latter in the outside world. A free agent is one who can stand back from the world and be responsible according to one's own agenda. Thus our very notion of freedom involves a distinction between inside and outside and a calculating self-reflexivity.

According to Taylor there are three aspects of this modern view of the self which are particularly bound up with the Cartesian, or epistemological, tradition:

> 'The first is the picture of the subject as ideally disengaged, that is free and rational to the extent that he has fully distinguished himself from the natural and social worlds, so that his identity is no longer to be defined in terms of what lies outside him in these worlds. The second, which flows from this, is a punctual view of the self, ideally ready as free and rational to treat these worlds – and even some features of his own character – instrumentally, as subject to change and reorganizing in order the better to secure the welfare of himself and others. The third is the social consequence of the first two: an atomistic construal of society as constituted by, or ultimately to be explained in terms of, individual, purposes.'
>
> (ibid.)

He maintains that to challenge one tradition automatically brings us into conflict with the other. The epistemological tradition gives support to the moral order of modernity and its ideals of disengaged rationalistic agency. In turn, this order gives support to the apparent clarity and naturalness of the Cartesian account of self and thought; and these traditions stand together in 'a complex relation of mutual support' (ibid.: 8).

In the technologies of psychiatry and psychotherapy, this mutuality becomes explicit in the credence our culture gives to analysis of the self. For example, the word 'insight' is a powerful metaphor of this inwardly directed gaze in search of self-awareness and self-understanding. Reflecting upon oneself in a detached and 'objective' manner has become a moral imperative. Analysing one's desires, motives, and aspirations through either cognitive forms of therapy or psychodynamic approaches is widely accepted as a 'good' way to deal with anxiety, depression, and, more recently, psychosis. In a wider field, the concept of 'counselling' has penetrated every aspect of personal and social life. However, it is CT which has a specific agenda of bringing a rational ordering to the world of unconscious 'scripts' and 'schemas', with the apparent objective of ridding ourselves of anxiety and despair through the Cartesian ideal of self-reflexivity. The end-result of therapy is a self which is more self-aware and detached, a self which can monitor itself in a rational way and detect emerging difficulties. A self which has loosened the bonds of dependency. A self which is more 'free' in every way.

CT FOR VOICES

It may be easier to understand the implications of the critique developed in this chapter if we examine recent work describing CT for people who hear voices. The origin of Chadwick and Birchwood's technique is deeply influenced by Aaron Beck:

> 'the belief that a voice comes from a powerful and vengeful spirit may make the person terrified of the voice and comply with its commands to harm others; however, if the same voice were construed as self-generated, the behaviour and affect might be quite different. This cognitive formulation of voices was inspired by Beck's cognitive model of depression (e.g. Beck et al. 1979) . . .'
>
> (Chadwick and Birchwood, 1994: 190–1)

Chadwick and Birchwood thus propose that distress associated with voices may be reduced by changing the subject's beliefs about the voices. First, they produce empirical evidence from interviews with voice hearers, which suggests that beliefs about voices' identities (whether they are malevolent or benevolent) determine how people respond to the voices. Their subjects engaged with positive voices, and they resisted malevolent ones. This observation establishes a rationale for the intervention:

> 'The cognitive treatment approach to hallucinations involves the *elucidation and challenging of the core beliefs that individuals have about their voices*. The weakening or loss of these beliefs is predicted to ease distress and facilitate a wider range of more adaptive coping strategies.'
>
> (ibid.: 195, emphasis added)

Therapy consists of three stages. In the opening phase, the therapist engages the voice hearer and establishes rapport. Education is an important component, and a tone of what is described as 'collaborative empiricism' (Beck et al., 1979) is established. The second stage involves disputing the subject's beliefs about voices, using two techniques drawn from CT – hypothetical contradiction and verbal challenge. The former 'measures' the voice hearer's willingness to accept evidence that challenges their beliefs, by considering their responses to hypothetical contradictory evidence. A verbal challenge is then used to challenge the subject's beliefs directly:

> 'The next stage in therapy is to question the beliefs directly. This involves first *pointing out examples of inconsistency and irrationality, and then, offering an alternative explanation of events*: namely that the voices might be self-generated and that the beliefs are an attempt to make sense of them.'
>
> (Chadwick and Birchwood, 1994: 196, emphasis added)

Finally, the therapist tries to test the subject's beliefs about voices by setting up situations in which the subject can discover that, for example, control can be exerted over the voices.

There are several ways in which our critique is relevant to this work. First is the importance attached in getting the subject to agree that voices are self-generated. The assumption here is that voices arise through faulty internal mental mechanisms. Cognitive science has expended much effort in seeking to establish the nature of these internal faults, although their nature varies (see, for example, Bentall and Slade, 1985; Frith, 1992). As far as therapy is concerned, the subject has to be persuaded that the voices are located internally, even though in many cases the subject's perception is that they are located externally. This is important: subjects then have to be convinced by the therapist that their beliefs about voices are erroneous, and that, if the correct beliefs can be established, then distress will be reduced. Thus the therapist has an important moral role, that of an arbiter, or judge, as to what might be rational or irrational beliefs for subjects to hold about voices.

Now there are serious difficulties with this position. The cognitivist insistence that voices are internally generated endorses the strong separation of 'inner mind' from 'external world' discussed earlier. As we have seen, this derives from a particular philosophical and cultural tradition and cannot be regarded as simply reflecting the objectively true nature of reality. In practice, this separation generates a therapeutic situation where little attention is paid to the subject's social reality, and the possibility that links may exist between the voices and events that have occurred in this reality. This is important because there is evidence that links hearing voices to trauma, such as bereavement (Rees, 1971) and sexual abuse (Ensink, 1993). It also disregards the view that voices can be seen to have *metaphorical* significance for subjects, and that the understanding of this metaphorical significance – in other words, relating the identity and content of voices to past experience – is important in helping the person to cope (Davies et al., 1999; Romme et al., 1992).

CT thus fails to contextualize the subject's voices, and disregards the possibility of understanding voices in terms of experience. This problem is compounded by the therapist's attempts to convince subjects that their beliefs about voices are wrong. For example, someone who has been abused in childhood may hear the voice of the devil telling them they are evil. The voice may share pragmatic features of the abuser (Leudar et al., 1997), which suggests that the identity of the voice (devil) is aligned with the abuser. From the voice hearer's position as an abused person, it is quite true to say that the voice represents the devil. Most people would agree that abuse is evil. If we attempt to persuade the subject that they are not really hearing the devil, and the voice comes from within, we are denying that aspect of the subject's reality that signifies the abuse. Some would regard such an act as itself abusive.

This demonstrates one of the fundamental difficulties within cognitivism as a clinical discourse. *Its preoccupation with interiority means that there is a systematic neglect of the social.* Cognitivism undermines the possibility of understanding voices, or, for that matter, any other aspect of human experience, within shared human contexts. To be fair, some cognitivists are aware of these shortcomings, and have become increasingly aware of them since we wrote the original version of this chapter. A subject in a study by Haddock et al. (1993) found it extremely difficult to accept that his voices were internally generated. The authors noted, though, that his voices were largely understandable in terms of the depressing social and material circumstances in which he was living at the time.

IMPLICATIONS

CT and other forms of self-reflective therapy endorse the two traditions described by Taylor, offering each other mutual support: viz. Cartesian notions of self and thought, and a moral order based upon individualism and atomism. Such theories and therapies are at home in a culture which strongly values and privileges the 'ideally disengaged' subject.

The first issue here concerns the extent to which such a view of self and agency can be regarded as universal, a question that can be answered only by reference to the literature of social anthropology. Our treatment of the issue here will not be extensive, and we will simply point to a few examples which make the point. The anthropologist Clifford Geertz defines the issue at stake in characteristic terms:

> 'the Western conception of the person as a bounded, unique, more or less integrated motivational and cognitive universe, a dynamic centre of awareness, emotion, judgement, and action organised into a distinctive whole and set contrastively both against other such wholes and against a social and natural background is, however incorrigible it may seem to us, a rather peculiar idea within the context of the world's cultures.'
>
> (Geertz, 1975: 48)

Arthur Kleinman has conducted extensive research on the problem of depression in Chinese and American patients. In his book *Rethinking Psychiatry* he writes:

> 'Psychiatry in the West is strongly influenced by implicit Western cultural values about the nature of the self and its pathologies which emphasize a deep, hidden private self. In contrast ... the Chinese view the self, to a large degree, as consensual – a sociocentrically oriented personality that is much more attentive to the demands of a particular situation and key relationships than to what is deeply private ... Social context, not personal depth, is the indigenous measure of validity.'
>
> (Kleinman, 1988: 98)

Laurence Kirmayer (1988) points out that in Japan, autonomy in interpersonal relationships is much less valued than in the West. For the Japanese, the moral value of the self is expressed through an idiom of social connectedness rather than personal achievement. He contrasts what he calls the 'sociosomatic' origins of distress in Japan with the more familiar psychosomatic framework developed in the West. Shweder and Bourne (1982) also distinguish two different approaches to the individual–social relationship: the 'egocentric contractual' and the 'sociocentric organic'. Societies endorsing the former as an ideal tend to emphasize the intrapsychic, promoting reflection upon the self and its desires and cognitions. Sociocentric societies have much less focus on the psychological realm, and instead there is an orientation toward individual integration with the natural, supernatural, and social worlds. This differentiation is now generally accepted in social anthropology, and is also increasingly accepted by mainstream transcultural psychiatrists (e.g. Leff, 1988).

Thus, the disengaged self, a basic assumption of Western psychiatry and psychology, is not a recognized notion in many world cultures. In multi-cultural modern Europe, the promotion of CT as an answer to distress entails promoting of a particular view of the self – with major implications for many ethnic minority communities struggling to maintain a sense of their own identity and ways of life. Because CT is presented as a 'scientific' enterprise, devoid of value orientations, these implications often remain unseen. The foregoing analysis therefore raises profound problems for the 'exporting' of therapies based on cognitivism to other parts of the world (Bracken and Petty, 1998).

The second issue can be formulated as a question: is the moral order predicated upon the philosophy of mind implicit in cognitivism the sort of order to which we should aspire?

Nikolas Rose has developed a sustained Foucauldian analysis of how psychology and psychotherapeutics have now penetrated into everyday life. He points to the political dimension of these developments, arguing that we are now substantially governed, ironically, through our own individual quests for freedom and self-expression:

> 'Psychotherapeutics is linked at a profound level to the socio-political obligations of the modern self. The self it seeks to liberate or restore is the entity able to steer its individual path through life by means of the act of personal decision and the assumption of personal responsibility. It is the self freed from all moral obligations but the obligation to construct a life of its own choosing, a life in which it realizes itself ... [T]he norm of autonomy secretes, as its inevitable accompaniment, a constant and intense self scrutiny, a continual evaluation of our personal experiences, emotions, and feelings in relation to images of satisfaction, the necessity to narrativize our lives in a vocabulary of interiority. The self that is liberated is obliged to live its life tied to the project of its own identity.'
>
> (Rose, 1989: 253–4)

Cognitive therapy, then, locates the problems of anxiety, depression, and psychosis firmly in the interior, with, the 'irrational' network of faulty schemata and dysfunctional beliefs giving rise to these problems allegedly being ordered by the exercise of reason alone. Distress can then be neutralized by looking within. Moreover, CT enthusiastically asserts the value of this move toward self-scrutiny. In doing so it not only connects the individual to the 'socio-political obligations of the modern self' but also works to devalue any contextualizing understanding of distress.

Such an understanding requires that we look in a quite different direction. Indeed, two of the greatest philosophers of the twentieth century, Martin Heidegger and Ludwig Wittgenstein, argued for a very different understanding of human reality, with both attaching particular importance to understanding, in terms of background (or social) context. This influence is now being felt in, for example, new phenomenological approaches (Csordas, 1994) the 'discursive turn' within psychology (Harré and Gillett, 1994) and latterly in a newly emerging 'post-existential' cosmology (Loewenthal, Chapter 12, this volume). While not without difficulties themselves, such approaches at least make it possible to lay open the moral assumptions and values which underpin cognitivism.

REFERENCES

Beck, A.T. (1972) *The Diagnosis and Management of Depression*, Philadelphia: University of Pennsylvania Press.

Beck, A.T. (1976) *CT and Emotional Disorders*, New York: Meridan–New American Library.

Beck, A.T., Rush, A., Shaw, B, & others (1979) *CT of Depression*, New York: Guilford.

Beeman, W. O. (1985) 'Dimensions of dysphoria: the view from linguistic anthropology', in A. Kleinman and B. Good (eds), *Culture and Depression: Studies in the Anthropology and Cross-Cultural Psychiatry of Affect and Disorder*, Berkeley: University of California Press.

Bentall, R. P. and Slade, P. D. (1985) 'Reality testing and auditory hallucinations: a signal detection hypothesis', *British Journal of Clinical Psychology*, 24: 159–69.

Bracken, P. and Petty, C. (1998) *Rethinking the Trauma of War*, London: Free Association Books.

Chadwick, P. and Birchwood, M. (1994) 'The omnipotence of voices: a cognitive approach to auditory hallucinations', *British Journal of Psychiatry*, 164: 190–201.

Chomsky, N. (1959) 'Review of B. F. Skinner's *Verbal Behaviour*', *Language*, 35: 26–58.

Churchland, P. and Sejnowski, T. (1992) *The Computational Brain*, Cambridge, Mass.: MIT Press.

Crane, T. (1995) *The Mechanical Mind*, London: Penguin.

Csordas, T. (1994) 'Words from the Holy People: a case study in cultural phenomenology', in T. Csordas (ed.), *Embodiment and Experience: The Existential Ground of Culture and Self*, Cambridge: Cambridge University Press, pp. 269–90.

Davies, P., Leudar, I., and Thomas, P. (1999) 'Dialogical engagement with voices: a single case study', *British Journal of Medical Psychology*, 72: 179–87.

Descartes, R. (1968) *Discourse on Method and the Meditations*, ed. E. E. Sutcliffe, London: Penguin.

Dreyfus, H. (1991) *Being-in-the-world. A Commentary on Heidegger's* Being and Time, Cambridge: MIT Press.

Dreyfus, H. (1994) *What Computers Still Can't Do: A Critique of Artificial Reason*, Cambridge: MIT Press.

Ensink, B. (1993) 'Trauma: a study of child abuse and hallucinations', in M. Romme and S. Escher (eds), *Accepting Voices*, London: MIND.

Fodor, J. (1995) 'The persistence of attitudes', in W. Lyons (ed.), *Modern Philosophy of Mind*, London: Everyman.

Foucault, M. (1967) *Madness and Civilization: A History of Insanity in the Age of Reason*, trans. R. Howard, London: Tavistock.

Frank, J. (1974) *Persuasion and Healing*, New York: Schocken.

Frith, C. (1992) *The Cognitive Neuropsychology of Schizophrenia*, London: Lawrence Erlbaum.

Geertz, C. (1975) 'On the nature of anthropological understanding', *American Scientist*, 63: 48.

Gergen, K. (1995) 'Metaphor and monophony in the 20th-century psychology of emotions', *History of the Human Sciences*, 8 (2): 1–23.

Goleman, D. (1985) *Vital Lies, Simple Truths: The Psychology of Self-deception*, New York: Simon & Schuster.

Harré, R. and Gillett, G. (1994) *The Discursive Mind*, Thousand Oaks, Calif.: Sage.

Harré, R and Secord, P. E. (1973) *The Explanation of Social Behaviour*, Oxford: Blackwell.

Janoff-Bulman, R. (1992) *Shattered Assumptions: Towards a New Psychology of Trauma*, New York: The Free Press.

Kant, I. (1992) 'What is Enlightenment?', in S. Eliot and K. Whitelock (eds), *The Enlightenment: Texts, II*, Milton Keynes: Open University Press.

Kelly, G. A. (1955) *The Psychology of Personal Constructs*, New York: Norton.

Kirmayer, L. J. (1988) 'Mind and body as metaphors: hidden values in biomedicine', in M. Lock and D. Gordon (eds), *Biomedicine Examined*, Dordrecht: Kluwer Academic.

Kleinman, A. (1988) *Rethinking Psychiatry: From Cultural Category to Personal Experience*, New York: The Free Press.

Layard, R. (2004) *Mental Health: Britain's Biggest Social Problem*, accessed on 8 August 2008 at: http://cep.lse.ac.uk/textonly/research/mentalhealth/RL414d.pdf.

Leff, J. (1988) *Psychiatry around the Globe*, London: Royal College of Psychiatrists.

Leudar, I., Thomas, P., McNally, D., and Glinski, A. (1997) 'What voices can do with words: pragmatics of verbal hallucinations', *Psychological Medicine*, 2: 885–98.

Levin J. D. (1992) *Theories of the Self*, Washington, D.C.: Hemisphere.

Lyons, W. (1995) 'Introduction', in W. Lyons (ed.), *Modem Philosophy of Mind*, London: Everyman.

Newell, A. and Simon, H. A. (1963) 'GPS: a program that simulates human thought', in E. A. Feigenbaum and J. Feldman (eds), *Computers and Thought*, New York: McGraw-Hill.

Olafson, E. (1987) *Heidegger and the Philosophy of Mind*, New Haven, Conn.: Yale University Press.

Putnam, H. (1975) *Mind, Language and Reality* (Philosophical Papers, Vol. 2), Cambridge: Cambridge University Press.

Rees, W. D. (1971) 'The hallucinations of widowhood', *British Medical Journal*, 4: 7–41.

Romme, M., Honig, A., Noordhoorn, E., and Escher, A. (1992) 'Coping with voices: an emancipatory approach', *British Journal of Psychiatry*, 161: 99–103.

Rose, N. (1989) *Governing the Soul*, London: Routledge.

Sass, L. (1989) 'Humanism, hermeneutics, and humanistic psychoanalysis: differing conceptions of subjectivity', *Psychoanalysis and Contemporary Theory*, 12: 433–504.

Schank, R. C. and Abelson, R. P. (1977) 'Scripts, plans and knowledge', in P. N. Johnson-Laird and P. C. Wason (eds), *Thinking: Readings in Cognitive Science*, New York: Cambridge University Press.

Shweder, R. A. and Bourne, E. J. (1982) 'Does the concept of the person vary cross-culturally?', in A. J. Marsella and G. M. White (eds), *Cultural Conceptions of Mental Health and Therapy*, Dordrecht: Reidel.

Soloman, R. C. (1988) *Continental Philosophy since 1750: The Rise and Fall of the Self*, Oxford: Oxford University Press.

Taylor, C. (1989) *Sources of the Self: The Making of the Modern Identity*, Cambridge, Mass.: Harvard University Press.

Taylor, C. (1997) *Philosophical Arguments*, Cambridge, Mass.: Harvard University Press.

Chapter 9

PSYCHOANALYSIS AND COGNITIVE BEHAVIOUR THERAPY:

RIVAL PARADIGMS OR COMMON GROUND?

Jane Milton

INTRODUCTION

Cognitive behaviour therapy (CBT) is hailed with great hope and enthusiasm as a means of rapidly alleviating mental distress. Its practice is seen in some quarters, for example in the UK public sector, as providing an alternative to psychoanalytically orientated therapy that is more rational, quick, and efficient, and regarded as of proven efficacy. This is similar to the early idealization of psychoanalysis, and may prove relatively short-lived. However, psychoanalysts need to take careful heed of this phenomenon, and be prepared to engage in debate about it, as it appears to be linked with a serious devaluation and erosion of the psychoanalytic perspective in health-care services worldwide.

In comparing and contrasting the two clinical paradigms, I will show how CBT practitioners are beginning to rediscover the same phenomena that psychoanalysts earlier faced, and are having to change and deepen both their theory and practice accordingly, and to modify their expectations. These rediscovered phenomena concern unconscious processes, the complexity of the internal world, and the intrinsic difficulties of psychic change. In a book about his work with personality-disordered patients (Beck and Freeman, 1990), one of the main originators of CBT, Aaron Beck, talks at times in a way reminiscent of the early Freud. Early psychoanalysis was itself more 'cognitive', and had to evolve to meet the challenges encountered in the psyche. We may find that CBT technique continues to become more 'analytic' as time goes by, and that accompanying this, the need for longer and more complex training of therapists, including substantial personal analysis, will be rediscovered.

The stance of the therapist in CBT is a socially acceptable one, which makes immediate intuitive sense. The psychoanalytic stance is much harder to swallow, and is maintained against the resistance of both the analyst and the patient. I will suggest that there is a constant tendency for 'decomposition' or collapse into something simpler during psychoanalytic work. The analyst is pushed constantly from without and within either into being more 'cognitive' or into a simpler counselling stance – in such ways the analytic stance is frequently in danger of being lost and having to be refound. When it can be achieved, the advantage is that through the discomfort and tension of the striving for analytic neutrality and abstinence, more disturbance becomes available in the room, within the therapeutic relationship itself,

An earlier version of this chapter appeared in the *International Journal of Psychoanalysis*, 82 (3), 2001, pp. 431–47. It was originally presented at a conference of the same title organized by the Association for Psychoanalytic Psychotherapy in the NHS on 3 March 2000 at St Anne's College, Oxford.

to be worked with and potentially transformed. CBT is far less disturbing and intrusive. It is worth noting that although it forfeits potential therapeutic power, it may be acceptable to some patients in a way that psychoanalytic therapy is not, protecting privacy and defences that the individual has good reasons for wishing to preserve.

A second, related point is that in my view, 'integration' of analytic and cognitive methods inevitably produces something more cognitive than analytic. Once cognitive or behavioural parameters are introduced by the therapist, I will argue that an analytic stance essentially ceases to exist, and the analytic paradigm and methodology again collapse into the cognitive one, with a loss of potential therapeutic power. This is worth exploring in view of the huge current enthusiasm for so-called 'integrated' treatments such as 'cognitive analytic therapy' (CAT).

One oft-quoted argument for offering CBT rather than psychoanalytic treatments to patients in the public sector is that there is so much more empirical research evidence for its efficacy – an issue several chapters address in detail in this book. On the surface, it also appears cheaper, as it is brief and needs less training to apply. It is worth noting, first of all, that where patients have freedom to choose, in the private sector, only a minority opt for CBT, with most patients preferring dynamic therapies. The alleged superior efficacy of CBT is also questionable empirically, and I will look briefly at the outcome research field in this connection.

COMPARING PSYCHOANALYTIC AND COGNITIVE BEHAVIOUR THERAPY

HISTORY OF THE SPLIT FROM PSYCHOANALYSIS

The biographical context for Freud's ideas is widely known, with important links between the ideas and Freud's personal experiences and his self-analysis. A similar context for Beck's ideas is less well-known and is worth outlining. Aaron T. Beck began as a psychoanalyst, graduating from the Philadelphia Psychoanalytic Institute in 1956. He became disillusioned and impatient with the psychoanalytic culture in which he found himself over the following decades – in his view unfocused, resting on dubious theoretical foundations, and insufficiently located in the patient's current reality. Psychoanalysis was very much the dominant, authoritative culture in psychiatry (a situation radically different from that in the UK then or now). Beck, in opposition to this establishment model, founded first a 'cognitive theory' of depression, then derived a brief therapeutic approach. Perhaps, as is not uncommon, innovation arose through the combination of a particular personality and a rather rigid or too-comfortable state of affairs in psychoanalysis at one place and time.

Beck's biographer (Weishaar, 1993) notes that Beck is open about having developed his theory and technique not just through his clinical work, but, like Freud, through introspection and analysis of his own neurotic problems. Born in 1921, the youngest of a sibship of five, Beck was according to family mythology the one who had 'cured' his mother by being born. Elizabeth Beck had been depressed since the loss of her first child, a son, in infancy, followed later by the death of a young daughter in the 1919 influenza epidemic. Described as a powerful matriarchal figure, overshadowing the quieter father, she remained an explosive person, whose unpredictable and irrational moods the young Aaron found troubling. She is described as having been 'overprotective' of her youngest son, who spent months in hospital with a life-threatening illness at the age of eight.

Beck describes the way he systematically desensitized himself to a serious 'blood/injury phobia' during his medical training, treating his fears of heights, tunnels, public speaking, and 'abandonment' with similar sorts of behavioural and cognitive strategies. He also described curing himself of 'moderate depression'. He is lukewarm about the effects of his training analysis. Weishaar quotes a colleague, Ruth Greenberg, as referring to Beck's restive rebelliousness about the psychoanalytic establishment. Greenberg suggests that being his own authority and being in control of himself were of overriding importance to Beck, and would have made the analytic training very problematic for him.

In the decade following his qualification as an analyst, Weishaar relates how Beck carried out empirical research into depression. Through examining the dreams of his depressed patients, he came to the conclusion that hypothesizing wish-fulfilment and hidden motivation was unnecessary, and indeed in time he came to dispense with the idea of an unconscious in Freud's sense at all. He also used more standard experimental-psychology procedures in his research, with one experiment involving a card-sorting test. The fact that depressed subjects did not react negatively to success in the task showed, Beck thought, that they did not have a need to suffer, and thus went toward disproving the psychoanalytic theory that depression was due to 'inverted hostility'. Many psychoanalysts might question this as a research paradigm for psychoanalytic concepts, isolated as it is from the context of a close interpersonal relationship. However, I think it illustrates how great the conceptual differences sometimes are between practitioners of the two treatments, which can lead to major difficulties in communication.

Beck began to develop a cognitive theory, and from that a cognitive therapy (CT) of depression. He was influenced by Kelly's (1955) personal-construct theory and by the idea that the patient could become his or her own 'scientist' of the mind. He was also influenced by the ideas of Adler, Horney, and Stack-Sullivan. Beck communicated with Albert Ellis, who was independently developing rational-emotive therapy, which shares some but not all of its features with cognitive therapy (Ellis, 1980). Beck, together with Ellis and Donald Meichenbaum (see, for example, Meichenbaum, 1985), is regarded as one of the 'founding fathers' of cognitive behaviour therapy (CBT), an umbrella term which covers this broad therapeutic approach, and which, in the UK at least, is now used more or less synonymously with CT. 'Behavioural' acknowledges the contribution of learning theory and classical behaviour therapy. I will continue to use the term CBT in this chapter.

Early theories underpinning CBT were relatively simple, with little emphasis on the precise mechanism of symptom causality, simply that things had been 'mis-learnt' through childhood experience. The emphasis was, rather, on the way symptoms were currently maintained and underpinned by 'negative cognitions', which were in turn generated by maladaptive internal 'schemas' – deep cognitive structures organizing experience and behaviour. (In recent years 'schemas' are seen in increasingly complex ways.) Beck believed that discovering and challenging negative cognitions was a simpler, shorter path to change than psychoanalysis, and made more theoretical sense. He saw himself as shifting away from the 'motivational' psychoanalytic model to an 'information processing' one – he directed attention away from 'why' on to 'how' distressed psychological functioning operates.

THE COGNITIVE BEHAVIOUR PARADIGM

In its classical form (Beck, 1979; Hawton et al., 1989; Moorey, 1991) CBT is a short-term, structured, problem-solving method by which a patient is trained to recognize and modify the maladaptive, conscious thinking and beliefs that are, it is argued, maintaining his or her problems and distress. This treatment/training is done first by educating the patient in the cognitive model of emotion, often with the help of written material. The patient is then helped to recognize negative automatic thoughts, then encouraged to use a process of logical challenging and reality-testing of thoughts, both in the session and in the form of between-session homework.

A vital feature of CBT is the sympathetic, collaborative therapeutic relationship, in which the therapist tries to be an inspiring and imaginative trainer in self-help skills. The patient is encouraged to become a scientific observer of him/herself and his or her thoughts, and to start to question the logical basis on which beliefs – for example, beliefs about being unlovable, or a failure – are held. Sessions are structured and directive, with the patient and therapist focusing general complaints down on to specific negative cognitions which can then give rise to experimental tasks to be carried out, and the outcome monitored. Thus, a depressed patient is found, for example, to have core beliefs that no one is interested in her, and that everyone else is having a better life. These core beliefs are found to generate day-to-day thoughts like 'no one talks to me at parties', and 'other people have much more interesting jobs'. Such beliefs can be specifically tested out both during discussion in sessions (often through a sort of Socratic dialogue) and then through carefully planned homework involving observations and, possibly, behavioural tasks. This hypothetical patient will be referred to again later.

The usual practice is to offer between ten and twenty sessions of treatment, with follow-up refresher sessions. Training required for the therapist is relatively brief, not requiring, for example, any personal therapy. Beck, however, stresses that it is far from enough for the therapist simply to learn a set of techniques – he/she needs to have an overall 'cognitive conceptualization', and to have well-developed interpersonal skills and sensitivity. Weishaar notes that Beck's treatment manual for depression fails to capture the heart of his own empathic therapeutic style, as seen on videotapes. This observation will be returned to later, when discussing what factors may really be therapeutic in CBT.

COMPARING THE PSYCHOANALYTIC PARADIGM

Contemporary psychoanalytic conceptualization and clinical technique mostly differ from that of 1950s Philadelphia. Beck, who was sceptical about classical drive theory, and the strong emphasis his psychoanalytic colleagues then placed on childhood reconstructions, might (or might not) have found a relatively active, 'here-and-now'-based object-relations approach more to his taste. I will lay out the basics of this contemporary psychoanalytic clinical paradigm so as to contrast it with the cognitive one. I approach this from the traditional 'positivist' rather than from an intersubjective 'constructivist' paradigm – that is, I see the primary object of study and discovery as being the inner world of the patient. While acknowledging the biases caused by our 'irreducible subjectivity' (Renik, 1998), I agree with Dunn (1995) that this does not reduce us to total ignorance. Thus I see the analyst as doing his or her best, with an imperfect and biased observing instrument, to strive toward understanding of the internal world of the other.

The CBT stance is intuitive and socially acceptable – indeed, it is a specialized form of a familiar tutorial relationship. The psychoanalytic stance is counterintuitive and less socially acceptable – much harder to swallow for both analyst and patient. The therapist offers close empathic attention, but leaves the agenda to the patient's free associations, becoming involved with the patient as participant-observer in an unfolding relationship. The analyst often has powerful wishes to respond naturally to the patient, to explain and to reassure. Giving way to such impulses relieves the analyst – it enables him or her to feel nicer and kinder. In particular, it spares the analyst the moral reproach intrinsic in being the negative-transference figure (Milton, 2000). The paradox is that although the analyst is apparently being more 'real', this is illusory. He or she has in fact, by fitting in with the patient's pressures, remained a transference object, and it is this familiar, relatively weak figure that the patient is left with externally and internally (Feldman, 1993). Collapse of the analytic stance has removed the potential for the analyst to become a truly surprising and new object (Baker, 1993). This is a new object for internalization, who can bear and reflect on the patient's projections, rather than quickly disowning them.

The analytic precepts of neutrality and abstinence do not refer to coldness, but to a striven-for personal unobtrusiveness that allows the analyst to become clothed in whatever the patient needs to bring. By reducing the extraneous 'noise' from one's own personality, a clearer field is provided for locating this. 'Live' emotional experiencing is allowed to occur, sometimes fraught, anxiety-provoking, or painful for analyst, patient, or both. However, by activating distorted internal object relationships in a live way, they are potentially able to be explored and gradually altered by experience. In contrast to CBT, change promoted by the work of psychoanalysis work is relatively independent of the conscious aspects of insight.

The analytic stance will frequently be lost, and have to be refound, as the analyst is subtly pulled into fulfilling the patient's unconscious scripts (Joseph, 1985; Sandler, 1976). There will be constant invitations, which the analyst will often partly accept, to become more prescriptive, or educational, more partisan, more emotionally reactive, and so on. One could say that the patient tries all the time to get the analyst to be a different sort of therapist – whether this is more of a humanistic counsellor, a gestalt therapist, a guru, a teacher, or, what I think is quite common, the patient unconsciously nudging the analyst into providing a weak version of cognitive therapy itself. All these therapies, including cognitive therapy but with the one exception of psychoanalytic therapy, use therapeutic stances that come more naturally because they are specialized forms of ordinary social contact. So it is always hard work, and work against the grain, to observe the collapse of the analytic stance, work it through in the countertransference, and re-establish its counter-intuitiveness and complexity again.

In CBT, the set-up is such that the patient and therapist talk together about a disturbed patient they mostly only hear reported, and try to think, with the sensible patient in the room, ways to help him or her feel, and be, more reasonable. The rational part of the self is strengthened, in order to get on top of the disturbance. This maintains, even strengthens, a division in the personality between rational and irrational, conscious and unconscious. Analytic conditions, by contrast, allow disturbed aspects of the patient to come right into the room, with all their passion and irrationality, loving, hating, destroying, and so on. The patient is encouraged to project, challenge, disrupt, complain, involve the analyst in myriad ways in the psychic drama. Primitive and disturbing phantasies, involving both body and mind, may come to light.

The analyst, then, has the advantage of a much greater range of orientations to the patient, and aspects of the patient, than the cognitive therapist has. Linked to this, an important but particularly intrusive feature of psychoanalysis is the analyst's frequent orientation toward what happens in the therapeutic relationship from an observing 'third position'. This triangularity can arouse the primitive feelings of oedipal exclusion which Britton (1989) describes. The analyst's reflective, independently thinking mind can seem an infuriatingly private, superior place where an excluding sort of 'mental intercourse' takes place. It is easier and more comfortable to flatten the triangle, to discuss things that are already visible, from a shared position, or to get together to discuss someone else. The 'collaborative colleague' stance of CBT, together with a setting that does not invite live manifestation of disturbance, can avoid triangularity almost completely.

I think this is a key issue in the difference. The psychoanalyst deliberately takes the risk at times of precipitating the patient's narcissistic indignation, or even rage, by speaking openly about things he or she sees that the patient cannot see, or half-sees and wants to keep hidden. Although this is uncomfortable for both, it means narcissistic parts of the personality are activated and may become gradually modified and integrated.

To consider now the case of the hypothetical depressed patient mentioned earlier who comes for help feeling no one is interested in her, and that other people are having better lives. A psychoanalyst with whom she consults will not actively encourage her to challenge and test this belief outside the room. Instead, a neutral, unstructured setting will be provided, in which the patient may quickly experience the analyst as uninterested, involved in his or her own thoughts, and speaking from a superior and privileged position – the analyst, like the people she meets outside, she believes to be having a much better and exciting time with other people, while she is left alone with an inferior sort of life. By not encouraging and reassuring, the analyst may quickly find him- or herself the target of this patient's miserable resentment. The nature and source of this resentment will become clearer, allowing it to be understood and questioned at a much deeper level. The patient's envious misery may prove linked to childhood feelings of exclusion from the parents' relationship and from the mother's relationship with other siblings. The 'other room' from which one by definition is always excluded (Britton, 1998) may, for many people, become idealized in a way that empties their own life of meaning, and halts the process of separation and independence. This deep sense of 'oedipal exclusion' may be linked to both childhood deprivations and a particular difficulty with tolerating separateness and difference. CBT is unlikely to reveal or to be able to address such complex dynamics.

It is certainly true that psychoanalysts reason with their patients, explain to them, make practical suggestions, and so on. Often, for example, I think this happens at the end of a bit of painful or stormy work in the transference. A narcissistic aspect of the patient has been finally understood and integrated (in Kleinian terms, for example, a move toward the depressive position) and the patient is thoughtful, curious, and collaborative about what has happened and how it relates to current and past relationships. I think this is often the organizing and contextualizing phase of a piece of work, which is in many ways a final 'cognitive' phase. At other times, though, I think analysts become 'cognitive' as a short circuit, to avoid a painful but necessary bit of emotional experiencing. Thus, a self-observing eye is needed, so the analyst can question whether he or she is beginning to sound very reasonable and sensible, trying to persuade the patient of some bit of reality, or push the patient into certain action. One might ask oneself at this point whether there is a wish to be seen as a good, blameless object – in which case it is worth wondering what form the bad object would take at this point that would feel so unbearable. It might also be that there is a larger picture to be seen in the transference and countertransference that is being missed. I will illustrate this latter possibility with the case of Mr A.

MR A

A 45-year-old man who was still living with his parents, working in a clerical job far below his capabilities, Mr A came to analysis for help to move on. He intermittently would come to a session in a particularly thinking and constructive mood, wanting help with a particular plan for change – such as learning to drive, applying for a new job, buying his own flat, and so on. I would feel encouraged and pleased for him, because he really was miserably stuck. I would join him in trying to analyse his difficulties with these tasks, linking things in, when I could, with the transference relationship and troublesome past relationships, in an ordinary sort of way. In subsequent sessions Mr A would have become very anxious and doubtful about the change. He would start to spin it all out – he would have a form to fill in but leave it at work, or lose it; he would tell me about a necessary phone call being put off, and so on, making sure I knew every stage of the postponement. He would still seem to want help with his fears. The nature of the scene-setting followed by the delays was such that I was often left with a very strong sense of thwarted desire.

At first I would find myself full of sensible and practical ideas and strategies for helping Mr A to challenge his fears, and (with a guilty sideways look toward my own analytic superego) I would slip into making interpretations which were really disguised practical suggestions, like 'it is interesting that you don't seem to feel that you could …'. At this stage we would enter, as I came to see, a 'cognitive' mode that was ultimately unproductive. Mr A would passively seem to accept my cognitive and behavioural suggestions, but continue to let the project slide. As Mr A became flatter and more passive, I would find myself more and more lively. I would now perhaps analyse his resistance in terms of his rebellious attitude to me, or to his disowning and projection of his mind into me, or perhaps in terms of his internal conflict.

Nothing would happen – that is, Mr A would still report to me flatly or hopelessly, or sometimes a tinge triumphantly, that he had still not done anything about the project. I would sometimes feel pushed beyond endurance at this stage. If I could not contain my countertransference, I would hear myself making a rather sharp and impatient interpretation about Mr A's passivity. In response, he would become either very weak and demoralized, or alternatively subtly excited and mocking. He would typically report dreams at times like these, in which someone was pursued or intimidated by gangsters or con men – it was often unclear which side he was on in these dreams.

By repeatedly working through these situations with Mr A, I came to understand a complex internal situation in which he was both trapped by, and took revenge upon, a monstrous internal figure which was partly a version of a very abusive stepmother. I came to see my 'cognitive' impulses as part of a larger picture in which we as an analytic couple enacted a sado-masochistic scenario that both trapped Mr A but also fulfilled a wish and need for a timeless infantile-like dependence on archaic objects. In phantasy, he seemed to have lodged himself inside me, projecting his active mind in a very wholesale way. Movement could only occur at times when I could get outside the situation, see the whole picture, and interpret it in a non-retaliatory way that Mr A could become really interested in, and concerned about. This work used to test my analytic capacity to the full, but it eventually enabled Mr A to experience his own mind more fully. This meant him having to face and mourn his own situation, internal and external, and experience his rage, guilt, sadness, and ultimately his own considerable strength.

In my work with Mr A I was thus periodically nudged into doing fragments of a weak version of CBT. This illustrates what I mean by 'collapse' of the analytic stance into something simpler and more apparently common-sense. It will inevitably occur in our work from time to time, and it needs hard work in the countertransference to notice and rebuild the tension and complexity inherent in productive analytic work.

COMPARING MODES OF LEARNING IN THE PSYCHOANALYTIC AND COGNITIVE BEHAVIOUR PARADIGMS

We know that both psychoanalysis and CBT involve learning. The main sort of learning hoped for in psychoanalysis is learning from emotional experience. This may be, for example, finding that one's worst fears in a relationship are not confirmed, or, when they are, that the experience can be survived and thought about. CBT therapists also hope their patients will learn from experience. The whole point of homework experiments is that the patient can test out distorted preconceptions outside the session. Some cognitive therapists, nowadays, may even say to the patient, '...and can't you see how you're doing it with me too?'. The analytic patient can, however, learn something quite subtle and complex through understanding, containment, repeated experiment, and sustained experience within the therapeutic relationship, that (for example in Mr A's case) giving up a dependent, sado-masochistic way of relating involves both some loss and a new sort of loneliness, but also a new freedom and independence of thought and action.

Implicit in CBT is that if one pays attention to modifying the patient's conscious distortions of reality, or 'dysfunctional assumptions', over a brief period, the deeper structures generating such assumptions will dissipate, or become far less powerful. Psychoanalysts are more sanguine about this. A patient Ms B may be relieved and encouraged to find as a result of a courageous homework exercise that her actual family are pleased about her applying for promotion at work. However, after a short remission she remains plagued and seriously inhibited in her life by a nightmarishly caricatured inner maternal figure who is weak, ill, and reproachful if her daughter leaves her own depression and self-doubt behind – it feels at a deep level as if she is 'abandoning' the mother. Another patient Mr C, who fears (he knows irrationally) that sexual intercourse will somehow damage either himself or the woman, may be able to reality-test his fears behaviourally only to a very limited extent. Unconsciously his childhood fury about being left out of his parents' bedroom and their smugly exclusive relationship, leading to a phantasy of violent intrusion into his mother's body, means that he superstitiously fears he will damage the woman, and/or provoke attack from an internal nightmarishly vengeful phantasy couple.

Having said this, cognitive therapists argue cogently for the efficacy of CBT in combating vicious cycles of symptom generation. Thus someone who suffers from panic attacks which are ultimately generated, say, by fearful unconscious phantasies is often then subject to further spiralling hypochondriacal fear at the feelings of breathlessness and palpitations generated. CBT can be very helpful in modifying such positive feedback loops in symptom generation. However, one would predict a less radical and enduring effect from CBT than from psychoanalytic work which would aim in such a situation to address structures earlier in the causal chain.

Psychoanalysis has shed light on some barriers we have to learning. Learning certain fundamental truths about self and others is a complex process – both sought after but also desperately hated and resisted (Money-Kyrle, 1968). It is hard to give up feeling omnipotent, the centre of the universe, rather than dependent on others, and fully to know we are the product of a couple who came together outside our control, and have minds that are separate and different from ours. This involves the triangularity I have referred to. Psychoanalytic research shows how very active a part we play in what we learn or mis-learn all our lives, and that this is the product of both environment and constitution. An implicit message in much CBT (but mostly not in psychoanalytic) writing is that somehow the therapist should be able simply to transcend and transform the patient's maladaptive internal schemas by being a good, reasonable person. This view of human nature sees the application of reason and the right external conditions as sufficient for healing. The assumption is that the patient is simply a good and reasonable victim of misunderstanding and neglect. Most psychoanalysts, in contrast, see man as subject to complex internal conflicts and strong tendencies toward unreasonableness – all needing to be understood and addressed in detail. This difference in philosophy, often unstated, has important clinical implications.

The factors that psychoanalysts suggest make learning so difficult may mean that certain patients will simply not be able to tolerate the sort of knowing and understanding that psychoanalysis offers. They will neither want it nor be accessible to it. In such cases it would be arrogant (as well as pointless) for a psychoanalytic therapist to attempt to impose such treatment. A patient must be free to choose a collaborative, less ambitious, and more directly educational approach that will not threaten needed defences. In a good assessment, one will hopefully be able to gauge how much intrusion a patient welcomes or is prepared to tolerate. This will mean, for example, that psychoanalytic psychotherapists in the public sector, funded to work only once a week with very disturbed patients, may find themselves introducing more cognitive parameters, and in effect collapsing the analytic stance. This collapse at least partially deprives the patient of a full opportunity to work in the negative transference – to project the very worst things in his or her internal world into the therapeutic relationship. Thus, one does limit the scope of the work that can be done. A therapist might judge with a particular patient that this is wise, as these terrible things might simply not be able to be contained within the limited setting available. However, I think it is always worth questioning this, and for the therapist to ask him- or herself whether it is really the patient being spared or the therapist – is one underestimating the patient's capacity to bear things, and avoiding an attack the patient really needs an opportunity to make?

There may be clinical reasons for knowingly collapsing the tension of the analytic stance in this way with particular patients, but collapse may also be part of ongoing debates and dialectics within the profession of psychoanalysis at different times and places. Abstinence and neutrality that harden into rigidity and arrogance may prompt some analysts to espouse 'human warmth' and experiment anew with gratification of the patient's infantile wishes. The pitfalls opened up by such an approach carried to extremes may then in turn provoke a countermovement. Partial collapses of analytic tension in one direction or another may become institutionalized in particular approaches. One analyst's collapse may be another's flexible and innovative experiment, and the debate thus launched may be creative within psychoanalysis, providing necessary challenges to stagnation. Moves toward more 'reasonable' and socially acceptable approaches may also be less creative, and related to analysts' own inevitable ambivalence about analysis and impatience with its slowness; its failure to live up to earlier, idealistic expectations.

'INTEGRATION' OF PSYCHOANALYTIC AND COGNITIVE THERAPIES

A number of psychotherapists believe you can combine all the advantages of the different techniques without losing power. Thus for example, 'cognitive-analytic therapy' (CAT) (Ryle, 1990) is a brief, flexible approach where the patient is encouraged to think about themselves and their relationships, and to formulate and monitor, with the therapist, what is habitually going wrong. The therapist may use classical CBT approaches such as encouraging the patient to keep a symptom diary and make homework experiments, while at the same time interpreting transference phenomena as they arise. The patient's resistances to diary-keeping and other tasks often (for example) quickly provide material for work in the transference.

CAT sessions are less structured than classical CBT sessions, and unconscious as well as conscious meanings are certainly sought, but CAT has certain hallmark structural features. There is, as in CBT, reading matter for the patient, and emphasis on early collaborative written formulation of the problems. The formulations can be referred back to when problems arise in the transference relationship or when difficulties outside are discussed. Another writing task is that both patient and therapist are supposed to write each other 'goodbye letters' expressing their views about the therapy as it comes to an end. Ryle (1995) describes CAT as a very useful and safe first intervention for patients referred for outpatient psychotherapy (in the UK health service).

Ryle (1995) regards the transference as a 'hardy plant' arising whatever one does, and certainly not requiring the therapist to be inactive. He regards the collaborative stance of CAT as less potentially dangerous than psychoanalysis, which he sees as placing the patient in quite a powerless position (Ryle, 1994). I agree with Ryle that bad psychoanalysis has more potential for harm than bad CAT. This is because conditions are created such that the 'hardy plant' of transference can flourish in a much fuller, often more disturbing way, much as the pot plants of colder climes become the bushes and trees of the tropics. In addition, many plants will not even germinate outside the tropics, and there will be important aspects of the transference and countertransference which will not come to light at all in the setting of CBT or CAT, which, in spite of superficial appearances to the contrary, I think have a fundamental similarity to each other and difference from a psychoanalytic approach. The therapist's active assertion of the benign colleague/teacher stance in CAT, as in CBT, and the structured nature of the work, help to limit the patient's regression, and the nature and intensity of the transference. This makes them on the whole safer therapies for relatively unskilled therapists to perform.

However, I think the same factors which limit the potential for harm and abuse to the patient in CAT and CBT also limit the potential power for good of the treatments, precisely because they restrict the nature and depth of the transference and countertransference. In both, a limit is put on the power and stature, both positive and negative, which the therapist can potentially have in the transference. The oedipal exclusion dynamic can be avoided or swiftly collapsed by the ready availability of cognitive escape routes – again, triangularity is bypassed. However, CAT, like CBT, will for these reasons be more accessible and user-friendly on initial contact, and will engage a greater variety of patients.

I think another linked and important limitation of both CAT and CBT, as compared with the analytic approach, is the therapist's non-neutral alignment in CAT and CBT with the ideal of 'progress'. Through the introduction of explicit tasks, pressure and expectation on the patient are implicit from the outset, in however gentle and understanding a form they might be couched, to conform and to improve. I think this makes good CBT and CAT both more paternalistic than good analysis, and introduces a subtle moral restrictiveness through its very reasonableness and friendliness.

Questions have also been raised (e.g. Scott, 1993) about the rather functionalist and benign model of the mind and of internal relationships which underpins CAT (and indeed, to my mind, CBT). The possibility of truly establishing and maintaining a task-orientated therapeutic alliance in deeply troubled and self-defeating patients seems too easily assumed. I think it is important for the therapist to be aware of the limitations of an approach such as CAT, and to be sensitive to some patients' longing and need for something more and different. As indeed with psychoanalysis, there is a danger of partisan idealization of one's own approach, without appreciation of both its advantages and its limitations.

THE REDISCOVERY OF TRANSFERENCE AND RESISTANCE IN CBT

I have argued that CAT (and other similar 'integrated' approaches) may be much nearer in their conceptualization to modern CBT than to psychoanalysis, in spite of their attention to the unconscious and use of the transference. I think this is becoming more obvious as CBT moves into the treatment of personality disorder, and becomes itself more experiential and emotive, and concentrates more on the therapeutic relationship. Beck himself has stated that CBT is an 'integrative therapy' par excellence (Beck, 1991).

Cognitive theory is evolving into something less mechanistic and more 'constructivist' – concerned with how the patient constructs reality. This moves from an idea of the therapist imposing their own 'rationality' on the patient. A number of authors (e.g. Power, 1991) have noted a 'psychoanalytic drift' in the practice of cognitive therapy, just as there was a 'cognitive drift' in the practice of behaviour therapy. Something a bit more object-related is seeping into schema theory also, via a flourishing of interest in Bowlby's ideas about attachment amongst cognitive theorists (e.g. Liotti, 1991). According to Weishaar (1993: 125), there is active debate amongst cognitive theorists at the moment as to 'whether clinical deficits are cognitive or interpersonal in nature'. However, in spite of this apparent 'analytic drift', I differ from Bateman (2000) in believing that the cognitive clinical paradigm remains fundamentally different from the psychoanalytic one, and that true rapprochement is more apparent than real. An examination of the way modern CBT therapists modify their technique will, I hope illustrate, this.

Alongside evolution in theory, therapists (e.g. Beck and Freeman, 1990) now suggest modifications to standard CBT technique (cf. the chapters by Clarke, Hemmings, and Mansell, this volume) when working with personality-disordered patients. They include careful attention to the relationship between patient and therapist, which, if it is not addressed, can lead to losing the patient prematurely, or the therapy getting stuck. The patient (we are told), for example, will not want to mention his or her troubling negative thoughts about the therapist, and instead will go silent, or show in other ways that something is being resisted, like pausing, clenching fists, stammering, changing the subject. To quote Beck: 'When questioned the patient may say, "It's not important, it's nothing". The therapist should press the patient nonetheless' (Beck and Freeman: 65). This is reminiscent of Freud's early 'pressure technique', when he would insist that the patient tell him what was in their mind, however much they would prefer not to. Freud describes (Breuer and Freud, 1895) how it is often the most significant things that are withheld from the physician, though the patient insists that they are insignificant. In other ways, too, I think CBT can be seen as re-creating earlier forms in the history of psychoanalysis. After all, at first Freud tried to cure patients using a simple cathartic method, and his initial attempts at dealing with transference were by explaining it to the patient as an archaic residue.

Giving a wealth of case examples, Beck describes how treatments have to be longer, and sometimes more than once a week. His therapeutic optimism is more guarded than before, and he talks of the difficulty of researching these longer-term, more complex treatments using the controlled trial format, suggesting that one should value single case studies and clinical experience much more. (This might strike psychoanalysts, who are often criticized for doing just this, as a bit ironic.) Beck talks about the importance of getting to know about the patient's total life, and exploring their childhood, and not just focusing down too much, or too prematurely, on cognitions and tasks. He emphasizes the importance of here-and-now affective experience, and the use of experiential techniques.

Beck points out that for the patient to re-experience relationship difficulties in relation to the therapist may be useful and 'grist to the mill'. However, in contrast to the analytic approach, the therapist is supposed swiftly to challenge these negative transference phenomena, in order to re-establish a benign working relationship. Beck says one should: 'be in the role of friend and advisor', 'draw on one's own life experience and wisdom' in order to 'propose solutions' and 'educate the patient regarding the nature of intimate relationships', and become a 'role model' for the patient (Beck and Freeman, 1990: 66). From the psychoanalytic angle, although the psychoanalyst may indeed at times be seen as a role model by the patient in the transference, one tries as an analyst to analyse rather than accept this sacrifice of the patient's autonomy. Analysts might see Beck's statement as claiming some unwarranted superiority over patients in knowing how a life should be lived. The following quotation from Beck perhaps illuminates this assumption, by illustrating the simple 'deficit' model assumed in CBT, which requires the therapist to be a sort of teacher of life-skills: 'This process of re-education is particularly important in treating patients with borderline personality disorder, whose own personality deficits may have prevented them from acquiring and consolidating many of the basic skills of self-control and stable relations with others' (ibid.).

In this recent work, Beck refers frequently to disappointment, frustration, and other negative feelings that will be induced in the therapist by these difficult patients. He emphasizes the importance of supervision in such cases, and also refers now and again in the book to the idea of the therapist dealing with his negative feelings and impulses toward the patient by keeping a 'dysfunctional thought record' of his own. Although Beck makes no mention of it, there is some indication nowadays that trainee CBT therapists are entering personal psychotherapy more often, albeit on a non-intensive basis, as an aid to their work. It seems to me that this has to be a logical progression of these new (re)discoveries in CBT. Without personal analysis, for example, most people are ill-equipped to make sustained clinical use of their countertransference rather than enacting it.

EMPIRICAL RESEARCH COMPARING PSYCHOANALYTIC AND COGNITIVE THERAPIES

Unfortunately, both professional rivalries and political pressures mean that something of a 'horse race' mentality can enter into the empirical comparison of outcome in cognitive and psychoanalytic treatments. Competition for scarce resources, for example in the UK public sector, can mean that clinicians using the different methodologies are eager to prove that their brand of treatment is more efficacious than the other. There are indications that clinicians of different temperament tend to be drawn toward the different modalities (Arthur, 2000), making it difficult for each to appreciate both the value of the other's way of working and the limitations of their own.

One oft-quoted argument for offering CBT rather than psychoanalytic treatments to patients in the public sector is that there is so much more empirical research evidence for its efficacy. It is also asserted as being cheaper, as it is brief and needs far less training to apply CBT, as a brief, focused therapy lends itself well to the popular randomized controlled trial (RCT) format, which has been repeatedly and enthusiastically undertaken, albeit often not with typical outpatient populations (Enright, 1999). Outcome measures are usually in the form of simple symptom scores, and follow-up periods short.

Psychoanalysis itself, of course, requires four- or five-times-weekly sessions over some years; one often sees radical changes in the patient's relationships, work capacity, and creative fulfilment, over and above 'symptom relief'. Such outcome criteria are difficult and complex to measure, though progress is being made in this area of 'objective measurement of the subjective' (Barber and Crits-Cristoph, 1993; Hobson and Patrick, 1998; Luborsky et al., 1986). Psychoanalytic psychotherapy as it is typically constrained within the public sector uses the same methodology, usually on a once-weekly basis over one or several years, and expects to foster the same sorts of changes to a lesser degree. My view is that what I was describing earlier – the striving toward the tension of the analytic stance – characterizes the psychoanalytic approach, whether it is carried out once or five times a week, and whether it is brief or long term. To my mind the vital factor is that for a therapist to be able to establish and maintain an analytic stance requires training on a very intensive, experiential, and long-term basis.

When attempts are made to fit psychoanalytic work into the extremely atypical sixteen-session format suited to CBT, most psychoanalysts would not predict more than symptomatic change, or a temporary alteration in surface cognitions, as there is no opportunity for vital working through. Thus, one might expect the efficacy of very brief psychoanalytic psychotherapy to resemble that of CBT. This is borne out in the relatively few circumstances where good quality comparative trials of CBT and brief psychoanalytic psychotherapy have been carried out – there is found to be essentially no difference in outcome (Crits-Cristoph, 1992; Luborsky et al., 1999).

One study attempting to link process and outcome in brief cognitive and dynamic therapies has suggested, interestingly, that it is the more typically 'dynamic' elements of therapy that are important (Jones and Pulos, 1993). These authors expected to find that cognitive therapy worked via cognitive procedures and dynamic therapy through dynamic ones. Instead they observed that 'evocation of affect', 'bringing troublesome feelings into awareness', and 'integrating current difficulties with previous life experience, using the therapist–patient relationship as a change agent' (ibid.: 315) all predicted improvement in both therapies. This was in contrast to the more typically 'cognitive' procedures of 'control of negative affect through the use of intellect and rationality' and 'encouragement, support and reassurance from therapists', (ibid.) which were not predictive of positive outcome.

Jones and Pulos suggest that all such treatments work via the provision of a unique, safe context within which relationships with the self and the world can be explored. They are aided by privileging emotional experience over rationality, and by emphasis on developmental history. According to this study at least, in so far as cognitive therapists take a 'rationalist' approach, in which affect is conceptualized and treated as the expression of irrational and unrealistic beliefs, and in so far as they view their role as one of imparting technical instruction and guidance, the therapy appears to be less successful.

Another study comparing process in 'dynamic-interpersonal' and cognitive behaviour therapies (Wiser and Goldfried, 1996) looked specifically at the types of interventions made in sections of sessions the experienced therapists themselves deemed change-promoting for their patients. Again, these researchers noted an unexpected tendency in the cognitive therapists toward both using and valuing more 'dynamic' techniques, and suggest that this is part of the recent shift in CBT toward a more interpersonal focus.

When we research outcome in more typical-length psychoanalytic treatments, the 'gold standard' RCT format, which works reasonably well for brief therapy, poses huge logistical problems, and may be quite inappropriate (Galatzer-Levy, 1995; Gunderson and Gabbard, 1999). We are dealing with a complex interpersonal process involving multiple variables. Controls may become impossible to achieve and randomization is a questionable activity in comparative trials where patients show marked preferences or aptitudes for different ways of working. The relative dearth of RCT evidence for the efficacy of psychoanalytic work is a function of the huge difficulties involved in researching typical psychoanalytic treatments in this way, and is often falsely equated with 'evidence against' (Parry and Richardson, 1996).

Having said this, there is a growing body of empirical research concerning more typical length public-sector psychoanalytic psychotherapy in adults and children (e.g. Bateman and Fonagy, 1999; Guthrie et al., 1999; Moran et al., 1991; Sandahl et al., 1998). Taken together with studies of psychoanalysis itself, the hardest of all to research, evidence begins to emerge that these lengthy, more ambitious treatments may indeed offer important additional benefit. Fonagy et al. (1999) have collected and critically reviewed 55 studies of psychoanalytic outcome. These authors, although they expose many methodological limitations in the data, adopt overall what they term a 'cautiously optimistic' attitude to psychoanalytic outcome, given the evidence available. Key provisional findings (which are fully referenced in the work itself) include the following:

1. intensive psychoanalytic treatment is generally more effective than psychoanalytic psychotherapy, the difference sometimes only becoming evident years after treatment has ended, this applying particularly to the more severe disorders.
2. Longer-term treatment has a better outcome, as does completed analysis.

3. There are findings that suggest psychoanalysis and psychoanalytic psychotherapy are cost-beneficial and perhaps even cost-effective, and that psychoanalysis can lead to a reduction in other health-care use and expenditure, although one study suggests an increase.
4. Psychoanalytic treatment appears to improve capacity to work, to reduce borderline personality-disorder symptomatology, and may be an effective treatment for severe psychosomatic disorder.

SUMMARY AND CONCLUSIONS

I have tried to show how I see the CBT paradigm as a useful but less complex paradigm than the psychoanalytic one, limited in its explanatory power and in terms of the change its therapeutic application can be expected to achieve. Its far less intrusive and threatening nature will, however, make it more acceptable for a number of patients. I have also tried to show how there is a strong attraction toward working in a 'cognitive' way, for both psychoanalyst and patient, and that the inherent tension and complexity of the analytic stance is constantly on the brink of decomposing, or collapsing, sometimes resulting in a weak version of cognitive therapy taking place. However, if the tension of psychoanalytic work can be borne by both patient and analyst, the reward can be experiential, emotional learning by the patient, which is likely to be deeper and more enduring than purely cognitive learning.

I have also suggested that, because psychoanalysts and cognitive behaviour therapists share the same field of study, they are increasingly going to discover the same clinical phenomena, and indeed are now doing so, although they may then approach these phenomena in fundamentally different ways. It is important, I think, both that the shared endeavour is recognized, to relieve the misery of psychic suffering, and also the differences, which will have important implications for which patients are treated, in what way, and with what aims. It is unfortunate that clinicians from the two groups are currently often pushed by external economic pressures to compete with one another in the public sector, which exacerbates the innate rivalries that are bound to exist between practitioners of two such very different sorts of treatment.

The selected empirical evidence I have quoted gives some interesting indications as to shared therapeutic factors in brief psychodynamic and cognitive therapies. In the relatively few instances in which comparative studies of CBT and very brief psychodynamic therapy have been carried out, there is found to be essentially no difference in outcome. This should be of no surprise to a psychoanalyst, as we would not predict deep and lasting change in inner-world structures without considerable opportunity for working through. We might, in fact, be rather surprised and impressed that psychodynamic therapy does as well as CBT under such circumstances. The claims I made earlier in the chapter about psychoanalysis as a method facilitating deep and lasting change certainly need substantiating empirically rather than simply asserting, and I think we are not yet able to do this with confidence and in detail. However, research evidence of the last couple of decades is beginning to confirm analysts' expectations that intensive and long-term psychoanalytic treatments have something substantial to offer over and above what brief treatments, whichever the modality used, can provide.

REFERENCES

Arthur, A. (2000) 'The personality and cognitive–epistemological traits of cognitive-behavioural and psychoanalytic psychotherapists', *British Journal of Medical Psychology*, 73: 243–57.

Baker, R. (1993) 'The patient's discovery of the psychoanalyst as a new object', *International Journal of Psycho-Analysis*, 74: 1223–33.

Barber, J. P. and Crits-Cristoph, P. (1993) 'Advances in measures of psychodynamic formulations', *Journal of Consulting and Clinical Psychology*, 61: 574–85.

Bateman, A. (2000) 'Integration in psychotherapy: an evolving reality in personality disorder', *British Journal of Psychotherapy*, 17: 147–56.

Bateman, A. and Fonagy, P. (1999) 'The effectiveness of partial hospitalisation in the treatment of borderline personality disorder – randomised controlled trial', *American Journal of Psychiatry*, 156: 1563–9.

Beck, A. (1991) 'Cognitive therapy as the integrative therapy: comments on Alford and Norcross', *Journal of Therapy Integration*, 1: 191–8.

Beck, A. and Freeman, A. (1990) *Cognitive Therapy of Personality Disorders*, New York: Guilford.

Beck, A., Rush, A. J., Shaw, B. F., and Emery, G. (1979) *Cognitive Therapy of Depression*, New York: Wiley.

Breuer, J. and Freud, S. (1895) 'Studies on hysteria', in the *Standard Edition* Volume 2,

Britton, R. (1989) 'The missing link: parental sexuality in the Oedipus complex', in R. Britton, M. Feldman, E. O'Shaughnessy, and J. Steiner, *The Oedipus Complex Today: Clinical Implications*, London: Karnac, pp. 83–101.

Britton, R. (1998) *Belief and Imagination*, London: Routledge.

Crits-Cristoph, P. (1992) 'The efficacy of brief dynamic psychotherapy: a meta-analysis', *American Journal Psychiatry*, 149: 151–8.

Dunn, J. (1995) 'Intersubjectivity in psychoanalysis: a critical review', *International Journal of Psycho-Analysis*, 76: 723–38.

Ellis, A. (1980) 'Rational-emotive therapy and cognitive behaviour therapy: similarities and differences', *Cognitive Therapy and Research*, 4: 325–40.

Enright, S. (1999) 'Cognitive-behavioural therapy – an overview', *CPD Bulletin of Psychiatry*, 1: 78–83.

Feldman, M. (1993) 'The dynamics of reassurance', *International Journal of Psycho-Analysis*, 74: 275–85.

Fonagy, P., Kächele, H., Krause, R., Jones, E., and Perron,R. (1999) 'An open-door review of outcome studies in psychoanalysis', London: International Psychoanalytical Association.

Galatzer-Levy, R. (1995) 'Discussion: The rewards of research', in T. Shapiro and R. Emde (eds), *Research in Psychoanalysis: Process, Development, Outcome*, Madison, Conn.: International Universities Press.

Gunderson, J. and Gabbard, G. (1999) 'Making the case for psychoanalytic therapies', *Journal of the American Psychoanalytic Association*, 47: 679–739.

Guthrie, E., Moorey, J., Margison, F., Barker, H., Palmer, S., McGrath, G., Tomenson, B., and Creed, F. (1999) 'Cost-effectiveness of brief psychodynamic–interpersonal therapy in high utilizers of psychiatric services', *Archives of General Psychiatry*, 56: 519–26.

Hawton, K.. Salkovskis, P. M., Kirk, J., and Clark, D. M. (1989) *Cognitive Behaviour Therapy for Psychiatric Problems*, New York: Oxford University Press.

Hobson, P. and Patrick, M. (1998) 'Objectivity in psychoanalytic judgements', *British Journal of Psychiatry*, 173: 172–7.

Jones, E. and Pulos, S. (1993) 'Comparing the process in psychodynamic and cognitive-behavioural therapies', *Journal of Consulting and Clinical Psychology*, 61: 306–16.

Joseph, B. (1985) 'Transference: the total situation', *International Journal of Psycho-Analysis*, 66: 447–54.

Kelly, G. (1955) *The Psychology of Personal Constructs*, New York: Norton.

Liotti, G. (1991) 'Patterns of attachments and the assessment of interpersonal schemata: understanding and changing difficult patient–therapist relationships in cognitive psychotherapy', *Journal of Cognitive Psychotherapy*, 5: 105–14.

Luborsky, L., Crits-Cristoph, P., and Mellon, J. (1986) 'The advent of objective measures of the transference concept', *Journal of Consulting and Clinical Psychology*, 54: 39–47.

Luborsky, L., Diguer, L., Luborsky, E., and Schmidt, K. A. (1999) 'The efficacy of dynamic versus other psychotherapies: is it true that "everyone has won and all must have prizes"? – an update', in D. S. Janovsky (ed.), *Psychotherapy: Indications and Outcomes*, Washington, D.C.: American Psychiatric Press.

Meichenbaum, D. (1985) *Stress Inoculation Training*, New York: Pergamon.

Milton, J. (2000) 'Psychoanalysis and the moral high ground', *International Journal of Psycho-Analysis*, 81: 1101-15.

Money-Kyrle, R. (1968) 'Cognitive development', *International Journal of Psycho-Analysis*, 49: 691–8.

Moorey, S. (1991) 'Cognitive behaviour therapy', *Hospital Update*, September: 726–32.

Moran, G., Fonagy, P., Kurtz, A., Bolton, A., and Brook, C. (1991) 'A controlled study of the psychoanalytic treatment of brittle diabetes', *Journal of the American Academy of Child Psychiatry*, 30: 926–35.

Parry, G. and Richardson, A. (1996) *NHS Psychotherapy Services in England: A Review of Strategic Policy*, London: Department of Health.

Power, M. (1991) 'Cognitive science and behavioural psychotherapy: where behaviour was, there shall cognition be?', *Behavioural Psychotherapy*, 19: 20–41.

Renik, O. (1998) 'The analyst's subjectivity and the analyst's objectivity', *International Journal of Psycho-Analysis*, 79: 487–97.

Ryle, A. (1990) *Cognitive Analytical Therapy*, Chichester: Wiley.

Ryle, A. (1994) 'Psychoanalysis and cognitive analytic therapy', *British Journal of Psychotherapy*, 10: 402–4.

Ryle, A. (1995) 'Psychoanalysis, cognitive-analytic therapy, mind and self', *British Journal of Psychotherapy*, 11: 568–74.

Sandahl, C., Herlitz, K., Ahlin, G., and Rönnberg, S. (1998) 'Time-limited group therapy for moderately alcohol-dependent patients: a randomised controlled trial', *Psychotherapy Research*, 8: 361–78.

Sandler, J. (1976) 'Countertransference and role-responsiveness', *International Review of Psycho-Analysis*, 3: 43–7.

Scott, A. (1993) 'Response to Anthony Ryle', *British Journal Psychotherapy*, 10: 93–5.

Weishaar, M. (1993) *Aaron T. Beck*, London: Sage.

Wiser, S. and Goldfried, M. (1996) 'Verbal interventions in significant psychodynamic–interpersonal and cognitive-behavioural therapy sessions', *Psychotherapy Research*, 6: 309–19.

Chapter 10

PERSON-CENTRED THERAPY, A COGNITIVE BEHAVIOUR THERAPY

Keith Tudor

> '...too many therapists think they can make something happen. Personally I like much better the approach of an agriculturalist or a farmer or a gardener: I can't make corn grow, but I can provide the right soil and plant it in the right area and see that it gets enough water; I can nurture it so that exciting things happen. I think that's the nature of therapy. It's so unfortunate that we've so long followed a medical model and not a growth model. A growth model is much more appropriate to most people, to most situations.'
>
> (Rogers, in Rogers and Russell, 2002: 259)

Many claims are made for cognitive behaviour therapy (CBT) – by cognitive behaviour therapists and researchers themselves, but also by politicians. Certainly in the United Kingdom (UK), in government circles, and in the National Health Service (NHS), CBT is the flavour of the moment, perhaps of the decade. The UK Government has announced that it wants to give patients greater access to 'talking therapies', by which it means CBT, in order to reduce rates of depression (Department of Health, 2006). Some researchers claim CBT to be an evidence-based and cost-effective cure for depression and other conditions. Cognitive behaviour therapists make claims about the efficacy, effectiveness, and efficiency of their approach – and in doing so, in effect claim proprietorial rights over the psychology of cognition and behaviour.

This chapter, written from a person-centred perspective, first examines the research basis, as well as the 'evidence' which favours CBT over other therapies, including person-centred therapy (PCT); and, secondly, as a counterpoint to the apparent dominance of CBT in the psychology of cognition and behaviour, elaborates the behavioural and cognitive aspects of PCT. Although I am also interested in the politics of CBT, this is well-covered elsewhere in this volume (e.g. Pilgrim's Chapter 21).

It is not my purpose or intention in this chapter to negate CBT. Clearly, it is an effective form of therapy, as are many other forms of therapy. Neither is it my intention to criticize a CBT which its exponents do not recognize. In the generic literature of psychotherapy there are enough 'straw arguments' based on ignorance and misunderstandings of, and projections on to, other therapeutic approaches. A common one which bedevils PCT is the erroneous view that the 'core conditions' (of congruence, unconditional positive regard, and empathy) are necessary and sufficient (for a response to which, see Tudor, 2000). CBT, as with all other theoretical orientations, has a history that includes different schools, traditions, or waves, which are the result of their exponents developing practice and theory in the light of experience and, often, integration insights from different orientations, disciplines (such as philosophy), and fields (such as neuroscience). Most cognitive behaviour therapists recognize three waves in the development of CBT: the first wave being the work of Beck and Ellis; the second being the schema-focused approach (e.g. Young, 1994); and the third being a focus on altering the person's relationship to both thought and feeling – a development which includes dialectical behaviour therapy (DBT) (see Linehan, 1993), Acceptance and Commitment Therapy (Hayes et al., 1999), and mindfulness (see Segal et al., 2000).

It *is* my intention to challenge the wilder claims made for CBT, which are of concern not only to those trained in other effective approaches, but also to cognitive behaviour therapists themselves who are coming under increasing pressure to cure all – and quickly. Also, on the basis of the research evidence of comparative studies and meta-studies, I do claim equivalence of therapeutic effectiveness; and, on the basis of client/patient choice, promote equal opportunities for equal and, indeed, increased access to a choice of psychological therapies in the public sector.

RESEARCH

In this part of the chapter I discuss the conceptual and methodological bias of the guidelines of the National Institute for Health and Clinical Excellence (NIHCE); the need for practice-based evidence and alternative methodologies in psychotherapy outcome research (see also Bohart and House's Chapter, 16 and 17, and Lees' Chapter 7, both in this volume); and research regarding the therapeutic relationship and client factors, both of which support person-centred approaches to research about therapy.

CONCEPTUAL AND METHODOLOGICAL BIAS

A major problem facing researchers in the field of psychotherapy is the clear bias in favour of certain methods of research. This derives from a traditional 'scientific' perspective, particularly influenced by medical science, and supported by the Government. Research in psychotherapy is still conceived within the medical model of diagnosis/treatment/cure (cf. Bohart and House's Chapter 16, this volume), and understood in terms of the 'drug metaphor', which seeks and implies that there is a specific 'treatment' for specific 'conditions' – a perspective which does not reflect, for instance, person-centred therapy. NIHCE guidelines follow and promote the medical model and not a growth model, so they are irrelevant to therapies based on growth models (see Rogers and Russell, 2002).

Furthermore, these guidelines are based on a clear hierarchy of evidence (or levels of evidence) assigned to studies, based on the methodological quality of their design, validity, and, in the field of health and medicine, their applicability to patient care. According to this hierarchy, the strongest level of evidence which guides decisions about practice is the systematic review or meta-analysis of randomized controlled trials (RCTs), or an individual RCT, and evidence-based practice. For issues of prognosis, the highest possible level of evidence is a cohort study. The weakest level of evidence is considered to be opinion from authorities and/or reports of expert committees. For its levels of evidence with regard to clinical guidelines, the NIHCE (2007) has adopted those of the Scottish Intercollegiate Guidelines Network (2002) (see Table 10.1).

Table 10.1 **Levels of evidence for intervention studies (Scottish Intercollegiate Guidelines Network, 2002)**

LEVEL OF EVIDENCE	TYPE OF EVIDENCE
1^{++}	High-quality meta-analyses, systematic reviews of RCTs, or RCTs with a very low risk of bias
1^{+}	Well-conducted meta-analyses, systematic reviews of RCTs, or RCTs with a low risk of bias
1^{-}	Meta-analyses, systematic reviews of RCTs, or RCTs with a high risk of bias*
2^{++}	High-quality systematic reviews of case-control or cohort studies High-quality case-control or cohort studies with a very low risk of confounding, bias, or chance and a high probability that the relationship is causal
2^{+}	Well-conducted case-control or cohort studies with a low risk of confounding, bias, or chance and a moderate probability that the relationship is causal
2^{-}	Case-control or cohort studies with a high risk of confounding, bias, or chance and a significant risk that the relationship is not causal*
3	Non-analytic studies (for example, case reports, case series)
4	Expert opinion, formal consensus

* Studies with a level of evidence ($^{-}$) should not be used as a basis for making a recommendation

This hierarchy promotes 'evidence-based medicine' and, more broadly, 'evidence-based practice', and privileges quantitative research (for a critique of which see Craig, 1996). The results of these evaluation techniques are, in the words of Leader (2007: 34), 'designed to avoid the complexity of human suffering' (see also Verhaeghe, 2007). Even the British Association for Counselling and Psychotherapy, not noted for its radicalism, has recommended (Rowland, 2007: 27) 'that NICE [sic] review its evidence evaluation process to admit a range of quantitative and qualitative evidence in the evaluation of psychological therapies'.

Moreover, this hierarchy of evidence – and the research it favours – is based on particular objectivist assumptions about the nature of science, especially regarding ontology, the essence of the phenomena under investigation; epistemology, that is, the grounds or theory of knowledge upon which we understand the world, and acquire, experience, and communicate this knowledge; and methodology, the nature of the investigation of knowledge (cf. Bohart and House's Chapters 16 and 17, this volume). Burrell and Morgan (1979) suggest that these assumptions about the nature of science, as well as assumptions about human nature, can be thought of in terms of a subjective–objective dimension (see Box 10.1). It is clear from this that, for instance, person-centred psychology and research would sit at the subjectivist end of this continuum or dimension.

Box 10.1 ***The nature of social science – the subjective–objective dimension***

The subjectivist approach to social science		*The objectivist approach to social science*
Voluntarism	Human nature	Determinism
Nominalism	Ontology	Realism
Anti-positivism	Epistemology	Positivism
Ideographic (symbolizing)	Methodology	Nomothetic (legislative)

The hierarchy of evidence favoured by NIHCE and other bodies that adopt a similar approach is not right or wrong, but it is biased as it represents a particular paradigmatic approach to research and to 'evidence'. Thus, for example, with regard to randomized controlled trials, as Freire (2006: 323) points out, 'the RCT is not a theory-neutral evaluative method but rather a research method shaped by assumptions that originate in behaviourist theories of therapy' (cf. Bohart and House, Chapter 16, this volume). Furthermore, as behaviourist and non-behaviourist therapies are grounded in what Freire (ibid.) refers to as 'incommensurable theories', then the methodology of an RCT cannot be used fairly to compare them. The issue here is that NIHCE presents its evidence base as neutral, and discounts qualitative research methods and other 'practice-based evidence' (Morgan and Juriansz, 2002).

PRACTICE-BASED EVIDENCE, ROGERS, AND ALTERNATIVE METHODOLOGY IN PSYCHOTHERAPY RESEARCH

The concept of practice-based evidence challenges the hegemony of evidence-based practice. As developed by Morgan (2004), it is a concept 'that has a specific approach (practice development in mental health), is based on solid principles (a strengths approach), and works in important areas of practice'. In many ways this concept describes the approach taken by Carl Rogers in his research. Rogers was the first psychologist to record therapeutic sessions – on glass-based disks at Ohio State University in 1939; and he also published the first complete set of therapeutic interviews ever recorded, the case of Herbert Bryan (Rogers,

1939). It was from listening to and reflecting on the recordings of his own therapeutic work, and that of his colleagues, that Rogers developed his hypothesis of the necessary and sufficient conditions of therapeutic personality change (Rogers, 1957, 1959) – a hypothesis which, in turn, formed the basis of further research (for a summary of which, see Bozarth, 1993), and which has been widely influential in the field of therapy across theoretical orientations. Rogers reflected on this in an interview recorded in the last year of his life and published posthumously (Rogers and Russell, 2002: 305):

> 'I believe that, by and large, what has been done in the field of client-centered therapy and the person-centered approach sets a good model for humanistic psychology because what we have done is based on a lot of clinical experience with all kinds and ages of people. And from that clinical experience we have drawn theoretical formulations which have really stood the test of time... and have been put to empirical and rigorous tests by researchers in a variety of fields and in a variety of countries.'

In 1967 Rogers et al. published the results of the Wisconsin project, a study of psychotherapy with schizophrenics which, for our present interest, considered behaviour, including quite disturbed behaviour, in its relational context, including how the patient influences the therapist. As one of the contributors (van der Veen, 1967: 353) puts it:

> 'In this study we have considered three possible sources of determinants for the behavior of each of the participants in the therapy relationship: the participant himself, the person with whom he interacts, and the particular combination of the two. Each of these sources of determinants is considered important for an understanding of what occurs in therapy.'

The research findings supported these hypotheses, including that change in patient level of experiencing from the initial to the subsequent interview was a function of the therapist's level of therapeutic behaviour.

Rogers's research in psychotherapy encompassed component factor methods and analysis, process scales, personality inventories, the Rorschach test, the Thematic Apperception Test, an adult intelligence scale, Q-sorts, and other methods – and was conducted in a way which reflected his fundamental philosophical position of open enquiry. Barrineau and Bozarth (1989) view this position, together with the therapist's conditions (of authenticity, acceptance, and empathy) as basic components for a qualitative research of a heuristic nature (on which, see Rogers, 1965, 1985; Moustakas, 1990). In promoting a human science of the person, Rogers (1968, 1985) is critical of traditional and confining research methods and statistical designs, and cites examples of new methods, designs within 'a new science' of humanistic research. More recently, a Task Force of the American Psychological Association's Division 32 (Humanistic Psychology) for the Development of Practice Recommendations for the Provision of Humanistic Psychosocial Services (2005) has developed an alternative and pluralistic perspective of psychotherapy research, and suggested research methods that should:

- Approach the person not just as a diagnostic category but as a whole;
- Consider therapy as an open dialogical process that is unpredictable and unmanipulable;
- Capture the non-quantifiable and the meaningful;
- Consider the participating individual as an agent and interpreter of the therapeutic situation;
- Focus descriptively and interpretively on individual persons in depth.

(ibid.: 16–17)

The richness of this history and diversity shows up the paucity of thinking and the limitations of the research methodology promoted by NIHCE and other bodies more concerned with 'governance' and economics than with open enquiry and integrity.

RESEARCH INTO THE THERAPEUTIC RELATIONSHIP AND CLIENT FACTORS, AND THERAPEUTIC EQUIVALENCE

It is now commonplace to cite research which demonstrates that the therapeutic relationship is a – or even *the* most – significant factor in determining the outcome of psychotherapy. What is most interesting about this, certainly from a client- or person-centred perspective, is the client's contribution to and perception of this.

The sixth of Rogers' necessary and sufficient conditions (Rogers, 1957, 1959) states clearly that the therapist's unconditional positive regard and empathic understanding be communicated to the client (Rogers, 1957) or perceived/experienced by the client (Rogers, 1959a). Indeed, in summarizing the therapeutic conditions, Rogers (1958/1967b: 130) refers to this condition as being fully *received* and, therefore, as the 'assumed' condition; and more recently, Toukmanian (2001) describes perception as the core element in person-centred and experiential psychotherapies. In early research on Rogers's therapeutic conditions, Barrett-Lennard designed a relationship inventory which, amongst other factors, measured the client's perceptions of the therapist's attitudes, initial results from which found that success in psychotherapy was positively related to the client's perception of the therapist conditions/attitudes (Barrett-Lennard, 1962). Other generic research also supports this view (see, for example, Luborsky et al., 1983; Horowitz et al., 1984).

In their review article, Stiles et al. (1986) cite studies which demonstrate a number of client behaviours or attitudes which influence the outcome of therapy:

- The client's involvement in therapy; and the verbal exploration of her or his internal frame of reference – which Stiles et al. (1986) view as major active ingredients of therapy outcome; and
- The overall level of patient participation; the patient's positive contributions; the total number of client utterances; moderate client expectancy (initial, and that developed during therapy); the client's self-efficacy, or her or his belief in self-efficacy – all of which Stiles et al. see as of therapeutic benefit.

More recent research has focused on the client factors which determine the outcome of therapy (Miller et al.,1995; Bohart and Tallman, 1999; Duncan et al., 2004). Client factors are characteristics or qualities of the client, such as level of motivation and commitment to change, inner strength, and religious faith; and extra-therapeutic factors in the life and environment of the client that impact change, such as social support, community involvement, and stressful events. Lambert (1992) refers to these as the major source of the variance in psychotherapy, and states that these factors account for about 40 per cent of psychotherapy outcome. Whatever the exact percentage, an increasing number of authors and clinicians agree with Miller et al. (1997: 25–6) that 'the research literature makes it clear that the client is actually the single, most potent contributor to outcome in psychotherapy'.

Research into the comparative effectiveness of different therapies shows equivalence – that is, that no one specific therapy can be distinguished as more effective than another (see Luborsky et al., 1975; Smith et al., 1980; Friedli et al., 1997; King et al., 2000; Stiles et al., 2006). This is sometimes referred to as 'the Dodo bird verdict', after the character in *Alice in Wonderland* who declares that 'All have won and all must have prizes'. Despite this, as Stiles et al. (2006) observe, the overwhelming quantity of published research on CBT gives CBT greater credibility than other approaches, and does not acknowledge equivalence. This gives the lie to the easy generalization that CBT is a 'more effective' therapy, a commonplace which is fuelled by political expediency and which, unfortunately, has become a public perception.

BEHAVIOUR AND COGNITION IN PERSON-CENTRED THERAPY

As a counterpoint to claims – or, at least, the implications – of exclusivity on the part of CBT on cognition and behaviour, in this second part of the chapter I elaborate a person-centred perspective on behaviour and cognition.

Person-centred therapy is based on organismic psychology which represents a holistic approach to human beings and to life (see Tudor and Worrall, 2006). This means that our behaviour and cognition, as well as our affect and other aspects and qualities, are features of a whole organism/person, and inextricably linked. In 1970 Rogers wrote a paper titled 'Bringing together the cognitive and the affective-experiential' (published two years later in 1972 – Rogers, 1972); and when asked by Russell whether the therapist's approach should be emotional rather than cognitive, Rogers responded by saying that it is both emotional and cognitive (Rogers and Russell, 2002). From a holistic perspective, the separation of behaviour and cognition is a conceptual abstraction; I separate them here only in order to elaborate Rogers's and person-centred thinking about behaviour and cognition – and as a part of a strategy to reclaim these aspects of the psychology of the person from the colonization of CBT.

BEHAVIOUR IN PERSON-CENTRED PSYCHOLOGY[1]

In his book, *Client-Centred Therapy*, Rogers (1951: 491–509) expounds his theory of personality and behaviour in a number of propositions, five of which explicitly refer to behaviour, and many others of which describe the behavioural actions of the human organism:

1. This section is based on work previously published in Tudor and Worrall (2006).

> 'Behavior is basically the goal-directed attempt of the organism to satisfy its needs as experienced, in the field as perceived [Proposition V] ... Emotion accompanies and in general facilitates such goal-directed behavior [Proposition VI] ... The best vantage point for understanding behavior is from the internal frame of reference of the individual her/himself [Proposition VII] ... Most of the ways of behaving which are adopted by the organism are those which are consistent with the concept of self [Proposition XII] ... Behavior may, in some instances, be brought about by organic experiences and needs which have not been symbolized. Such behavior may be inconsistent with the structure of the self, [and thus] is not "owned" by the individual [Proposition XIII].'

There are a number of implications which follow from these propositions:

1. That behaviour is the expression of the organism which tends to actualize – that is, to maintain, enhance, and reproduce itself.
2. That behaviour is inextricably linked to needs – that is, that it is needs-driven and goal-directed, even when those needs are difficult to ascertain or understand, and the goal is not known or perceived; and that all behaviour is enacted in order to meet a present need, although past experience, and our understanding of that experience, may modify the present meaning given to experience.
3. That behaviour is a reaction to the environmental field, *as perceived*. Evans and Zarate (1999: 160) state that:

   > 'Every kind of behaviour results from the way our minds interact with our environment, and the mind results from the interaction of the environment with our genes. Different environments will lead the mind to develop differently and change the way in which the mind causes behaviour.'

4. That all needs have what Rogers refers to as 'a basic relatedness' (ibid.: 491), and spring from and refer to the human organism's tendency to actualize. Individual behaviour is, thus, dialogic, in that it cannot be understood without being symbolized and, at least initially, a baby cannot symbolize on her or his own. She or he needs the 'abstract', empathic, and symbolizing attitude of another. As Goldstein (1934/1995: 19) puts it:

   > 'Thus the behaviour of the infant is not at all an expression of his concrete capacity alone *but also of the abstract attitude of someone else*. Thus normal behavior in infancy becomes comprehensible as the result of the activity of two persons.' (my emphasis)

5. That, in pursuing the satisfaction of needs, the organism *is* its behaviour at any one moment, an implication which provides further support for the importance of the interchange between organism and environment and the inseparability of the holistic mind/body organism/environment from its behaviour. It is this final implication that is the most radical and controversial. If behaviour is an organismic attempt to satisfy current need, then a person *is* her or his behaviour, whether that is loving, hating, generous, jealous, aggressive, or even violent. This has huge implications, especially for

those humanistic psychologists, therapists, and trainers who seek to separate the person from her or his behaviour, as in the instruction 'Criticize the behaviour, not the person'. From an organismic and holistic perspective, this separation is artificial, unhelpful, and misses the point. It is artificial in that it is the person who is behaving in the way which is being criticized. It is unhelpful in that the separation doesn't work: when faced with criticism, most people do take it personally – because it *is* personal! The attempt to separate behaviour from the person misses the point: faced with cruelty, oppression, nastiness, or evil in the world, the issue is how to respond to, deal with, and work with people who are, *at that moment when they do something cruel*, themselves cruel.

It is, therefore, unrealistic to suggest that, in some way, everyone is 'in essence' simply 'good'. Human organisms are more complex and life is more complicated than that. Such liberalism about ontology (the essence of things) sets up a false idealism about human nature and life itself. Finally, the attempt to claim a comforting 'niceness' about an essence of human nature does not allow for entropy, or disorder, alongside syntropy, or unity. Equally, it is simplistic and naïve to offer unconditional positive regard for the person but not for her or his behaviour. This constitutes an untenable dichotomy, in that a person's behaviour is an intimate and accurate expression of who she is as a person in the moment of her behaving. Elsewhere, Tudor and Worrall (2006) offer a solution to this dichotomy, and argue that:

> 'It makes more sense to say that we hold unconditional positive regard for the fact that a person tends to actualise, and to see that she or he is tending to actualise whatever she, he or others may think of the behavioural manifestations of that tendency.'
>
> (ibid.: 74)

In a paper written a few years after his 1951 paper on personality and behaviour, Rogers (1967a: 194–5) concludes his view of 'the good life' and the 'fully functioning person' with the following lines, which describe a tension between organismic functioning and consciousness:

> 'Man's behaviour is exquisitely rational, moving with subtle and ordered complexity toward the goals his organism is endeavoring to achieve. The tragedy for most of us is that our defenses keep us from being aware of this rationality, so that consciously we are moving in one direction, while organismically we are moving in another.'

Following Goldstein, Rogers distinguishes between defensive and disorganized behaviours. The distinction is based on a description of a gradual process from discrepancy, threat, and defence to a distinct point at which a person's process of defence no longer holds. This experience and concept of disorganization includes many of the more 'irrational' and 'acute' psychotic behaviours. Rogers argues both that this is a more fundamental classification than the neurotic–psychotic one, and that it avoids the concepts of neurosis and psychosis being viewed as entities in themselves.

Rogers' ideas about behaviour are clearly different from those of behavioural psychologists such as B. F. Skinner, with whom he had a number of encounters or dialogues (in 1956, 1960, and 1962) (see Kirschenbaum and Henderson, 1990; Nye, 2000). Whilst Rogers acknowledges that objective, quantitative approaches to the study of human behaviour are important means of obtaining certain knowledge, he places more emphasis on subjective knowledge (knowing oneself) and on empathic, intersubjective knowledge (knowing the subjective states of the other), and thus represents a different view of scientific knowledge (Rogers, 1985; Box 10.1). He also represents a different view from that of behaviourism regarding the 'control' of human behaviour (Rogers and Skinner, 1956; see also Nye, 2000); and views of 'reality' (Rogers, 1974/1980). For further reading on the distinctions between person-centred psychology and behaviourism and behavioural methods see Rice (1984) and Nye (2000).

COGNITION IN PERSON-CENTRED PSYCHOLOGY

Not many people would classify person-centred therapy as a cognitive therapy as such, yet it has a theory of cognition. In Rogers's (1959) major formulation of client-centred theory, he discusses cognition in terms of perceptions, constructs, self-concept, and intensionality. Here I summarize these concepts, and discuss the cognitive strand of person-centred psychology.

PERCEPTIONS

Rogers (1959: 199) defines a perception as 'a hypothesis or prognosis for action which comes into being in awareness when stimuli impinge on the organism'. As such, perception is almost synonymous with awareness, but is a more specific term which relates to the importance of the usually external stimulus.

CONSTRUCTS

A construct is a certain idea, the basis on which a prediction about the world is made. It is a term which Rogers borrowed from George Kelly (Kelly, 1955) and used in his process conception of psychotherapy, one element of which is the concept of constructs which Rogers (1958/1967b: 157) refers to as 'the cognitive maps of experience'. Rogers sees the seven stages of his process conception as describing a movement from construing experience in rigid ways to developing constructions which are modifiable by each new experience (see Rogers, 1958/1967b; Tudor and Worrall, 2006).

SELF-CONCEPT

According to Rogers (1951: 136–7) a self-concept is:

> 'an organized configuration of perceptions of the self which are admissible to awareness, it is composed of such elements as the perceptions of one's characteristics and abilities; the percepts and concepts of the self in relation to the environment; the value qualities which are perceived as associated with experiences and objects; and goals and ideals which are perceived as having positive or negative value'.

In person-centred psychology, the term 'self-concept' is used mainly synonymously with self and self-structure. However, 'self-concept' is also used to refer to a person's view of her- or himself, as distinct from his or her self-structure which is used more precisely to refer to the internalized view someone has of her- or himself which derives from another. Rogers also discusses the defence mechanism of distortion – that is, the distortion of perception. As Thorne (1996: 128) puts it, 'perceptual distortion takes place whenever an incongruent experience is allowed into conscious awareness but only in a form that is in harmony with a person's current self-concept'. This is similar to Beck's (1967) concept of 'cognitive distortion'. In his 1959 paper, Rogers describes the process of breakdown and disorganization of the personality in terms of the tension between the concept of self with its distorted perceptions, and experiences which are not accurately symbolized; and the process of reorganization, which includes the creation of conditions under which experiences, including threatening ones, are accurately symbolized.

Rogers drew his ideas on the self-concept from Victor Charles Raimy, one of his students whose doctoral thesis on the subject, 'The self-concept as a factor in counselling and personality organization', was published in 1971. In a subsequent work, Raimy (1975: xi) defines self-concept as 'composed of more or less organized notions, beliefs, and convictions that constitute an individual's knowledge of himself and that influence his relationships with others'. Raimy also developed 'the misconception hypothesis', which proposes that psychological disturbances are the result of faulty beliefs or convictions, and that: 'if those ideas or conceptions of a client or patient which are relevant to his psychological problems can be changed in the direction of greater accuracy where his reality is concerned, his maladjustments are likely to be eliminated' (ibid.: 7). Commenting on Raimy's work, Patterson (1986) identifies a number of diagnostic clusters which are, or which involve, cognitive misconceptions – see Table 10.2.

Raimy's approach is based on the view that one of the goals of most therapies is to help the client recognize and change such misconceptions, and that one of the major 'contentions' of therapy is that such misconceptions can be changed by evidence or information presented by the therapist by means of:

- client self-examination;
- therapist explanation, through reflection of feelings, asking questions, and making suggestions and exhortations;
- self-demonstrations, whereby the client, through reflecting on either real or imagined situations, can observe her or his own misconceptions; and
- vicariation or modelling.

Whilst many person-centred practitioners would find some of Raimy's – and Patterson's – language a long way away from traditional or classical person-centred principles and thinking, it is interesting that the concept of the 'self-concept' has been developed in a way which offers a precise understanding of cognitive processes. Cartwright and Graham (1984) develop this cognitive approach to self-concept in their work on and research into self-concept and identity as overlapping portions of a cognitive structure of self. They base their argument on cognitive theory, and elaborate Rogers' (1951) model of personality to include concepts, categories, instance categories, and perceived social images.

***Table 10.2* Diagnostic clusters and cognitive misconceptions (based on Patterson, 1986)**

Diagnostic cluster	*Cognitive misconceptions*
Paranoid cluster	Delusions involving failure of reality testing; disordered content of thought; delusions of persecution; and ideas of reference.
Depressive neurotics	Being hopeless, helpless, or worthless; that they will never recover; and are not 'normal'.
Obsessive neurotics	That they have to be punctual, orderly, conscientious, and reliable.
Hysterical personalities	That they are effective (only) when flirtatious, seductive, vivacious, and/or dramatic; and that they cannot tolerate frustration and disappointment.
Phobia reactions	That the feared object is dangerous; that they will probably collapse when the feared object is present; and that they cannot overcome their fear reaction to the object.
Phrenophobia	The false belief that there is something wrong with one's mind.
Being special (narcissism)	That they must control others; that they are superior to others; that they should not compromise; that they suffer from more frustrations than others do; that they must strive to be perfect; and that others cannot be trusted.

INTENSIONALITY

This term, taken from general semantics, describes the specific types of behaviour of an incongruent individual and, as Rogers (1959: 205) describes it, is characterized by a person who tends 'to see experience in absolute and unconditional terms, to overgeneralize, to be dominated by concept or belief, to fail to anchor his reactions in space or time, to confuse fact and evaluation, to rely upon abstractions rather than reality-testing'. Intensionality is a term which encompasses the characteristics of the behaviour – and cognition – of the individual who is in a defensive state; and, together with other terms – defence, defensiveness, distortion, and denial – describes the organism's response to threat.

COGNITION IN PERSON-CENTRED THINKING SINCE ROGERS

There is in the history and the literature of client-centred therapy, then, a distinct cognitive strand. According to Lietaer (1990), following the termination of the Wisconsin project, the emergence and later consolidation of four strands or 'factions' within client-centred therapy (CCT) can be discerned. One of these was a group around David Wexler and Laura Rice, who chose cognitive learning psychology as a theoretical framework for their development of CCT, whereby they recast client-centred concepts of growth and actualization in a framework drawn from cognitive and information-processing psychology.

This shift is represented in a volume edited by Wexler and Rice in 1974: *Innovations in Client-Centered Therapy*. In his own contribution to this volume Wexler (1974) critiques Rogers' theorizing on self-actualization and experiencing, and argues that a cognitive view helps explain the process of change in the moment-to-moment interaction between client and therapist. In the same volume, Zimring (1974) also takes a cognitive view of CCT, arguing that both the practice of CCT and the cognitive framework in scientific psychology emphasize the knowing rather than the known. According to Zimring, the goal of CCT is an increase in the client's experiential organization. He asserts that 'the therapist achieves this goal through an interaction involving joint processing of the client's experience. The therapist works both at the same time level with and slightly ahead of the client's ability to organize, thus facilitating his processing' (ibid.: 136).

In a subsequent volume on CCT and the person-centred approach, Rice (1984) distinguishes CCT from cognitive behaviour approaches in which cognitive structures are examined and compared with 'reality' in a way which makes cognitive behaviour therapy a kind of 'learning lab'. Rice compares this kind of CBT with therapies at the other end of a conceptual continuum which focus and even encourage the client's expression of strong affect and impulses. Rice views good CCT as somewhere in the middle of this continuum as, according to her (ibid.: 183), it involves 'the resolution of a series of cognitive-affective reprocessing tasks'. Whilst Rice does identify a series of these tasks, she distances herself from cognitive behaviour methods used to effect change. Although she does not name it, her reluctance is presumably to do with wanting to maintain a non-directive attitude or an identification with non-directive therapy. Rice's conceptualization of therapeutic change in terms of cognitive theory comprises four phases:

1. *Positioning for exploration* – in which the client describes a particular experience which is problematic and a reaction which she or he views as problematic in that she or he considers it to be peculiar, unreasonable, exaggerated, or inappropriate.

2. *Exploring the two sides* – of the client's inner reaction and perceptual processing, an exploration which involves:

   'the discovery of a *meaning bridge* between the quality of one's affective reaction and the idiosyncratic, subjective nature of one's construal of salient elements of the stimulus situation; that is, one's reaction is seen to fit the stimulus situation as construed.'

   (ibid.: 193)

3. *Recognition and exploration of self-schemas* – which represents an explicit attempt to understand and re-evaluate the relatively enduring clusters of cognitive and affective structures by which we assimilate input and organize output. (Some writers and clinicians, including Rice [1974], consider that the word 'scheme' is a more accurate translation of Piaget's term *schème* than 'schema'.)

4. *Awareness of new options* – viewed in the light of 'loosening and reorganized self-schemas' (Rice, 1984: 201).

This structured approach is similar to the description of therapeutic work offered by those associated with the experiential faction or tribe of person-centred and experiential therapies (see, for instance, Leijssen and Elliott, 2008).

Whilst there is no sense of a strong cognitive 'faction' within the person-centred approach or within the World Association of Person-Centred and Experiential Psychotherapy and Counselling, there are a number of articles within the approach on cognition. One paper on the relationship between emotions and cognitions (Tausch, 2002) includes an analysis of Rogers's interactions with a client, 'Gloria' (Rogers, 1965), in which the author suggests that in 67 per cent of his responses, Rogers attends more to the client's cognitions than emotions, responses which seem to have had a parallel effect on the client. Comparing Rogers's responses to those of two other therapists, Tausch observes that: '*Carl Rogers' empathic understanding of the client's cognitions ... seems to be an appropriate and helpful therapeutic approach*, since it avoids the disadvantages that arise with the exclusive attention to cognitions or emotions only' (ibid.: 139, original emphasis). Other articles on cognition focus on a cognitive perspective on borderline personality development (Bohart, 1990); focusing and cognitive functions (Iberg, 1990); cognitive processes as a cause of psychotherapeutic change (Zimring, 1990); the importance of empathy in cognitive restructuring (Vanaerschot, 1993); incongruence and social cognition (Hoyer, 1996); and cognition patterns in a client-centred therapy session in the context of a schizophrenic client process (Trytten, 2003).

CONCLUSION: WE'RE ALL COGNITIVE BEHAVIOUR THERAPISTS NOW

Just as each school of therapy has its theory of human development, health and psychopathology, and change, so too it has a theory of cognition and of behaviour. However, the term 'cognitive behaviour therapy' and the identity 'cognitive behaviour therapist' imply that only cognitive behaviour therapists do CBT, and that CBT is the exclusive territory of cognitive behaviour therapists. Of course, most therapists don't 'do' cognitive and behavioural therapy using CBT techniques, and in that sense are not cognitive behaviour therapists; but, as all therapists work with cognition and behaviour, in this sense we *are* all cognitive and behavioural therapists. This is an argument in favour of sharing conceptual and clinical space rather than claiming territory.

Of course, the same argument may be made about the term 'person-centred therapy' and the identity 'person-centred therapist'. Many if not most therapists would argue that they are 'person-centred' in that they centre on the person or client – 'though this may reflect a 'one-person' or 'one-and-a-half person' approach to psychology rather than a more 'two-person' relational perspective (Stark, 1999). Person-centred therapists have tended to defend their person-centredness by referring to person-centred principles – such as the fact that the human organism tends to actualize, the non-directive attitude of the therapist, and the necessity and sufficiency of certain conditions of therapy – in order to define and claim what is meant by 'client-centred' or 'person-centred'. However, in my view, this is an equally defensive, territorial, technical, and, ultimately, narcissistic position. Being client- or person-centred is not – or should not be – exclusive to any one approach to therapy and, in any case, runs counter to Rogers's own research and integrative statement about psychotherapy in general (Rogers, 1957), and his non-dogmatic stance. Over the years the approach has been referred to by a number of terms: 'non-directive therapy' (Rogers, 1939), 'relationship therapy' (Rogers, 1942), 'client-centred therapy' (Rogers, 1951), and, most recently, 'person-centred therapy' and, more widely, the person-centred *approach*. These terms carry different meanings for different practitioners, and there is little agreement amongst therapists and trainers within the broad church or nation of person-centred and experiential therapies, let alone clients, as to what these terms mean. In the field of psychotherapy and counselling, the term 'person-centred' has become as meaningless as the designation 'integrative'; both require further clarification, definition, and explanation.

If we are to make an impact where it matters, both in the clinic and in society, we need to make certain changes. As therapists we need to get over ourselves specifically with regard to rigid allegiances to unhelpful labels, and with regard to a kind of psychological sectarianism. Researchers need to be more impartial and to be open to diverse and multiple evidence bases and methods. Finally, 'though perhaps firstly, politicians need to be more honest about the ideological and economic basis of their policies, to take a long-term view about health and health care, and to promote improving access to psychological therapies (plural) rather than restricting access to one favoured form of therapy.

REFERENCES

American Psychological Association Division 32 (Humanistic Psychology) Task Force for the Development of Practice Recommendations for the Provision of Humanistic Psychosocial Services (2005) *Recommended Principles and Practices for the Provision of Humanistic Psychosocial Services: Alternatives to Mandated Practice and Treatment Guidelines*. Document available online at: www.apa.org.divisions/div32/pdfs/taskfrev.pdf; retrieved 31 August 2008.

Barrett-Lennard, G.T. (1962) 'Dimensions of therapist response as causal factors in therapeutic change', *Psychological Monographs*, 76 (43).

Barrineau, P. and Bozarth, J. D. (1989) 'A person-centered research model', *Person-Centered Review*, 4 (4): 465–74.

Beck, A. T. (1967) *Depression: Clinical, Experimental and Theoretical Aspects*, New York: Harper & Row.

Bohart, A. C. (1990) 'A cognitive client-centered perspective on borderline personality development', in G. Lietaer, J. Rombauts, and R. Van Balen (eds), *Client-Centered and Experiential Psychotherapy in the Nineties*, Leuven: Leuven University Press, pp. 599–621.

Bohart, A. C. and Tallman, K. (1999) *How Clients Make Therapy Work*, Washington D.C.: American Psychological Association.

Bozarth, J. D. (1993) 'Not necessarily necessary, but always sufficient', in D. Brazier (ed.), *Beyond Carl Rogers*, London: Constable, pp. 92–105.

Burrell, G. and Morgan, G. (1979) *Sociological Paradigms and Organizational Analysis*, London: Heinemann.

Cartwright, D. S. and Graham, M. J. (1984) 'Self-concept and identity: overlapping portions of a cognitive structure of self', in R. S. Levant and J. M. Shlien (eds), *Client-Centered Therapy and the Person-Centered Approach*, New York: Praeger, pp. 108–30.

Craig, G. (1996) 'Qualitative research in an NHS setting: uses and dilemmas', *Changes*, 14 (3): 180–6.

Department of Health (2006) 'End of the "prozac nation" – more counselling, more therapy, less medication to treat depression', press release, 12 May; Ref no. 2006/0177.

Duncan, B. L, Miller, S. D., and Sparks, J. A. (2004) *The Heroic Client: A Revolutionary Way to Improve Effectiveness through Client-Directed, Outcome-Informed Therapy* (rev. edn), San Francisco: Jossey-Bass/Wiley.

Evans, D. and Zarate, O. (1999) *Introducing Evolutionary Psychology*, Cambridge: Icon Books.

Freire, E. S. (2006) 'Randomized controlled clinical trial in psychotherapy research: an epistemological controversy', *Journal of Humanistic Psychology*, 46 (3): 322–35.

Friedli, K., King, M., Lloyd, M., and Horder, J. (1997) 'Randomised controlled assessment of non-directive psychotherapy versus routine general practitioner care', *Lancet*, 350: 1662–5.

Goldstein, K. (1995) *The Organism*, New York: Zone Books (original work published 1934).

Hayes, S., Strosahl, K. D., and Wilson, K. G. (1999) *Acceptance and Commitment Therapy*, New York: Guilford.

Horowitz, M. J., Marmar, C., Weiss, D. S., DeWitt, K., and Rosenbaum, R. (1984) 'Brief psychotherapy of bereavement reactions: the relationship of process to outcome', *Archives of General Psychiatry*, 41: 438–48.

Hoyer, J. (1996) 'Incongruence and social cognition', in U. Esser, H. Pabst, and G.-W. Speierer (eds), *The Power of the Person-Centered Approach: New Challenges–Perspectives–Answers*, Köln: GwG, pp. 3–22.

Iberg, J. R. (1990) 'Ms. C's focusing and cognitive functions', in G. Lietaer, J. Rombauts, and R. Van Balen (eds), *Client-Centered and Experiential Therapy in the Nineties*, Leuven: Leuven University Press, pp. 173–203.

Kelly, G. A. (1955) *The Psychology of Personal Constructs. Vol. 1*, New York: W. W. Norton.

King, M., Lloyd, M., Sibbald, B., Gabbay, M., Ward, E., Byford, S., and Bower, P. (2000) 'Randomised controlled trial of non-directive counselling, cognitive behaviour therapy and usual general practitioner care in the management of depression as well as mixed anxiety and depression in primary care', *Health Technology Assessment*, 4 (19).

Kirschenbaum, H. and Henderson, V. L. (eds) (1990) *Carl Rogers: Dialogues*, London: Constable.

Lambert, M. J. (1992) 'Psychotherapy outcome research: implications for integrative and eclectic therapists', in J. C. Norcross and M. R. Goldfried (eds), *Handbook of Psychotherapy Integration*, New York: Basic Books, pp. 94–129.

Leader, D. (2007) 'A dark age for mental health', The *Guardian*, 13 October: 34.

Leijssen, M. and Elliott, R. (2008) 'Integrative experiential psychotherapy in brief', in K. Tudor (ed.), *Brief Person-Centred Therapies*, London: Sage, pp. 31–46.

Lietaer, G. (1990) 'The client-centered approach after the Wisconsin project: a personal view on its evolution', in G. Lietaer, J. Rombauts, and R. Van Balen (eds), *Client-Centered and Experiential Therapy in the Nineties*, Leuven: Leuven University Press, pp. 19–45.

Linehan, M. M. (1993) *Cognitive-behavioural Treatment of Borderline Personality Disorder*, New York: Guilford.

Luborsky, L., Singer, B., and Luborsky, L. (1975) 'Comparative studies of psychotherapies', *Archives of General Psychiatry*, 32: 995–1008.

Luborsky, L., Crits-Cristoph, P., Alexander, L., Margolis, M., and Cohen, M. (1983) 'Two helping alliance methods for predicting outcomes of psychotherapy: accounting signs vs. global rating method', *Journal of Nervous and Mental Disorders*, 171: 480–92.

Miller, S. D., Duncan, B. L., and Hubble, M. A. (1997) *Escape from Babel: Toward a Unifying Language for Psychotherapy Practice*, New York: W. W. Norton.

Miller, S., Hubble, M., and Duncan, B. (1995) 'No more bells and whistles', *The Family Therapy Networker*, March/April: 53–63.

Morgan, S. (2004) 'Practice Based Evidence', website, at: www.practicebasedevidence.com/home/home_pbe.htm; retrieved 31 August 2008.

Morgan, S. and Juriansz, D. (2002) 'Practice-based evidence', *OpenMind*, 114: 12–13.

Moustakas, C. (1990) 'Heuristic research: design and methodology', *Person-Centered Review*, 5 (2): 170–90.

NIHCE (2007) *Developing NICE Clinical Guidelines*. Document available online at: http://www.nice.org.uk/aboutnice/howwework/developingniceclinicalguidelines/developing_nice_clinical_guidelines.jsp; retrieved 31 August 2008.

Nye, R. D. (2000) *Three Psychologies: Perspectives form Freud, Skinner, and Rogers*, 6th edn, Belmont: Wadsworth/Thomson.

Patterson, C. H. (1986) *Theories of Counseling and Psychotherapy*, New York: Harper Collins.

Raimy, V. (1971) *The Self-Concept as a Factor in Counselling and Personality Organization*, Ohio: Ohio State University.

Raimy, V. (1975) *Misunderstandings of the Self: Cognitive Psychotherapy and the Misconception Hypothesis*, San Francisco: Jossey-Bass.

Rice, L. N. (1974) 'The evocative function of the therapist', in D. A. Wexler and L. N. Rice (eds), *Innovations in Client-Centered Therapy*, New York: Wiley, pp. 289–311.

Rice, L. N. (1984) 'Client tasks in client-centered therapy', in R. F. Levant and J. Shlien (eds), *Client-Centered Therapy and the Person-Centered Approach: New Directions in Theory, Research and Practice*, New York: Praeger, pp. 182–202.

Rogers, C. R. (1939) *The Clinical Treatment of the Problem Child*, Boston: Houghton Mifflin.

Rogers, C. R. (1942) *Counseling and Psychotherapy: Newer Concepts in Practice*, Boston: Houghton Mifflin.

Rogers, C. R. (1951) *Client-Centered Therapy*, London: Constable.

Rogers, C. R. (1957) 'The necessary and sufficient conditions of therapeutic personality change', *Journal of Consulting Psychology*, 21: 95–103.

Rogers, C. R. (1959) 'A theory of therapy, personality and interpersonal relationships, as developed in the client-centred framework', in S. Koch (ed.), *Psychology: A Study of a Science. Vol. 3: Formulation of the Person and the Social Context*, New York: McGraw-Hill, pp. 184–256.

Rogers, C. R. (1965) *Three Approaches to Psychotherapy* (E. Shostrom, Producer) [film], Santa Ana, Calif.: Psychological Films.

Rogers, C. R. (1967a) 'A therapist's view of the good life: the fully functioning person', in his *On Becoming a Person*, London: Constable, pp. 183–96 (original work published 1957).

Rogers, C. R. (1967b) 'A process conception of psychotherapy', in his *On Becoming a Person*, London: Constable, pp. 125–59 (original work published 1958).

Rogers, C. R. (1969) 'Toward a science of the person', in A. J. Sutich and M. A. Vich (eds), *Readings in Humanistic Psychology*, New York: Macmillan.

Rogers, C. R. (1972) 'Bringing together ideas and feelings in learning', *Learning Today*, 5: 32–43.

Rogers, C. R. (1978) *Carl Rogers on Personal Power*, London: Constable.

Rogers, C. R. (1980) 'Do we need "a" reality?', in his *A Way of Being*, Boston: Houghton Mifflin, pp. 96–108 (original work published 1974).

Rogers, C. R. (1985) 'Toward a more human science of the person', *Journal of Humanistic Psychology*, 25 (4): 7–24.

Rogers, C. R., Gendlin, E. T., Kiesler, D. J., and Truax, C. B. (eds) (1967) *The Therapeutic Relationship and its Impact: A Study of Psychotherapy with Schizophrenics*, Madison: University of Wisconsin Press.

Rogers, C. R. and Russell, D. E. (2002) *Carl Rogers The Quiet Revolutionary: An Oral History*, Roseville, Calif.: Penmarin Books.

Rogers, C. R. and Skinner, B. F. (1956) 'Some issues concerning the control of human behaviour. A symposium', *Science*, 124: 1057–66.

Rowland, N. (2007) 'BACP and NICE', *Therapy Today*, 18 (5): 27–30.

Scottish Intercollegiate Guidelines Network (2002) SIGN 50. *A Guideline Developer's Handbook*, Edinburgh: Scottish Intercollegiate Guidelines Network.

Segal, Z. V., Williams, J. M., and Teasdale J. D. (2000) *Mindfulness-Based Cognitive Therapy for Depression: A New Approach to Relapse Prevention*, New York: Guilford.

Smith, M. L., Glass, G. V., and Miller, T. I. (1980) *The Benefits of Psychotherapy*, Baltimore: Johns Hopkins University Press.

Stark, M. (1999) *Modes of Therapeutic Action: Enhancement of Knowledge, Provision of Experience, Engagement in Relationship*, Northvale: Jason Aronson.

Stiles, W. B., Shapiro, D. A., and Elliot, R. (1986) 'Are all psychotherapies equivalent?', *American Psychologist*, 41 (2): 165–80.

Stiles, W. B., Barkham, M., Twigg, E., Mellor-Clark, J., and Cooper, M. (2006) 'Effectiveness of cognitive-behavioural, person-centred and psychodynamic therapies as practised in UK National Health Service settings', *Psychological Medicine*, 36: 555–66.

Tausch, R. (2002) 'The relationship between emotions and cognitions: implications for therapist empathy', in D. Cain (ed.), *Classics in the Person-Centered Approach*, Ross-on-Wye: PCCS Books, pp. 134–42 (originally published 1988).

Thorne, B. (1996) 'Person-centred therapy', in W. Dryden (ed.), *Handbook of Individual Therapy*, London: Sage, pp. 121–46.

Thorne, B. (2003) *Carl Rogers*, 2nd edn, London: Sage (originally published 1992).

Toukmanian, S. (2002) 'Perception: the core element in person-centered and experiential psychotherapies', in G. Wyatt and P. Sanders (eds), *Contact and Perception*, Ross-on-Wye: PCCS Books, pp. 115–32 .

Trytten, J. D. (2003) 'Schizophrenic Client Process: Phase and Cognition Patterns in a Client-Centered Therapy Session', unpublished Ph.D. thesis, Chicago: Argosy University.

Tudor, K. (2000) 'The case of the lost conditions', *Counselling*, 11 (1): 33–7.

Tudor, K. and Worrall, M. (2006) *Person-Centred Therapy: A Clinical Philosophy*, London: Routledge.

van der Veen, F. (1967) 'The effects of the therapist and the patient on each other', in C. R. Rogers, E. T. Gendlin, D. J. Kiesler, and C. B. Truax (eds), *The Therapeutic Relationship and its Impact: A Study of Psychotherapy with Schizophrenics*, Madison: University of Wisconsin Press, pp. 353–66.

Vanaerschot, G. (1993) 'Empathy as releasing several micro-processes in the client', in D. Brazier (ed.), *Beyond Carl Rogers*, London: Constable, pp. 47–71.

Verhaeghe, P. (2007) 'Chronicle of a death foretold: the end of psychotherapy' – keynote address, Health4Life Conference, Dublin, 11th September.

Wexler, D. A. (1974) 'A cognitive theory of experiencing, self-actualization and therapeutic process', in D. A. Wexler and L. N. Rice (eds), *Innovations in Client-Centered Therapy*, New York: Wiley, pp. 49–116.

Wexler, D. A. and Rice, L. N. (eds) (1974) *Innovations in Client-Centered Therapy*, New York: Wiley.

Young, J. E. (1994) *Cognitive Therapy for Personality Disorders: A Schema-Focused Approach*, Sarasota: Professional Resource Press.

Zimring, F. (1974) 'A cognitive theory of experiencing, self-actualization and therapeutic process', in D. A. Wexler and L. N. Rice (eds), *Innovations in Client-Centered Therapy*, New York: Wiley, pp. 49–116.

Zimring, F. (1990) 'Cognitive processes as a cause of psychotherapeutic change', in G. Lietaer, J. Rombauts, and R. Van Balen (eds), *Client-Centered and Experiential Therapy in the Nineties*, Leuven: Leuven University Press, pp. 361–80.

CHAPTER 11

COGNITIVE BEHAVIOUR THERAPY:

FROM RATIONALISM TO CONSTRUCTIVISM?

DAVID A. WINTER

INTRODUCTION

Treatment guidelines indicate that the treatment of choice for most psychological problems is cognitive behaviour therapy. This chapter suggests that there are alternative constructions of the evidence base from which such guidelines are drawn, and reviews another relevant evidence base, concerning the relationship between clients' and therapists' philosophical beliefs, personal styles, and treatment preferences. One distinction that will be drawn, and illustrated by approaches to the 'resistant' client, is that between rationalism and constructivism; and possible constructivist trends in cognitive behaviour therapy will be discussed.

With at least 500 psychological therapies available (Karasu, 1986), the choices faced by clinicians, clients, and health-service commissioners in selecting a therapeutic approach would appear to be bewildering. However, relief is provided from making such complex decisions by guidelines and reviews indicating that the treatment of choice for most psychological (Chambless et al., 1998; National Institute for Health and Clinical Excellence, 2005; Roth and Fonagy, 2005), not to mention economic (Centre for Economic Performance's Mental Health Policy Group, 2006), ills is cognitive behaviour therapy. Such assertions, generally framed within a discourse of evidence-based practice and empirical validation, may appear rooted in scientific considerations. However, the situation is not quite so simple, since therapies differ not only in terms of technical features but also in underlying philosophical assumptions, which may be at least as relevant to treatment selection as is scientific evidence concerning therapeutic efficacy.

This chapter will review an alternative evidence base, which concerns the relationship between philosophical beliefs and clients' and therapists' preferences for different therapies, as well as the practice of, and clients' response to, these therapies. It will also indicate that the more familiar evidence base concerning the outcome of cognitive behaviour and other therapies is open to alternative constructions, which call into question the treatment guidelines that have been derived from it. Finally, the chapter will consider the implications for this debate of the increasing diversification of cognitive behaviour therapies.

An earlier version of this chapter appeared in the *European Journal of Psychotherapy and Counselling*, 10 (3), 2008, pp. 221–30.

PHILOSOPHICAL BELIEFS, PERSONAL STYLES, AND THERAPEUTIC PREFERENCES

A research programme that commenced in the 1960s has provided consistent evidence that, whether they be staff or clients, people's preferences for different treatments for psychological problems reflect their 'personal styles' (Caine et al., 1981; Caine and Winter, 1993). Two dimensions of personal style that are of particular relevance are inner- versus outer-directedness, a focus on subjective concerns or on the external world; and radicalism versus conservatism. People who preferred, chose to practise, were allocated to, or improved in more structured, directive therapies (such as behaviour therapy) were found to be more outer-directed and conservative than those who preferred, practised, were allocated to, or improved in less directive, more interpersonally focused approaches (such as group-analytic therapy).

A related body of research concerns the epistemological positions characterizing different therapies. Schacht and Black (1985) found behaviour therapists to have an empirical 'epistemic style' (concerned with the correspondence of beliefs with observations), in contrast to the predominantly metaphorical style (concerned with symbolic representations and the ability to generalize from beliefs) of psychoanalytic therapists. Arthur (2000), as well as confirming the difference between these therapists on the metaphorical style dimension, showed cognitive behaviour therapists to be characterized by the objectivist worldview described as mechanism, in contrast to the organicism, or subjectivist worldview, of psychoanalytic psychotherapists. Neimeyer et al. (1993) also found that individuals preferred therapeutic approaches matching their epistemic styles.

Another distinction is that between rationalist and constructivist epistemological positions, essentially whether people are viewed as passively perceiving an independently existing real world or actively constructing their realities. It has been found that rational-emotive therapists are more rationalist and less constructivist than personal-construct psychotherapists (Neimeyer and Morton, 1997); and that therapists' epistemological positions are reflected in their personal characteristics, therapeutic styles, and choice of interventions, with rationalists being more likely to use cognitive behaviour techniques (Neimeyer et al., 2006). A further indication of the rationalist position of cognitive behaviour therapists was provided by Winter et al. (2006), who, comparing them with psychotherapists of eight other orientations, found them to be more rationalist than all except hypnotherapists. They were also more outer-directed than all other therapists, and more likely to construe therapy in technical terms.

PHILOSOPHICAL BELIEFS IN PRACTICE

Psychotherapists' philosophical beliefs would be expected to be reflected in their therapeutic practice, and distinctions between rationalist and constructivist therapies have been delineated in this regard (Mahoney, 1988). Fundamental to these distinctions is rationalist therapists' primary concern with the validity of the client's view of the world, and hence with the correction of 'cognitive errors', as opposed to constructivist therapists' primary concern with the viability of this view.

There is some evidence of distinctive features of constructivist and rationalist therapies. Vasco (1994) found that the therapeutic practice of constructivist psychologists was characterized by low levels of structure, directiveness, focus on current issues, and confrontation regarding resistance. Viney (1994) demonstrated that personal-construct and client-centred therapy sessions showed greater acknowledgement than rational-emotive therapy sessions of clients' emotional distress, which tended to be regarded as indicating irrationality in rational-emotive therapy. Winter and Watson (1999) found that, compared to cognitive-therapy sessions, personal-construct psychotherapy sessions were characterized by a less negative therapist attitude, greater therapist exploration and client participation, greater use of less structured response modes and less use of directive responses, and greater use by the client of complex levels of perceptual processing. The two types of therapist also held different views of the therapeutic relationship.

It is in their approach to the client who is considered resistant to therapy that differences in practice between therapists of different orientations often come into the sharpest focus. The difference between rationalist and constructivist therapists may be framed in terms of Liotti's (1989) distinction between pedagogical and exploratory approaches. The former is nowhere more vividly presented than in Albert Ellis's (1980) remark that resistance may be due to 'the therapist's engaging in… therapy in a namby-pamby, passive way instead of vigorously getting after clients' (ibid.: 256). Compare this, and the battlefield metaphors often used by rationalist therapists in describing work with resistant clients, with Mahoney's (1988) description of the constructivist view:

> 'that resistance to core psychological change is a natural and healthy expression of an individual's attempt to protect and perpetuate his systemic integrity.… For the constructivist therapist, then, resistance to change is not the enemy in counselling. It is not something to be "overcome", but a healthy self-protective process that is to be respected and worked *with* rather than *against*.'
>
> (ibid.: 306, original emphases)

Rationalist therapists' approach to resistance may be illustrated by the following extract from a session concerning a client's failure to comply with homework strategies suggested by her cognitive behaviour therapist to tackle her trichotillomania (Watson and Winter, 2000):

Therapist (T): *So, did you manage to wear the gloves while you were driving?*

Client (C): *No, I didn't.*

T: *Any problem with that?*

C: *To be quite honest I didn't really think about it because I'm always in a rush…*

T: *Right, I see, but I think that would be a very good way of stopping that when you're driving.*

C: *Mm.*

T: *Because to overcome this problem you have to have a strategy otherwise nothing is going to change for you… have you been breathing?*

C: *Yeah sometimes.… But I can't see how doing all this wearing gloves and breathing and so forth is going to stop me hair pulling, because it won't.*

T: *I know about these problems and there's a whole range of things that one needs to do together to get a grip on these problems, because the problem is very difficult and therefore you need a sledgehammer to crack it, it's a very evasive problem and you can't have half-hearted attempts at dealing with it.*

It was perhaps unsurprising that the client dropped out of therapy after this session.

In contrast, a constructivist approach is illustrated by a session with a client who did not comply obediently with the instructions of fixed-role therapy (Kelly, 1955), requiring him to take on a new role. Rather than fully adopting this role, a character named Barry, he had held a conversation between Barry and his angry self, whom he named Billy (Winter, 2008). The client, who had previously been through the mill of cognitive behaviour and other approaches to therapy, recounted this to the therapist, and the following interaction ensued:

C: *...I don't know where that quite leaves us with it because there's been some moderate benefit at least in the short term, but I'm aware that it isn't doing as you had intended.*

T: *It doesn't need to be.*

C: [laughs] *Say it again.*

T: *It doesn't need to be done in a very prescriptive way. A conversation, albeit a short one, between Barry and Billy might be.*

C: [laughs] *Well, perhaps that's the other novelty of a personal-construct approach because if it's fair to characterize a personal-construct approach as a cognitive approach... other cognitive approaches are extraordinarily directive.*

T: *Which is why I would say that it isn't a cognitive approach.*

C: [laughs] *...once again I've sabotaged the therapy, which has been the accusation in the past, resistance, not wanting to do as you're told, all these kind of things.*

T: *It could be looked at in that way, but it could also be seen that you've done something quite novel, which seems to have had some effect.*

A constructivist approach such as this to the 'resistant' client may be less likely to lead to therapeutic casualties than the 'ballistic' (Stiles et al., 1996), invalidating approach demonstrated in the first example (Winter, 1997).

THERAPEUTIC OUTCOME

Lists of 'evidence-based' or 'empirically supported' therapies are dominated by cognitive behaviour approaches. However, the evidence on which such lists are based is open to alternative constructions, and different interpretations of research findings in this area have been apparent at least since Eysenck's (1952) assertions concerning the ineffectiveness of psychotherapy. While early meta-analyses of outcome research did indicate some superiority of cognitive behaviour over other approaches, such differences could be attributed to features of research design favouring cognitive behaviour therapy. More generally, the very criteria for what constitutes an empirically validated therapy (Chambless et al., 1998), emphasizing quantitative, randomized controlled trials of manualized therapies for clients with specific diagnoses, may be considered biased toward cognitive behaviour approaches, and to lead to the 'empirical violation' of humanistic and constructivist therapies (Bohart et al., 1998; Bohart and House, Chapters 16 and 17, this volume). As Slife (2004: 51–2) has asked,

> 'Is it merely coincidental that the therapies that match the values of objectivist science are those that are most scientifically supported?... Is it merely coincidental that cognitive behavioural therapy has virtually the same epistemological assumptions (values) as traditional science (i.e., a wedding of empiricism and rationalism). The positive empirical evaluations of this therapy may be the result of systematic bias rather than efficacy without such bias.'

Roth and Fonagy (2005) concede this point in the second edition of their influential book, *What Works for Whom?*, where, commenting upon research on personal-construct psychotherapy (PCT), they remark that

> 'what is available is philosophically at variance with a conventional review such as this one. This latter point could be used to argue that the absence of reports of evidence for PCT in this book reflects our selection bias rather than a real absence of evidence.'
>
> (ibid.: 492)

Meta analyses have, indeed, suggested that this form of therapy is at least as effective as other approaches, including cognitive behaviour therapy (Metcalfe et al., 2007; Viney et al., 2005).

Even when the focus is upon comparative outcome studies conducted according to traditional scientific method, which might be expected to favour cognitive behaviour therapy, recent meta-analyses have indicated little or no difference between therapies (Wampold, 2001). Furthermore, there is little or no evidence for the effects of specific ingredients of therapy, leading Wampold (ibid.: 147–8) to conclude that 'the ingredients of the most conspicuous treatment on the landscape, cognitive-behavioral treatment, are apparently not responsible for the benefits of this treatment'.

VARIETIES OF COGNITIVE BEHAVIOUR THERAPY

Cognitive behaviour therapy has diversified considerably over the last half century, the 'first wave' of empirically based behaviour therapies being succeeded, during the 'cognitive revolution', by a 'second wave' of therapies which, while incorporating attention to cognitions, were still essentially mechanistic (Hayes, 2004). The more recent 'third wave' of cognitive behaviour therapies, regarded as contextualist (viewing events within their total context) and more concerned with process than with content, are so varied that one wonders at what point the cognitive behaviour label becomes so permeable as to be no longer useful. They include Dialectical Behaviour Therapy (Linehan, 1993), mindfulness-based cognitive therapy (Segal et al., 2002), and Acceptance and Commitment Therapy (Hayes et al., 1999). As

Watson (2005) indicated, cognitive behaviour therapy is 'no longer about correcting cognitive errors', unlike the rationalist therapies which she had previously differentiated from personal-construct psychotherapy. Nevertheless, there is some evidence that at least one 'third-wave' approach, Dialectical Behaviour Therapy, differs from personal-construct psychotherapy in ways which are not inconsistent with her earlier study (Winter et al., 2003).

Nor is it easy to accept the claims of leading cognitive 'second-wave' therapists such as Beck (Weishar, 1993) and Ellis (1990) that their approaches are constructivist. Indeed, Ellis's (1990: 118) assertion that rational-emotive therapy 'is not only nonrationalist but... is in several important respects more constructivist and more process-oriented than just about all of the other cognitive therapies' perhaps only goes to prove his thesis that all of us, even rational-emotive therapists, are prone to irrationality!

CONCLUSIONS

Psychological therapies differ markedly in their underlying philosophical assumptions, and individuals, whether clients, therapists, health commissioners, or policy makers, tend to favour approaches with assumptions matching their own beliefs and 'personal styles'. These beliefs are also likely to influence constructions placed on the 'evidence base' for psychological therapies. For example, since 'the science of economics has largely endorsed empiricism and the operationalization of nonmaterialist constructs', as well as hedonism (Slife, 2004: 54), it is not surprising that an economic reading of this evidence base might view cognitive behaviour therapies as a panacea. This has been graphically demonstrated in England by the Government's recent commitment of £300 million to improve access to predominantly cognitive behaviour psychological therapies on the basis of a report by an economist, who has also authored a book on happiness (Layard, 2005; see also Pilgrim's Chapter 21, this volume). The language used by the British Minister of Health in introducing this initiative clearly reflects the rationalist philosophy on which it is based: 'Successful psychological therapies ensure that the *right number* of people are offered a choice of the *right services* at the *right time* with the *right results*' (Hewitt, 2007: 2, emphasis in original).

However, although there is little doubt that cognitive behaviour approaches are effective with some problems, it can no longer be confidently asserted (admittedly in the view of this particular reader of the 'evidence') that these therapies are generally more effective than any other, or that their effects are due to their specific cognitive behaviour ingredients (cf. Bohart and House, Chapters 16 and 17, this volume). In addition, the diversification of cognitive behaviour therapies, while perhaps to be welcomed in making them more contextualist and constructivist and less likely to subject the resistant client to a 'ballistic' approach, might also be viewed as rendering them so indistinct that one might ask when is such a therapy no longer cognitive behavioural.

REFERENCES

Arthur, A. R. (2000) 'The personality and cognitive-epistemological traits of cognitive behavioural and psychoanalytic psychotherapists', *British Journal of Medical Psychology*, 73: 243–57.

Bohart, A. C., O'Hara, M., and Leitner, L. M. (1998) 'Empirically violated treatments: disenfranchisement of humanistic and other psychotherapies', *Psychotherapy Research*, 8: 1–57.

Caine, T. M. and Winter, D. A. (1993) 'Personal styles and universal polarities: implications for therapeutic practice', *Therapeutic Communities*, 14: 91–102.

Caine, T. M., Wijesinghe, O. B. A., and Winter, D. A. (1981) *Personal Styles in Neurosis: Implications for Small Group Psychotherapy and Behaviour Therapy*, London: Routledge & Kegan Paul.

Centre for Economic Performance's Mental Health Policy Group (2006) *The Depression Report: A New Deal for Depression and Anxiety Disorders*, London: London School of Economics.

Chambless, D. L., Baker, M. J., Baucom, D. H., Beutler, L. E., Calhoun, K. S., Crits-Christoph, P., Daiuto, A., DeRubeis, R., Detweiler, J., Haaga, D. A. F., Johnson, S. B., McCurry, S., Mueser, K. T., Pope, K. S., Sanderson, W. C., Shoham, V., Stickle, T., Williams, D. A., and Woody, S. R. (1998) 'Update on empirically validated therapies, II', *The Clinical Psychologist*, 51: 3–16.

Ellis, A. (1980) 'Treatment of erectile dysfunction', in S. R. Leiblum and L. A. Pervin (eds), *Principles and Practice of Sex Therapy*, London: Tavistock, pp. 235–61.

Ellis, A. (1990) 'Is rational-emotive therapy (RET) "rationalist" or constructivist? in A. Ellis and W. Dryden (eds), *The Essential Albert Ellis: Seminal Writings on Psychotherapy*, New York: Springer, pp. 26–32.

Eysenck, H. J. (1952) 'The effects of psychotherapy: an evaluation', *Journal of Consulting Psychology*, 16: 319–24.

Hayes, S. C. (2004) 'Acceptance and commitment therapy, relational frame theory, and the third wave of behavioral and cognitive therapies', *Behavior Therapy*, 35: 639–65.

Hayes, S. C., Strosahl, K .D., and Wilson, K. G. (1999) *Acceptance and Commitment Therapy: An Experiential Approach to Behavior Change*, New York: Guilford.

Hewitt, P. (2007) 'Foreword', in *Commissioning a Brighter Future: Improving Access to Psychological Therapies Positive Practice Guide*, London: National Health Service, p. 2.

Karasu, T. B. (1986) 'The psychotherapies: benefits and limitations', *American Journal of Psychotherapy*, 40: 324–43.

Kelly, G. A. (1955) *The Psychology of Personal Constructs*, New York: Norton.

Layard, R. (2005) *Happiness: Lessons from a New Science*, London: Penguin.

Linehan, M. M. (1993) *Cognitive-Behavioral Treatment of Borderline Personality Disorder*, New York: Guilford.

Liotti, G. (1989) 'Resistance to change in cognitive psychotherapy: theoretical remarks from a constructivist point of view', in W. Dryden and P. Trower (eds), *Cognitive Psychotherapy: Stasis and Change*, London: Cassell, pp. 28–56.

Mahoney, M. J. (1988) 'Constructive metatheory: II. Implications for psychotherapy', *International Journal of Personal Construct Psychology*, 1: 299–315.

Metcalfe, C., Winter, D. A., and Viney, L. L. (2007) 'The effectiveness of personal construct psychotherapy in clinical practice: a systematic review and meta-analysis', *Psychotherapy Research*, 17: 431–42.

National Institute for Health and Clinical Excellence (2005) *Compilation Issue 10: Mental Health*, www.nice.org.uk

Neimeyer, G. J. and Morton, R. J. (1997) 'Personal epistemologies and preferences for rationalist versus constructivist psychotherapies', *Journal of Constructivist Psychology*, 10: 109–23.

Neimeyer, G. J., Lee, J., Aksoy, G., and Phillip, D. (2006) 'Epistemic styles among seasoned psychotherapists: some practical implications', in J. Raskin and S. Bridges (eds), *Studies in Meaning, Vol. 3*, New York: Pace University Press.

Neimeyer, G. J., Prichard, S., Lyddon, W. J., and Sherrard, P. A. D. (1993) 'The role of epistemic style in counselling preference and orientation', *Journal of Counseling and Development*, 71: 515–23.

Roth, A. and Fonagy, P. (2005) *What Works for Whom? A Critical Review of Psychotherapy Research*, New York: Guilford.

Schacht, T. E. and Black, D. A. (1985) 'Epistemological commitments of behavioural and psychoanalytic therapists', *Professional Psychology: Research and Practice*, 16: 316–23.

Segal, Z. V., Williams, J. M. G., and Teasdale, J. D. (2002) *Mindfulness-Based Cognitive Therapy for Depression: A New Approach to Preventing Relapse*, New York: Guilford.

Slife, B. D. (2004) 'Theoretical challenges to therapy practice and research: the constraint of naturalism', in M. J. Lambert (ed.), *Bergin and Garfield's Handbook of Psychotherapy and Behavior Change*, New York: Wiley, pp. 44–83.

Stiles, W. B., Honos-Webb, L., and Surko, M. (1996) 'Responsiveness as a challenge to process research', paper presented at 27th Annual Meeting of Society for Psychotherapy Research, Amelia Island, Florida.

Vasco, A. B. (1994) 'Correlates of constructivism among Portuguese therapists', *Journal of Constructivist Psychology*, 7: 1–16.

Viney, L. L. (1994) 'Sequences of emotional distress expressed by clients and acknowledged by therapists: are they associated more with some therapist than others?', *British Journal of Clinical Psychology*, 33: 469–81.

Viney, L. L., Metcalfe, C., and Winter, D. A. (2005) 'The effectiveness of personal construct psychotherapy: a meta-analysis', in D. A. Winter and L. L. Viney (eds), *Personal Construct Psychotherapy: Advances in Theory, Practice and Research*, London: Whurr, pp. 347–64.

Wampold, B. E. (2001) *The Great Psychotherapy Debate: Models, Methods, and Findings*, Mahwah, NJ: Erlbaum.

Watson, S. (2005) 'Personal construct therapy and the cognitive therapies revisited: how different are they in the 21st century?', paper presented at the 16th International Congress of Personal Construct Psychology, Columbus, Ohio.

Watson, S. and Winter, D. A. (2000) 'What works for whom but shouldn't and what doesn't work for whom but should?', *European Journal of Psychotherapy, Counselling and Health*, 3: 245–61.

Weishar, M. E. (1993) *Aaron T. Beck*, London: Sage.

Winter, D. A. (1997) 'Everybody has still won but what about the booby prizes?', *British Psychological Society Psychotherapy Section Newsletter*, 21: 1–15.

Winter, D. A. (2008) 'Personal construct psychotherapy in a National Health Service setting: does survival mean selling out?', in J. D. Raskin and S. K. Bridges (eds), *Studies in Meaning 3: Constructivist Psychotherapy in the Real World*, New York: Pace University Press, pp. 229–52.

Winter, D. A. and Watson, S. (1999) 'Personal construct psychotherapy and the cognitive therapies: different in theory but can they be differentiated in practice?', *Journal of Constructivist Psychology*, 12: 1–22.

Winter, D. A., Tschudi, F., and Gilbert, N. (2006) 'Psychotherapists' "personal styles", construing and theoretical orientations', in D. Loewenthal and D. A. Winter (eds), *What is Psychotherapeutic Research?*, London: Karnac.

Winter, D. A., Watson, S., Gillman-Smith, I., Gilbert, N., and Acton, T. (1993) 'Border crossing: a personal construct psychotherapy approach for clients with a diagnosis of borderline personality disorder', in G. Chiari and M. L. Nuzzo (eds), *Psychological Constructivism and the Social World*, Milan: FrancoAngeli, pp. 342–52.

Chapter 12

POST-EXISTENTIALISM AS A REACTION TO CBT?

Del Loewenthal

INTRODUCTION

The purpose of this chapter is to describe a place for exploring notions of well-being at the start of the twenty-first century that is in contrast to the increasing cultural dominance of cognitive behaviour therapy (CBT). Whilst, however, post-existentialism can be held as an alternative to CBT, it is of course far more than this. An attempt is made to offer such an alternative place where we might still be able to think about how alienated we are through valuing existential notions such as experience and meaning, whilst questioning other dimensions, such as existentialism's inferred narcissism and the place it has come to take up with regards to – for example – psychoanalysis and the political.

The chapter describes an approach that is being developed, in part as a reaction to CBT, where existentialism and phenomenology are critically revisited and, as a result, post-existentialism is offered in terms of its implications for practice. It is argued that post-existentialism also has significant implications for our cultural practices in general, including the current interest in 'well-being', enabling the psychological therapies to have a quite different emphasis to that provided by CBT.

It is considered by many that the German philosopher Heidegger (1962) is a – if not *the* – foremost writer on the subject of being. Heidegger is associated with existentialism, and in many ways post-existentialism implies a combination of both Heideggerian and some post-Heideggerian approaches. One feature of key importance to post-existentialism is that we *start with* considering such notions of being, rather than attempting to add them on afterwards to a technique that is based on more rational assumptions regarding what it means to be human, as some more recent CBT theorists have done. This chapter is part of work-in-progress at the Research Centre for Therapeutic Education at Roehampton University, London, where we are re-looking at existentialism in a post-Heideggerian era, with particular reference to the psychological therapeutic practices of counselling and psychotherapy (see, for example, the special issue of the journal, *Philosophical Practice* – Loewenthal, 2008).

THE CHANGING NATURE OF ESCAPISM

In keeping with the post-existential, including something of the phenomenological, I would like to start by describing an experience I had whilst preparing this chapter. At the time I was visiting a Canadian University, and on my first evening after returning to my hotel I switched on the TV. The first programme focused on a section of road where, one by one, people in cars picked up other people whom they made carry out various sexual acts that one did not see in close-up; but one did subsequently see, in detail, these victims being horrendously beaten up. I changed channels, and it was an evangelical preacher entrancing his audience. The next time I watched TV, it was a programme advertizing sleeping tablets that showed beautiful people waking up in beautiful houses to the background of sweet music and the enticing voice-over saying 'this could be addictive'! As someone who watches very little TV, I still feel traumatized by the first programme. I am not suggesting that this is only a North American problem: on returning to London I went into a pub (bar) where there were at least two TV programmes and two different sound systems on concurrently: I assume that this entertainment is provided in order to anaesthetize the clients in the name of relaxation. Is it that the dose of these different stimuli (as with the evangelical preacher, medication, and simultaneous entertainments) are having to be continually increased in order for people not to think? Is CBT, when it becomes the main State-approved approach to our well-being, a logical development of this need to take our mind off those thoughts that might otherwise come to us – thoughts that are individually and culturally too much?

In a previous era, many spoke of alienation, and existentialists spoke of self-estrangement: Heidegger (1962), for example with 'the crowd', and Sartre (1943) in terms of 'bad faith'. However, it would appear, as in the Canadian examples above, that new ways of dealing with our increasing alienation have been established which include no longer naming it as such. Thus, such ways of reduced awareness – what I have termed 'escape motivation' (whether it be of death, nothingness, oneself, others, or the world) – and which organizations including the State can use to manipulate us (Loewenthal, 2002), are no longer in our everyday vocabulary. Perversely, it is as if the better the escape, the better our level of so called 'well-being'. For example, it is as if the more CBT and its equivalents can help to take our minds off our problems, the better-off we will be. CBT may well be helpful individually, but when adopted as *the* main mode of 'treatment' by a society, then individually and collectively the implications are that we cannot allow thoughts to come to us, and we will not therefore be able to come to our senses – with potentially catastrophic consequences. There would be, for example, no point in worrying about our and others' responsibilities for how we are – indeed, such concepts as alienation are, in an age of happiness (Layard, 2006; Seligman 2002), not only unnecessary but counterproductive!

DEVELOPMENTS IN THE UNITED KINGDOM

In the UK, the so-called 'British school of existentialism' (Van Deurzen, 1997, 2001; Spinelli, 1989, 2007), which has done so much to put existentialism on our map, initially favoured Boss over Binswanger (Cooper, M., 2003), as they were influenced by Heidegger working with Boss; whereas Binswanger had said that he had misunderstood Heidegger, although the misunderstanding was a fruitful one (Friedman, 1991: 414, 426). However, what then seems to have developed is a reaction to the psychoanalytic influences on Boss. Whilst what I am calling the 'post-existential' would not want to get caught up in Freud's (and particularly his later) universalizing, meaning-making schemas, it would also not wish to ignore the writings of psychoanalysis, in that, for example, our past can unknowingly influence the present, and we will always be subject to something 'life-giving' in ourselves that we are not in control of. It is therefore considered unhelpful to attempt to deny this in therapy.

In some ways the work of R. D. Laing (1967, 1969, 1990) would come close to one attempt to keep open (with failings) what is being termed here a post-existential approach. There are those at the Philadelphia Association, which Laing founded, who continue this tradition (Cooper, D., 1990; Gordon and Mayo, 2004), registering their students as psychoanalytical psychotherapists. Here, psychoanalysis is considered together with philosophy. The Roehampton University programme, with which the term 'post-existential' is primarily associated (Loewenthal, 2007), is also influenced by Laing. (I, for one, trained at the Philadelphia Association.) However, there are significant differences in that, for example, at Roehampton, phenomenology is initially explored with an emphasis on practice through Carl Rogers, and then existentialism, followed by a phenomenological reading of Freud. What happened to phenomenology is then followed through those who might be labelled 'post-modern', such as Lacan, Derrida, Levinas and French feminists like Kristeva, Cixous, and Irigaray, before examining the implications of all this for carrying out 'relational research'. Previous descriptions of this learning process have been given in terms of theory (Loewenthal and Snell, 2003), research (Loewenthal, 2007), and training (Loewenthal and Snell, 2008).

At Roehampton, with post-existentialism and 'post-phenomenology' as the particular focus, the psychotherapy students are registered as integrative, and the counselling-psychology students take relational approaches as their major model, and contrast this with CBT. Thus, besides its relationship with psychoanalysis, our post-existential training may have a greater emphasis on starting with the experiential and exploring what is meant by research than most other UK trainings in existentialism. There is also less enthusiasm for incorporating the existential with the cognitive (Spinelli and Worrell, 2009, forthcoming).

RESEARCH AND THE POST-EXISTENTIAL

Does this need increasingly to escape from what Aristotle called the 'what is' also apply to what we regard as research? 'Positive psychology', together with positivism and, as already mentioned, such techniques as cognitive behaviour therapy, are increasingly dominating our culture. Indeed, are such rarely questioned contemporary approaches as 'evidence-based practice' the only way we can think about things such that we ensure that thoughts do not come to us? It seems that if those supporting a particular therapeutic approach can afford randomized controlled trials, it cannot then be said that this therapeutic approach is better or worse than another (Seligman, 1995), and the research methods currently in fashion seem not to be able to allow for all the significant variables, such as the characteristics of the therapists (or 'therapist factors') – not to mention their supervisors. Also, what is presented is so often not scientific – for example, Rogerians suddenly have 'treatment goals' (Elliott, 2002); and Freud is also being manualized (for example, Allen and Fonagy, 2006), perhaps in the hope of ensuring public funding.

As a prominent researcher said to me when I questioned what the evidence-based research she had successfully carried out for her modality had to do with truth and justice, 'not a lot about truth but it is justice, as my approach has been accepted'. Of course, selective watering-down is in some ways not new; not only can it be seen to have happened to Freud and Rogers but also to the founding fathers of psychology, like Wilhelm Wundt and William James. Indeed, those like Wundt (1904) insisted that psychology should be not only about the experimental (of which he is regarded as the founder), as this must always be accompanied by the historical and the cultural (a point which will be developed later with regard to Foucault). However, as with positivistic research which is meant to come up with rules of thumb as an aid, instead the measurement becomes the goal, and in this case the treatment goal, thus fundamentally altering the very essence of the original endeavour. What has essentially happened is that the measuring tool now determines the therapy, even though Physis or Phusis is what comes from itself; yet it seems increasingly too difficult for most people to be able to hear what is coming from themselves or from another. It is as if we are now so alienated that we are unable to explore our alienation.

PRACTICE, THE POST-EXISTENTIAL, AND THE TRAINING OF PSYCHOLOGICAL THERAPISTS

The previous discussion with regard to, for example, science has particular implications for the development of practitioners. Whilst existentialism can be seen as healing various dualisms – for example, subject vs object, mind vs body, reason vs passion, fact vs value (Cooper, D., 1990) – neither existentialism nor post-existentialism can, or should, give a primacy to the scientific/technical over the soul. It is vital that the soul comes first. There are of course many ways of facilitating the development of post-existential practitioners, but such programmes may, in their different ways, need to start with, again in different ways, what is increasingly being termed 'relational practice', and find a way of considering science not as technique or positivism, but including the experimental with the cultural and social, yet recognizing that the soul can never be incorporated even by the latter.

Post-existential approaches are likely to attempt to start with practice, and explore what it might mean to be human whilst accepting that we will never fully understand. Indeed, at times considering the writings of those like Merleau-Ponty (1962) who suggests that mystery (not to be confused with mystification) sometimes defines the very thing itself, and Levinas (1989), who warns us of the potential violence through attempting to know. Thus, theories including the psychoanalytic and the post-modern can then come to mind on a case-by-case basis as implication rather than application. There is therefore an important distinction to be made here from the work of those like Askay and Farquhar (2006) who, in contrast to the post-existential, first take psychoanalysis and then examine the existential-phenomenological.

QUESTIONS OF DEFINITION

One way of looking at the Greek roots of existentialism is that it is about something that is both astonishing and ever changing (Heaton, 1990); yet has existentialism got stuck in the nostalgia of the 1950s and 1960s, thus no longer forever changing? What, then, would we need to re-look at? There is also the very question of definition in a post post-modern era. By locating post-existentialism with both some aspects of existentialism and some of post-modernism, this raises the question as to the appropriateness of universalizing definitions. Rather, the attempt here is to locate an approach that is broadly defined and forever open to new possibilities (but not all possibilities).

In fact, existentialism was never clearly defined. It appears to be a term used by the French philosopher Marcel to describe the work of those like Sartre (1943) and De Beauvoir (1972), even though they initially disagreed with being labelled in this way. Heidegger is thought of as probably the most important thinker on existentialism, particularly for psychotherapy. Both Heidegger (1962) and, before him, Kierkegaard (1941, 1980) saw our being as always in the process of becoming, and as such it fundamentally questioned technical categorization. (Besides Heidegger and Kierkegaard, Nietzsche (1883, 1974) can also be seen as an important influence in the development of existentialism.)

In some ways, the method of existentialism might be seen as phenomenology, but again, there has never been agreement about its definition. Husserl's (1983) idea of 'to the things themselves' is grounded in the notion of intentionality, which others, like Sartre, were not at one with. It was however Foucault (1974) who, whilst initially being a strong adherent, criticized phenomenology in the light of developments in structural linguistics. But would it not be possible to take, for example, Merleau-Ponty's notion of phenomenology being to do with what emerges in 'the between', and at times also then consider the implications of Saussure and others for helping us make sense of our being-in-the-world? In fact, it may be even more important to consider what is being suggested in this chapter as not only being post-existential, but in particular post-phenomenological.

What we will then have for post-existentialism is some aspects of existentialism in terms of experience and meaning, together with something from post-phenomenology of what emerges in the between, whilst at the same time allowing to come to mind the developments that have been termed post-modern without getting stuck in them.

FURTHER DIFFERENCES OF POST-EXISTENTIALISM FROM EXISTENTIALISM AND POST-MODERNISM

The post-existential would challenge existentialism, particularly in terms of questions of choice, politics, psychoanalysis, and feminism. Sartre's 'I am my choices' has been taken by many to be about the development of autonomy, for some to the extent that one could almost decide what one wanted to be. The post-existential might be more about finding ourselves taking a certain place where we will have some agency but never full agency: we will always be *subject to*. What we might be subject to can be explored in various ways – for example, heteronomy and ethics (Levinas), an unconscious (Freud), writing and difference (Derrida), and language (Lacan).

From a post-existential perspective we might look at the implications of an aspect of one of these authors for our practice without being fully caught up by a Levinasian, Freudian, Lacanian, or Derridean mode of thought (see Loewenthal, 2006). Indeed, Derrida (1990) acknowledged this in showing us how we are always caught up in a way of looking. So we would end up being destructured, but not to the extent that this makes communication impossible and destabilization too much to take. In some ways it would appear that post-modern ideas on their own have also become too much for people to take, and what we seem to have done is culturally to return to the straightjacket of the positivistic. The post-existential might therefore be seen to lie somewhere between the existential and the post-post-modern.

Other important difference between post-existentialism and existentialism would include greater political awareness. In some ways it seems too easy for existentialists to be fascists or royalists, and for psychotherapists to say that they are not interested in the political. Feminism, as developed by those like Cixous (1975), Irigaray (1977, 1990), and Kristeva (1986), can provide important insights for the post-existential, and some understanding of Lacan would be necessary to reach these important cultural developments.

APPROACHING, POST-PHENOMENOLOGICALLY, THE INDIVIDUAL WITH THE HISTORICAL/CULTURAL

Foucault became interested in power and knowledge and the political status of psychiatry as science. Questioning, through post-existentialism, issues such as well-being, power, and knowledge, and the political nature of psychology as science, would be, in some ways, similar to how Foucault and some existentialists questioned the political status of psychiatry as science. In this, at least a primacy would be given to first thinking of what is termed 'mental illness' as not like a physical illness but more to do with relations with others. Yet there would be vitally important distinctions.

Foucault's (1974) abandonment of his early interest in phenomenology was, as Hoeller (1986) points out, because he took Husserl's notion of transcendental phenomenology, which does not really allow for the historical and cultural. Yet Heidegger, with his *dasein* as being in the historical/cultural world with others, enables phenomenology to be released from Husserl's attempts to show a pure subjectivity, and thus 'a universal doctrine of the structures of individual subjectivity and intersubjectivity' (Hoeller, 1986: 7). Binswanger, Boss, and Laing further developed this opening up of phenomenology for psychotherapy.

Thus, if we could perhaps both be attentive to what emerges in the between of client and therapist and be aware of what is regarded culturally and historically as common sense, we could have an interest in how both our clients and those around them have brought and bring pressures on each other. This meeting, which could include the implications for the present of the client's history and the history of the culture, without being caught up in a potentially totalizing Foucauldian genealogical approach, would be an example of post-phenomenology, and might also be closer to what those like Wilhelm Wundt saw as psychology.

CBT VS POST-EXISTENTIALISM IN PRACTICE

It is suggested here that the underlying assumptions behind CBT are fundamentally different to those behind post-existentialism. If we take the often-quoted scenario where a client speaks of six colleagues, five of whom cheerfully say 'good morning', with one who appears to ignore this particular client: It would appear that there is far less likelihood that the therapist influenced by post-existentialism, as opposed to CBT, will focus on the five colleagues who have been pleasant, or will wonder with the client whether perhaps the one who ignored him was preoccupied with something completely different. There is also a greater likelihood that the post-existential rather than CBT therapist will be influenced by, for example, Kierkegaard's (1944) education by dread (rather than attempting to shore the client up with positive thinking, which some would consider to be part of a systematic attempt to govern through developing a climate of false security); and notions of Lacan (1977), such as that we will never know what the other person thinks, and it is only through allowing a gap, with all its associated anxieties, that desire will emerge. Not only is it important for the individual to be able to doubt if thoughtfulness is to be enabled to flourish, but it is also particularly true for us as a society, otherwise it is more likely that catastrophe will be inevitable.

CONCLUSION

Post-existentialism can therefore be seen, on the one hand, to be attempting to find a place between existentialism and post-post-modernism. Enabling us to take from the existential and the post-modern that which can be helpful to us in exploring our existence at the start of the twenty-first century? Another dimension of post-existentialism is to find a place between natural and social science, though by starting with notions of existence is to imply starting with the human soul (Plato, in Cushman, 2001) and the historical and cultural aspects of social (rather than starting with the natural) science. With this emerges the possibilities of a political viewpoint which, unlike CBT, could engage with various notions of democracy, as well as an unconscious – coming more from those like Kierkegaard (1941, 1980) and Nietzsche (1883, 1974).

I would like to emphasize, again, however, that in developing post-existentialism in part as a reaction to CBT, I am not doubting the integrity of people who are cognitive behaviour therapists, nor that some clients will benefit more from CBT; and furthermore, that in terms of conventional costings it can be more cost effective (but see Chapter 24). There is, however, the danger of any approach, including that of post-existentialism, being a totalizing move; and whilst there have been the dangers of this previously with both psychoanalysis and humanism, CBT (despite the unheard protestations of some of its adherents) appears particularly susceptible to being used in this way.

I have previously attempted to explore some of these dimensions – initially through how individuals and structures in society conspire to produce a form of alienating escape motivation (Loewenthal, 2002). More recently, I have been interested in exploring how post-modernism has emerged from phenomenology (Loewenthal and Snell, 2003), with particular reference to Levinas as a post-existential philosopher (Loewenthal, 2007). There are, of course, others who are developing interesting ideas that have some similarities to what I have described here. For example, there are those who are considering some of Wittgenstein's ideas to question the very nature of how we use theory (Heaton, 2000; House, 2008); whilst, with regard to research, Heideggerian ideas are becoming increasingly in evidence – for example Polkinghorne (2000) and Rennie (2007). Certainly, what these approaches do have in common is a concern with the humanness of the human, which is different from a managerialism based on very narrow notions of so-called evidence with which CBT has come to fit so well. The danger is that rather than being useful for the specific, we are making CBT culturally dominant in a way such that we can no longer recognize ourselves, and are too frightened at any possibility of doing so.

REFERENCES

Allen, J. G. and Fonagy, P. (2006) *The Handbook of Mentalization-based Treatment*, Oxford: Blackwell.

Askay, R. and Farquhar, J. (2006) *Apprehending the Inaccessible: Freudian Psychoanalysis and Existential Phenomenology*, Evanston, Ill.: Northwestern University Press.

Cixous, H. (1975 [1991]) 'The laugh of the Medusa', in R. R. Warhol and D. P. Herndl (eds), (1991) *Feminisms: An Anthology of Literary Theory and Criticism*, NJ: Rutgers University Press.

Cooper, D. E. (1990) *Existentialism: A Reconstruction*, London: Blackwell Publishing.

Cooper, M. (2003) *Existential Therapies*, London: Sage.

Cushman, R. (2001) *Therapeia: Plato's Conception of Philosophy* (new edn), Piscataway, NJ: Transaction Publishers.

De Beauvoir, S. (1972 [1949]) *The Second Sex* (trans. H. M. Parshley), London: Penguin.

Derrida J. (1990) *Resistances to Psychoanalysis*, Stanford: Stanford University Press.

Elliott, R. (2002) 'Hermeneutic single-case efficacy design', *Psychotherapy Research*, 12 (1): 1–21.

Foucault, M. (1974 [1954]) *The Psychological Dimensions of Mental Illness* (trans. A. M. Sheridan-Smith), New York: Harper & Row.

Friedman, M. (1991) *The Worlds of Existentialism: A Critical Reader*, New York: Humanity.

Gordon, J. and Mayo, R. (eds) (2004) *In Between Philosophy and Psychotherapy: Essays from the Philadelphia Association*, London: Whurr Publications.

Heaton, J. (1990) 'What is existential analysis?', *Journal of Existential Analysis*, 1 (1): 1–5.

Heaton, J. (2000) *Wittgenstein and Psychoanalysis*, New York: Totem Books.

Heidegger, M. (1962 [1927]) *Being and Time* (trans. J. Macquarrie and E. S. Robinson), London: Harper & Row.

Hoeller, K. (1986) 'Editor's Foreword – Dream and existence', special issue of *Review of Existential Psychology and Psychiatry*, 23 (1–2): 7–17.

House, R. (2008) 'Therapy's modernist "regime of truth": from scientistic "theory-mindedness" towards the subtle and the mysterious', *Philosophical Practice*, 3 (3): 343–52.

Husserl, E. (1983) *Ideas Pertaining to a Pure Phenomenology and to a Phenomenological Philosophy* (trans. F. Kersten), Nijhoff: The Hague.

Irigaray, L. (1977) *Ce Sexe qui n'en est pas un*, Paris: Editions de Minuit.

Irigaray, L. (1990[1993]) *Je, tu, nous: towards a culture of difference* (trans. A. Martin), London: Routledge.

Kierkegaard, S. (1980 [1844]) *The Concept of Anxiety* (trans. R. Thomte), Princeton, NJ: Princeton University Press.

Kierkegaard, S. (1941 [1855]) *The Sickness unto Death* (trans. W. Lowrie), Princeton, NJ: Princeton University Press.

Kierkegaard, S. (1944 [1848]) *The Concept of Dread* (trans. W. Lowrie), Princeton, NJ: Princeton University Press.

Kristeva, J. (1986) *The Kristeva Reader* (ed. T. Moi), Oxford: Blackwell.

Lacan, J. (1977) *Ecrits: Selected Writings* (trans. A. Sheridan), London: Routledge.

Laing R. D. (1967) *The Politics of Experience*, London: Tavistock Publications.

Laing, R. (1969) *Self and Others*, 2nd edn, London: Routledge.

Laing, R. (1990) *The Divided Self: An Existential Study in Sanity and Madness*, London: Penguin.

Layard, R. (2006) *Happiness: Lessons from a New Science*, London: Penguin.

Levinas, E. (1989 [1984]) 'Ethics as first philosophy', in S. Hands (ed.), *The Levinas Reader*, Oxford: Blackwell, pp. 75–87.

Loewenthal, D. (2002) 'Involvement and emotional labour', *Soundings*, 20: 151–62.

Loewenthal, D. (2006) 'Counselling as a practice of ethics: some implications forTherapeutic Education', *Philosophical Practice*, 2 (3): 143–51.

Loewenthal, D. (2007) *Case Studies in Relational Research*, Basingstoke: Palgrave Macmillan.

Loewenthal, D. (2008) 'Introducing post-existential practice: an approach to wellbeing in the 21st century', *Philosophical Practice*, 3 (3): 316–21.

Loewenthal, D. and Snell, R. (2003) *Postmodernism for Psychotherapists*, London: Routledge.

Loewenthal, D. and Snell, R. (2008) 'The learning community and emotional learning in a university-based training of counsellors and psychotherapists', *International Journal for the Advancement of Counselling*, 30: 38–51.

Merleau-Ponty, M. (1962) *The Phenomenology of Perception* (trans. C. Smith), London: Routledge & Kegan Paul.

Nietzsche, F. (1974 [1882]) *The Gay Science* (trans. W. Kaufman), New York: Vintage Books.

Nietzsche, F. (1883) *Thus Spoke Zarathustra* (trans. A. Tille), New York: Dutton, 1933.

Polkinghorne, D. (2000) 'Psychological inquiry and the pragmatic and hermeneutic traditions', *Theory and Psychology*, 10 (4): 453–79.

Rennie, D. (2007) 'Methodical hermeneutics and humanistic psychology', *The Humanistic Psychologist*, 35 (1): 1–14.

Sartre, J.-P. (1943) *Being and Nothingness: An Essay on Phenomenological Ontology*, trans. H. Barnes, New York: Philosophical Library, 1956.

Seligman, M. (1995) 'The effectiveness of psychotherapy: The Consumer Reports Study', *American Psychologist*, 50 (12): 965–74.

Seligman, M. E. P. (2002) *Authentic Happiness: Using the New Positive Psychology to Realize Your Potential for Lasting Fulfillment*, New York: Free Press.

Spinelli, E. (1989) *The Interpreted World: An Introduction to Phenomenological Psychology*, London: Sage.

Spinelli, E. (2007) *Practicing Existential Psychotherapy: The Relational World*, London: Sage.

Spinelli, E. and Worrell, M. (2009) *Existentially Focused Cognitive Behavioural Therapy*, New York: Wiley.

Van Deurzen, E. (1997) *Everyday Mysteries: Existential Dimensions of Psychotherapy*, London: Routledge (2nd edn, 2006).

Van Deurzen, E. (2001) *Existential Counselling and Psychotherapy in Practice*, London: Sage Publications.

Wundt, W. (1904 [1874]) *Principles of Physiological Psychology* (trans. E. B. Tichener), London: Allen.

CHAPTER 13

DIALOGIC COGNITIVE THERAPY?

TOM STRONG, MISHKA LYSACK,
& OLGA SUTHERLAND

INTRODUCTION

We have been encouraged by continued developments within cognitive behaviour therapy (CBT) and offer 'our' dialogic and discursive (i.e. social constructionist) ideas as resources for where CBT might yet develop. In this chapter we show how these ideas might further critical examination of CBT, should it be narrowly practised in monologic or ideological ways that obscure client preferences and resourcefulness. We also turn a discourse-analytic lens on therapeutic dialogue itself to consider ways CBT could be practised in ways that are collaborative and generative. For us, CBT takes place in dialogues that discursive insights can help to optimize.

The possibility of dialogue has not been ended by those who plan continually for monologue to be followed by cheers of acceptance (Billig, 1996: 109). Cognitive therapy, along with so many other recent cultural developments, has been a site of diversity and hybridity. More a family of theoretically affiliated approaches to therapy than a singular method (e.g. Dobson, 2001), what has been hybrid about CBT is its evolving inclusion of new theoretical and clinical ideas, such as Ellis's (1993) integration of constructivist ideas. We consider CBT a dialogic practice where language use in clinical conversation is its focal activity, and we bring a discourse-analysis and social-constructionist view to CBT. We share our concerns for non-dialogic variants of practice, and in particular for technologizing CBT into a cultural prescription, and will examine conversational practices that show some of CBT's therapeutic aims being met.

We write from a preference for a collaboratively practised CBT that conversationally mobilizes the expertise and resourcefulness of both clients and therapists. For us, therapy is a dialogue occurring at the nexus of many dialogues in which clients and therapists are already engaged. This extends to how we regard 'cognition' since we see it as inseparable from these dialogues (Billig, 1996). Consistent with these different dialogues in which we find ourselves are different ways of understanding and orientating to experience, and to each other. CBT is one such dialogue, one in which client and therapist could refract meanings and other ways of talking in which they are also engaged, and from which they could beneficially talk.

Given our preference for dialogue we are concerned about where CBT has been and could be taken. CBT, practised monologically, could be seen as an ideological instrument

An earlier version of this chapter appeared in the *European Journal of Psychotherapy and Counselling*, 10 (3), 2008, pp. 207–20.

for holding others to particular understandings of reality or particular ways of engaging with it (cf. Bakhtin, 1984; Eagleton, 1991). Variations on this theme come up when practice is reduced to scripts for therapists and clients, or to cultural prescriptions for self-conduct (Layard, 2005). It also comes up in ways CBT might be used with clients: 'administered', 'implemented' – as if therapy were about doing something to a merely receptive client. Closer to our dialogic views are practices within the CBT literature that speak to actively engaging clients in *co*-developing preferred and viable ways of understanding and acting.

We will say more about how we position ourselves within CBT's therapeutic approaches in ways we think are useful for the continued development and hybridization of CBT. We elaborate on what we mean by 'dialogical' practice, relating this to the meaning-making of both clients and therapists, particularly in how they make sense of and respond to each other in clinical interviews. Seeing cognition, discourse, and dialogue as related, we share how relationships between them can generatively inform the practice of CBT. In the other direction, we further articulate our concerns and objections with reducing the practice of CBT to narrow cultural and therapeutic prescriptions. We aim to add to CBT's discussions with our focus on resourceful and collaborative dialogues with clients.

POSITIONING OURSELVES AND CBT

We can't use our minds at full capacity unless we have some idea of how much what we think we're thinking is really thought, and how much is familiar words running along their own familiar tracks. Nearly everyone does enough talking, at least, to become fairly fluent in his own language, and at that point there's always the danger of automatic fluency, turning on a tap, and letting a lot of platitudinous bumble emerge. The best check on this so far discovered is some knowledge of other languages, where at least the bumble has to fit into a different set of grammatical grooves (Frye, 1962: 50).

Our position with respect to CBT is that it involves particular kinds of conversations, the kinds that develop 'their own familiar tracks', as Frye suggests above. So we will link our intentions to some possibly unfamiliar tracks for readers, and relate these to the conversations we aim to have with clients. Each of us has been fortunate to work with the renowned family therapist, Karl Tomm. Tomm (as cited in Godard, 2006) has conceptualized such conversations in terms of the intentions held by therapists as they work with clients, interactions he classifies into four ethical quadrants as seen below in Figure 13.1.

OPENING SPACE, OR INCREASING OPTIONS

The figure is delineated by two continua. The vertical axis refers to the degree to which therapists promote options of practice that restrict or increase client options on the matter of clinical interest. This extends to how therapists might hold clients to their particular therapeutic initiatives or conceptualizations or, conversely, 'open space for' client initiatives and conceptualizations. The horizontal access reflects the degree to which therapists make their knowledge shared, transparent, and contestable; and the degree to which decisions about therapy's goals, procedures, and interventions are shared or expertly prescribed by the therapist.

***Figure 13.1* Karl Tomm's grid of ethical postures as delineated by two continua (axes). Closing Space, or Decreasing Options**

Manipulation	*Confrontation*
Separate, Professional Knowledge, Hierarchical Relationship Succorance	Shared Knowledge, Collaborative Relationship Empowerment

Tomm's quadrants thus make explicit the choices therapists can make in how they 'position' themselves with clients in terms of their use of professional knowledge within therapeutic conversations. We locate our approach to CBT primarily in the lower 'Empowerment' quadrant and see our expertise as focused on collaboratively eliciting and mobilizing clients' expertise in addressing their presenting concerns (Anderson, 1997; Strong, 2002). We focus our expertise on hosting generative therapeutic conversations where decisions about the interview's conduct and progress are made transparently and mutually.

CBT practised from this 'position' requires improvising skill by responsive therapists who open themselves and the therapeutic process to client direction. In our dialogic and constructionist view of CBT, the interview is a construction (or deconstruction) zone collaboratively constructed and maintained (Strong, 2004). CBT's primary focus, the meanings and ways of thinking clients bring to therapy, find their inadequacies or fit in this construction zone. For us, however, thinking and meaning are linked to language as the primary means by which people not only represent their experiences, but influence them as well. We borrow from Wittgenstein (1958), for whom the aptness of language was a paramount concern, and from narrative therapists for whom there can be 'better' discourses or stories for experience (Freedman and Combs, 1996; White and Epston, 1990). CBT, as we envision it, is a collaborative and critically informed search – not for better thinking, but for more viable language (in clients' eyes) to articulate ways forward where clients have been experiencing concerns.

THOUGHT AS DIALOGUE AND DISCOURSE

> 'Reality does not happen "behind the back of language"; it happens rather behind the backs of those who live in the opinion that they have understood "the world" (or can no longer understand it); that is, reality happens precisely *within* language.'
>
> (Gadamer, 1976: 35)

We agree with writers who see thoughts as extensions of dialogue (Beck, 1975; Edwards, 1994; Maranhão, 1986), and find it odd that thoughts could be seen as being apart from dialogue when they are discussed as a part *of* dialogue. We agree with writers such as Vygotsky (1987) that any 'intra'-mental representation or activity begins 'inter'-mentally – between people. Cognition in this sense is a representational activity sustained in dialogue. But there is another dimension brought out by writers such as Michael Billig (1996,

1999), for whom this activity remains rhetorical, not merely representational. By this we refer to how thoughts are partly developed in anticipation of how they might be received in the interactions where they might be put to use. Billig (1999) used the example of repression to illustrate how a repressive style of talking or interacting parallels the internal dynamics (i.e. way of thinking) associated with that style of talking. This is a significant shift away from locating maladaptive thinking in particular constructs or evaluations made by the individual. Rhetorically, the same style of participating in dialogue that preceded a particular thought or way of thinking could sustain it in later dialogues. For us, therefore, *how* conversations occur are as important, if not more important, for therapeutic dialogue as *what* gets discussed in such dialogues.

What therapy can offer is a dialogue outside the hurly-burly of habitual, everyday conversation – a break from the kinds of conversations where others hold us to particular accounts and ways of interacting (Shotter, 1993). Therapists can offer proxy dialogues for those where therapy's outcomes can hopefully be talked into being, while exploring possibilities seemingly unavailable to clients in their everyday conversing. Practised in this way, therapy hinges on a question: how can we have a dialogue different from the ones you have been having with yourself and others, on the matter which brought you to therapy? A therapeutic conversation that occurs in new ways, ways different from one's prior internal and external dialogues, affords possibilities for new mental connections (Wittgenstein, 1958), and new ways of thinking at the same time. Therapy can help clients overcome their stalled projects in dialogue, where lines of talk or inquiry lack a satisfactory resolution until helpful dialogue facilitates this occurring. Not surprisingly, internal dialogue can sometimes be seen as unspeakable dilemmas (Griffith and Griffith, 1994), unspeakable for how what gets said is expected to be received by others. Our CBT reverses Vygotsky's inter- to intra-mental trajectory, by eliciting the not-yet-said aloud, or by welcoming efforts to talk beyond prior dialogic impasses that got similarly stuck internally.

We are of course not alone in seeing cognition as inner dialogue. However, such inner dialogues are often portrayed as eccentric projects hived off from real-world interaction. That doesn't square with our sense of dialogue, or how individuals create and convey understandings via the discourses accessible to them. Emotional life thus finds its meanings and performances in particular discourses, 'language games' (Wittgenstein, 1958), or in what Harré (1986) termed 'emotionologies'. For us, the notion that a construct or schema could be extricated, collaboratively evaluated, or re-construed, to 'therapeutically' be placed back in unchanged patterns or dialogues in clients' lives, comes up short. Thoughts are contextually linked to the inner and outer dialogues where they find their currency. Thus, therapy is a dialogue to transform such contexts.

MOVING FROM MONOLOGIC TO DIALOGIC INTERACTION IN CBT

> 'Individual consciousness is not the architect of the ideological superstructure, but only a tenant lodging in the social edifice of ideological signs.'
>
> (Volosinov, 1986: 39)

There is little doubt that CBT's attention to inner 'talk' and careful use of questions assists clients to construct useful knowledges and actions for making differences in their lives. How this talking occurs merits consideration. Meichenbaum (1996) distinguishes 'rationalist' and 'constructive' perspectives taken up within CBT (Ellis, 1993; Wessler, 1992). Bruner (1990) highlights these differences by contrasting computational knowledges and narrative knowledges. Therapy focused on thought as rationally computed positions both client and therapist differently from therapy that is focused on client story-making. Sampson's (1981) concerns relate to the former stance: cognitive psychology has tended toward subjectivism in granting 'primacy to the structures and processes of the knowing subject' (ibid.: 730) and individualism for centring on the individual knower apart from relationship. Such a view of cognition breaks it into discrete components and mechanisms located *in* individuals. Instead, Sampson (1993) highlighted a relational and social character to human knowing that arises in and from interactions between persons in social and cultural contexts, culminating in an emergence of individuals' unique perspectives or '*voices*' (Bruner, 1990: 77).

MONOLOGUE AND DIALOGUE

Bakhtin's (1984, 1986; Lysack, 2002) distinction between monologue and dialogue has helped us to distinguish differences between *hierarchical* and *collaborative* forms of therapeutic interaction. Bakhtin (1984) outlined the main characteristics of a monologic orientation: 'Monologue manages without the other, and therefore to some degree materializes all reality ...[and] pretends to be the ultimate word' (ibid.: 293–4). However, in relationships orientated by dialogue, human consciousness, life, and relationships combine to construct a shared dialogic space: 'The single adequate form for *verbally expressing* authentic human life is the *open-ended dialogue*. Life by its very nature is dialogic. To live means to participate in dialogue' (ibid.: 293; original emphases). Bakhtin's (1984) distinction between monologue and dialogue relates to an accompanying ethics. It is 'one thing to be in relation to a dead thing, to voiceless material that can be molded and formed as one wishes, and another thing to be active *in relation to someone else's living, autonomous consciousness*' (ibid.: 285; original emphasis). Consistent with a view that knowledge is relational and transactional, he also wrote, 'Truth is not born nor is it to be found inside the head of an individual person, it is born *between people* collectively searching for truth, in the process of their dialogic interaction' (ibid.: 110; original emphasis). For Bakhtin, dialogue is where and how a person is 'constructed'.

DIALOGIC RELATIONSHIP AND EMERGENCE OF VOICE

A dialogical perspective also entails an awareness of the co-presence of voices within language and conversation. This occurs between people *and* within the inner speech of one's consciousness which points to other voices, and to other consciousnesses. For Bakhtin, these voices are not content simply to co-exist alongside of one another, but gravitate to an intense interanimation with one another in what he calls a 'microdialogue' where 'They hear each other constantly, call back and forth to each other, and are reflected in one another' (ibid.: 75).

Like others (Hermans and Kempen, 1993; Hermans et al., 1992; Paré and Lysack, 2004), Penn and Frankfurt (1994) explored therapeutic possibilities of clients shifting from monologue to dialogue in their inner conversations:

> 'Frequently, clients ... tell their first stories as though they were monologues: single-voiced, absolute and closed ... Unlike the monologue, dialogical conversation is many-voiced. It listens to others and is open, inviting, relative, and endless because it is future-oriented. It awaits an answer.'
>
> (ibid.: 223)

We have also found that clients can be dominated by negative inner 'voices', initially experiencing these voices to the exclusion of others. Penn and Frankfurt suggest that in struggling with problems, we construct

> 'an internal monologue that is often experienced as a negative, self-accusing voice: "You're hopeless, you've failed, you're incompetent, unlovable," and so on. However, given the ability to reply to ourselves, we can create a balance of power, so to speak, through the discovery or invention of our other voices – more positive, confident, even ecstatic voices – that can converse with our negative monologue.'
>
> (1994: 218)

Similarly, Meichenbaum (1996) found that clients suffering PTSD from the effects of abuse described themselves as 'spoiled goods', 'damaged property', or 'useless'. He suggests that a client 'may inadvertently reproduce the "voice" of the perpetrator, as in the case of victims of domestic violence. She needs to develop her own voice' (ibid.: 135). For Penn and Frankfurt (1994), this is where a beneficial plurality of voices can come into contact and engage with each other interactively, in what might be called a 'dialogic space' (ibid.: 222).

Such ideas inform our participation in therapy as a dialogic interaction which can generate multiple perspectives while expanding on existing meanings with other possible meanings through responsive dialogue between client and therapist (Lysack, 2005; Paré and Lysack, 2004, Strong, 2003). Therapy can enact a polyphony of voices that Bakhtin saw as crucial to a dialogic orientation. We share Meichenbaum's (1996) view when he suggested that therapists working with clients, '...should not do the thinking for them, nor put words in their mouths' (ibid.: 140).

COGNITIVE MODIFICATION AS DIALOGICAL ACCOMPLISHMENT

> 'Thought is restructured as it is transformed into speech. It is not expressed but completed in the word.'
>
> (Vygotsky, 1987: 251)

One of the significant contributions of CBT has been its focus on 'common-sense psychology' or on people's attempts to define their problems in their own terms (Beck, 1976; Ellis, 1962; Meichenbaum, 1977). Proponents of behaviourist or bio-psychiatric approaches too often dismissed as irrelevant the value of exploring clients' judgements and understandings of their problems. CBT practitioners made people's routine meaning-making a primary target of investigation and intervention. However, many CBT practitioners adopt a correspondence theory of truth, and evaluate clients' appraisals of events and experiences by comparing them to their (purportedly) objectively known reality (Lyddon, 1995). Such therapists assessed and challenged 'incorrect meanings' implicit in clients' reports (Beck, 1976: 95).

In contrast to an 'objectivist' approach, social constructionists (Berger and Luckmann, 1967; Gergen, 1999) focus on meaning as it arises in social interaction. Similarly, discursive psychologists (Edwards, 1994, 1995; Edwards and Potter, 1992) regard meanings as accounts introduced by clients in accomplishing situated interactional work (e.g. such as a question being answered). Discursive psychologists argue that such meanings or accounts evolve over time, and change according to the contexts in which they are occasioned. Different therapists, or even the same therapist on a different occasion, is likely to elicit (or co-articulate) a different account of the client's problem or experience.[1] Hence, discursive and constructionist psychologists maintain that clients' thoughts, attitudes, memories, or even identities are not private events but are communicative accomplishments (Edwards and Potter, 1992; Gergen, 1999). What matters is how participants (therapists and clients) produce their descriptions. The *function* of a client's evaluative or experiential report in interacting with a therapist, as well as the *context* of its production, shapes the precise nature of the report.

Constructionist and critical movements in psychology focus on how socio-cultural, familial, and (inter)personal circumstances occasion particular meanings (cognitions), and how prior meaning shapes such circumstances (Gergen, 1999; Prilleltensky and Nelson, 2002). Some CBT writers also warn against considering cognition, affect, and behaviour apart from contexts that shape and sustain them (Alexander et al., 1996; Baucom et al., 1996; Linehan, 1993; Neimeyer and Cabanillas, 2004; Safran and Segal, 1990). Critically orientated CBT practitioners attend to factors that shape (or constrain) how clients come to cognize themselves and their life situations, aiming to minimize power differentials in the therapeutic relationship (Doherty, 1995; Dunst et al., 1988; McWhirter, 1994; Safran and Muran, 2000). Instead, they promote a dialogic context where clients' problematic meanings and experiences are welcomed, then collaboratively formulated, evaluated, and modified.

Consistent with some approaches to CBT (e.g. Meichenbaum, 1977), constructionists propose that peoples' cognition is derived, created, and maintained in and through interpersonal processes across the lifespan. A common assumption among CBT practitioners is that clients' experiences and appraisals of them are private and relatively stable. Social constructionists 'externalize' clients' 'internal communication system' (Beck, 1976: 26), maintaining that clients' rationality is not internally 'pre-packaged'. Instead, the reality that clients utter has many discursive articulations for understanding and describing that reality, some being formulated and unpacked in the back-and-forth of clients' communication with others, including therapists. Viewing clients' voiced cognitions as emergent in and through interactions of therapist and client challenges traditional conceptions of the therapist as a neutral and objective elicitor and describer of intrapsychic reality. From our perspective,

1. For example, researchers who study discourse of couples therapy demonstrate how systemic therapists deploy specific linguistic devices to transform couples' 'individualist' accounts of their predicaments (he is too distant; she is too critical) into systemic or relational terms (Buttny, 1996; Edwards, 1994).

therapists co-articulate clients' cognitive material, and neither can objectively 'discover' that material (Guidano and Liotti, 1983; Lyddon, 1995; Mahoney, 1988; Safran and Segal, 1990). While clients are conceived as active and purposeful interpreters of events and circumstances, their constructions of reality will overlap in some ways and differ in others from those of the therapist (Neimeyer, 1993). Collaborative and dialogically orientated cognitive behaviour therapists are often pragmatists who recognize that the value and utility of the client's cognitions are established and evaluated conjointly by the client and therapist as they talk (Neimeyer, 2002). They propose to view cognitive-behavioral intervention as *a relational act* (Safran and Muran, 2000; Safran and Segal, 1990) of meaning construction and negotiation. They join clients in their unique ways of construing their lives and experiences, and expand collaboratively on those ways by encouraging clients to step into, or 'try on,' alternative meanings and experiential descriptions (Strong, 2000).

CBT AS IDEOLOGY?

> 'Human beings have largely conquered nature, but they have to still conquer themselves.'
>
> (Layard, 2005: 9)

It may seem a heavy-handed criticism, but some see therapists as being ideological in how their notions and ways of practice can become complicit with dominant cultural aims and norms (Foucault, 1990; Rose, 1990). Typically one associates therapy with expanding one's possibilities for freedom and happiness, not hitching these to some restrictive practice of ideas. Feminists (Brown, 1994; Miller, 1976) and 'radical' psychiatrists (Laing, 1967; Szasz, 1970) have long taken issue with therapy 'helping' clients to adjust to unjust realities. Linking such realities to practised ideologies, however, is a move that makes some uncomfortable, and others suggesting activism (Gergen, 2000). Quite a literature has developed examining therapists' power vis-à-vis that of the client (e.g. Proctor, 2002), particularly in how therapy's dialogues often tilt asymmetrically toward therapist control of the interview and its content (e.g. Antaki, 2001; Davis, 1986). However, the reality–ideology critique, extended to the practice of therapy, has some important implications for the practice of CBT.

In his popular book, *Happiness*, Layard (2005), an economist, invites readers to find their happiness internally. He also argues that depression is of greater concern than poverty (ibid.: 181), and that CBT holds potential to enhance inner control for overcoming moodiness and attaining happiness. Two streams of critique converge for us here (Foucault, 1990; House, 2003; Newman and Holzman, 1997) because therapy can – intentionally or inadvertently – become a quintessential activity in upholding particular moral and cultural orders. CBT's 'realist' approaches can position therapists as expert 'arbiters of correct subjectivity' (Rose, 1990) as if there were correct ways of understanding reality or conducting oneself in it. Our other concern is with turning inward, when addressing what is outward and unjust might be a client preference. At worst, therapists can ignore the external realities of clients' lives, 'helping' them instead *internally* to cope with their thoughts and feelings.

Within the CBT spectrum of approaches, we recognize a range of approaches and opinions on the kinds of concerns we have been raising. Within constructivist CBT circles, one finds construals of reality important, with no focus on correctly articulating reality (as if this could be adjudicated by a knowing therapist). Thus, the dialogical empiricism we see in Beck's practice of Socratic questioning (DeRubeis et al., 2002) can fit here as a means to contest problematic linguistic constructions while searching for *viable* and fitting constructions of reality (Parker, 1998). Realists would see things differently, inviting clients to dispute distortions or maladaptive beliefs, so who decides what is (or whether one has) a distortion or maladaptive belief is therefore of no small concern to us. Within more behaviourally focussed CBT approaches, one finds problem-solving and skill-developing approaches to addressing client-defined realities (e.g. Goldfried, 1995). The client-centred challenge is in tailor-making skills and problem-solving strategies to address client circumstance.

CBT practices of 'self-management', however, are where our Foucaultian concerns and Layard's cultural prescription for happiness collide. Foucault (1994) partly focussed his later career on 'biopower' and 'technologies of the self'. These notions refer to living 'correctly' or 'appropriately', denoting how correctness or appropriateness have specific personal requirements in differing historico-cultural contexts. These are moral requirements as much as they are prescriptions for proper living. Once embedded in psychological discourse, they take on a prescribed and presumed scientific correctness (Cushman, 1995; Danziger, 1997), not unlike the moral correctness one associates with religious practices of confession followed by spiritual direction (Foucault, 1990). CBT's practices of 'self-management' (e.g. Rokke and Rehm, 2001) focus on 'self-instruction', 'self-monitoring', and 'self-control'. The problem here is with the word 'self'. From Foucault's perspective, extended to considering CBT 'self-management practices', this involves taking on CBT in apprenticing oneself to its practices of 'self-subjectification', and policing or disciplining oneself accordingly. Said another way, this is how one learns to be a person on CBT's terms.

Ideology can creep into CBT in insidious ways, even though the intentions behind Layard's prescriptions of CBT are obviously meant to be helpful. The practices and philosophy of certain approaches to CBT, applied as a personal technology for self-conduct, can be seen as a kind of ideology. Where things can get problematically ideological is when, in a sense, clients are instructed to disattend to certain features of their realities that can't be remedied with thought modification (e.g. poverty) or in forms of 'self-monitoring' and 'self-control' that preclude other avenues to happiness and contentment.

CODA

> 'For words only have meaning in the stream of life.'
>
> (Wittgenstein, 1988: aphorism 687)

Our aim here has been to share our dialogic and discursive views on CBT since it has become a dominant and pluralistic presence. We identify with some aspects of CBT's pluralism more strongly than others, and admire its creative hybridity in incorporating research and theoretical developments. Particularly dear to us have been the growing efforts to collaborate with clients in aspects of practice formerly deemed the therapists' prerogatives. In this regard, we have shared our ideas and concerns from social-constructionist theory, dialogue theory, and discursive research, to further discussion on potential new hybrids of CBT. For us, it is fundamentally important to locate the practice of CBT as a dialogic practice, as an activity that takes place in 'streams' of respectful and generative dialogues. We extend this to our thinking about our part in dialogues that might further the practice of CBT in ways we have described.

REFERENCES

Alexander, J. F., Jameson, P. B., Newell, R. M., and Gunderson, D. (1996) 'Changing cognitive schemas', in K. S. Dobson and K. D. Craig (eds), *Advances in Cognitive-behavioural Therapy*, London: Sage, pp. 174–92.

Anderson, H. (1997) *Conversation, Language and Possibilities*, New York: Basic Books.

Antaki, C. (2001) '"D'you like a drink then do you?" – dissembling language and the construction of an impoverished life', *Journal of Language and Social Psychology*, 20: 196–213.

Bakhtin, M. (1984) *Problems of Dostoevsky's Poetics*, Minneapolis: University of Minnesota Press.

Bakhtin, M. (1986) *Speech Genres and Other Late Essays*, Austin: University of Texas Press.

Baucom, D. H., Epstein, N., Raskin, L. A., and Burnett, C. K. (1996) 'Understanding and treating marital distress from a cognitive-behavioral orientation', in K. S. Dobson and K. D. Craig (eds), *Advances in Cognitive-behavioural Therapy*, London: Sage, pp. 210–36.

Beck, A. T. (1976) *Cognitive Therapy and the Emotional Disorders*, New York: International Universities Press.

Berger, P. and Luckmann, T. (1967) *The Social Construction of Reality*, New York: Doubleday.

Billig, M. (1996) *Arguing and Thinking* (2nd revised edn), Cambridge: Cambridge University Press.

Billig, M. (1999) *Freudian Repression: Conversation Creating the Unconscious*, Cambridge: Cambridge University Press.

Brown, L. S. (1994) *Subversive Dialogues: Theory in Feminist Therapy*, New York: Basic Books.

Bruner, J. (1990) *Acts of Meaning*, Cambridge, Mass.: Harvard University Press.

Buttny, R. (1996) 'Clients' and therapist's joint construction of the clients' problems', *Research on Language and Social Interaction*, 29: 125–53.

Cushman, P. (1995) *Constructing the Self, Constructing America: A Cultural History of Psychotherapy*, Cambridge, Mass.: Perseus Publishing.

Danziger, K. (1997). *Naming the Mind: How Psychology Found its Language*, London: Sage.

Davis, K. (1986) 'The process of problem (re)formulation in psychotherapy', *Sociology of Health and Illness*, 8: 44–74.

DeRubeis, R. J., Tang, T. Z., and Beck, A. T. (2002) 'Cognitive therapy', in K. S. Dobson (ed.), *The Handbook of Cognitive Behavioral Therapies* (2nd edn), New York: Guilford, pp. 246–94.

Dobson, K. S. (ed.) (2001) *The Handbook of Cognitive Behavioral Therapies* (2nd edn), New York: Guilford.

Doherty, W. J. (1995) *Soul Searching: Why Psychotherapy Must Promote Moral Responsibility*, New York: Basic Books.

Dunst, C. J., Trivette, C. M., and Deal, G. (1988) *Enabling and Empowering Families: Principles and Guidelines for Practise*, Cambridge, Mass.: Brookline Books.

Eagleton, T. (1991) *Ideology: An Introduction*, London: Verso.

Edwards, D. (1994) 'Script formulations: a study of event descriptions in conversation', *Journal of Language and Social Psychology*, 13: 398–417.

Edwards, D. (1995) 'Two to tango: script formulations, dispositions and rhetorical asymmetry in relationship trouble talk', *Research on Language and Social Interaction*, 28: 319–50.

Edwards, D., and Potter, J. (1992) *Discursive Psychology*, London: Sage.

Ellis, A. (1962) *Reason and Emotion in Psychotherapy*, New York: Lyle Stuart.

Ellis, A. (1993) 'Constructivism and rational-emotive therapy: a critique of Richard Wessler's critique', *Psychotherapy*, 30: 531–2.

Foucault, M. (1990) *The History of Sexuality: An Introduction. Volume 1*, New York: Vintage.

Foucault, M. (1994) *Ethics: Subjectivity and Truth. Essential Works of Michel Foucault 1954–1984*. Volume I (ed. P. Rabinow), New York: The New Press.

Freedman, J. and Combs, G. (1996) *Narrative Therapy: The Social Construction of Preferred Realities*, New York: Norton.

Frye, N. (1962) *The Educated Imagination*, Concord, Canada: House of Anansi Press.

Gadamer, H.-G. (1976) *Philosophical Hermeneutics* (ed. and trans. D. E. Linge), Berkeley: University of California Press.

Gergen, K. (2000) 'From identity to relational politics', in L. Holzman and J. Morss (eds), *Postmodern Psychologies, Societal Practise, and Political Life*, New York: Routledge, pp. 130–50.

Godard, G. (2006) *Love, Violence and Consciousness: Ethical Postures for Therapist Positioning*, Final Project submitted for the Master of Counselling degree, Campus Alberta Applied Psychology: Counselling Initiative.

Goldfried, M. R. (1995) *From Cognitive Behavior Therapy to Psychotherapy Integration*, New York: Springer.

Griffith, J. and Griffith, M. (1994) *The Body Speaks*, New York: Basic Books.

Guidano, V. F. and Liotti, G. (1983) *Cognitive Processes and Emotional Disorders*, New York: Guilford.

Harré, R. (ed.) (1986) *The Social Construction of Emotions*, Oxford: Blackwell.

Hermans, H. and Kempen, H. (1993) *The Dialogical Self: Meaning as Movement*, San Diego, Calif.: Academic Press.

Hermans, H., Kempen, H., and van Loon, R. (1992) 'The dialogical self: beyond individualism and rationalism', *American Psychologist*, 47 (1): 23–33.

House, R. (2003) *Therapy Beyond Modernity: Deconstructing and Transcending Profession-centred Therapy*, London: Karnac Books.

Laing, R. D. (1967) *The Politics of Experience and the Bird of Paradise,* Baltimore: Penguin.

Layard, R. (2005) *Happiness: Lessons from a New Science*, London: Penguin.

Linehan, M. M. (1993) *Cognitive-behavioral Treatment of Borderline Personality Disorder*, New York: Guilford.

Lyddon, W. J. (1995) 'Cognitive therapy and theories of knowing: a social constructionist view', *Journal of Counseling and Development*, 73: 579–85.

Lysack, M. (2002) 'From monologue to dialogue in families: internalized other interviewing and Mikhail Bakhtin', *Sciences pastorales/Pastoral Sciences*, 21 (2): 219–44.

Lysack, M. (2005) 'Empowerment as an ethical and relational stance: some ideas for a framework for responsive practices', *Canadian Social Work Review*, 22(1): 31–51.

McWhirter, E. H. (1994) *Counseling for Empowerment*, Alexandria, Va.: American Counseling Association.

Mahoney, M. J. (1988) 'Constructive metatheory: basic features and historical foundations', *International Journal of Personal Construct Psychology*, 1: 1–35.

Maranhão, T. (1986) *Therapeutic Discourse and Socratic Dialogue*, Madison: University of Wisconsin Press.

Meichenbaum, D. (1977) *Cognitive Behavioral Modification*, New York: Plenum.

Meichenbaum, D. (1996) 'Cognitive-behavioral treatment of Posttraumatic Stress Disorder from a narrative constructivist perspective: a conversation with Donald Meichenbaum', in M. Hoyt (ed.), *Constructive Therapies: Volume 2*, New York: Guilford, pp. 124–47.

Miller, J. B. (1976) *Toward a New Psychology of Women*, Boston, Mass.: Beacon.

Neimeyer, R. A. (1993) 'An appraisal of constructivist psychotherapies', *Journal of Consulting and Clinical Psychology*, 61: 221–34.

Neimeyer, R. A. (2002) 'The relational co-construction of selves: a postmodern perspective', *Journal of Contemporary Psychotherapy*, 32 (1): 51–9.

Neimeyer, R. A. and Cabanillas, W. E. (2004) 'Epistemology and psychotherapy: a constructivist conversation', in J. D. Raskin and S. K. Bridges (eds), *Studies in Meaning 2: Bridging the Personal and Social in Constructivist Psychology*, New York: Pace University Press, pp. 69–83.

Newman, F. and Holzman, L. (1997) *The End of Knowing*, New York: Routledge.

Paré, D. and Lysack, M. (2004) 'The willow and the oak: from monologue to dialogue in the scaffolding of therapeutic conversations', *Journal of Systemic Therapies*, 23 (1): 6–20.

Parker, I. (ed.) (1998) *Social Constructionism, Discourse and Realism*, London: Sage.

Penn, P. and Frankfurt, M. (1994) 'Creating a participant text: writing, multiple voices, narrative multiplicity', *Family Process*, 33: 217–31.

Prilleltensky, I. and Nelson, G. (2002) *Doing Psychology Critically: Making a Difference in Diverse Settings*, New York: Palgrave Macmillan.

Proctor, G. (2002) *The Dynamics of Power in Counselling and Psychotherapy*, Ross-on-Wye: PCCS Books.

Rokke, P. D. and Rehm, L. P. (2001) 'Self-management therapies', in K. S. Dobson (ed.), *The Handbook of Cognitive Behavioral Therapies* (2nd edn), New York: Guilford, pp. 173–210.

Rose, N. (1990) *Governing the Soul: The Shaping of the Private Self*, New York: Routledge.

Safran, J. D. and Muran, J. C. (2000) *Negotiating the Therapeutic Alliance: A Relational Treatment Guide*, New York: Guilford.

Safran, J. D. and Segal, Z. V. (1990) *Cognitive Therapy: An Interpersonal Process Perspective*, New York: Basic Books.

Sampson, E. (1981) 'Cognitive psychology as ideology', *American Psychologist*, 36: 730–43.

Sampson, E. (1993) 'Identity politics: challenges to psychology's understanding', *American Psychologist*, 48(12): 1219–30.

Shotter, J. (1993) *Conversational Realities*, London: Sage.

Strong, T. (2000) 'Six orienting ideas for collaborative counselors', *European Journal of Psychotherapy, Counselling and Health*, 3 (1): 25–42.

Strong, T. (2002) 'Collaborative "expertise" after the discursive turn', *Journal of Psychotherapy Integration*, 12: 218–32.

Strong, T. (2003) 'Dialogue in therapy's "borderzone"', *Journal of Constructivist Psychology*, 15: 245–62.

Strong, T. (2004) 'Ethical "construction zones" in Psychology's big tent', *International Journal of Critical Psychology*, 11: 131–52.

Szasz, T. S. (1970) *The Manufacture of Madness*, New York: Delta.

Volosinov, V. N. (1986) *Marxism and the Philosophy of Language*, Cambridge, Mass.: Harvard University Press.

Vygotsky, L. S. (1987) *The Collected Works of L. S. Vygotsky. Volume 1. Problems of General Psychology*, New York: Plenum.

Wessler, R. L. (1992) 'Constructivism and rational-emotive therapy: a critique', *Psychotherapy*, 29: 620–5.

White, M. and Epston, D. (1990) *Narrative Means to Therapeutic Ends*, New York: Norton.

Wittgenstein, L. (1958) *Philosophical Investigations* (3rd edn) (trans. G. Anscombe), New York: MacMillan.

Wittgenstein, L. (1988) *Remarks on the Philosophy of Psychology*, Volume II (ed. H. Nyman and G.H. von Wright; trans. C. G. Luckhardt), Chicago: University of Chicago Press.

CHAPTER 14

THINKING THOUGHTFULLY ABOUT COGNITIVE BEHAVIOUR THERAPY

JOHN D. KAYE

> 'In the varied topography of professional practice, there is a hard, high ground, which overlooks a swamp. On the high ground, manageable problems lend themselves to solution through the use of research based theory and technique. In the swampy lowlands, problems are messy and confusing and incapable of technical solution... in the swamp lie the problems of greatest human concern.'
>
> (Donald A. Schön)

INTRODUCTION

The past decade in Australia has witnessed an increasing realization of the prevalence of high rates of depression in the community, inadequate treatment opportunities, and the associated social, familial, and economic costs to the community. As a result of this awareness, together with pressing concern and representations to the Federal Minister of Health on the part of health and welfare bodies including the Australian Psychological Society, the Australian Government legislated for the 'Better Outcomes in Mental Health Care' programme. Under this initiative, patients referred by their General Practitioner were enabled to claim a rebate under Australia's universal Medicare system for psychological services, including psychotherapy provided by registered psychologists. This latter reflects acceptance by the authorities of the claim that the treatment programmes offered by psychologists have a scientific basis. Given that cognitive behaviour therapy (CBT) is the most validated psychotherapeutic modality in the research literature (or, rather, given its claims to be evidence based), it has gained the status as the 'treatment of choice' for conditions such as depression, anxiety, obsessional-compulsive disorder, and social phobia.

My aim in this chapter is not to engage in a detailed deconstruction of the paradigm governing CBT, as this has been fully addressed elsewhere in this book. Nor is it critically to deconstruct the 'Scientist Practitioner' model which forms the foundation of most Clinical Masters and Ph.D. degrees in Australia, and to which most practising psychologists pay lip-service while also employing methods drawn from other schools of therapy (e.g. Solution Focussed Therapy, Systemic Family Therapy, Collaborative Therapy, Narrative Therapy) when confronted with the exigencies of practice. Rather my aim is to:

- critique some of the governing paradigm's limits and consequences;
- question the privileged status granted to CBT; and
- briefly consider innovations such as Mindfulness-based Cognitive Behaviour Therapy (MCBT) and Acceptance and Commitment Therapy (ACT).

ON THE RHETORICAL CONSTRUCTION OF THE SCIENTIST PRACTITIONER MODEL AND CBT

In advocating for Psychology's rightful place as a preferred provider of psychotherapeutic treatment and in establishing Psychology's scientific credentials, the Australian Psychological Society has constructed a base of scientific credibility drawing on positivist and empiricist views of what constitutes scientific knowledge and legitimate research. In achieving this, it has based itself on positivist and empirical views of the nature of scientific knowledge and within that frame, legitimate scientific research. Its advocatory role in employing legitimating rhetoric drawing on the authority of science as the underpinning of the much-vaunted 'Scientist Practitioner' model cannot be underestimated. Its rhetoric has certainly proved to be invaluable in establishing Psychology's stake in the provision of therapeutic services, its place in the market-place, and its reputation for accountability.

In turn, the acceptance by the mainstream profession of the Scientist Practitioner model, and the nature of the evidence supporting the efficacy of CBT, is obdurately maintained in spite of consistent critique of its governing positivist paradigm (Gergen, 1985, 1987; Hoffman, 1993; John, 1987, 1998; Kaye, 2003; Martin, 1989); in spite of critiques of the nature of the evidence cited in support of CBT (Bohart, 2002; Wampold, 2001); and in spite of evidence from meta-analytic studies of therapeutic efficacy citing outcome equivalence across all therapies (Ahn and Wampold, 2001; Luborsky et al., 1975; Smith and Glass, 1997). That is, despite differing theoretical orientations between schools of therapy, research has not yielded demonstrable differences in effective outcomes. Thus, contemporarily there is no conclusive evidence of differential effects between therapies, despite consistent research efforts to establish primacy of the medical-model based CBT approaches.

This being so, it can be said with reasonable certainty that the primacy granted CBT by its proponents is based more on obstinate true belief in its governing scientistic paradigm and its accompanying legitimizing rhetoric, rather than on hard evidence – a somewhat savage irony for a discipline that prides itself on being empirically supported! The privileged status granted to the category 'CBT', while definable in terms of a set of attributes and methods (e.g. Beck 1972, 1976; Greenberger and Padesky, 1995; Wells, 1997) is the result of a particular form of rhetorical advocacy on the part of behavioural scientists with interests to serve, and a stake to protect. As John (1987: 227) puts it:

> '...what is ultimately to be resolved is who is to be authorised or legitimated to adjudicate claims for inclusion in the category and how this is to be justified. The definition of the term is a political, rather than an empirical matter, and the meaning accorded to it can only be grasped in relation to the wider social historical context in which it is embedded.'

To quote John further:

> 'That is, the portrayal or representation of psychotherapy as an applied science serves an ideological function of legitimating particular claims concerning the nature of psychotherapy and in doing so of advancing and securing political

> objectives, amongst which are the social and economic interests of various groups of psychologists.'
>
> (ibid.: 283)

If Psychology's mission is to generate knowledge about human behaviour and to apply this knowledge to the promotion of human welfare, the question arises whether the specification of CBT as the authorized treatment modality to the exclusion of other therapies necessarily benefits those people who approach us for help in overcoming the full range of psychological/ emotional dilemmas, relationship problems, and problems in living. What is considered to be evidence-based practice mandates only those therapies utilizing a particular set of methodologies established and assessed by randomized controlled trials aimed at specific disorders (Chambless and Ollendick, 2001). The research methodology in many studies utilizes experimental manipulations under control conditions vastly different to those in 'real life' clinical conditions – conditions that meta-analyses have shown to be effective. In this sense, the evidence favouring empirically supported treatments can be construed as evidence *biased* – biased against other forms not similarly tested. Attention focuses on methodological critique rather than on outcome as a way of discrediting the efficacy of therapies outside of the parameters set by the empirically supported treatments (EST) lobby (Westen et al., 2004). In this sense a pro-EST, politically driven ideology militates against the acceptance of such therapies.

A further question arises then of the *ethic* of authorizing CBT at the expense of other therapies when (a) therapeutic modalities emerging from other traditions such as the post-foundational turn to language have been shown to produce positive outcomes, and (b) there are problems in restricting practice to CBT techniques. To address this issue it is necessary to discuss the role of paradigms.

ON PARADIGMS AND PARADIGMATIC ASTIGMATISM: A BRIEF CRITIQUE

All psychotherapies are governed by a paradigm – a disciplinary narrative consisting of a set of interlinked propositions undergirded by presuppositions which together constitute the boundaries of its knowledge domain, and which direct its practice. As I have written elsewhere (Kaye, 2005: 180):

> '...these presuppositions produce and sustain what Foucault (1980) labels "truth effects" and as Parker (1995) points out they function as a necessary part of the "regime of truth" that is at work. They are constructed assumptions that shape our view of phenomena and within the parameters of the paradigm are held to be true – impervious to criticism and inviolable. The paradigm also mandates rules of procedure governing sanctioned research and practice to which members of the discipline are constrained to adhere. In turn it guides the assumptions made by the practitioner, the questions he or she might ask and the interpretations made. Unfortunately, just as the presuppositions and rules that govern a model

> (in this case one such as the "scientist practitioner" and its offspring, mainstream CBT) define its boundaries, so they also constitute limits.'

In the case of psychotherapy, these limits disqualify phenomena that, from the viewpoints of alternate paradigms, are crucial to the understanding of human experience – or indeed those core anxieties, and profound, deeply embodied experiential and existential fears that so trouble people. They also exclude consideration of the socio-cultural networks of ideas, values, and practices by which people are positioned – let alone the interactional nature of the problems people experience in their relationships. In this regard, it is crucial to understand that problems do not necessarily reside *within* the individual – they are the product of the relationship between people and how they interact around issues, and are thus not simply attributable to any one person. According to the Emergent Principle (Checkland, 1988), relational problems are an emergent – with the interrelatedness of units in a system giving rise to new qualities that are a function of that very relatedness. Bearing this in mind, any problem assessment that focusses solely on individual characteristics, cognitions, or construals is of necessity limited and misleading.

However, the paradigm that informs cognitive behaviour therapy is predominantly essentialist and individual focussed. That is, it assumes:

1. an underlying cause or basis of pathology
2. the location of this cause within individuals, their behaviour, and cognitions
3. the diagnosability of the problem
4. treatability via a specifically designed set of techniques.

According to the current author:

> 'Implicit in these suppositions are the concepts of normality and abnormality, the normatively good or bad and the presumption of a true root cause that can be objectively established, known and remediated. Within this frame, therapy can be seen as an instrumental practice consisting of the treatment of what is judged to be mental disorder and abnormal or dysfunctional behaviour. Therapists working within these parameters seek to bring about a restructuring or reprogramming of behaviour ... against some criterion of the normal, the deviant, the well-adjusted, the problematic and the non-problematic.'
>
> (Kaye, 2003: 227)

It follows that therapeutic activity in this frame involves the translation of the consultee's story into the therapist's frame of reference, and engages them actively in reinterpreting their narrative within the therapist-provided frame.

This process, further, is potentially prejudicial to the consultee's interests. In translating a client's account of experience into the concepts governing their model, clinicians impose their theoretical structure on the client's account such that the person's views are perceived through the monocular funnel of the therapist's theoretical lens and rendered secondary – a form of hegemonic psychological colonization. The translation, too, circumscribes the possible ways in which the problem can be construed, and the nature of the therapist's questioning itself helps forge the causal link to the conclusion drawn by the practitioner. As Spence (1982: 29) puts it:

> '[The therapist] is constantly making decisions about the form and status of the patient's material. Specific listening conventions... help to guide these decisions. If, for example, the analyst assumes that contiguity indicates causality, then he will hear a sequence of disconnected statements as a causal chain... If he assumes the transference predominates and that the patient is always talking, in more or less disguised fashion, about the analyst, then he will hear the material in that way and make some kind of ongoing evaluation of the state of the transference.'

In this way, therapists, guided by the categories mandated by their theory, *produce* what is taken to be the problem, and may well devise ingenious solutions to the wrong problem.

Seeking to establish the nature of the problem can be pathologizing in a further way. Berg and De Shazer (1993: 8) writing about 'problem talk' put it this way:

> 'As we listen to people describe their problems and search for an explanation, "fact" piles up upon "fact" and the problem becomes heavier and heavier. The whole situation can quickly become overwhelming, complicated and perhaps even hopeless... Such problem-talk, talking more about what is not working is doing more of the same of something that has not worked. ...Simply, the more clients and therapists talk about so-called facts the greater the problem they jointly construct.'

This, together with the assumption of a problem residing in the individual, as well as its expression in a language of deficit or deficiency, can indeed prove iatrogenic, leading the consultee directly into what Gergen (1991) has called a spiral of infirmity. In this interaction, the therapist is positioned as the knowing expert while the client, implicitly informed of his or her deficiency, is furnished a lesson in inferiority.

The individualization of distress, further, can divert attention from the socio-cultural siting of a consultee's problem, subtly in turn enjoining him or her to adjust to the unjust – unemployment for example, redundancy, marginalization, or discrimination.

MODERNIST THERAPY AS REGULATIVE PRACTICE

The majority of mainstream cognitive behaviour therapies draws on socio-culturally derived or disciplinary discourses embodying what constitutes 'normality' or 'abnormality', adjustment or maladjustment. Given also their assumed value neutrality, they tend to be blind to the broad cultural conditions that govern their precepts and practices. In this way, they are unknowingly infused with ideologically saturated 'regimes of truth' specifying particular power relations between consultant and consultee, and governing the nature of the interaction. The process is vested with particular techniques of discursive regulation or practices of power, that in turn produce, maintain, and reproduce particular rules and practices, including specific 'technologies' of self.

In this light, modernist CBT therapies may be seen as socially regulative in that they may position their subjects to become complicit in their own subjugation by being recruited into conforming to particular specifications of personhood carried in dominant assumptions of normality and the moral codes governing exemplary being – discursive formations which problematized their experience in the first place. As Rose (1990) asserts, therapy may well co-opt people into engaging in practices or technologies of the self in which they attempt to discipline, govern, or change themselves in relation to mandated specifications of personhood, while attention is drawn away from socially oppressive structures and practices.

If, as a socially sanctioned disciplinary technology, modernist CBT psychotherapy does unreflectively reproduce dominant discourses and mechanisms of control while masking inegalitarian regimes of truth, if the practice implicates the subjects of the discipline in their own subjection (Foucault, 1979, 1988), it thereby exercises limiting and subjugating effects. Its very instantiation of self-examination draws attention to the personal while excluding attention to discursive positioning, thereby immuring people within essentialist identities that constrain change.

Within the above frame, mainstream CBT may be construed as an ideologically infused practice which: (a) supports the social order; (b) may serve as an instrument of social control preserving the dominant culture; and (c) maintains inequitable social conditions and arrangements which may be constitutive of the problems people experience (White, 1991). On this view, such treatments may unwittingly act to perpetuate the causes of the problem they seek to treat by confirming and normalizing oppressive or problematizing social beliefs, norms, and mores.

FROM FIRST-ORDER TO SECOND-ORDER CBT

Traditional or what I call first-order CBT seeks to alter what is seen to be maladaptive behaviour by means of modifying its underpinnings in the form of associated thoughts and assumptions presumed to be 'dysfunctional'. It involves acting on peoples' accounts of their problem through the narrow lens of cognitive theory. However, amidst the ranks of CBT's true believers are some practitioners who have become aware of problems with this approach both conceptually and in practice.

First, there is the problem of engaging in 'more of the same' problem talk as that which in itself is part of the problem, and acts to maintain and even intensify it (Hayes and Batten, 1999) – a fact that strategic and solution-focussed therapies, emerging as they do from an alternate non-linear post-foundational paradigm, have argued for some years. Secondly, there is empirically established evidence of resistance to CBT's emphasis on change (Linehan, 1993) – especially, I believe, where embodied emotion-saturated core beliefs central to a person's sense of psychological safety are threatened. This is likely to trigger defence or resistance – engaging the protagonists in a counter-therapeutic battle for control of the 'symptom'. *Symptoms, symptomatic behaviour, and their thought associations have a function* – they can serve a protective purpose, for example, or, in the consultee's mind, are the only way of dealing with anxieties and shame, or life circumstances and occurrences seen as intolerable or threatening. Put another way, they are emotionally clung to, being central to the person's sense of self-preservation, well-being, and indeed their very sense of existential being. In this sense *they are functional rather than dysfunctional* and stubbornly defended against intrusion. Insistence on change invites resistance! And unfortunately, where the therapist acts unwittingly to induce change, this can lead to its opposite – problem maintenance, in which the person persists in the pattern of thinking and acting that reinforces the problem!

Some understanding of the above has led to a shift from first-order to what I call second-order CBT – a move from a focus on the *category* of problem 'dysfunctional thoughts/ dysfunctional behaviour/intersection' to a focus on the *superordinate class* 'thinking'.Thus, mindfulness-based cognitive therapy (MCBT) (Segal et al., 2002) and Acceptance and Commitment Therapy (ACT) (Hayes and Batten, 1999) have adopted an approach in which the attention is not on acting to modify thoughts considered dysfunctional, but rather on the superordinate concept of how they are maintained. In essence this constitutes a shift in paradigm. Both approaches *defocus* from the problem – the link between thinking and feeling – to how feelings are maintained (e.g. by experiential avoidance), and both focus on acceptance of whatever is experienced.

Mindfulness is an experiential approach utilizing awareness exercises with an emphasis on the development of a non-judgemental, curious, receptive attitude via a structured programme. In this, it fosters self-acceptance as against rejection/avoidance of experience, with the core aim being

> 'to help participants develop a different way of relating to sensations, thoughts, and feelings - specifically, mindful acceptance and acknowledgement of unwanted feelings and thoughts, rather than habitual, automatic, pre-programmed routines that tend to perpetuate difficulties'.
>
> (Segal et al., 2002: 86)

The approach is not crudely to work to overcome negative thoughts (first order) but to attend to these with interest and comfort, and for this sense to spread to a general sense of well-being as an embodied counter to negative or depressive ideation. In this, it is apparent that there is not only a similarity to exposure approaches but to Victor Frankl's paradoxical intention, the paradoxical methods used by the Mental Research Institute (MRI) school at Palo Alto, and the Gestalt focus on awareness-raising in the here and now. Mindfulness seeks to enable a different stance toward troubling issues and emotions: the ability to adopt a state of reflective awareness toward feelings, as opposed to one of non-reflective awareness in which one is engulfed by them.

In turn, for Acceptance and Commitment Therapy, 'seeing thoughts and feelings as the problem is itself part of the problem, and solutions based on this analysis is also part of the problem' (Hayes and Batten, 1999: 2). In common with MCBT, ACT seeks to counteract coping strategies that focus on avoidance of experience, and to develop the willingness to remain in touch with private experiences construed as negative. Beyond this, ACT has a characteristic focus on language and the meanings people attribute to their experience, differentiating between what people take to be 'givens' and pragmatic truth and how we become fused with the meanings socially given to particular experiences. Thus, according to Hayes and Batten (1999: 1), 'One of the core elements of ACT is undermining this type of cognitive fusion by altering the normal verbal context provided by the social/verbal community.'

From this it is clear that ACT's guiding principles are consistent with both the turn to language in the social sciences, and the constructivist and social constructionist concepts that our realities are socially constructed and language-constituted. Thus, the constructs that govern peoples' experience, and indeed our psychological practices, are just that – constructs, and not invariant truths.

It should be clear, finally, that CBT, given theoretical developments based on constructs outside its original governing paradigm and utilizing techniques drawing from therapeutic models inconsistent with that paradigm, is not a homogeneous static entity. The field known as CBT has undergone a process of transformation in which one or more of its parameters have been altered. Thus, it is no longer restricted to the set of procedures so proudly touted as the one uniquely evidence-based method of therapy, even while its enhanced intervention repertoire is still conveniently gathered under the rubric 'CBT' for public consumption and the benefit of the industry. Ironically, what could simply be called Mindfulness Therapy still seeks the security and respectability conferred by the 'CBT' acronym!

Finally, one can only applaud those innovators who have had the courage to step outside of the limited view of therapy and the impoverished conceptualization of human ways of being imposed by traditional cognitive behaviour thinking, with its narrow concept of the cognition/behaviour nexus. This model can no longer claim to be to be *the* preferred method of choice. The contemporary contextual therapies (such as MCBT and ACT), with their enriched but still systematic approach to therapy, offer expanded possibilities, and the ability creatively to confront life's more profound existential and emotional challenges, problems of spiritual emptiness, or the sense of meaninglessness and disconnection that afflict so many – Schön's swamplands. This can only be to the benefit of consumers – those who come to us for help, and deserve better than the rigid methodologies imposed by the unimaginative guardians of the original CBT faith!

REFERENCES

Ahn, H. and Wampold, B. E. (2001) 'Where oh where are the specific ingredients? A meta-analysis of component studies in counselling and psychotherapy', *Journal of Counselling Psychology*, 48 (3): 251–7.

Beck, A. T. (1972) *Depression: Causes and Treatment*, Philadelphia: University of Pennsylvania Press.

Beck, A. T. (1976) *Cognitive Therapy and the Emotional Disorders*, New York: International Universities Press.

Berg, I. K. and De Shazer, S. (1993) 'Making numbers talk: language in therapy', in S. Friedman (ed.), *The New Language of Change*, New York, Guilford Press.

Bohart, A. (2002) 'A passionate critique of empirically supported treatments and the provision of an alternative paradigm', in J. C. Watson, R. N. Goodman, and M. S. Warner (eds), *Client-centered and Experiential Psychotherapy in the 21st Century: Advances in Theory, Research and*

Practice, Llangarron, UK: PCCS Books, pp. 258–77.
Chambless, D. and Ollendick, T. (2001) 'Empirically supported psychological interventions: controversies and evidence', *Annual Review of Psychology*, 52: 685–716.
Checkland, P. (1988) *Systems Thinking, Systems Practice*, Chichester: Wiley.
Foucault, M. (1979) *Discipline and Punish: The Birth of the Prison*, Middlesex: Peregrine Books.
Foucault, M. (1988) *The Care of the Self: The History of Sexuality, Vol. 3*, London: Allen Lane/ Penguin Press.
Gergen, K. J. (1985) 'The social constructionist movement in modern psychology', *American Psychologist*, 90: 266–75.
Gergen, K. J. (1987) 'The language of psychological understanding', in H. J. Stam, T. B. Rogers, and K. J. Gergen (eds), *The Analysis of Psychological Theory*, Cambridge: Hemisphere.
Gergen, K. J. (1991) *The Saturated Self: Dilemmas in Identity in Contemporary Life*, New York: Basic Books.
Greenberger, D. and Padesky, C. A. (1995) *Mind over Mood: Change How You Feel by Changing the Way You Think*, New York: Guilford Press.
Hayes, S. C. and Batten, S. V. (1999) 'Acceptance and Commitment Therapy', *European Psychology*, 1 (1): 2–9.
Hoffman, L. (1993) *Exchanging Voices: A Collaborative Approach to Family Therapy*, London: Karnac Books.
John, I. D. (1987) 'The social construction of psychotherapy and psychological practice', *Australian Psychologist*, 22 (3): 275–89.
John, I. D. (1998) 'The scientist-practitioner model: a critical examination', *Australian Psychologist*, 33 (1): 24–30.
Kaye, J. D. (2003) 'Psy no more: toward a non-iatrogenic psychotherapy', in Y. Bates and R. House (eds), *Ethically Challenged Professions: Enabling Innovation and Diversity in Psychotherapy and Counselling*, Ross on Wye: PCCS Books.
Kaye, J. D. (2005) 'Reconstituting psychology's paradigm: toward a reformulated disciplinary practice', in A. Gülerce, A. Hofmeister, I. Staeuble, G. Saunders, and J. Kaye (eds), *Contemporary Theorising in Psychology: Global Perspectives*, Concord, Canada: Captus Press.
Linehan, M. M. (1993) *Cognitive Behavioural Treatment of Borderline Personality Disorder*, New York: Guilford Press.
Luborsky, L., Singer, B., and Luborsky, L. (1975) 'Comparative studies of psychotherapies', *Archives of General Psychiatry*, 32: 995–1008.
Martin, P. R. (1989) 'The scientist-practitioner model and clinical psychology: time for a change?', *Australian Psychologist*, 24: 71–92.
Rose, N. (1990) 'Psychology as a social science', in I. Parker and J. Shotter (eds), *Deconstructing Social Psychology*, London: Routledge.
Schön, D. (1992) 'The crisis of professional knowledge and the pursuit of an epistemology of practice', *Journal of Interprofessional Care*, 6 (1): 49–63.
Segal, Z., Williams, J., and Teasdale, J. (2002) *Mindfulness-based Cognitive Therapy for Depression: A New Approach to Preventing a Relapse*, New York: Guilford Press.
Smith, M. L. and Glass, G. V. (1997) 'Meta-analysis of psychotherapy outcome studies', *American Psychologist*, 32: 752–60.
Spence, D. (1982) *Narrative Truth and Historical Truth*, New York: Norton.
Wampold, B. (2001) *The Great Psychotherapy Debate: Models, Methods and Findings*, Mahwah, NJ: Erlbaum.

Wells, A. (1997) *Cognitive Therapy of Anxiety Disorders*, Chichester: Wiley.

Westen, D., Novotny, C. M., and Thompson-Brenner, H. (2004) 'The empirical status of empirically supported psychotherapies: assumptions, findings and reporting. I. Controlled clinical trials', *Psychological Bulletin*, 130 (4): 631–63.

White, M. (1991) 'Deconstruction and therapy', *Dulwich Centre Newsletter* (Adelaide), 3: 21–40.

Chapter 15

CBT AND EMPIRICALLY VALIDATED THERAPIES:

INFILTRATING CODES OF ETHICS

Christy Bryceland & Henderikus J. Stam

INTRODUCTION

Codes of ethics have begun to refer to preferences that interventions be 'empirically supported'. The movement toward Empirically Supported Treatments (ESTs) is based on a medical model of intervention using randomized controlled trials as the prime method. Cognitive behavior therapies are the most prominent of the ESTs, and threaten to dominate the field of psychotherapy by virtue of their easily measurable and limited outcomes. Alternative practices are at risk of being considered unethical within this framework because their practitioners are unlikely to conduct the kind of outcome research that is considered necessary to demonstrate efficacy. In this chapter, we consider the symbiotic relationship of CBT in supporting the dominance of ESTs.

Professions are normally defined by their utilization of a publicly recognized and expert body of knowledge and skills, their control of a labour market based on credentials obtained through specialized training programmes typically associated with universities, and autonomy in the workplace, including evaluative autonomy, along with a public service ideal (e.g. Freidson, 1999). Autonomy is increasingly threatened in contemporary professions by the interventions of state agencies and by market-place considerations. For example, the organizational settings in which professionals find themselves have become vastly more complex in recent decades, making the control of professional work no longer the exclusive purvey of peers and professional organizations, but instead nesting it with professional managers of employing organizations (e.g. Leicht and Fennell, 1997). As Miller and Magruder (1999) have put it, psychotherapy has gone through a 'metamorphosis ... from a decentralized, fee-for-service cottage industry, to a massive market-driven, largely for-profit, health care system' (p. xv).

Threats to autonomy are amongst the most serious recent threats for professionals. This is largely because professionals' work is based on 'theoretically based discretionary specialization' (Freidson, 1999: 119). In addition to the complexity of organizational settings in which professionals are employed, consumer pressure can also place demands on a profession. More likely, however, it is managerial and bureaucratic pressure to contain costs and limit what may be unlimited services that most directly restrain professionals. In the health and service professions, these constraints have come in the form of guidelines or other

This chapter is a revised and shortened version of a paper which originally appeared in the *Journal of Constructivist Psychology*, 18, 2005: 131–55. We thank Taylor & Francis for permission to reprint segments of the original paper.

forms of prescriptive advice to limit variation in diagnostic and therapeutic practice, and to develop so-called 'standards of care'.

Evidence-based medicine was the first to demand that practice not be dominated 'by opinion (possibly ill-informed) and by consensus formed in poorly understood ways by "experts". [Instead] the idea is to shift the centre of gravity of health care decision making towards an explicit consideration and incorporation of research evidence' (Sheldon, 1997: vii). As Berg et al. (2000) have noted, there is an implicit tension in the demand for 'objectivity' wherein the enhancement of the scientific status of the discipline may in fact lead to a reduction in the autonomy of the professional, at the same time as the increasing transparency of the decision-making process makes it more vulnerable to scrutiny and to interference by outsiders, particularly managers. This dilemma is also clearly visible in the psychotherapeutic domain, as the push to treatments with empirical support gains momentum. This issue has been widely discussed on both sides of the Atlantic, and will continue to be worked out in local as well as national and international contexts.

This chapter is addressed specifically to the role played by codes of ethics in these debates, and their utilization as support for empirically validated therapies. Recent discussion on the use of codes of ethics clearly reflects differing moral views on what constitutes proper, effective, and ethical practice. More important, this has implications for therapies that are not cognitive behavioural, such as psychodynamic and constructivist approaches. We will argue that it is a misuse of codes of ethics to co-opt them into debates that are essentially professional and bureaucratic, but are not primarily about proper or ethical conduct in the field of therapy.

PSYCHOLOGY ASSOCIATIONS AND EVIDENCE-BASED PRACTICE

Psychological associations such as those in the United Kingdom, the United States, and Canada have become more outspoken regarding the need for psychologists to provide interventions that have empirically supported efficacy. Psychologists in the UK led the move toward empirically based psychological treatments, part of a larger movement known initially as 'evidence-based medicine' (EBM; Sackett et al., 1997).

In 1993, the American Psychological Association's (APA) Division 12 (Clinical Psychology) developed a task force to define, identify, and disseminate information about empirically supported interventions. The Task Force (1993) made controversial recommendations that the APA develop and maintain a list of empirically validated treatments for distribution, and that training programmes include training in empirically validated treatments. The Task Force also had as an initial goal that the criteria be used to develop practice guidelines for government, professionals, managed-care organizations, and mental-health insurers. However, political pressure from within the APA led Division 12 to renounce this goal (Chambless et al., 1996). Despite the controversy, particularly over the development and use of an empirically supported treatment list, the group issued the first of a series of reports in 1995, identifying a number of psychological interventions as 'empirically validated'. Later, these became known as 'empirically supported treatments' (ESTs). The APA Committee on Accreditation decided in 1996 to include training in ESTs as part of the guidelines for accreditation of doctoral and internship training programmes.

The Clinical Section of the Canadian Psychological Association (CPA) has also entered the debate. In a key paper, a CPA task force recommended the explicit endorsement by the Clinical Section of CPA of the APA Division 12 work on ESTs, encouraging CPA as a whole to endorse the Division 12 list, and encouraging CPA accreditation to require training in ESTs as a mandatory criterion for accreditation of doctoral programmes and internships in clinical psychology (Hunsley et al., 1999). In addition, the task force recommended that CPA work with provincial regulatory bodies to require knowledge of and training in empirically supported treatments, as part of the assessment of suitability to independently provide health services to the public.

In the UK, the National Institute for Health and Clinical Excellence (NICE) has developed clinical-practice guidelines intended to provide 'national guidance on promoting good health and preventing and treating ill health'. Their guidelines include treatment for mental-health and behavioural disorders such as anxiety, depression, eating disorders, and schizophrenia. Many of the guidelines specify CBT as the psychological treatment of choice, and go so far as to suggest the necessary number of sessions required (e.g. NICE, 2007). Recently, these guidelines have taken on a new level of significance in reference to Lord Layard's agenda on happiness and the provision of widespread psychological services for the treatment of disorders such as depression and anxiety. He wholeheartedly takes up the NICE guidelines in specifying CBT as the treatment of choice for these disorders, and recommends a large expansion of psychological services providing 'predominantly' CBT (Layard, 2006).

CRITIQUES OF THE EMPIRICALLY SUPPORTED TREATMENT MOVEMENT

Critics have noted that empirically supported treatment, as it has been defined by APA's Division 12 Task Force, encompasses a narrow field of practice and leaves much beyond its scope. The vast majority of interventions listed fall within the domain of cognitive behaviour therapy or CBT. It has also been argued that the EST list systematically discriminates against certain classes of research, treatment, and patients, including non-English-language research and the treatments of ethnic minorities and children, as well as psychodynamic and experiential treatments which have different assumptions about the nature of treatment, the manualizability of treatment, and research design (Elliott, 1998). The criteria for which treatments are selected to the list have also been criticized for being too restrictive, because they limit empirical support to include only a particular kind of research trial, based on the methodology used in drug trials.

The criteria have also been criticized for focusing on therapy technique and manualization, and downplaying more important research findings, such as the general equivalence of most treatments, or the importance of client and therapist variables. Henry (1998), for example, is critical of the EST movement for tacitly ignoring 'the vast bulk of empirical psychotherapy and psychopathology research' (p. 128). There is great variation in the degree to which different theoretical approaches to psychotherapy embrace conceptions of disorder and treatment. The Division 12 criteria only apply to a very narrow conception of psychotherapy: models that fall outside this conception are not considered to have 'empirical support', despite the fact that in many cases they have large bodies of supporting empirical evidence. Critics contend that the EST movement is deeply embedded in the concern for professional autonomy on the one hand, and controlling other, non-EST therapies on the other.

REACTIONS FROM THERAPIES MARGINALIZED BY THE EST MOVEMENT

The implications of the EST movement have not gone unnoticed by those who adhere to theoretical perspectives that are essentially marginalized by it, such as psychodynamic, systemic, humanistic, and postmodern therapeutic practitioners and theorists. Bohart et al. (1998) argue that the Division 12 Task Force criteria for ESTs could 'disenfranchise therapies that do not share [their] assumptions about the nature of psychotherapy and will stifle psychological research' (p. 141; see also Bohart and House, Chapter 16, this volume). The authors' primary critique of the Division 12 criteria is their basis in a 'medical-like meta-model of psychotherapy', designed to appeal to the market forces of managed care. Such a model is 'inappropriate for therapies whose primary focus is not to cure disorder', such as humanistic, constructivist, and feminist approaches (p. 141). They criticize the Division 12 criteria because they are driven by what the authors consider to be 'obviously financial and territorial' considerations (p. 142). Bohart et al. (1998) articulate the fear that Division 12's EST list, with its implication that unlisted treatments are either 'experimental' or not empirically supported, will be used to 'expose persons practicing from alternative theories to the possibility of malpractice suits' (p. 141). Henry (1998) articulated a related concern, stating that as the EST list becomes entrenched and taken up by managed care, 'it would be reasonable from the standpoint of a consumer or a third-party payer to increasingly look askance at therapies that were not on the list' (p. 130).

'ETHICS' AND EMPIRICALLY SUPPORTED TREATMENT

Is there legitimacy in the fears that EST lists and criteria will become regulatory tools – used to de-legitimate particular therapies by either disciplinary or financial means? One sign that positions are becoming entrenched is that the language of ethics is being recruited to the debate on empirically supported treatments. Proponents of ESTs have begun to argue that the practice of empirically supported or evidence-based treatment constitutes ethical practice, and that by implication, practising a therapy that does not have empirical support is unethical. It is important to recognize the gravity of this move. One of the features of professions is a service ethic. Professions provide a public service based on specialized education and training. In return, professions are largely self-governing, a privilege upheld by codes of ethics and professional conduct that are used to impose sanctions for misconduct. The prescriptive use of particular forms of therapy has not traditionally been part of these codes.

This may change, however. For example, in a special issue of *Canadian Psychology*, covering the debate on Empirically Supported Treatment, Morin wrote 'practitioners have an ethical responsibility to use EST, whenever such treatment is available' (1999: 314). Similarly, the authors of the CPA task force report on ESTs, Hunsley et al. (1999), indicated that

> 'It is an ethical requirement that Canadian psychologists keep informed of relevant knowledge and progress in their areas ... [T]hat health services be based on sound scientific evidence should, therefore, not only pose no threat to the practices of psychologists, it should be warmly embraced by psychologists.'
>
> (ibid.: 316)

Likewise, Australian psychologist Gavin Andrews (2000) argues that

> 'any clinician, asked by a client what other treatments there are for their "disorder", would be ethically obliged to mention treatments listed as supported by Type 1 [supported by at least two rigorous randomized controlled trials showing superiority to placebo or another treatment] evidence before offering advice about the treatment to be preferred'.
>
> (p. 265)

At the moment these claims remain at the level of rhetorical flourish. Indeed, 'sound scientific evidence' is a contestable phrase, and is entirely non-threatening on a broad understanding of 'science'. Nor is the notion of 'empirical status' particularly problematic, so long as we understand by it that empirical content is always theory-laden. It is the conflation of these notions with specific lists generated around narrower considerations of psychotherapy that signal the appropriation of the language of ethics to the debate – Andrews is a very clear example in this regard. The problematic assumption is that 'mechanical objectivity', or the agreement to follow certain rules and methods for the collection and evaluation of evidence, can solve problems of a broader disciplinary and judgemental nature.

The language of 'empirical support' has appeared in more recent code revisions for a number of psychological associations and regulatory bodies. Whether or not references to empirical support in these documents are intended to specify Empirically Supported Treatment as defined by the Division 12 Task Force is unknown; more important may be whether these ethical principles will come to be interpreted in a manner reflective of the Division 12 criteria.

The 2002 revision of the APA code does not explicitly use the language of 'empirical support', but it does include a number of revisions that increase the emphasis on science or research-based evidence for practice of both assessment and therapy (APA, 2002). The Code of Ethics of the British Psychological Society also does not explicitly use the language of empirical support. However, it requires that psychologists 'value and have respect for all relevant evidence and the limits of such evidence when giving psychological advice or expressing a professional opinion'; as well as 'value and have respect for scientific evidence and the limits of such evidence when making public statements that provide psychological information' (BPS, 2000: 5).

The Canadian Code of Ethics for Psychologists also contains revisions to reflect greater emphasis on the ethics of evidence-based practice, and actually incorporates the language of empirical support, recommending that psychologists choose interventions with 'reasonable theoretical or empirically supported efficacy' (CPA, 2000: 18). The New Zealand Code of Ethics for Psychologists (2002) was modelled on the Canadian Code. Similar to the Canadian Code, it contains a clause that refers to expectations for competence in terms of 'scientifically derived knowledge' (p. 10).

Codes of ethics do not necessarily serve a role as regulatory documents that specify disciplinary action; in fact, they are often presented as educational and aspirational documents. However, a number of Codes of Conduct developed by the provincial regulatory bodies in Canada have also come to reflect the language of empirical support. These codes take up language such as 'empirical foundation of intervention', demanding that registrants be familiar with reliability, validity, standardization, and outcome research for their techniques, and be trained in their proper application (e.g. College of Psychologists of British Columbia, 2005; College of Psychologists of Ontario, 2005). These codes of conduct are where disciplinary 'teeth' may be found. The encroachment of the EST language into these codes may lay the grounds for real fear of disciplinary action, by those who practise therapies labelled as 'experimental' by Division 12, or for those that practise therapies that are not on the EST list at all.

While there is clearly variation in the degree to which codes discuss or even suggest the need for empirical support for interventions, there is a trend within these codes to emphasize psychologists' responsibility to base their practices on scientific evidence. We believe that it is reasonable and just to expect psychologists to be knowledgeable on questions of evidence, outcome studies, reliability, validity, and so on. Moreover, what is meant by terms such as 'science', 'research', or 'evidence' in these codes is open to interpretation. However, could such terms come to be interpreted to reflect the narrow demands of the EST movement as defined by APA's Division 12 Task Force? Or will codes move toward mandating that psychologists inform their clients whether the therapy they provide has empirical support, or one step further, mandate the practice of empirically supported treatment?

CODES OF ETHICS AND PSYCHOTHERAPY'S PROFESSIONALIZATION AGENDA

Disciplinary measures are not the only concerns related to these semantic shifts in codes of ethics and conduct. A number of theorists have argued that codes of ethics play a central role in the professionalization of groups and the development of their political power. Dunbar (1998) has argued that the professionalization goals of codes of ethics include the marketing of psychology, establishing the exclusive rights of psychologists to certain areas of practice, and influencing public policy and decision-making. Codes of ethics are important indicators and legitimators of professional autonomy and self-governance.

Based on the perspective of professionalization, the worries about the incorporation of the language of ESTs in codes of ethics may reflect more than a worry of certain practices themselves becoming labelled unethical and vulnerable to disciplinary action. Viewing codes of ethics as tools of professionalization, it becomes apparent that they also serve to designate professional boundaries. The inclusion of the language of empirical support in codes of ethics may serve a number of purposes for the psychology profession, including that of laying claim to particular technologies as the domain of psychologists and underscoring psychologists' unique role as 'scientist-practitioners' who ground their interventions in a particular kind of empirical support. Henry (1998) argued that the political agenda of the EST movement includes the promotion of the survival of professional psychology and academic research in psychology. Including the practice of ESTs in codes of conduct would only serve to further this political agenda by legitimizing the EST agenda within the regulatory mechanisms of the psychology profession.

THE INFILTRATION OF ESTS: NARROWING THE FIELD

The inclusion of ESTs in codes of ethics is not based on considerations that necessarily address issues of moral hazard or protect the public interest. Instead, they bring concerns with quantification, legitimation, and bureaucratic efficiency together with mechanical objectivity and the limits of human judgement, into the centre of the client–therapist relationship. We do not argue that these considerations should not be of concern or debated – quite the contrary. They should in fact be discussed for what they are: historically specific disputes concerning the nature and function of therapy, the relationship between therapist and client, and arguments about what constitutes the best form of therapy for what kinds of problems. We also believe that psychotherapists should be accountable and knowledgeable, and up to date in their use of techniques in so far as they are relevant to their practice. But efficiency in technique is not the same as psychotherapy, and accountability is not the same as being current in the research, as some commentaries have argued.

CONCLUSION

Our argument against the inclusion of ESTs in codes of ethics rests not on their inherent instability as scientific and rational indicators (that is a debate going on elsewhere), nor primarily on their political uses to strengthen psychology as a discipline (a question worthy of further discussion in its own right), or their bureaucratic uses in managed care organizations (where they serve to enhance efficiency and ultimately reduce costs). Instead, we feel that ESTs may become confused with the ends of therapy, and by finding their way into the language of ethics, have already pushed the debate in a direction inimical to the aims of psychotherapy. Particularly by potentially foreclosing 'other' therapies, they threaten the very enterprise of therapy itself by promising technique above what is, after all, a moral vocation. Moreover, those 'other' therapies are precisely those that are not cognitive and behavioural. Their demise would greatly restrict the discourse of therapy, if not our conceptual resources.

REFERENCES

American Psychological Association (2002) *Ethical Principles of Psychologists and Code of Conduct 2002*, retrieved 1 February 2004 from: http://www.apa.org/ethics/code2002.html.

Andrews, G. (2000) 'A focus on empirically supported outcomes: a commentary on search for empirically supported treatments', *Clinical Psychology: Science and Practice*, 7: 264–8.

Berg, M., Horstman, K., Plass, S., and van Heusden, M. (2000) 'Guidelines, professionals and the production of objectivity: standardisation and the professionalism of insurance medicine', *Sociology of Health & Illness*, 22: 765–91.

Bohart, A., O'Hara, M., and Leitner, L. (1998) 'Empirically violated treatments: disenfranchisement of humanistic and other psychotherapies', *Psychotherapy Research*, 8: 141–57.

British Psychological Society (2000) *A Code of Conduct for Psychologists*, Leicester: British Psychological Society.

Bryceland, C. and Stam, H. J. (2005) 'Empirical validation and professional codes of ethics: description or prescription?', *Journal of Constructivist Psychology*, 18: 131–56.

Canadian Psychological Association (2000) *Canadian Code of Ethics for Psychologists* (3rd edn), Ottawa, ON: Canadian Psychological Association.

Chambless, D., Sanderson, W., Shoham, V., Johnson, S., Pope, K., Crits-Christoph, P., Baker, M., Johnson, B., Woody, S., Sue, S., Beutler, L., Williams, D., and McCurry, S. (1996) 'An update on empirically validated therapies', *The Clinical Psychologist*, 49: 5–18.

College of Psychologists of British Columbia (2005) *Code of Conduct*, retrieved 22 October 2006, from: http://www.collegeofpsychologists.bc.ca/codeofconduct.

College of Psychologists of Ontario (2005) *Standards of Professional Conduct*, retrieved 22 October 2006, from: http://www.cpo.on.ca/BylawRegStdGuide/Standards/Standards.pdf.

Dunbar, J. (1998) 'A critical history of CPA's various codes of ethics for psychologists (1939–1986)', *Canadian Psychology*, 39: 177–86.

Elliott, R. (1998) 'Editor's introduction: A guide to the empirically supported treatments controversy', *Psychotherapy Research*, 8: 115–25.

Freidson, E. (1999) 'Theory of professionalism: method and substance', *International Review of Sociology*, 9: 117–29.

Henry, W. P. (1998) 'Science, politics, and the politics of science: the use and misuse of empirically validated treatment research', *Psychotherapy Research*, 8: 126–40.

Hunsley, J., Dobson, K. S., Johnston, C., and Mikail, S. F. (1999) 'The science and practice of empirically supported treatments', *Canadian Psychology*, 40: 316–19.

Layard, R. (2006) 'The Case for Psychological Treatment Centres', retrieved 21 October 2006, from: http://cep.lse.ac.uk/layard.

Leicht, K. T. and Fennell, M. L. (1997) 'The changing organizational context of professional work', *Annual Review of Sociology*, 23: 215–31.

Miller, N. E. and Magruder, K. M. (1999) 'Introduction', in N. E. Miller and K. M. Magruder (eds), *Cost-effectiveness of Psychotherapy*, New York: Oxford University Press, pp. xv–xxx.

Morin, C. (1999) 'Empirically supported psychological treatments: a natural extension of the scientist-practitioner paradigm', *Canadian Psychology*, 40: 312–15.

National Institute for Health and Clinical Excellence (2007) *Depression (amended): Management of Depression in Primary and Secondary Care*, retrieved 6 September 2008 from the National Institute for Health and Clinical Excellence at http://www.nice.org.uk/guidance/index.jsp?action=download&o=29615.

New Zealand Psychological Society (2002) *Code of Ethics for Psychologists Working in Aotearoa/New Zealand*, Aukland, NZ: Author.

Sackett, D., Richardson, W., Rosenberg, W., and Haynes, R. (1997) *Evidence-based Medicine*, New York: Churchill Livingstone.

Sheldon, T. (1997) 'Introduction', in L. Grayson (ed.), *Evidence-based Medicine*, London: British Library, pp. vii–xi.

Task Force on Promotion and Dissemination of Psychological Procedures (1993) *A Report to the Division 12 Board*, Washington, D.C.: American Psychological Association.

CHAPTER 16

EMPIRICALLY SUPPORTED/VALIDATED TREATMENTS AS MODERNIST IDEOLOGY, I:

DODO, MANUALIZATION, AND THE PARADIGM QUESTION

ARTHUR C. BOHART & RICHARD HOUSE

INTRODUCTION

For philosopher of science Kuhn (1977), it is commonly difficult for those speaking from different paradigms or 'world-views' to understand one another, not least because of the incommensurable and often unarticulated assumptions from which each speaks and thinks (rather like Ludwig Wittgenstein's lion, and how it structures its world – 'Even if a lion could speak, we could not understand him [because we don't know how he structures his world]' – Wittgenstein, 1973/1958: 223). What we will term the 'Empirically Supported/Validated Treatments' (ESVT) approach, like any and every research approach, necessarily entails a paradigm underpinned by assumptions about what psychotherapy, and research into it, are concerned with. From within its own internal logic, the ESVT approach seems so self-evidently rational that its advocates have difficulty grasping any objections to it. Thus, its proponents commonly fail to recognize the paradigmatic or ontological level from which objections to its approach are being raised, with attempts therefore being made to assimilate and deal with those objections from within their own paradigm. Not that those of us who subscribe to an alternative paradigm are immune from this very same process! – so it may be that ESVTers feel misunderstood by us, too. In this chapter, we present one view of what the ESVT paradigm looks like, and how it is experienced, from the different paradigmatic standpoint which we share.

When confronted with objections, ESVT proponents sometimes claim that their opponents' motivation is to advance what the former view as 'unscientific' practice, defining 'science' as they do in terms of manualized clinical practice, with randomized controlled clinical trials (RCTs) methodology being seen as *the* valid route to scientifically legitimate practice.

Alternatively, ESVTers sometimes maintain that any objections can be dealt with from within their own paradigm. However, the ways in which issues are framed, and even thought about, is different in different paradigms; and whilst it may be true that in some cases, analogues of some therapeutic approaches can be created within the ESVT paradigm, it

---

This chapter is based upon, and is a substantial elaboration of, Arthur C. Bohart's chapter entitled 'A passionate critique of empirically supported treatments and the provision of an alternative paradigm', which first appeared in J. C. Watson, R. N. Goldman, and M. S. Warner (eds), *Client-centered and Experiential Psychotherapy in the Twenty-first Century: Advances in Theory, Research, and Practice*, Ross-on-Wye: PCCS Books, 2002, pp. 258–77.

does not follow from this that their real spirit or essence can be captured within, or effectively represented by, such analogues.

From a more post-modern perspective, it is not wise prematurely to impose a unitary paradigm on to a field, especially when that paradigm has not been consensually arrived at, but has, rather, been created by a minority of people in a narrowly circumscribed part of the field. Furthermore, as we will see both in this and our next chapter, and in the rest of this book, the impetus to the development of ESVT standards is arguably far more economic, political, and interest driven, than it is scientific (Beutler, 1998; Hubble et al., 1999). Thus, those of us subscribing in a principled way to different paradigmatic assumptions view attempts to entrench ESVT assumptions as *the* (only) route to legitimate practice as a hegemonic attempt to impose on both science and practice what is to us, at least in part, an alien and epistemologically unsustainable world-view.

A few words about the notion of a 'paradigm'. The term commonly denotes a set of background assumptions about whatever 'reality' is being studied (including a theory of what exists, and what it might mean to say that something 'exists') – a way of conceptualizing the world which underlies, informs, and to some extent determines specific theories and practices. According to Kuhn (1970), our routine procedural paradigms substantially control the ways in which we study the world during periods between what he termed 'scientific revolutions'. A paradigm can therefore both constrain and constructively influence the kinds of theories that are developed, how research is done, and what is to be considered as legitimate research-based knowledge. In psychotherapy, for example, a 'paradigm' might refer to a model of what the process of providing help consists in – for example, therapy as 'treatment' for a 'psychopathological disorder' (the medical-model paradigm), contrasted with therapy viewed as interpersonal encounter, intersubjective dialogue, and/or consultation.

Another key issue is the underlying metaphysical model influencing both practice and research. Thus, we could counterpose a 'modernist', Newtonian view of the universe, with its goal of increasing control over dependent variables by specifying and manipulating independent variables – contrasted with, say, a more 'post-modern' systemic cosmology, where we can never totally predict or control the phenomena being studied, and where 'science' is acknowledged, but without it necessarily determining or dominating practice.

In what follows, we will first examine the so-called 'Dodo bird verdict' in psychotherapy, and its paradigmatic significance. We then outline the implicit but unarticulated logic of the paradigm underlying the ESVT approach, along with the implicit logic of an alternative plausible paradigm. We maintain that there are paradigms at least as plausible as an ESVT-driven one, which we here loosely term a 'relational meta-paradigm'. We maintain that the latter can convincingly be argued to underlie, and make sense of, psychotherapy experience and practice, of which the ESVT criteria seem to make at best only limited sense. The research and practice of psychotherapy, we argue, needs to remain open to a rich diversity of alternative paradigms (House and Totton, 1997) until, through the slow, steady accumulation of results and by emerging common consent, one or another paradigm begins to take prominence. Finally, we maintain that there exist 'evidence-based' ways of practising therapy that do not depend upon the ESVT world-view – looking in particular at the manualization issue and that of Randomised Control Trial (RCT) methodology, about which significant reservations have already been expressed in the literature (e.g. Persons and Silberschatz, 1998).

Although we make comparatively limited direct reference to CBT *per se*, it should be clear that many if not most of our arguments have direct relevance to CBT, given its current place as modernity's paradigm-crowning modality, and its inextricable intertwining with questions of 'evidence-based practice', RCT research methodology, and so on.

For two writers from different continents to co-author a chapter which they can both stand by, in what is such a controversial area as contesting psychotherapy paradigms, is a challenging experience. And whilst we may have some differences in terms of nuance, emphasis, or detail, what is more notable is that we have quite effortlessly found extensive common ground on which we can stand together – which in turn reaffirms our confidence in the paradigmatic challenges and alternatives which we offer in both this and in the following chapter.

THE DODO BIRD: AN EXAMPLE OF A PARADIGM CLASH

The so-called 'Dodo bird verdict', that all therapies are for the most part equally effective, beautifully illustrates the difference between competing psychotherapy paradigms. For purposes of this discussion, we set aside for a moment the methodological complication that it might not be meaningful to speak of distinctive approaches' or modalities per se, as this assumes that comparison between what are assumed *from the outset* to be distinct modalities is a legitimate object of study, and/or a more valid comparative metric than is, for example, differences in level of experience, or whether the practitioner has had a personal therapy, or whether s/he holds any spiritual world-view – and so on. The Dodo verdict certainly illustrates very clearly the phenomenon of *incommensurable psychotherapy paradigms*.

For ESVT proponents, the Dodo bird verdict, if true, would be catastrophic. First, there would be no point in developing and studying different treatments for different labelled 'disorders'. Secondly, the ESVT paradigm is a quintessentially 'technological' view of therapy – assuming that it is the technical aspects of therapy that are the primary cause of therapeutic change. The 'scientific' ESVT approach aspires to developing and testing specific technologies, which are then manualized for the various 'disorders'. Under this appoach, even 'the therapeutic relationship' itself is treated as a kind of 'thingified' manipulable 'variable', to be studied and then differentially 'delivered' for different 'disorders'. It comes as little surprise, therefore, that ESVT advocates maintain that the Dodo bird verdict is 'flawed' (Lampropoulos, 2000) or that it has been superceded (Task Force, 1995).

A plausible alternative paradigm might conceive of therapy as a fundamentally interpersonal/dialogical process, with technology perhaps being utilized, but always being of secondary or incidental importance. Advocates of 'relational' paradigms can easily accept the Dodo bird verdict, not being in the least surprised that different modalities, often using very different (or no) therapeutic 'techniques', may have only minimal differential treatment effects.

It is unlikely that the Dodo bird question can ever be resolved until – if ever – one therapy paradigm prevails or predominates. In our view, from any dispassionate standpoint the Dodo bird evidence is so compelling that, were its conclusions in accord with 'mainstream' beliefs and theories, it would surely long ago have been accepted as a major finding, and then built upon (Bohart and Tallman, 1999). What is arguably the overbearing arrogance of 'paradigmatic hegenomy' is surely clear in paradigm-bound assertions like that of Lampropoulos (2000), that therapists should not be allowed to rely exclusively upon the therapeutic relationship, powerful placebos, and other ill-defined 'common factors' (e.g. van Kalmthout et al., 1985), which, he argues, seem to be major assumptions shared by most opponents of ESVTs.

The opposite of the Dodo bird verdict, that differential treatment effects have been scientifically demonstrated, has been equally strongly challenged. Wampold (1997), for example, points out that the number of such findings does not exceed what one would expect by chance; and findings of 'experimenter allegiance effects' cast further doubt on differential treatment findings. We maintain, and seek to show in this and the next chapter, that those practitioners who pursue a therapeutic approach that is different from the medical-model differential-treatment approach, relying upon more 'post-modern' notions like 'ill-defined' or 'non-specific' common factors, are at least as defensible and legitimate as are ESVT-driven approaches.

A NON-BELIEVERS' PERSPECTIVE ON THE ESVT PARADIGM

In its underlying logic, the ESVT paradigm is a particular model concerning the nature of psychotherapy, underpinned in turn by a more general metaphysical position which necessarily entails implicit and interconnected assumptions about reality, science, knowledge, and truth. Mainstream psychotherapy practice is routinely viewed through an analogy to the medical model (e.g. Bohart and Tallman, 1999; House, 1996; Stiles and Shapiro, 1989), with a central focus upon *treatment*, which is viewed as analogous to drug treatment, and which seeks to 'correct' abnormal, so-called 'psychopathology' (Parker et al., 1995; House, 2001), just as drugs are supposed to correct or cure 'pathology'. On this, modernist view, it is believed that the treatment *qua treatment* is somehow *applied to* the problem or 'disorder' in a causal way, so as to eradicate it. As in mainstream allopathic medicine, it is further assumed that the more specifically tailored the treatment is to the 'disorder', the more likely it is to be effective. It is taken as axiomatic that differential treatment must *by definition* be more effective than so-called 'non-specific' treatment, with research then becoming a matter of demonstrating differential treatment effects. Within this world-view, therapy therefore becomes a technological enterprise, with, at worst, therapists viewed as '"behavioral engineers" rather than storytellers or moral guides' (Johnson and Sandage, 1999: 4).

A central sequela of a treatment-driven approach is that treatments must necessarily be content-described with as much specificity as possible, with, above all, a need for a standardizable application – and with the predictable concomitant: manualization. Various ESVTers even imply that such specificity is the ideal. If a manual were 'merely' a general statement of therapeutic principles which could be operationalized by different practitioners in different ways and contexts, then it would of course be impossible to research specific 'treatments'. This highlights a key issue so often neglected in the literature – viz. the many individuals within the 'professionalized' therapy field (House, 2003) with a powerful vested interest in the medical-model world-view and its accompanying 'treatment' ideology.

The metaphor of a manual-driven therapy implies an approach in which the practitioner follows what are imported, externally generated rules which do not emerge from the specificity and arguable uniqueness of a therapeutic encounter, and where those rules are reasonably specific. A manual is effectively a set of relatively specific rules and prescriptions for action, a 'how-to' or rule book of operating procedures. Many practitioners, including the present authors, view this guiding metaphor as strongly contradicting widespread viewpoints and intuitions in the field about the nature of therapeutic experience, and how therapy can be most appropriately conducted and researched.

THE METAPHYSICS OF THE ESVT PARADIGM AND ITS RELATION TO RESEARCH

The ESVT research paradigm is based on conventional natural-scientific experimental logic, which many in the field believe to be quite inappropriate for therapy work. First, an attempt is made at the outset to specify a so-called 'independent variable', with other variables allegedly controlled or 'held constant', and using standardized measures of the dependent variable, so that one can claim to demonstrate a so-called 'linear causal relationship' between the independent and dependent variables. Such a procedure entails a whole host of highly questionable ontological assumptions, with an underpinning and routinely implicit linear-causal, mechanistic view of how psychotherapy – and the universe – works. In stark contrast, Stiles et al. (1998), for example, refer to what they call 'a responsive view' of therapy as an *ongoing intersubjective experience*, where issues and experiences emerge and change, often in response to what has gone before. On this latter view, the therapeutic encounter is therefore *invented*, at least in part, as therapist and client respond to emerging and co-created contingencies.

RANDOMIZED CONTROLLED TRIAL (RCT) METHODOLOGY

In the ESVT paradigm, the *randomized controlled clinical trial* (RCT) methodology is routinely seen as the 'method of choice'. Because the RCT is the 'gold standard' in medicine, it is also assumed *a priori* to be the gold standard in psychotherapy research too (e.g. Persons, in Persons and Silberschatz, 1998) – arguably a glaring example of the colonizing hegemony of a positivistic, control-orientated modernity which assumes its one-size-fits-all methodologies to be universally applicable to all dimensions of reality.

Yet the RCT approach to research may well not be a particularly valid or useful tool for the study of complex ecological systems (e.g. DeGreene, 1991): for example, 'Group designs, in which patients are randomly assigned to treatment conditions, simply do not generalize to how we practice clinically' (Goldfried and Wolfe, 1996: 1015). There is indeed a long list of objections which, taken together, constitute a devastating 'case against' the embracing of RCT methodology in psychotherapeutic research. For RCT methodology is open to a range of compelling challenges which have never been satisfactorily refuted (House and Loewenthal, 2008; cf. Hemmings, pp. 46–8, this volume) – not least, that:

1. its methodology hides, through the comparison of means, what actually happens to *individuals* in the research trial – with the consequence, for example, that there may well be people in both groups who are worse off after 'treatment';

2. RCT methodology ignores the different responses of different individuals to the same treatment, so that, as Heron has convincingly argued, it simply 'cannot help with the everyday question, "What is the treatment of choice for this individual patient?"' (1996: 198);

3. it routinely ignores the powerful effect of the mind on the body (assuming we accept that ontological distinction), and the latent, subtle, and often mysterious phenomenon of self-healing;

4. RCT methodology unquestioningly assumes the validity of its univariate approach, which separates out the single treatment variable from all other influences in order to assess its causal impact (as if real, lived life were remotely like that);

5. it objectifies suffering as a 'thingified' process, inappropriately reifying 'external' causal influence and ignoring subjective illness categories experienced and made sense of by the client, and ignoring the meaning or tacit intentionality of the illness; and finally

6. RCT methodology ignores the possibility that its so-called 'statements of fact' (including variable specification and measurement) may be unavoidably theory- and value-laden, and can only be formulated *within a pre-existing (and therefore self-fulfilling) set of theoretical assumptions*, which can then so easily become a circular proving of what was assumed to exist at the outset (cf. Parker et al., 1995).

In drug-dominated allopathic scientific medicine with its cause-and-effect billiard-ball cosmology, in contrast, the 'independent variable' is allegedly controlled as tightly as possible, a major drive being to identify the medication's 'active ingredients'. In uncritically mimicking a procedure which is even open to challenge within natural-science methodology, psychotherapy research duly proceeds to conduct dismantling studies which claim to identify active 'operative ingredients'. Moreover, the unquestioned underpinning assumption, that the best way to practise therapy is to discover general nomothetic laws and then treat individual cases as specific instances of these general laws or categories (Schön, 1983), never seems to be questioned by ESVT proponents.

The 'treatment', then, is the independent variable, which is applied to the 'dependent variable' – *the client* (or the client's 'disorder'), the goal being to 'operationalize' the treatment clearly and unambiguously. The more precisely the independent variable can be operationalized, the better for plotting predictable linear-causal relationships between it and the dependent variable. As already mentioned, ESVTers routinely criticize 'ill-defined' or 'non-specific' common factors, such as 'the relationship' dimension, presumably because the latter cannot be specified as a series of unambiguously definable, measurable, and controllable therapist strategies. In short, a kind of epistemologically naïve 1930s Logical Positivism seems to dominate the research consciousness of the ESVT tendency, as they dismiss as meaningless, concepts that cannot be easily operationalized within their cosmology. Yet if, as many practitioners believe, it is precisely these difficult-to-define 'imponderables' that are *most* important in many a healing and change experience (see our Chapter 17, this volume), then to embrace a methodology which systematically rules them out of account, and which privileges, instead, only that which is measurable and controllable, may well be to do a kind of methodological *violence* to the reality we are interrogating, and certainly radically to misrepresent it – and in what is, ironically, a most unbefitting *un*scientific way!

We can predict that in this positivistic instrumental universe, any findings that 'the relationship' plays an important role in therapeutic change will likely lead to a fundamentally misguided attempt to 'technologize' the relational – which in turn betrays a fundamental misunderstanding of what we might call 'the efficacy of the relational'. For at worst, it too will then be studied so that it can be 'manipulated' as a form of 'treatment' – and the intangible '*healing through relationship*' experience will inevitably be lost; and if such healing still manages somehow to occur, it will be *in spite of* rather than because of any positivistic atomizing of 'the relationship' that is attempted.

We view ESVT proponents as inhabiting a modernist, mechanistic, linearly determined world, where perfect predictability and control are at least in principle achievable. Underlying this world-view appears to be a traditional Newtonian cosmology of the universe as a giant clock. It can of course be dismantled; and how each part contributes to the operation of the whole can be accurately specified. Using a simple additive model of main effects and interactions, ultimately the whole clock can be known theoretically, and its workings predicted and controlled without remainder. Further, because it is a completely deterministic universe, as discussed earlier the goal of research is to establish the independent variable's *control* over the dependent variable. In sum, the client becomes truly a 'dependent variable' (a *live* dependent variable, to be sure!) on which the independent variable is then operating to bring about its effects.

INTIMATIONS OF AN ALTERNATIVE PARADIGM

A paradigm very different from that just described can be derived from two (and by no means only two) prominent therapeutic approaches: viz. client- or person-centred therapy, and the so-called 'constructive' therapies (e.g. strategic/solution-focussed therapy and its descendants). As with the ESVT paradigm, we can distinguish both a practice level and an underlying philosophical or metaphysical level.

THE NATURE OF THERAPY: PRACTICE LEVEL

Client-centred therapy and strategic therapy share some common assumptions. Both adopt a holistic attitude: the therapist *as person* is working with a whole person in order to help the latter remove obstacles to living what, for them, is a more fulfilling life. This contrasts markedly with an approach in which a 'treatment' is being applied to 'dysfunctional' *parts* or aspects of the person (egos, schemas, conditioned responses, etc.). Secondly, the therapist relies upon clients' own capacities for self-healing (Bohart and Tallman, 1996), and works within the client's frame of reference. The client's own 'generativity' is an integral part of this process, and insights and solutions emerge from therapist and client interrelating, rather than being dictated *a priori* by a 'cookbook' list of treatments matched up to problems, conditions, or diagnoses. Thirdly, the practitioner is guided by a set of *broad relational principles*, which can be embodied or actualized by different practitioners in relation with different clients in different ways. The resultant therapy experience will therefore often look very different from one therapist–client pair to another, while still being principle-guided.

Moreover, therapy is not really seen as a *treatment* in the medical-model sense of that term. In contrast to the idea that the therapist is 'treating' a 'disorder', therapy becomes a co-created dialogue between two (or more) intelligent, living, embodied beings. The guiding metaphor for this approach is therefore *conversation* and *dialogue* (e.g. Anderson, 1997), and therapy is no more seen as a medical-like treatment. To try to manualize a co-created and inherently unpredictable dialogue is contrary to what intuition suggests genuine, authentic dialogue might consist in. The metaphor of manualization is therefore fundamentally antithetical to the guiding metaphor of this alternative approach.

Since, in this cosmology, successful therapy relies crucially upon clients' active, creative intelligence, interventions become ways that therapist *and* client invoke to fashion therapeutic movement or 'solutions' (Bohart and Tallman, 1999). Contary to the ESVT paradigm explored earlier, it is neither helpful nor accurate to conceptualize these 'ways of being' as 'independent variables' which operate on 'dependent variables' (clients) in order to give rise to therapeutic 'effects'.

In such an alternative paradigm, then, solutions are in no way 'applied' to quasi-passive clients. From a systemic perspective, for example, two clients with what is notionally 'the same' problem (for instance, 'depression') may differ considerably in how the problem was generated, how it is maintained, and how it interacts with their life spaces (Kleinman, 1988). Solutions, or paths to progress, will therefore accordingly vary, and it would most certainly do a kind of violence to this paradigm's core ethos to apply a standardized solution to them. Rather, solutions *emerge* out of an intelligent interrelational dialogue, and are in that sense emergent and necessarily idiosyncratic.

With client-centred therapy in particular, it is the 'being' of the therapist and client in indissoluble relationship which is assumed to be therapeutic, and not specific 'therapist operations', skills, or programmatic interventions. This kind of view is very difficult to understand from a modernist paradigmatic position, which claims that only what is definable and measurable has meaning and effectivity – or even can be said to exist! There may be, and probably is, a potentially *infinite* set of different ways in which therapists could embody and actualize the relational qualities of warmth, empathy, and genuineness with different clients. Therapy 'works' through the interrelational *presence* of the therapist, rather than through specific technological or skill-based operations. It is very difficult to imagine, for example, how one could measure, specify, control, or manualize *authenticity*, or 'being yourself' in therapy! Yet there does now seem to be some empirical support for this view of therapy (e.g. Elliott et al., 2004). Finally, both person-centred and constructive-therapy approaches place *responsiveness* first. That is, they rely upon moment-to-moment phenomenological sensitivity to the subtlety and complexity of the emerging process, and upon their ability to respond appropriately in that moment (cf. our Chapter 17).

Kinds of interventions, then, emerge out of the dialogue with the client, with the therapist effectively utilizing the resources in/of the moment. A client's difficulty or problem would not therefore be treated merely as an instance of a more generalized category of 'disorder'; and nor would any standardized 'treatment' be applied to the client for a given 'disorder'. Indeed, a completely different kind of intervention (or intervention*s*) might have been used with different clients who were describing *the same* 'symptoms' or 'disorder', depending upon the client and her or his life, how client and therapist met and what they co-created together, and on the particular therapeutic experience that their unique meeting generated. Further still, a different therapist working with the same client might have productively utilized an entirely different approach or interventions, while still being faithful to general strategic principles – and still being effective. Viewed from within such a paradigmatic world-view, then, the very project of generalization-driven manualization is quite literally non-sensical and fundamentally wrong-headed – and it is exceedingly difficult if not impossible to imagine how the kinds of approaches described above could be manualized in any meaningful sense. To quote Rosenbaum (1994: 248), 'Therapy requires a constant, ongoing process where the therapist adjusts to the client, and the client adjusts to this adjustment. This makes the manualizing of therapy precisely the wrong strategy for psychotherapy research.'

Some attempts *have* of course been made to manualize client-centred therapy (e.g. Greenberg and Watson, 1998). What they create is an excellent *analogue* of client-centred therapy mapped into a different intellectual universe; but they certainly do not fully represent client-centred therapy as we understand it. In sum, the very idea of following a manual is antithetical to the fundamental nature of client-centred therapy.

The alternative paradigm we are describing here has *subtlety* at its core – along the kind of lines written about by educationalists Max van Manen and Rudolf Steiner (cf. van Manen, 1986; see our Chapter 17, this volume). On this view, to call what therapists do in their work 'interventions' fundamentally misrepresents it in ways that distort the human, experienced meaning of it for both therapist and client. Therapists do not typically do or say something deliberately in order to 'intervene': rather, for example, they will often be genuinely interested and curious, and respond from that experience – albeit in a way that pays attention to the therapeutic helping context in which the experience is unfolding. Yet this perspective is certainly *not* a recipe for an undisciplined '*anything* that is experiential, goes'! (cf. Norcross, 1999: xviii).

In sum, it seems to us particularly absurd to think of many therapists all trying to 'provide' the same 'intervention' in a standardized fashion, when what is so clearly healing about a given unique contextual experience is arguably its natural spontaneity and human quality. This may sound rather like a straw-man caricature – but we are merely describing the logical implications stemming from the world-view entailed in the ESVT paradigm. In terms of research implications, all this is to argue that we would do well to come up with meaningful ways to study client-centred therapy phenomenologically in its 'natural setting' (cf. van Manen, 1997), rather than to distort its nature by manualizing it to fit into a paradigm whose very nature is really alien and even procedurally 'violent' to it.

METAPHYSICAL LEVEL

At the metaphysical or philosophical level, there are two key aspects to the alternative paradigm we are propounding.

THE NATURE OF PROFESSIONAL PRACTICE AND THE 'UNIQUENESS' ASSUMPTION

First, psychotherapy is conceived of, above all, as *a practice*. The kinds of knowledge and the way knowledge is utilized within a given practice are different from the goals of acquiring scientific or theoretical knowledge (Schön, 1983). The goal of conventional 'scientific knowledge' is the nomothetic one of formulating general laws, while the goal of practice is the idiographic one of focusing on the unique, particular individual case or situation.

The approach to practice described above is highly compatible with what a number of writers have described as the real nature of professional practice across all professions (e.g. Bourdieu, 1990; Schön, 1983; Sundararajan, 2002). In any walk of life or profession, practice is fundamentally different from the approach to practice implied by the ESVT approach. The manualization mentality is an instance of what Schön, Habermas (e.g. 1972), the Frankfurt school, and others have called 'technical rationality', being an example of the traditional way in which science is to be applied to practice. However, based on Schön's studies of practitioners in a variety of professions, it does not represent how expert professionals actually practise, even – tellingly – professionals who utilize conventional scientific knowledge, such as architects and engineers. The manualization approach (and ESVT in general) is also an example of what Nadler et al. (1995), in their studies of how professionals creatively solve problems in business, call the 'traditional' problem-solving model, and in no way represents how creative business professionals develop effective solutions to problems.

According to Schön, Nadler et al., and others, effective and successful professionals treat each new problem or case as unique; while in stark contrast, the manualization approach starts out from an (often implicit, unarticulated) *assumption of similarity* (i.e. 'this case is merely an instance of a more general category'), and only embraces uniqueness when the manual fails. In real life, however, it is, at the very least, frequently not so that one case is sufficiently like another to lead to the mechanistic generalization of a thought-replacing rule from one case to another. Manualized generalizing may in some sense 'work' sometimes, or *appear* to work (which is different); but in all cases it is argued to be the judgement of the practitioner which transcends and supersedes the application of any such rules.

To use the language of positivism for a moment, uniqueness exists in the real world because each individual case is a complex combination of many different 'variables', with 'more variables – kinds of possible moves, norms, and interrelationships of these – than can be represented in a finite model' (Schön, op. cit.: 79). And to quote DeGreene, 'The concept of clearly definable and correlatable independent, intervening and dependent variables may be completely inappropriate in a dynamic, mutually causal world' (DeGreene, 1991, as quoted in Nadler, p. 89). Phenomena in the real world are characterized by '. . . complexity, uncertainty, [and] instability' (Schön, 1983: 39); and for Robert Sternberg, 'Real problems are often poorly structured and hard to define . . .' (1987, as quoted in Nadler et al., 1995: 273).

In medical practice, for example, patient care is seldom a simple matter of prescribing precise treatments for distinct, unambiguously definable disease states. Rather, patients typically present as 'polysymptomatic', with complaints often being vague and of an emotionally tinged nature; and neat, clearly identifiable syndromes/diseases often fail to emerge from the review of symptoms (e.g. Sobel, 1995). Indeed, doctors use hunch and intuition far more often than 'medical science' cares to acknowledge (Scovern, 1999: 287) – with 'the art of the healer' and/or culturally sanctioned or legitimated healing practices (Frank, 1973) perhaps being far more significant and efficacious than the 'objective' diagnoses of the scientist-practitioner. Schön refers to an ophthalmologist (more of a 'scientist' than a psychotherapist, one might plausibly assume) who says, 'In 80 or 85 percent of the cases, the patient's complaints and symptoms do not fall into familiar categories of diagnosis and treatment....' (op. cit.: 64).

The uniqueness assumption therefore means that the practitioner focuses on the particulars of each individual case, rather than on how a given case fits into a general category (Schön, 1983). Both general principles and prior knowledge are drawn upon to help understand the unique case, but do not override the necessity of dealing with the uniqueness. Thus, Schön maintains that '[The practitioner] is not dependent on the categories of established theory and technique, but constructs a new theory of the unique case....' (ibid.: 68). Actual solution-finding in real-life situations therefore involves a complex and normally quite unpredictable blend of nomothetic knowledge, the use of prior exemplars, intuition (however we might try to define it – Alexander and Claxton, 2000; see our Chapter 17), and considerable tacit knowledge (Polanyi, 1966) gained through experience – all applied to understanding each unique case. In addition, practice involves an ongoing experimental self-correcting *dialogue* with the situation itself. Through such a dialogue, solutions (if appropriate) are frequently forged which, at the least, are creative modifications of old solutions, and at best are often entirely new solutions that are discovered through that dialogue (or emergence).

Schön also refers to something akin to the so-called 'law of unintended consequences', noting that,

> 'Because of this complexity, the designer's moves tend, happily or unhappily, to produce consequences other than those intended. When this happens, the designer may take account of the unintended changes he has made... by forming new appreciations and understandings and by making new moves. He shapes the situation... the situation "talks back", and he responds . . .'
>
> (op cit.: 79)

Such a description of practice is compatible with our earlier description of practice in client-centred and strategic/solution-focussed therapy. In this alternate paradigm, then, the therapist treats each case as unique – meaning that each case is its own unique blend of what is similar to other cases, and what is different. Any solution developed is developed by a process of ongoing experimentation and *judgement* by the professional and client, wherein prior knowledge and ideas are tested, modified, and so on, until new ways forward or solutions are developed.

Standardized nomothetic knowledge is one possible aspect of what might be used to develop an approach or a solution with an individual client. ESVT- and RCT-based information would then be just one source of information factored into the professional's and client's decision-making process; but there would certainly be no automatic assumption that just because a particular treatment has been manualized and found through an RCT to 'work' for a given 'disorder', that this is what the professional and client would necessarily use in this particular instance. Given that the description of practice presented here is compatible with how Schön (1983) and others have found that practitioners *in general* function, this seems an entirely reasonable way to conceptualize a way of practice, notwithstanding its being antithetical to programmatic manualization. Accordingly, if we wish really to learn how to be effective practitioners, it would be counterproductive, and potentially disastrous, to force both research and practice into a mould which does not represent and do justice to real, effective practice.

CONCLUSIONS

In what is the first part of this two-chapter essay (part II of which follows in Chapter 17), we have looked in some depth at the question of contested paradigms in psychotherapy, through the media of the troublesome (for some!) Dodo bird verdict, the issue of common or 'non-specific' factors, the ontological and methodological shortcomings of positivistic approaches to research, and the mentality and practice of clinical 'manualization'. As made clear in a number of chapters in this volume, CBT is very much a creature of 'modernity', and all that goes with the modernist world-view or paradigm. As such, if it can be demonstrated that the epistemological and ontological assumptions of a modernist cosmology itself, and certainly as applied to psychotherapy experience, are open to severe challenge – not least from incommensurable paradigms which are, at the very least, as legitimate as modernist ones – then it follows from this that we can by no means take at anything like face value the hegenomic claims of 'scientific' superiority that routinely emanate from the ESVT tendency in general, and from the CBT practitioner-field in particular.

In our next chapter, we consider further the fascinating phenomeon of what has been termed 'the intuitive practitioner' (Atkinson and Claxton, 2000), as just one example of the kinds of key relational qualities which the positivist research mentality finds it extremely difficult if not impossible to encompass; and in the process we also look to re-claim for alternative, post-modern therapy paradigms the 'empirically supported treatment' label which has been quite unjustifiably colonized and annexed by the modernist ESVT tendency in the psychotherapy field.

REFERENCES

Anderson, H. (1997) *Conversation, Language and Possibilities: A Postmodern Approach to Therapy*, New York: Basic Books.

Atkinson, T. and Claxton, G. (eds) (2000) *The Intuitive Practitioner: On the Value of Not Always Knowing What One Is Doing*, Buckingham: Open University Press.

Beutler, L. E. (1998) 'Identifying empirically supported treatments: what if we don't?', *Journal of Consulting and Clinical Psychology*, 66: 113–20.

Bohart, A. C. and Tallman, K. A. (1996) 'The active client: therapy as self-help', *Journal of Humanistic Psychology*, 36 (3): 7–30.

Bohart, A. and Tallman, K. (1999) *How Clients Make Therapy Work: The Process of Active Self-healing*, Washington, D.C.: American Psychological Association.

Bourdieu, P. (1990) *The Logic of Practice* (trans. R. Nice), Stanford, Calif.: Stanford University Press.

DeGreene, K. B. (1991) 'Rigidity and fragility of large sociotechnical systems: advanced information technology, the dominant coalition, and paradigm shift at the end of the 20th century', *Behavioral Science*, 36: 64–79.

Elliott, R., Greenberg, L. S., and Lietaer, G. (2004) 'Research on experiential psychotherapies', in M. J. Lambert, A. E. Bergin, and S. L. Garfield (eds), *Handbook of Psychotherapy and Behavior Change* (5th edn), New York: John Wiley & Sons.

Frank, J. D. (1973) *Persuasion and Healing*, Baltimore: Johns Hopkins University Press.

Goldfried, M. R. and Wolfe, B. E. (1996) 'Psychotherapy practice and research: repairing a strained alliance', *American Psychologist*, 51: 1007–16.

Greenberg, L. S. and Watson, J. (1998) 'Experiential therapy of depression: differential effects of client-centered relationship conditions and process-experiential interventions', *Psychotherapy Research*, 8: 210–24.

Habermas, J. (1972) *Knowledge and Human Interests*, London: Heinemann.

Heron, J. (1996) *Co-operative Inquiry: Research into the Human Condition*, London: Sage.

House, R. (1996) 'Counselling in general practice: a plea for ideological engagement', *Counselling*, 7 (1): 40–4.

House, R. (2001) 'Psychopathology, psychosis and the Kundalini: postmodern perspectives on unusual subjective experience', in I. Clarke (ed.), *Psychosis and Spirituality: Exploring the New Frontier*, London: Whurr, pp. 107–25 (plus composite references); retrievable at: http://www.uea.ac.uk/~wp276/article.htm.

House, R. (2003) *Therapy Beyond Modernity: Deconstructing and Transcending Profession-centred Therapy*, London: Karnac Books.

House, R. and Loewenthal, D. (2008) 'Editorial', in special issue on 'CBT in Question', *European Journal of Psychotherapy and Counselling*, 10 (3): 181–6.

House, R. and Totton, N. (1997) *Implausible Professions: Arguments for Pluralism and Autonomy in Psychotherapy and Counselling*, Ross-on-Wye: PCCS Books.

Hubble, M. A., Duncan, B. L., and Miller, S. D. (eds) (1999) *The Heart and Soul of Change: What Works in Therapy*, Washington, D.C.: American Psychological Association.

Johnson, E. L. and Sandage, S. J. (1999) 'A postmodern reconstruction of psychotherapy: orienteering, religion and the healing of the soul', *Psychotherapy: Theory, Research, Practice, Training*, 36: 1–15.

Kleinman, A. (1988) *The Illness Narratives: Suffering, Healing, and the Human Condition*, New York: Basic Books.

Kuhn, T. S. (1970) *The Structure of Scientific Revolutions* (2nd edn), Chicago: University of Chicago Press.

Kuhn, T. S. (1977) *The Essential Tension: Selected Studies in Scientific Tradition and Change*, Chicago: University of Chicago Press.

Lampropoulos, G. K. (2000) 'A reexamination of the empirically supported treatments critiques', *Psychotherapy Research*, 10: 474–87.

Nadler, G., Hibino, S., and Farrell, J. (1995) *Creative Solution Finding: The Triumph of Breakthrough Thinking over Conventional Problem Solving*, Rocklin, Calif.: Prima Publishing.

Norcross, J. C. (1999) 'Foreword', in M. A. Hubble, B. L. Duncan, and S. D. Miller (eds), *The Heart and Soul of Change: What Works in Therapy*, Washington, D.C.: American Psychological Association, pp. xvii–xix.

Parker, I., Georgaca, E., Harper, D., and McLaughlin, T. (1995) *Deconstructing Psychopathology*, London: Sage.

Persons, J. B. and Silberschatz, G. (1998) 'Are results of randomized controlled trials useful to psychotherapists?', *Journal of Consulting and Clinical Psychology*, 66: 126–35.

Polanyi, M. (1966) *The Tacit Dimension*, New York: Doubleday.

Rosenbaum, R. (1994) 'Single-session therapies: intrinsic integration?', *Journal of Psychotherapy Integration*, 4: 229–52.

Schön, D. A. (1983) *The Reflective Practitioner: How Professionals Think in Action*, New York: Basic Books.

Scovern, A. W. (1999) 'From placebo to alliance: the role of common factors in medicine', in M. A. Hubble, B. L. Duncan, and S. D. Miller (eds), *The Heart and Soul of Change: What Works in Therapy*, Washington, D.C.: American Psychological Association, pp. 259–96.

Sobel, D. S. (1995) 'Rethinking medicine: improving health outcomes with cost-effective psychosocial interventions', *Psychosomatic Medicine*, 57: 234–44.

Stiles, W. B. and Shapiro, D. A. (1989) 'Abuse of the drug metaphor in psychotherapy process outcome research', *Clinical Psychology Review*, 9: 521–44.

Stiles, W. B., Honos-Webb, L., and Surko, M. (1998) 'Responsiveness in psychotherapy', *Clinical Psychology: Science and Practice*, 5: 439–58.

Sundararajan, L. (2002) 'Humanistic psychotherapy and the scientist-practitioner debate: an "embodied" perspective', *Journal of Humanistic Psychology*, 42 (2): 34–47.

Task Force on Promotion and Dissemination of Psychological Procedures, Division of Clinical Psychology of the American Psychological Association (1995) 'Training and dissemination of empirically validated psychological treatments: Report and recommendations', *The Clinical Psychologist*, 48: 3–23.

van Kalmthout, M. A., Schaap, C., and Wojciechowski, F. L. (eds) (1985) *Common Factors in Psychotherapy*, Lisse, The Netherlands: Swets & Zeitlinger.

van Manen, M. (1986) *The Tone of Teaching*, Richmond Hill, Ontario: Scholastic/TAB Publications.

van Manen, M. (1997) *Researching Lived Experience: Human Science for an Action Sensitive Pedagogy*, 2nd edn, New York: SUNY Press.

Wampold, B. E. (1997) 'Methodological problems in identifying efficacious psychotherapies', *Psychotherapy Research*, 7: 21–43.

Wittgenstein, L. (1973) *Philosophical Investigations*, Oxford: WileyBlackwell (orig. 1958).

CHAPTER 17

EMPIRICALLY SUPPORTED/VALIDATED TREATMENTS AS MODERNIST IDEOLOGY, II:

ALTERNATIVE PERSPECTIVES ON RESEARCH AND PRACTICE

RICHARD HOUSE & ARTHUR C. BOHART

'What is most tangible has the least meaning and it is perverse then to identify the tangible with the real.'

(Michael Polanyi)

INTRODUCTION

In Chapter 16 we looked in some depth at how CBT is just a part of a wider paradigmatic world-view which we can (rather inadequately) term 'modernity' (e.g. Toulmin, 1990). A strong theme that comes out of that discussion is that, as Brazier and Lees make clear in their Chapters 6 and 7 of this volume, *not* to attempt to locate therapeutic practices and their assumptive philosophies within the evolution of ideas and human consciousness is a major (and telling) omission. For if we fail to seek, and gain, some kind of philosophical purchase on, just what is entailed in the assumptive world-views and practices to which we adhere, then this can at worst lead to a kind of uncritically damaging, *paradigm-bound 'acting-out'*, which will tend to be self-reinforcing and 'status-quo preserving' – that is, generating an inherently conservative 'status quo theory', to use the term coined by theorist of post-modernity, David Harvey (Harvey,1973). This is surely the very antithesis of the kind of critical, deconstructive thinking that is arguably the way in which human consciousness can and does healthily evolve (Tarnas, 1996).

In this chapter we will look more closely at the kinds of phenomena that could be argued to be central in an alternative paradigmatic world-view and its associated research undertaking – paying special attention to issues like subtlety, intuition, discernment, and 'the tacit' in human relational experience (Polanyi, 1966) – *phenomenological* qualities *par excellence* that rarely if ever figure in the kinds of scientistic research that regrettably dominates our field.

This chapter is based upon, and is a substantial elaboration of, Arthur C. Bohart's chapter enitled 'A passionate critique of empirically supported treatments and the provision of an alternative paradigm', which first appeared in J. C. Watson, R. N. Goldman, and M. S. Warner (eds), *Client-centered and Experiential Psychotherapy in the Twenty-first Century: Advances in Theory, Research, and Practice*, Ross-on-Wye: PCCS Books, 2002, pp. 258–77.

THE ROLE OF SCIENCE

The realization that therapy is the *practice* of a professionional activity leads us to view the role of science in a different way. In a practice-view of what therapists are doing in their work, the practice itself is not, nor can it ever be, mechanistically scientific. Artists and artisans use science inventively and unpredictably to solve real-life problems in ways that simply cannot be specified beforehand (e.g. Lawrence, 2005); and any such knowledge is certainly not 'manualistically' applied.

It is interesting and illuminating to imagine a thought-experiment world in which an alternative paradigm such as the one we are advocating here were routinely accepted, and in which no one might even think of doing ESVTs. For a start, they would ask very different research questions – for example, they might want to know about the principles of change involved in helping, and how expert practitioners blend tacit and explicit knowledge to co-create ways of being with, or make productive decisions with, individual clients. Or they might inquire into whether there is any causal connection between the kinds of experiential practices undertaken by therapy trainees and their capacity for intuitive relating and tacit knowing. Alternatively again, they might be interested in questions concerning sensitivity to individual cases; or they might be interested in how practitioners learn from, and adjust to, ongoing feedback they receive in sessions. Such knowledge would certainly not then be manualized, because it would be understood that *practice knowledge* is different from (but includes) scientific knowledge (Schön, 1983; Sundararajan, 2002). This is the kind of research that would tend to be pursued, then, rather than writing theory-based treatment manuals and then engaging in RCTs to test these manuals for so-called 'standardized disorders'.

In short, research would tend to investigate *principles and processes of change*. What would be useful to practitioners, for example, might be to study the tacit-knowing processes used by successful practitioners to discover whether they can be explicitly improved upon or deepened. Beginning attempts have already been attempted in this regard. We can say, for instance, with some degree of scientific backing, that therapists who (a) are adept at facilitating the formation of a good therapeutic alliance; (b) are adept at dialoguing with the client, empathically listening, and taking the client's frame of reference into account (Duncan et al., 1997); (c) who are adept at supporting client involvement (Bohart and Tallman, 1999) and mobilizing their hope and optimism (Duncan et al., 1997; Greenberg, 1999; Snyder et al., 1999); (d) adept at fostering the developing of insight, development of new perspectives, and clarification of the problem (Grawe, 1997); (e) who allow or foster problem actuation in the learning environment of therapy (Grawe, 1997); and (f) who provide the opportunity for mastery experiences (Grawe, 1997) will be more likely to be successful.

In this sense, practitioners who work with these kinds of experiences could legitimately be said to be practising therapy in an 'empirically supported' fashion, although they do not necessarily practise empirically supported *treatments*! If it turns out that these are indeed the kinds of qualities that are more important than are standardized treatment packages for specific 'disorders', then the whole modernist ESVT approach may well turn out to have been an unfortunate and highly wasteful distraction – a mystifying detour that has actually taken us *further away from* a 'scientific' understanding (broadly defined) of therapy and relational experience.

THE NATURE OF THE HUMAN RELATIONAL EXPERIENCE

At a deeper level still, our alternative paradigm is arguably far more compatible with a post-modern, non-deterministic, post-foundational view of the universe (House, 2003) than it is with nineteenth-century Newtonian mechanics. Post-modernism is in fact not an 'ism', or any kind of thing, but rather, a key transitional moment in the evolution of ideas and human consciousness – a moment denoting both an important disillusionment with the objectivist Enlightenment project of modernity, and a liminal potential space which presages something that is as yet unknown and undefined (and may, of course, remain intrinsically so, as 'knowing' and 'definition' themselves are increasingly problematized – see, for example, Clarke, 2005; Hart et al., 1997). Not only, then, is there the question of the place of the transpersonal and the spiritual in forms of knowing (see, for example, Baruss, 1996; Clarke, 2005; and Hart et al. 1997, 2000), but even at the level of modernist science, there is a degree of indeterminacy in the universe, and reality will never be known with 100 per cent predictability – *not* because we simply don't possess the computational capacity to learn everything (a purely practical problem), but because of the very nature of knowing itself. Complete predictability is not even in principle possible.

Our alternative paradigmatic approach has some affinity with a systems view that is, in turn, compatible with Stiles et al.'s (1998) notion of responsiveness. The two complex intersubjective 'systems' that are therapist and client influence one another and psychically interpenetrate in a multitude of different and often unspecifiable ways: verbally, non-verbally, emotionally, cognitively, perceptually, behaviourally, and even, some might argue, spiritually or transpersonally. These multiple paths of influence cross and re-cross in dynamic, circular, non-linearly causal ways. On this kind of view, *a 'meeting of persons' is a complex, indissolubly holistic phenomenon which simply cannot be dismantled into component, linear causal parts.* There are just far too many ways in which two individuals can 'meet' and psychically interpenetrate; and 'meeting' even within the 'system' of the same two individuals can vary from moment to moment, as these two systems themselves change, mutually influence one another, and evolve.

Talking about 'meeting' or encounter in this way may seem too 'ill-defined' and wishy-washy to ESVT advocates, but that is because its very nature is that of a complex, interlocking, shifting phenomenon, not reducible to easily specified behaviours or their combinations. What is easily forgotten is that the label of 'wishy-washiness' is nothing more than a paradigm-bound belief underpinned by a modernist ideological mentality that ontologically assumes (often in an unexamined way) that 'reality' is necessarily sharply and easily definable and capturable. As critics of logical positivism have relentlessly pointed out, it is also a move of faulty logic to assume that that which cannot be measured and accurately specified therefore doesn't exist. Thus, because of what we believe to be the mutual, ongoingly reciprocal influence of the dynamic system which constitutes a therapeutic meeting or encounter, we maintain that an operationalizable 'independent variable' cannot sustainably exist in psychotherapy research.

Again, manualization may offer some kind of reassuring illusion that such a variable is validly specifiable, but within our paradigm, this is merely an illusion. When complex systems interpenetrate, it is both in principle philosophically incoherent and impossible in practice to chart simple linear-causal relationships between input from one system to another system. Therapeutic interventions simply do not map in a one-to-one fashion into client effects, but rather set up perturbations in complex ecological systems where, at best, all we will ever be able to expect are partial, incomplete, and therefore *quite possibly misleading* correlations between inputs and ultimate outputs. Predictability is sometimes possible, but it is inherently imperfect and probabilistic.

Further, and to add to the complexity, because of the systemic nature of the co-creating intersubjective meeting, along with the phenomenon of emergence, the very meaning of any intervention shifts and changes as an ongoing function of its place in that evolving complex system. Because we realize that we can never have perfect predictability, and that there is no necessary standard solution for a given problem, we need to just try things out, trusting our phenomenological experience and intuition, experimenting, self-correcting, and so on. This in turn leads us to operating *intelligently*; and it then becomes important, in practice and in research, to *consult* with the system being worked with (cf. Heron, 1996). Thus, one works *with* the system, not *on* the system. The systems involved must therefore be viewed as self-correcting systems – both therapist and client. The process is inherently *discovery-oriented*, including creative generation of new solutions through processes of dialoguing with the challenge or problem, and then reflexively correcting in an ongoing way. Ultimately, each approach or solution will be unique to that system's intersubjective nature and unfolding, sometimes in very obvious ways, sometimes in relatively subtle ways. This also implies that there is no one solution to any given problem: many different solutions may 'fit' a given problem (equifinality) – if indeed we are even to speak the discourse of 'problems'.

Thus, this approach is much more based on metaphors of *responsiveness* and *resonance.* Moreover, responsiveness and resonance are primary, and not additions or bolt-ons to a standardized format. The client is not a 'dependent variable' to be operated on by an 'independent variable'.

TACIT KNOWLEDGE AND ROLE OF THE THERAPY PRACTITIONER

In Chapter 16 we referred in passing to the issue of tacit knowledge. Effective practitioners do not practise by following manuals, but learn how to use their intuition to transcend rules. Internalized rules become progressively irrelevant because, through practice, practitioners progressively acquire a much more subtle and differentiated *tacit knowledge* of the terrain of practice than can ever, *in principle*, be expressed in explicit rules. Once again, therefore, we can see how a manualization approach fundamentally misrepresents what *actually happens* in therapy practice. In reality, we should note in passing that it is also unlikely that actual therapy practice in any ESVT research project is actually guided by manualization either. Rather, it is guided by the considerable tacit learning that has occurred through training, and then through ongoing supervision by experienced practitioners. One of us (ACB) has personally observed Leslie Greenberg train therapists for his manualized research studies, and it was clear that Greenberg was using considerable tacit, fine-grained understanding in training his therapists in subtleties that went well beyond the descriptions in the training manual.

On this view, then, manuals therefore merely give *an illusion* of the comforting specificity sought after by researchers, but are actually nothing more than 'pretend pseudo-science' – a grand scientific 'emperor' with no clothes on. It is also quite illusory to believe that the immense degree of tacit knowledge often *mysteriously* conveyed by experienced practitioners in their tutoring process will ever be able to be specified well enough in manuals to render practice as 'scientific' as those who advocate ESVTs seem to be pursuing (Schön, 1983). Despite manualization, it will be expected that effective practitioners will practise differently, as they do in all other professions. The same melody played by two different musicians, or conducted by two different conductors, is always different. It is the player him- or herself that really matters, and not the technical, procedural content of what is played, to anything like the same extent.

We therefore support the radical conclusion that in the real world of actual therapy practice, there is no standardized 'treatment' which is being applied *even in the case of manualized therapies*. In our paradigm, a starting assumption is that each practitioner–client pair will generate its own unique ways of working effectively. Different practitioners will embody practice principles in different ways; and in all cases of practice, the role of the practitioner is crucial. Put somewhat differently, one might say that *diversity* (House and Totton, 1997) rather than *standardization* 'rules' – however much the attempt is made to shoe-horn the subtleties and complexities of therapeutic experiencing into a measurable, predictable metric. Or as Moen (1991: 6) evocatively puts it, 'Selective analysis of general properties is not a substitute for the aesthetic intuition of a concrete and particular presence'.

SUBTLETY, INTUITION, AND THERAPEUTIC EXPERIENCE

In the kind of alternative, 'transmodern' paradigm we are exploring both here and in the previous chapter, the phenomenon of *subtlety* and its experiential handmaiden, the virtue of *discernment*, can be seen as key aspects of a therapeutic experience that a modernist, ESVT- and CBT-orientated worldview would find exceedingly difficult if not impossible to encompass. The *Concise Oxford Dictionary* defines 'subtle' thus: 'pervasive or elusive owing to tenuity; evasive, mysterious, hard to grasp or trace; making fine distinctions, having delicate perception; acute; ingenious, elaborate, clever; crafty, cunning'. This is a useful starting-point – though the very nature of subtlety perhaps renders any attempt at a dictionary definition less than satisfactory.

Subtlety, then, is a quality of a kind of human consciousness that is tragically absent from the technocratic *Zeitgeist* of 'modernity' that still *dominates* modern consciousness. It is a telling commentary on the prevailing paradigmatic *Zeitgeist* that the book *The Subtlety of Emotions* (Ben-Ze'ev, 2000) is one of the very few books that seems to have been written which explicitly addresses the question of subtlety.

In his voluminous writings, educationalist and polymath Rudolf Steiner (whose work Lees discusses in Chapter 7) repeatedly emphasized how modern materialistic natural science is incapable of the kind of subtle insight with which an alternative paradigm for psychotherapy is explicitly concerned. In April 1924, for example, he said that '...the kind of intimate observation that reveals fine and delicate changes in man's soul or his bodily structure does not evolve out of scientific ideas' (1968: 28); and 'The interests of this materialistic conception of the world... have developed in the educationist a terrible indifference to the more intimate and delicate impulses in the soul of the human being who is to be educated' (1926: 18) – with the result that 'materialistic thought is unpractical when the need is to enter into life in a living way' (1938: 60).

The educationalist and phenomenologist Max van Manen also explicitly addresses what we might call, after Steiner, the 'intangibles' or 'imponderables' in his writings on pedagogy. Van Manen was Professor of Education at the University of Alberta when he wrote a number of deeply insightful books on 'pedagogical subtlety' – the kind of subtleties which are notably absent, or at best neglected, in mainstream education (see Brown, 1992; van Manen, 1986, 1991).

Founding editor of the journal *Phenomenological Pedagogy*, van Manen's contributions are deeply influenced by hermeneutical-phenomenological thinking (where 'hermeneutics' refers to 'the process of describing the "essence" of something' – Brown, 1992: 47). His two major studies, *The Tone of Teaching* (1986) and *The Tact of Teaching* (1991) are veritable goldmines of wisdom and insight on the 'soul-subtleties' of teaching as practice and experience; and his seminal text *Researching Lived Experience: Human Science for an Action Sensitive Pedagogy* (1990) gives us a glimpse of what research might begin to look like within a 'post-foundationalist' alternative paradigm. Rather than setting out manipulatively to control the world (as the technocratic objectivist does), the sensitive phenomenologist offers the possibility of in-touch contact with, and full participation in, the 'life-world'. In short, the approach privileges sensitivity, openness to existential experience, and a commitment to inquire into lived, revealed meaning, and to illuminate 'contextualized humanity' (Brown, op. cit.: 49-51 *passim*).

Van Manen's book *The Tone of Teaching* is full of wisdom about an attuned pedagogy's intangible subtleties. He writes, for example, that '"Atmosphere"... is a vaporlike sphere which envelops and affects everything... *Mood is a way of knowing* and being in the world... Atmosphere is a complex phenomenon... – the way human beings experience the world' (van Manen, 1986: 31, 32, emphasis added). Van Manen also pays attention to the critical question of 'presence'. Within the field of counselling and psychotherapy, *presence* refers to the Buberian I–Thouness of the therapeutic relationship (e.g. Robbins, 1997) – the capacity to relate in a relatively undefended, open, non-projecting way which encourages real human contact, intimacy, and genuine encounter. Just as the teacher's presence with and for the children in her charge is a vital aspect of their pedagogical identity, so it can be argued that a *passionate presence* (Natiello, 2001), or encountering the other at *relational depth* (Mearns and Cooper, 2005), constitute core dimensions of what we might call 'trans-modern' therapy practice from the kind of paradigmatic stance we are attempting to articulate.

Here is van Manen on presence – with the words 'therapist' and 'client' substituted for his terms, 'teacher' and 'child' (with our apologies to Max):

> 'The most important aspect of our living hope is a way of being with clients. It is not what we say and do, first of all, but a way of being present to the client... When a therapist fails to be what ostensibly he or she *does*, then the therapist is really an absence... We may be physically present to clients while something essential is absent in our presence.'
>
> (1986.: 27, 43, his emphasis)

Sardello (2002: 118) is surely referring to something very similar when he writes of 'a letting-be-present of the soul-being of the other in radical proximity to our own soul-being'. Buber wrote similarly about what he called 'contact' (a term also used, incidentally, in Gestalt psychotherapy): 'through his mere existence, only he must be a really existing man and he must be really present to his pupils; *he educates through contact*' (Buber, 1990/1967: 102, emphasis added).

Van Manen proceeds to make an even more subtle link between atmosphere and presence – for 'atmosphere is also the way a teacher [therapist] is present to children [clients], and the way children [clients] are present to themselves and to the teacher [therapist]' (1986: 36). Certainly, 'Pedagogic thoughtfulness and tact are not simply a set of external skills to be acquired in a workshop' (ibid.: 50), and 'A professional can act first because his or her body has been readied by thoughtfulness' (ibid.: 53).

Van Manen also has a strongly non-instrumental approach to teacher competency that is very different from the current mainstream ideology:

> 'Methods or techniques of teaching cannot be adequately described by external knowledge... Teacher competency has more to do with pedagogical tactfulness, having a sensitivity to what is best for each child [client], having a sense of each child's [client's] life and his or her deep preoccupation.'
>
> (ibid.: 49, 46)

Van Manen is also not afraid to enter the political arena: '…the "administrative" and "technological" have so penetrated the very lifeblood of our existence that parents and teachers are in danger of forgetting a certain other type of understanding…' (ibid.: 29).

In sum, 'teaching [or doing therapy] is much more than the dutiful execution of technical acts' (Brown, 1992: 56): it involves an improvisational thoughtfulness involving 'the corporeal being of the person; an active sensitivity toward the subjectivity of the other' (van Manen, quoted in ibid.).

TOWARD THE INTUITIVE PRACTITIONER: BEYOND 'COMPETENCIES', TOWARD BEING

> 'Generalizable knowledge about teaching and learning will never fully reflect or be reflected in the individual cognitive framework of practitioners.'
>
> (Atkinson and Claxton, 2000: 4)

The role of intuition (however we might attempt to define what it consists in) within the professions – most notably in teaching – has recently been recognized in an important book, tellingly titled *The Intuitive Practitioner: On the Value of Not Always Knowing What One Is Doing* (Atkinson and Claxton, 2000). Though focussing primarily on education, we maintain that this edited collection has great relevance to the work of psychotherapy and counselling as well. It starts from the observation that, for much of the time, experienced professionals are unable to account for and explain what they are doing, or, indeed, tell us what they 'know'. Yet within the pravailing 'audit-culture' values (Power, 1997) of the crass positivistic specification of measurable so-called 'competencies', professional development and practice are routinely discussed as if conscious understanding and specification are of central relevance and importance. *The Intuitive Practitioner* addresses the relationship between rational or explicit ways of knowing and learning, on the one hand, and inarticulate, intuitive, or implicit ones on the other – embracing what is a seeming paradox, and exploring the dynamic relationship that exists between reason and intuition within the realm of professional practice. The book's contributors delve deeply and revealingly into the much-neglected nature of intuition, and illustrate the crucial role that it plays in the exercising and development of professional decision-making and judgement.

The 'modernist' tendency to 'fetishize' the conscious and the declarative, and to interpret reflection solely in terms of conscious articulation, is fundamentally questioned, and the value of forms of reflection that are not necessarily articulatable is strongly asserted. We should note in passing that the book has considerable relevance to therapy training in its offering of diverse practical lessons for the initial training and continuing professional development of educators that takes full account of the import of the intuitive.

The chapter by Broadfoot (2000) is especially pertinent to our current concerns in our two chapters in this volume. Broadfoot opens up the question of the effect of what we might term 'assessment-mindedness' on intuitive capacity. There are important parallels here with so-called 'evidence-based practice' and the associated near-obsession with the need for certain kinds of research in the therapy world. It is virtually unheard of for anyone to challenge *the very idea* of 'research' (as currently conceived as hypothesis-testing quantification) in our field, but that is precisely what we are going to do here. First, we think it is important to be aware of the *emotional dynamics* that may well be driving, at least in part, the field's current obsession with research, accountability, and 'evidence-based practice' – rooted in part, one of us (RH) suggests, in a culturally pervasive and essentially unprocessed anxiety to do with loss of control, a phantasy of powerlessness, and cultural and spiritual anomie. An anxiety, moreover, which therapy practitioners would normally be expected to be particularly aware of and able to contain, and certainly not to 'act out' from. Yet in the field's uncritical embracing of the 'audit culture', the New Managerialism, and the New Public Management (House, 2008; Power, 1997), the grave concern is that we are unawarely colluding with these pernicious cultural forces in our obsession with accountability, efficacy, and 'scientific evidence' cast in a positivistic mould.

It is important not to assume, of course, that merely because a process may be anxiety- and unconsciously driven, that this *de facto* renders it necessarily invalid; but it certainly does cast considerable doubt on the essentially uncritical way in which research- and efficacy-mindedness have been embraced by the field without any critical debate as to their relevance and appropriateness in our peculiar field. One might reasonably ask why it is that, to date, there has been comparatively little engagement with these crucial issues in the therapy world. Might it be that there is some kind of insidious process operating in modern culture such that we all end up '*thinking like a state*' (Scott, 1999) – with all of the deadly limiting and distorting consequences of that surreptitious mentality? Broadfoot puts it thus:

> 'assessment is... so central to the discourse of contemporary culture that [quoting Wittgenstein] we find ourselves in a "linguistic prison"; we have been "bewitched" by the concepts of... assessment ... to such an extent that even what we are able to think is constrained by the boundaries of that conceptual language.'
>
> (2000: 207)

These are surely the kinds of questions that culturally, critically, and *politically* engaged psychotherapeutic thinking at its most incisive is very best placed to engage in; and to the extent that we don't do it, the therapy field could be in for very big trouble indeed. After all, the 'audit culture' and its accompanying ideology are systematically saturating every aspect of public and, increasingly, private life, and therapy is by no means immune from these arguably toxic developments. With the current obsession with 'evidence-based practice', for example, the very notion of 'evidence' itself is routinely taken for granted and uncritically assumed to be unproblematic. There are at last some welcome signs that the audit culture and its control-obsessed managerialist ideology is beginning to fall apart at the seams – certainly in the post-Blair UK; yet should not the insight that a psychotherapeutic ethos and sensibility affords us have led to a forensically critical deconstructive spotlight being shone upon the way in which the audit culture has been infecting the therapy world in all manner of ways? – not least through the CBT/happiness agenda (see Pilgrim's Chapter 21, this volume) and the extraordinarily naïve 'outcomes' claims that have been made for the superiority of CBT-type approaches over other modalities (see various chapters in this volume).

Just as there has been a kind of 'trance induction' involved in the seemingly inexorable move toward the state regulation of the psychological therapies in Britain, a similar kind of trance induction has arguably been active in the case of the audit culture within therapy, with erstwhile critically minded practitioners seemingly taking the notion of 'evidence' and 'evidence-based practice', and the underlying dynamics driving these preoccupations, as unproblematic givens.

The other important point to make here is the impact of what, elsewhere, I (RH) have called 'audit-mindedness' (House, 1996a) on the very subtle practitioner qualities that we are discussing here. For if, as we strongly believe, qualities like subtletly, discernment, and intuitive capacity are key common-factor 'ingredients' of effective practionership, and if those very qualities are not only *not* amenable to the positivistic 'violence' that is 'variable specification' and all that goes with it, but are actually *adversely affected by* such an 'evidence-based' mentality, then it may well be that the very act of importing a 'politically correct' preoccupation with accountability into our work substantially compromises it – and even ends up with the grotesque outcome that our anxiety-driven need to somehow guarantee the efficacy of our work, and the armamentarium of procedures that we adopt to prove it, *actually do far more net damage to the quality of therapy work than any improvements brought about by the assessment and accountability regime itself.*

We also surely have enough experience by now to know that virtually all technocratic intrusions into human systems generate all manner of normally unconscious 'material' around power (cf. Guilfoyle's and Proctor's Chapters 19 and 20, this volume), and routinely precipitate quite unpredictable side-effects which commonly do more net harm than did the pre-existing shortcomings the interventions were supposed to address. Crassly positivistic and technocratic conceptions of service evaluation – what Kilroy et al. (2004: 1) refer to as 'the reduction of (qualitative) thought to (quantitative) product, (critical) education to (utilitarian) skill-set' – are surely singularly inappropriate means of evaluating efficacy in the peculiarly unique and idiosyncratic field of psychotherapeutic help. As Broadfoot has it, 'attempts to pretend that a human being's achievements, or even more, their potential, can be unambiguously measured, are doomed from the outset' (2000: 215). Again, within the field of education Fendler (1998: 57) develops the kind of critique that has been notably missing in the mainstream therapy world. Below, we reproduce an aspect of her incisive critique, substituting 'therapy' for 'education' terms (as precisely the same arguments apply in both fields):

> 'Now there is a reversal; the goals and outcomes are being stipulated at the outset, and the procedures are being developed post hoc. The "nature" of the [client's experience] is stipulated in advance, based on objective criteria, usually statistical analysis. Because the outcome drives the procedure (rather than vice versa), there is no longer the theoretical possibility of unexpected results; there is no longer the theoretical possibility of becoming unique in the process of becoming ["treated"]... In this new system, evaluation of [psychotherapeutic] policy reform is limited to an evaluation of the degree to which any given procedure yields the predetermined results...'

What our field should surely be embracing is the most radical thinking in relevant and associated fields (e.g. Trifonas, 2004), rather than uncritically mimicking the worst features of the 'surveillance culture' and the souless technocracies of 'high modernity'. The kinds of epistemological and methodological critques that will be necessary are at last beginning to be made within the field, but we find ourselves asking, where have they been all these years?... Might it be the case, for example, that some process commonly occurs in which we are all in some sense infantilized by the state, and haven't yet found a mature place to take up in relation to overweening state intrusion into human experience, and into life itself? – and might this be especially so in the post 9/11 cultural milieu of acute and often largely unprocessed anxiety, which may well have triggered off all manner of unconscious phantasies?

These are the kinds of questions to which analytic and psychotherapeutic thinking might have a significant contribution to make, if we are not to sleepwalk into a thorough-going 'surveillance society'. And to follow Samuels' important work in this realm (e.g. Samuels, 2001), as the anxiety-saturated 'audit culture' proceeds to penetrate every aspect of public and private life, these are also questions that will surely manifest in the consulting room itself, and with which politically committed and aware practitioners surely cannot fail to engage with their clients and patients. There are also interesting institutional questions about the extent to which a *radical countercultural space* can be preserved in a psychotherapy field which becomes increasingly professionalized and subject to the all-pervasive audit culture.

Over a decade ago now, Spinelli provocatively wrote that '[T]here exists precious little about therapy that we can say with any certainty... therapists really don't know what they're doing – even if they insist upon pretending ... they are "experts"' (Spinelli, 1996: 56, 59). We strongly concur with this view, which paradoxically further entails that the more we are able to admit to our 'ignorance' – albeit it in a 'disciplined' way, perhaps – then the more likely it will be that we will discover the requisite abilities and capacities really to help our clients in a sensitive and effective way.

DISCUSSION

At the risk of oversimplification, we can say that the main culprits in the ESVT paradigm ultimately reduce to two tendencies: first, the underlying mechanistic assumptions upon which the ESVT paradigm appears to be based, which erroneously presume that greater and greater specificity will lead to better and better predictability and control, based on the research model wherein an independent variable is manipulated to 'control' the dependent variable; and the misguided metaphorical identification of psychotherapy with a medical-model, drug/treatment/cure ideology (e.g. House, 1996b; Stiles and Shapiro, 1989). In regard to the former, the ESVT paradigm can be argued to be based upon a traditional Newtonian, billiard-ball view of the universe, in which it is in principle conceivable (if not actually possible) to know everything, so that one can predict and control everything. From this paradigmatic vantage-point, science is only imperfect because we haven't yet discovered and identified everything – while in principle, complete predictability is assumed to be possible.

In contrast, we maintain that in a complex, systemic, non-linear view of the universe, more compatible with post-modern, New Paradigm thinking, one will never *even in principle* be able to know with any degree of certainty how 'A' affects 'B' (if that is the causal-determinsitc way we presume to chop up the universe), certainly where complex systems are involved. In other words, even within in its own terms, the linear-deterministic approach is quite inadequate for producing the kind of knowledge to which it claims to aspire.

Thus, simple input–output models of research, while perhaps useful as 'rough cuts', are positively misleading in understanding the complex nature of the phenomena involved (or more accurately, perhaps, they *may well* be – and we have no way from within the positivist world-view to ascertain the degree of misleadingness). When two complex non-linear systems 'bump up' against one another, one can perhaps hope for research to show an increase in probability that an input 'A' may increase the probability of an effect 'B'; but the idea that one can successively dismantle and disaggregate the phenomenal 'whole' and move closer and closer to complete mechanistic predictability is unrealistic and ontologically unsustainable. In sum, then, we can say that pro-ESVT advocates live in a modernist universe, while those sceptical of the ESVT ideology, like the present authors, inhabit something more akin to a post- or trans-modern one – however we might attempt a definition-*which-is-not-one* of the philosophically challenging post-modern mentality.

The second culprit appears to be the medical-model drug metaphor. In medicine, when a new drug comes along, RCTs are carried out to test its effects. However, when a medical doctor encounters a patient with a problem, in practice she or he does not mechanistically apply the drug and simply do nothing else. The drug, which has been validated in a drug trial, is used as a *part* of treatment (and of course we are ignoring here the crucially important question of the placebo effect – Shepherd and Sartorius, 1989). Note that *the whole course* of treatment is not in itself manualized. In contrast, because the whole course of a psychotherapy experience (e.g. a treatment for a 'disorder') is made analogous to a drug, in the psychotherapy domain, those who want to adopt the drug metaphor make the quite unwarranted jump of *manualizing the whole course of treatment.*

From the kind of paradigmatic perspective adopted in this and the previous chapter, it is a form of scientific hegemony, and an epistemologically naïve and unsustainable position, to suggest that all research should be carried out within the ESVT paradigm – and anyone that claims that it should be is either uncritically caught up in the 'ideology of modernity' (cf. Woolfolk and Richardson, Chapter 5, this volume), or else caught up in parochial vested interests or configurations of institutional power (cf. Guilfoyle's Chapter 19, this volume). It is equally hegenomous, and again a scientifically unsustainable position, to argue that practice should be based on therapies that meet ESVT criteria, or, by extension, to argue that it is unethical if one does not use an RCT-supported therapy where appropriate (e.g. Persons, in Persons and Silberschatz, 1998; Bryceland and Stam, Chapter 15, this volume).

ESVTers would no doubt raise objections to what we have argued here. First, it might be objected that the 'ideal-typical' picture we have painted of contesting paradigms in psychotherapy is oversimplified to the point of caricature, and that as a consequence, our critiques have a 'straw-man' quality which bears little relation to what actually happens in the world of therapy practice. We would certainly be committing precisely the error which we attribute to the modernist mentality if we were to assert a dichotomous, mutually excluding categorization of therapy approaches into 'modernist' and 'post-modernist' ones. Not least, we are *all* in some quite unavoidable sense creatures of 'modernity', and it is arguably impossible to absent ourselves from modernity's culturally pervasive influences and effects.

However, we do maintain that the epistemological *tendencies* that we have identified and elaborated upon in this and the previous chapter do have a very real and demonstrably tangible presence in modern therapeutic practice, and we base this on our own personal experience of both practising as therapists and reflecting deeply upon this peculiar work we do. We maintain, further, that if any coherent sense is to be made of the efficacy controversies that currently beset our field, then a full engagement with the *level* and the *nature of argument* developed in these chapters is an essential necessary condition if any progress toward insight and understanding is to be made.

ESVTers might propose a head-to-head test of a manualized empirically supported treatment versus therapy carried out from within the alternative paradigm propounded here. But this simply won't do; for the troubling question would then be: which set of research criteria from which paradigm would be used to answer the question? – or in other words, how do we decide which paradigmatic criteria should be given precedence in order to give an 'objective' answer to the question? Of course, we are entering the thorny and highly contested philosophical field of relativism here, which is a discussion well beyond the scope of this chapter. Yet we can see the kinds of philosophical and epistemological arguments that need to be engaged with to address the efficacy question in the therapy field – and to date, ESVTers have, tellingly, shown no inclination to enter and engage with these difficult arguments.

It is highly likely that framing of such a question in a way that would satisfy advocates of the ESVT approach would not satisfy advocates of the alternative, post-modern paradigm – and, of course, vice versa. Moreover, and based on what we know about therapy research, the most likely outcome would be the Dodo bird verdict. And even if one approach could somehow be shown to be superior to the other, advocates of which ever approach had 'lost' would argue that the test wasn't fair. Surely a far better way to proceed is for researchers from different paradigms to pursue their varying ends, and somewhere, down the road, the slow, steady accumulation of results will decide the issue – with a Kuhnian paradigm shift perhaps being the outcome (Kuhn, 1970), should post-modernist approaches prevail in the broad sweep of the evolution of ideas and human consciousness (cf. Lees' Chapter 7, this volume). So – let us allow the rich diversity of therapy approaches to flourish, and let us dare to trust the paradigmatic outcome!

Finally, and in relation to this book, what are the implications of our arguments for CBT and its mounting hegemony in the therapy world, driven as it is by complex cultural and political-economic forces (e.g. Pilgrim, Chapter 21, this volume), and the overriding 'ideology of modernity' (cf. Woolfolk and Richardson, Chapter 5, this volume)? Briefly, we maintain – with no little irony – that the detailed arguments developed in this and the previous chapter cast considerable doubt on, if not constitute a devastating undermining of, the allegedly *scientific* legitimacy that is routinely and uncritically claimed for CBT by its proponents. We maintain that at the very least, philosophers of CBT and its theorists urgently need to construct a viable and defensible *metaphysical underpinning* for its theory and practice – for it seems clear from the many critical arguments in this book that, as yet, no one in the field seems to have attempted to construct such a metatheory that is able to make a coherent and sustainable case against the kinds of epistemological arguments and paradigmatic critiques presented in this book. Until such an attempt is made, it seems to us that at the very least, a far greater degree of modesty is called for from those who aspire to entrenching CBT as *the* therapy of choice across the therapeutic realm. As Woolfolk and Richardson (see Chapter 5) articulated so clearly a quarter century ago, what is at stake in all this is a veritable Kuhnian 'paradigm war' between the forces of modernity and post- or trans-modernity; and we maintain that it is impossible to understand the precipitate rise of CBT without locating it within such a cultural and paradigmatic world-view (cf. Lees' Chapter 7, this volume).

CONCLUSION

> 'The need to recoup the loss of depth and particularity is urgent if we are not to treat fellow human beings as abstract objects or lapse into anesthetic and destructive indifference to the natural environment.'
>
> (Marcia K. Moen, 1991: 6)

A 'trans-modern' world-view calls forth the imperative to move far beyond therapy as *technology* and a medical-model 'diagnosis-and-treatment' model of care, as envisaged in the world of cognitively biased CBT and postivistic evidence-based practice, to embrace instead the often uncomfortable reality that therapy as a healing practice entails many practitioner qualities that are *in principle* beyond rational 'modernist' specification – as a number of writers in diverse fields well beyond therapy have argued (cf. Michael Polanyi's notion of 'tacit knowledge' and Donald Schön's 'reflective practitioner', for example). As Frank put it, '[P]sychotherapy transpires in the realm of meaning.... [I]n contrast to facts, meanings cannot be confirmed or disconfirmed by the objective criteria of the scientific method' (Frank, 1989: 144).

In their excellent anthology *The Intuitive Practitioner*, we find Atkinson and Claxton arguing that there is a great value in 'not always knowing what one is doing', and that *intuition* is often the key to effective and successful practitionership in the human caring vocations. Such radical counter-cultural perspectives on therapy in the twenty-first century clearly have major implications for the be-coming of therapy practitioners, for the kinds of training experiences that might be most effective and enabling – and of course for the practice of psychotherapy research itself.

REFERENCES

Atkinson, T. and Claxton, G. (eds) (2000) *The Intuitive Practitioner: On the Value of Not Always Knowing What One Is Doing*, Buckingham: Open University Press.

Baruss, I. (1996) *Authentic Knowing: Convergence of Science and Spiritual Aspiration*, West Lafayette, Ind.: Purdue University Press.

Ben-Ze'ev, A. (2000) *The Subtlety of Emotions*, MIT Press: Bradford Books.

Bohart, A. and Tallman, K. (1999) *How Clients Make Therapy Work: The Process of Active Self-healing*, Washington, D.C.: American Psychological Association.

Broadfoot, P. (2000) 'Assessment and intuition', in T. Atkinson. and Claxton, G. (eds), *The Intuitive Practitioner: On the Value of Not Always Knowing What One Is Doing*, Buckingham: Open University Press, pp. 199–219.

Brown, R. K. (1992) 'Max van Manen and pedagogical human science research', in W. F. Pinar and W. M. Reynolds (eds), *Understanding Curriculum as Phenomenological and Deconstructed Text*, New York: Teachers College Press, Columbia University Press, pp. 44–63.

Buber, M. (1990) *A Believing Humanism: My Testament, 1902–65*, New Jersey: Humanities Press Int. (orig. 1967).

Clarke, C. (ed.), (2005) *Ways of Knowing: Science and Mysticism Today*, Exeter: Imprint Academic.

Duncan, B. L., Hubble, M. A., and Miller, S. D. (1997) *Psychotherapy with 'Impossible' Cases: The Efficient Treatment of Therapy Veterans*, New York: Norton.

Fendler L. (1998) 'What is it impossible to think? A genealogy of the educated subject', in T. S. Popkewitz and M. Brennan (eds), *Foucault's Challenge: Discourse, Knowledge and Power in Education*, New York: Teachers College Press, Columbia University, pp. 39–63.

Frank, J. D. (1989) 'Non-specific aspects of treatment: the view of a psychotherapist', in M. Shepherd and N. Sartorius (eds), *Non-Specific Aspects of Treatment*, Toronto: Hans Huber Publishers, pp. 95–114.

Grawe, K. (1997) 'Research-informed psychotherapy', *Psychotherapy Research*, 7: 1–20.

Greenberg, R. P. (1999) 'Common psychosocial factors in psychiatric drug therapy', in M. A. Hubble, B. L. Duncan, and S. D. Miller (eds), *The Heart and Soul of Change: What Works in Therapy*, Washington, D.C.: American Psychological Association, pp. 297–328.

Hart, T., Nelson, P., and Puhakka, K. (eds) (1997) *Spiritual Knowing: Alternative Epistemic Perspectives*, Carrollton, Ga.: State University of West Georgia, Studies in Social Sciences, Vol. 34.

Hart, T., Nelson, P., and Puhakka, K. (eds) (2000) *Transpersonal Knowing: Exploring the Horizon of Consciousness*, Albany: State University of New York Press.

Harvey, D. (1973) *Social Justice and the City*, London: Arnold.

Heron, J. (1996) *Co-operative Inquiry: Research into the Human Condition*, London: Sage.

House, R. (1996a) '"Audit-mindedness" in counselling: some underlying dynamics', *British Journal of Guidance and Counselling*, 24 (2): 277–83.

House, R. (1996b) 'General practice counselling: a plea for ideological engagement', *Counselling*, 7 (1): 40–4.

House, R. (2003) *Therapy Beyond Modernity: Deconstructing and Transcending Profession-centred Therapy*, London: Karnac Books.

House, R. (2008) 'The dance of psychotherapy and politics', *Psychotherapy and Politics International*, 6 (2): 98–109.

House, R. and Totton, N. (eds) (1997) *Implausible Professions: Arguments for Pluralism and Autonomy in Psychotherapy and Counselling*, Ross-on-Wye: PCCS Books.

Kilroy, P., Bailey, R., and Chare, N. (2004) 'Editorial sounding: auditing culture', *Parallax*, Issue 31, 10 (2): 1–2.

Kuhn, T. S. (1970) *The Structure of Scientific Revolutions* (2nd edn), Chicago: University of Chicago Press.

Lawrence, R. L. (2005) *Artistic Ways of Knowing: Expanded Opportunities for Teaching and Learning*, San Francisco: Jossey-Bass.

Mearns, D. and Cooper, M. (2005) *Working at Relational Depth in Counselling and Psychotherapy*, London: Sage.

Moen, M. K. (1991) 'Introduction', in B. den Ouden and M. Moen (eds), *The Presence of Feeling in Thought*, New York: Peter Lang, pp. 1–9.

Natiello, P. (2001) *The Person-Centred Approach: A Passionate Presence*, Ross-on-Wye: PCCS Books.

Persons, J. B. and Silberschatz, G. (1998) 'Are results of randomized controlled trials useful to psychotherapists?', *Journal of Consulting and Clinical Psychology*, 66: 126–35.

Polanyi, M. (1966) *The Tacit Dimension*, New York: Doubleday.

Power, M. (1997) *The Audit Society: Rituals of Verification*, Oxford: Oxford University Press.

Robbins, A. (1997) *Therapeutic Presence: Bridging Expression and Form*, London: Jessica Kingsley.

Samuels, A. (2001) *Politics on the Couch: Citizenship and the Internal Life*, London: Karnac.

Sardello, R. (2002) *The Power of Soul: Living the Twelve Virtues*, Charlottesville, Va.: Hampton Roads Publ. Co.

Schön, D. A. (1983) *The Reflective Practitioner: How Professionals Think in Action*, New York: Basic Books.

Scott, J. C. (1999) *Seeing Like a State: How Certain Schemes to Improve the Human Condition Have Failed*, New Haven: Yale University Press.

Shepherd, M. and Sartorius, N. (eds) (1989) *Non-Specific Aspects of Treatment*, Toronto: Hans Huber Publishers.

Snyder, C. R., Michael, S. T., and Cheavens, J. S. (1999) 'Hope as a psychotherapeutic foundation of common factors, placebos, and expectancies', in M. A. Hubble, B. L. Duncan, and S. D. Miller (eds), *The Heart and Soul of Change: What Works in Therapy*, Washington, D.C.: American Psychological Association, pp. 179–200.

Spinelli, E. (1996) 'Do therapists know what they're doing?', in I. James and S. Palmer (eds), *Professional Therapeutic Titles: Myths and Realities*, Leicester: British Psychological Society, Div. Couns. Psychol., Occasional Paper 2, pp. 55–61.

Steiner, R (1926) *The Essentials of Education: Five Lectures…*, London: Anthroposophical Publ. Co.

Steiner, R. (1938) *The Education of the Child in the Light of Anthroposophy*, London: Rudolf Steiner Press; New York: Anthroposophic Press.

Steiner, R. (1968) *The Roots of Education*, London: Rudolf Steiner Press.

Stiles, W. B. and Shapiro, D. A. (1989) 'Abuse of the drug metaphor in psychotherapy process outcome research', *Clinical Psychology Review*, 9: 521–44.

Stiles, W. B., Honos-Webb, L., and Surko, M. (1998) 'Responsiveness in psychotherapy', *Clinical Psychology: Science and Practice*, 5: 439–58.

Sundararajan, L. (2002) 'Humanistic psychotherapy and the scientist-practitioner debate: an "embodied" perspective', *Journal of Humanistic Psychology*, 42 (2): 34–47.

Tarnas, R. (1996) *The Passion of the Western Mind: Understanding the Ideas That Have Shaped Our World View*, London: Pimlico.

Toulmin, S. (1990) *Cosmopolis: The Hidden Agenda of Modernity*, New York: Free Press.

Trifonas, P. P. (2004) 'Auditing education: deconstruction and the archiving of knowledge as curriculum', *Parallax*, Issue 31, 10 (2): 37–49.

van Manen, M. (1986) *The Tone of Teaching*, Richmond Hill, Ontario: TAB Publishers.

van Manen, M. (1990) *Researching Lived Experience: Human Science for an Action Sensitive Pedagogy*, Albany: SUNY Press.

van Manen, M. (1991) *The Tact of Teaching: The Meaning of Pedagogical Thoughtfulness*, New York: SUNY Press.

CHAPTER 18

WHERE IS THE MAGIC IN COGNITIVE THERAPY?

A PHILO/PSYCHOLOGICAL INVESTIGATION

FRED NEWMAN

'Effective therapy often seems magical.'

(Kenneth Gergen, 2006: 28)

WHAT IS THE RELATIONSHIP BETWEEN COGNITIVE THERAPY AND COMMON SENSE?

Is cognitive therapy an effort to analyse common sense and to show how and when commonsensical thinking can go astray and lead to emotional disorders? Or is cognitive therapy an effort to make use of common sense in dealing with those emotional disorders? Or is cognitive therapy an effort to do both of those and more?

Aaron Beck's seminal work on cognitive therapy (1979) begins its very first chapter, 'Common Sense and Beyond', with a quotation from the distinguished British philosopher Alfred North Whitehead:[1]

> 'Science is rooted in what I have just called the whole apparatus of common sense thought. That is the datum from which it starts, and to which it must recur ... You may polish up common sense, you may contradict it in detail, you may surprise it. But ultimately your whole task is to satisfy it.'
>
> (p. 6)

There is, of course, a colossal irony here. For one of Whitehead's great intellectual contributions (albeit a very early one) was *Principia Mathematica* (written in collaboration with Sir Bertrand Russell, also a philosopher). *Principia* was a monumental effort to show that all of mathematics could be reduced to logic (in particular, to mathematical logic, provided that mathematical logic included, as supposed by Russell and Whitehead, the unassailable concept of a set: Russell and Whitehead's assumption being that nothing could be more *intuitively* obvious than the notion of a collection of things or a group, which is what they and most everyone else meant by a set). Yet starting with Frege through Gödel and beyond, this commonsensical

1. Alfred North Whitehead was President of Section A of the British Association for the Advancement of Science. In September 1916 Whitehead addressed Section A – Mathematical and Physical Sciences – at the Association meeting in Newcastle-on-Tyne, UK. His talk was entitled 'The Organization of Thought'. It was printed in *Science,* Vol. 44, no. 1134 (22 September), 1916: 409–19.

notion of a set appeared to introduce paradoxes which rendered implausible Russell and Whitehead's, and dozens of other mathematical logicians' reductionistic projects.

WHAT IF ANYTHING DOES COMMON SENSE HAVE TO DO WITH SCIENCE?

Whitehead's observations seem commonsensically sound, yet serious efforts to deconstruct and analyse science and the scientific method (a project which consumed the minds of many philosophers in the first half of the twentieth century) yield distinctly uncommonsensical (and unacceptable) results. This came as a surprise to some, but by no means to all, for the historical and mathematical roots of science, complex as they may be, are arguably as much in magic (somewhat broadly interpreted) as they are in common sense.[2] Pythagoras seemed to have gained genuine insight by exploring magical numerological connections. And when Newton wasn't downstairs 'wowing' the Royal Academy, he was apparently upstairs exploring ancient alchemic relationships. And even today, if common sense alone could do it, what need of the most interesting esoteric elements that make up modern science from quanta to quarks to string theory?

The first half of the twentieth century was marked by many philosophers serving as the self-appointed handmaidens of science, attempting to articulate a logical and empiricistic model of science which would be rigorous and unassailable. Logical positivism was its name. Its fame was worldwide; Vienna was its home and – while he himself denied it adamantly – the early writings of Ludwig Wittgenstein were its inspiration. But that project (especially in the USA) came crumbling down rather forcefully to the ground by the 1950s with the appearance of W.V.O. Quine's 'Two Dogmas of Empiricism' (1951) and 'meta-ironically' with Wittgenstein's posthumous publication *Philosophical Investigations* (1953).

QUINE'S AMERICAN REVOLUTION

Quine, at once a first rate logician, a philosopher of science and, as well, situated at Harvard, fully in the tradition of American psychological pragmatism (from William James to C. I. Lewis), summed up almost a half-century of positivistic self-criticism in his revolutionary essay. What he showed with remarkable eloquence was that logical empiricism, which purported to be in some version or another the model for all of science (including mathematics), was itself a methodology which rested firmly yet fatuously on two dogmas.

The first, the so-called (dogma of the) distinction between analytical propositions and so-called synthetic propositions, went back at least to Kant. The distinction claimed that there were basically two kinds of scientific propositions that could be articulated. One kind, the analytical, was definitional in character (in many cases mathematical) and was true (or false) by virtue of the language and definitions employed (Euclidean geometry was the best example). The other, the synthetic, was true or false by virtue of its relationship to empirically verifiable conditions (direct observation is the paradigm here). These two radically different kinds of propositions, the analytic and synthetic, constituted what most people accepted as the terrain of science, if not the broader terrain of knowledge. What Quine showed was that

---

2. See, for example, Styers (2004); or, pertaining to the medical sciences, Thorndike (1941).

the commonsensical notion that these two kinds of propositions were clear and distinct (from each other) was not at all clear and distinct.

The second and related dogma of empiricism, the dogma of reductionism, was a critique of the commonsensical belief that complex propositions – be they analytic or synthetic – could be reduced to the smallest elements of which they consisted, and that this process made visible the significance of the more complex proposition.

Finally, in the last sections of his essay, Quine lays down guidelines for the creation of a science (or a conception of science) free of dogmas. His student Thomas Kuhn, more a sociologist than a philosopher, and many, many others advanced this conception. Quine's and Kuhn's (1970) work shaped a new philosophical foundation of philosophy of science, though whether they have anything to do with, or impact at all on, science as practised is difficult to say. Yet beginning in the 1960s in *both* the Anglo-American tradition and the continental–existential tradition there has been a persistent reconsideration of what science is, of what common sense is, and of whether these two have anything to do with each other. Some have considered these explorations a component of an intellectual movement known as 'post-modernism'. Others have taken great pains to distinguish their research from that appellation. Yet what is most interesting to me is the extent to which contemporary science and contemporary philosophers of science and others move along parallel tracks while seemingly oblivious to each other.

Most relevant to this chapter, the evolution, practice, and influence of cognitive therapy grow abundantly while philosophers of psychology seriously question and advance the concept of cognition itself. (It is as if Lewis and Clark insisted that there be two different trails because they did not walk in each other's precise footsteps.)

TURN, TURN, TURN

The cognitive turn, the linguistic turn, and the post-modern turn are obviously interrelated. How is not the least bit clear to many, and probably excessively clear to some. To me, all seem a reaction to the arrogant and radical 'deductiveness' of a great deal of nineteenth and early twentieth century thought, be it positivistic or idealistic or Marxist – they are all modernist. Many if not most reactions come from those quite familiar with the approaches they are unraveling. So with Quine and Kuhn and many of those who pursued their work; so, of course, with Wittgenstein who, in his *Philosophical Investigations*, was in fact deconstructing his own earlier work in the *Tractatus* (1921); and so with the therapeutic cognitivists who had grown up under the influence of Freudian analytical theory, behavioural theory, and neuropsychological theories. (So with me as an orthodox Marxist-turned-post-modern Marxist.) Indeed, Beck's somewhat *defensive* beginning (pardon the therapeutics) over-connecting, in my opinion, science and common sense reveals his concern to reassure the world that a return to cognition as both a subject and a mode of study is not to be seen as any kind of rejection of science.

From a broader perspective of the 'turns of the century', such defensiveness was (and remains), of course, unnecessary. For not only was consciousness in one form or another, from radical existentialism to Quine and Gödel (who was, after all, a self-identified Platonist), coming back into fashion, but theoreticians as well as practitioners in all these fields were beginning to violate the constraining and narrow-minded prohibitions of late nineteenth and early twentieth century positivistic thought.

These successful revolutions (or turns, if you like) in physics, mathematics, psychiatry, philosophy (particularly philosophy of science), linguistics, etc. essentially occurred (as I have said) simultaneously, without very much of an awareness of each other, and eventually resulted in overstatements to the detriment of each of the particular revolutions. By the way, the intellectual revolutions of this period (which have been vastly more successful than the much more publicized and deadly on-the-ground revolutions of the same period) have yet to be synthesized, or in the minds of some, to be correctly characterized or labelled.

It is not within the scope of this chapter to do so (or even want to), but the critique being offered of cognitive therapy is that *it has, in general, gone way too far in an effort to preserve a scientific character that science no longer has.* And so while it is a most significant advance in psychotherapeutics (as well as in psychotherapeutic theory), it has done so at the expense of taking the magic out of science and, thereby, for their purposes out of the examination of consciousness and, therefore (and this concerns me most), out of therapy where magic is what makes it work. Some have gone to other extremes, characterizing consciousness in such a way as to make it incomprehensible (or, at least, barely recognizable as consciousness). The failing and irony of the cognitive therapy movement is its *excessive* comprehensibility, particularly in light of the revolutionary world, the ever turning anti-positivist world, into which it was born.

This formulation might well seem to many like philosophical claptrap, so abstract as to be of no value to anyone. So let me put it another way, less precise, but more to the point. Cognitive behaviour therapy is overly decidable (in Gödel's sense of the word; Nagel and Newman, 2001). It is thereby insufficiently magical (in my sense of the word) and, finally, cognitive behaviour therapy is insufficiently political in the broadest sense of the word. It is *unrelentingly* apolitical.

And this is a serious flaw. For not only is all science magical and virtuously undecidable (Newman, 2003), all science is political. And the three are related. For it is a proper combination of magic (properly understood) and politics (properly understood) and undecidability (properly understood) that relates science, and indeed all thought, to the world and, thereby, to the lives of people.

POLITICS PROPERLY UNDERSTOOD

I have spent a lifetime writing about and, more importantly, trying to perform 'politics properly understood'. It is, first and foremost, an *activity*; a collective, humanistic, creative building of new things – large and small, *mental* and *physical.* Science should not be performed in the service of partisan politics; nor should it be carried out in the name of ideologically driven politics. It must 'serve the people'. While I have worked hard for almost four decades to create projects which do just that, I have never been able to put into words this humanistic ideal. Perhaps the closest I have come are in my psychological plays (mainly comedies) written for and performed at several meetings of the American Psychological Association

(APA). Others have expressed the humanism of psychology better than I – none better, in my view, than Dr Martin Luther King, Jr in the following statement, made on 25 April 1957 at the Conference on Christian Faith and Human Relations,Nashville:

> 'There are certain technical words in the vocabulary of every academic discipline which tend to become stereotypes and clichés. Psychologists have a word which is probably used more frequently than any other word in modern psychology. It is the word "maladjusted". This word is the ringing cry of the new child psychology. Now in a sense all of us must live the well-adjusted life in order to avoid neurotic and schizophrenic personalities. But there are some things in our social system to which I am proud to be maladjusted and to which I suggest that you too ought to be maladjusted. I never intend to adjust myself to the viciousness of mob-rule. I never intend to adjust myself to the evils of segregation and the crippling effects of discrimination. I never intend to adjust myself to the tragic inequalities of an economic system which take necessities from the many to give luxuries to the few. I never intend to become adjusted to the madness of militarism and the self-defeating method of physical violence. I call upon you to be maladjusted. The challenge to you is to be maladjusted – as maladjusted as the prophet Amos, who in the midst of the injustices of his day, could cry out in words that echo across the centuries, "Let judgment run down like waters and righteousness like a mighty stream"; as maladjusted as Lincoln, who had the vision to see that this nation could not survive half slave and half free; as maladjusted as Jefferson, who in the midst of an age amazingly adjusted to slavery could cry out, in words lifted to cosmic proportions, "All men are created equal, and are endowed by their creator with certain unalienable rights, that among these are Life, Liberty and the pursuit of Happiness". As maladjusted as Jesus who dared to dream a dream of the Fatherhood of God and the brotherhood of men. The world is in desperate need of such maladjustment.'
>
> (King, 1992)

What Dr King is saying with his usual extraordinary eloquence is that psychology must never become so scientific as to abandon its humanism. I could not agree more. Moreover, if 'scientific' is properly (contemporaneously) understood, it need not.

ADDING WITTGENSTEIN TO QUINE

Though it is a decade-and-a-half since it appeared on the bookshelves of the world, John R. Searle's *The Rediscovery of the Mind* (1992) still amazes and delightfully confuses those of us, like me, who began a philosophical career in the dying moments of logical positivism. My first philosophical trick was to point a finger at my imaginary debating opponent while not quite screaming, 'That's a category mistake you've made', and then laughing ever so quietly under my breath. This admonition came, of course, from Gilbert Ryle. His famous though, as it turned out, faddish, book, *The Concept of Mind* (1949), certainly did not envision a rediscovery of mind four decades later.

Ryle's work, a British combination of A. J. Ayerian-style logical positivism in its death knell and the later Wittgenstein in its birth moment, was designed to celebrate the human intellectual capacity finally to get rid of mind. 'Mind' itself was a category mistake, according to my reading of Ryle, or at a minimum it was a result of centuries of category mistakes. It was ultimately indistinguishable from Hegel's Absolute and Heidegger's Nothingness. It was *unverifiable*; invoking the positivist cross to the devil of meaninglessness.

But even as Ryle and his friends at Cambridge and Oxford were playing with this new idea, Quine at Cambridge, Mass., was pragmatizing the entire issue, and showing in some way that the concept of science (or at least its foundations) suffered from as much metaphysicality as the most boring existentialist on the Left Bank of the Seine.

Forty years later, which philosophically speaking is a drop in the historical bucket, John Searle, knowing a good deal of all of this tradition and even something of neuropsychology, authors *The Rediscovery of the Mind* (1992).[3] Searle, known for his contributions to philosophy of mind and consciousness, rejects dualism; seems, to me, more comfortable with paradoxicality; and considers language (and the ontological commitments of our discourse) carefully – although not with Quine's logicality and pragmatism. (Searle, as I recall, a student of J. L. Austin, is more an ordinary-language realist.) Searle locates the mind–body problem in the obsolete vocabulary and false assumptions that philosophers and psychologists accept, and with which they perpetuate dualism:

> 'We've inherited this vocabulary that makes it look as if *mental* and *physical* name different realms ... I'm fighting against that. The way I solve [the mind-body problem] is to get rid of the traditional categories. Forget about Descartes' categories of *res existence* and *res cogitance*, that is, the extended reality of the material and the thinking reality of the mental.'
>
> (Searle, 1999: web-accessed)[4]

Searle's own view, which he terms 'biological naturalism', asserts that 'the brain is the only thing in there, and the brain causes consciousness' (Searle, 1992: 248). What is most critical here is that in Searle's conception of causation (at least psychological causation), there is no dualistic cause–effect divide; consciousness is not an effect separate from the processes producing it.

Holding to dualism, no matter how sublimated, frequently forces philosophers and cognitive scientists alike to posit ontological units that violate common sense (such as it is) and ordinary experience (ontological subjectivity) – units such as mental rules and patterns, unconscious mental phenomena – and some kind of mental content to mental processes are conjured up (magically and/or pseudo-scientifically) in order to 'make intelligible' the relationship between the dualisms – mind–body, cognition–behavior, and so on. (In

3. More recent publications of Searle's include *Mind: A Brief Introduction* (2005) and *Freedom and Neurobiology: Reflections on Free Will, Language and Political Power* (2006).

4. Richard Rorty's dismissal of the concept of truth on the grounds that he is no longer interested in it may sound like Searle's dismissal of mind–body, but they are quite different. For Searle is accepting the magicality of science, while Rorty is simply defending the failure of pragmatism to understand truth.

psychotherapeutics, witness the *DSM-IV*; Newman and Gergen, 1999.) It is an error, Searle says (seemingly in a partial rejection of Hume), to assume that if a patterned or meaningful relationship can be said to exist between entities or events, then the process producing that relationship must be equally patterned or meaningful. If a person thinks of B when seeing A, which resembles B, we should not (but too many do) assume there is either any content or a particular form to the mental process that results in relating A and B. We are not following any mental rules when we think of B; there is no extra mental logic needed to account for the phenomenon in question.

In sum, Searle's point is that there is no mind–body problem. Indeed, there is no mind–body distinction. So we should stop talking as if there is one, and move on to the best we have at the moment – neuropsychology. The mind is rediscovered in this interesting relationship between the brain and conscious thought, and consciousness, like mind, has (to vary the use of Ryle's extraordinary metaphor) 'no ghosts in its machinery' (Ryle, 1949: 15-16). The brain produces thoughts which are transmitted to others via behaviour, most especially linguistic behaviour which stimulates other brains to produce other thoughts and so on. No mystery. A little magic, but no mystery.

DONALD DAVIDSON TO THE RESCUE

Another of Quine's students, perhaps his most brilliant (in the name of full disclosure, he was my mentor and tennis partner at Stanford University in the early 1960s) takes it upon himself to rehabilitate some of the critical conceptions that, for example, Rorty and Searle are justifiably if not rigorously abandoning. In particular, Donald Davidson seeks to reintroduce into the ontology of philosophical thought some notion of truth (a weak one), some conception of cause (a strong one), and an idea of deducibility which goes back at least to Hempel (a logical positivist) and perhaps to Plato and Aristotle (Greeks). Davidson's conservatism is formidable if not, to me, ultimately convincing.

THE MAKING OF A CONSERVATIVE

After his work on decision theory (done early in his career) Davidson published little for many years, focusing his attention on brilliant teaching. When he returned to publishing in 1963 with his seminal essay, 'Actions, Reasons and Causes' (Davidson, 1980), his mission appeared to be to salvage from the critical writings of the many anti-positivists, pro-late Wittgensteinian critical authors of the period those key concepts we, the people, would be *lost without*. Indeed, his real mission, it seems to me, was to salvage philosophy itself. Wittgenstein, on his death-bed, had left it on its death-bed.

Davidson's brilliant analyses of various features of mental activities (intentional acts, desires, wilful acts, etc.), contained as they are in separate and discrete essays written over an extended period, make it difficult to see his overall perspective. But it is there. And for me, it became more apparent in viewing a dialogue that Philosophy International (PI) from the London School of Economics produced of him and Quine in their later years before a group of scholars and students at the London School of Economics (Davidson and Quine, 1997). Much of what Davidson pursues in this discussion with his former teacher is what he calls a third dogma of empiricism which Quine (claims Davidson) overlooked (indeed, committed).

Davidson, who in the LSE discussion claimed he had spent half a century trying to convince 'Vann' of his 'missing dogma', focused not on Quine's critical analysis in the first half of 'Two Dogmas' (which most agree is analytically valid), but rather on Quine's efforts in the final sections to metaphorically characterize a dogma-free sense of science.

There, Quine invokes a C. I. Lewis-like 'buzzing, blooming confusion' (a flux) upon which varying conceptual frameworks from the gods of Homer to modern science somehow impose order. But Davidson insists that this formulation (the idea of a flux), while perhaps useful in certain ways, invokes a third empiricistic dogma, namely the dogma of the flux.

Davidson says, correctly it seems to me, that there is no flux: that whatever the ordering mechanisms may be, gods, nature, particles, or quanta, the world appears to us and is, ontologically speaking, 'already ordered'. It is a fiction and a dogma to suppose that we humans must order a flux of subjective experience (sense datum, phenomenological experience, or whatever). I can recall Davidson, himself a radical naturalist, approvingly teaching in his epistemology class of a little-known medieval theologian (Bishop Butler) who is said to have said, 'Everything is what it is and not another thing!'

Lewis, Quine's teacher and very much a Kantian *and* a Humean (a modernist), apparently felt a pragmatic need to include in his ontology a 'buzzing, blooming confusion' to justify the function of whatever conceptual apparatus history (and geography), i.e. culture, happens to provide us with. Quine, according to Davidson, uncritically carries on this tradition (dating back at least to Plato), but it is as much a dogma of empiricism (deriving from its idealistic roots) as either the analytic/synthetic distinction or reductionism. It is classical Davidson; for the rejection of 'the flux' is not ultimately ontological; it is epistemological. The human capacity, if you will, to *connect* the 'flux' and the 'conceptual framework' would itself require a connector, and so on, and so on. No, says Davidson, the *connection* must be as fundamental as the *connected* and, moreover, it *must* be causal. For even as Davidson is cleaning out the flux, he is constructing the broom, *connecting* all of his writings on these matters by saying in his introduction to *Essays on Actions and Event* (the first collection of his essays):

> 'All the essays in this book have been published elsewhere, and each was designed to be more or less free standing. But though composed over a baker's dozen of years, they are unified in theme and general thesis. The theme is the role of causal concepts in the description and explanation of human action. The thesis is that the ordinary notion of cause which enters in to scientific or common-sense accounts of non-psychological affairs is essential also to the understanding of what it is to act with a reason, to have a certain intention in acting, to be an agent, to act counter to one's own best judgment, or to act freely. Cause is the cement of the universe; the concept of cause is what holds together our picture of the universe, a picture that would otherwise disintegrate into a diptych of the mental and the physical'.
>
> (1980: xi)

And so we more clearly discover Davidson's philosophical conservatism. He is, ultimately, an *anti-disintegrationist,* a rehabilitationist. For all his radical analysis of particular mental acts, he must ultimately pull everything together. He is a systematic philosopher defending philosophy for philosophy's sake. Using the Wittgensteinian idea (developmental in my view) of employing philosophy to escape the limits of philosophy is turned (reacted to) by Davidson into using philosophy to clean up the mess made by philosophy. And then what? Presumably, wait passively for the next mess.

I, of course, do not favour disintegration or rehabilitation. I favour development and, thereby, growth. Davidson seems to feel it is essential constantly to clarify philosophy, while I feel – deriving from Wittgenstein, Marx, and Vygotsky – that humankind must build a new world, not make up fantastical categories to explain or interpret or 'cement' the old one. We don't have to hold, and therapy must not seek to hold, the world together; i.e. we neither need the flux nor the cement, we need to develop.[5]

PHILOSOPHY GOES THERAPEUTIC

Davidson's assault on Wittgenstein is equally a serious and formidable defence of the roots of modernism. Not only is it reactionary, it is a reaction formation (pardon the therapeutics again), and indeed it does not stand alone. For the reaction to the post-modern assault has been powerful and, arguably, somewhat successful, though exposing (Newman and Holzman, 1997).[6]

Certainly in psychology, post-modern thinking and ideas are still relegated to the fringe, while neuropsychology in its modernist guise dominates. All the more reason why cognitive behaviour therapy (and more generally all forms of therapy) must take a political stand. In some ways, the point of this chapter is to give therapy, a very critical component of psychology, a theoretical basis for 'going post-modern'. Cognitive behaviour therapy, the dominant therapeutic form, must lead the way.

WHAT IS SOCIAL THERAPY?

Social therapy is, to my way of thinking, a cognitive behaviour form of therapy. It is, after all, about helping people understand better (though not necessarily cognitively) and thereby do better (as in performing better). But it endeavours to return the necessary magic to therapy by insisting on its revolutionary nature. 'Revolution' as used here means neither an ideologically driven (determined) set of views imposed on people in as traditionally an authoritarian a manner as the market will bear; nor is it an appeal to some highly abstract spirit best understood by studying the history of the world's varied religions. Rather, it is a conceptual revolution we seek; not a new therapy but a new way of looking at therapy and, thereby, of practising it. It is a practice of method shaped by activity theorists going back at least to Vygotsky and Marx (Newman and Holzman, 1993). Its tools (and results) are an updated, indeed postmodernized, dialectic, greatly influenced by Wittgenstein and other relatively

5. 'The philosophers have only *interpreted* the world, in various ways; the point, however, is to *change it*' (Marx, 1845: 15).

6. 'In response to the postmodernist "attitude", they [the scientists] have given up objectivity, empirically based findings, and logical argumentation in favor of hyperbole, emotional outbursts, and arguments *ad hominem*' (Newman and Holzman, 1997: 1).

contemporary philosophers of mind. As well, it relies a good deal on the concept/activity of performance and has taken much from contemporary theatre and dramaturgy (Holzman and Mendez, 2003; Newman and Holzman, 1996).

But for all that, it remains a cognitive behaviour therapy. Hopefully, it is a positive advance, but as with all positive advances, it is to some extent a critique of what came before.

WHAT IS THAT CRITIQUE?

Let us go back to the beginning of our remarks. Cognitive therapy, we are told, is scientific in that it is based on common sense. But Gödel, Wittgenstein, Einstein, Heisenberg, and others have taught us that common sense is often less than commonsensical. The view of science invoked by the theoreticians and practitioners of traditional cognitive behaviour therapy is based on an ignorance or misunderstanding of contemporary thinking about the philosophy of mind, and more generally, philosophy of science. By way of summing up my own brief account of that history, a revolutionary turn from modernism to a sometimes muddled post-modernism, let us consider a final and critical element in Davidson's defence of modernism.

MORE ON ME 'N DONALD

My earliest discussions with Davidson on these matters came early in the 1960s, while I was still a graduate student and he was justifiably identified as the genius of Stanford's philosophy department, just about to set out to conquer the philosophical world. He did. Meanwhile, I sought to turn my intellectual efforts to radical organizing and psychology. I did not presume that Davidson and I would run into each other again. But we have.

My Ph.D. dissertation, written under the direct supervision of Daniel Bennett, a brilliant young Wittgensteinian at the time and ironically a former student and then a colleague of Davidson, was a study of the concept of explanation in history. And an analytical consideration of such matters required a reading of Carl Hempel's 'The function of general laws in history' (1942). Davidson, a friend of Hempel, very much admired some of the positions that Hempel took in his important essay and, naturally, to begin with (this is the first law of graduate school), so did I. But as I proceeded in studying what was then contemporary philosophy of history reading Scriven, Dray, and others, I grew more and more wary of Hempel's logical-positivist position.

Davidson and I sadly parted ways before anything resembling a deepening of that discussion happened. But in my own mind I have been having it with Donald ever since. It is something like Donald's discussion with 'Vann' on 'the flux'. In many of my imaginary discussions, I say to Donald: 'But look, Carl Hempel was a highly dedicated empiricist and yet he speaks of the function of general laws in history. But there are no general laws in history.'

Perhaps a rare historian seeks to speculate on the existence of such a law, but in almost 100 per cent of historical writings there are no such laws to be found. How odd, then, that Hempel, a confirmed radical empiricist, is seeking to discover the function of the non-existent laws. Perhaps Hempel's essay might have been called 'Why there should be' or 'How there could be' general laws in history. But not 'The function of general laws in history'. Many years ago, Scriven made something very close to this point (Scriven, 1958).

I, of course, do not know Davidson's response to my imaginary polemic since we never had it. But in my reconsideration of Davidson's lifelong defence of modernism, I see what he found attractive in Hempel's almost bizarrely entitled paper, for the most essential claim in Hempel's view is that there must be a connection between what is explained and its explanation (in Hempel's Latin, the 'explanans' and the 'explanandum'). For in the final analysis, while causality might be the cement, connectedness (in Hempel's case, deducibility) is the justification for the logical positivist and indeed for the modernist, and eventually for the early scientist's claim that everything must be connected. But if and when everything is connected, we lose the magic (or more accurately put, we lose the space for the magic) that is necessary for human development. Surely therapists must be sensitive to this.

Vygotsky speaks to the child's learning–developing process in such language as the child growing 'a head taller than him/[her]self' (Vygotsky, 1978: 102). Some may write this off as metaphor; I do not. I think it points to an essential feature of growth. And it is equally applicable to cognitive growth and to emotive growth, and to grown-ups as well as to the child.

In my view, Davidson betrays the depth of his commitment to modernism by his dogmatic defence of *connectedness*. There are, it seems to me, two major arguments against *connectedness*. The first is that there is no need for *connectedness* because everything is connected. This argument is something like (bears a family resemblance to) Davidson's argument against the flux/conceptual framework picture. The second argument is that everything *isn't* connected. Why? Because there must be room for development.

Cognitive behaviour therapy (indeed, all therapy) requires a theoretical basis to move in a post-modern direction. Modernist science and the demand for everything being 'connected' costs us the space for magic, not tricks and games, but the real magic of real science. Cognitive behaviour therapy's argument that science and scientific psychology is commonsensical not only eliminates the magic, but that framework adds to people's neuroses. For in eliminating the 'space for magic', a concept critical for understanding human development, it seems to me, we eliminate the possibility of cure. Vygotsky's idea of performing a head taller than one's self is based on the notion of performing what one is becoming. Is Vygotsky suggesting that one literally grows a second head, making one a 'head taller'?

In social therapy – once again a cognitive behaviour therapy, but primarily a group therapy – the second head is the creating of the group. And both from the personal or individual point of view and from the broader social point of view, it is the creating of the group that is the revolutionary activity necessary for further human development.

DIALECTICS AND PERFORMANCE (SOCIAL THERAPY, PART II)

Aristotle, who knew a great deal about both ethics and logic (indeed, a case could be made that he invented both), noted famously that the conclusion of a practical syllogism was an *action*, not another proposition. It is within that overall spirit that several thousand years later in what is now a *post*-modern period as opposed to a *pre*-modern period, we consider the relationship between dialectics and performance. Aristotle set in motion an extraordinary conversation (actually several) which ran its course throughout the entire history of modernist thought, for it was never apparent how propositional thinking could lead to action, any more than it was apparent how mental activity could produce physical activity. The mind and the body, which obviously work together, seem, conceptually, to keep getting in each other's way.

For the pre-modernist, God was allowed to solve this puzzle as well as all other problems. But modernism's rejection of God re-raised the problem and, roughly speaking, starting with Descartes, the mind–body issue has dominated epistemology/psychology. The writings of Searle, Rorty, Davidson, and others represent, to me, the best of late modernism's efforts to solve the Aristotelian problem. But post-modernism both requires and makes possible a new way of looking at this whole matter. And the location of such discussions requires stepping outside of the cognitive sciences and into the therapeutic arts; for although therapeutics are very much a product of cognitive thinking (witness Freud and many other things as well), they are in practice most fundamentally an art form. Such is the case with social therapy.

An anti-dichotomist (a post-modernist) point of view such as mine would hardly permit a rock-hard differentiation between art and science. On the other hand, these two central phenomena in Western history have very different cultural histories and, as such, play very different roles in the life of the society, most significantly in the lives of the masses of the society. Ask two people – ordinary citizens – one of whom is off to an art exhibition and the other to a science show, what their expectations are.

Psychotherapeutics may not be Western society's only art/science crossover phenomenon (witness poker playing), but it is surely one of the most important. Attempting to deconstruct a phenomenon so large and so ontologically and methodologically confused is not only daunting; it provides no obvious starting point. We leave ourselves open to the charge that we are fundamentally mixing apples and oranges – and, of course, we are at least doing that. All those authors whom we have considered (Ryle, Wittgenstein, Quine, Rorty, Searle, Davidson, and hundreds of others) have all recognized these issues and attempted to evolve a method for even considering the mind–body relationship. Aristotle's several-thousand-year-old provocation about the practical syllogism seems more bold to me than all the others. I seek a post-modern version of his pre-modern audacity.

Of course I'm mixing apples and oranges (post-modernism is a fruit cocktail).

Sentence NAD (Not a definition):

Within a performatory (as opposed to a cognitive) modality (community), we (social therapy/social therapists) seek to help create a pointless dialectical (a mixture of Plato's and Marx's) group conversation (a conversation oriented toward discovery/creation) in order to generate a new game (a Wittgensteinian game) which completes (in a Vygotskian sense) the thinking, and is itself (by magic, aka art) a performance (though more activity than an action).

That might well be the most complex sentence I have ever intentionally created. I normally prefer simple sentences. I am very much scientific in my orientation, and such has been the case all of my intellectual, and perhaps my pre-intellectual, life.

What is the essence of that posture, of that attitude? Well, I've always felt very close to the hardness of the subject matter of science, and the effort to account for or explain that unbelievably complex body of knowledge by the simplest of means, namely science. That has always been my ideal; but when Carl Hempel and many others started to speak of the general laws in history (when there are no such things), a philosopher of science like myself with a modicum of intelligence and a reputable Ph.D. had to put his foot down… even if it meant taking on the most intelligent man I had ever met in my life, viz. Donald Davidson.

And so, some 50 years ago, I began that process for a variety of reasons, in a variety of ways, which, at its most fundamental level, involved taking on philosophy itself. For science, which in some ways emerged as a challenge to philosophy, had itself gone too far. It was insisting that its methodology, probably the most brilliant in all of Western thought, somehow had gained the privilege of applying itself to every thing in Western thought.

The next thing I knew, I was a practising therapist. And as such I was introduced to *DSM-IV*. The authors of *DSM-IV* make Carl Hempel look very modest indeed, for though he spoke as if they existed, Hempel did not make up any historical laws. *DSM-IV*, while it does not quite make up laws of psychology, more precisely laws of emotionality, comes very close to doing so. It is something of a *Poor Richard's Almanac* of mental disturbances designed apparently for therapists of all stripes to identify what is mentally wrong with a client, and to explain to the client what is wrong with her or him.

Gergen and I considered it in our paper on diagnosis (1999), which we speak of as 'The Rage to Order' – it might as well be called the 'Rage to *Connect*'. These pseudo laws (perhaps they should be called pre-laws) are surely not scientific. Even the psychiatrists who authored *DSM-IV* would agree with that. But in relatively ordinary language they as much insist upon a connectedness as laws of optics.

The pseudo laws suggested by *DSM-IV* are perhaps not a bad bunch of cracker-barrel ideas in relatively ordinary language about emotional pain within our culture. But even cracker barrels have a history. And even *Poor Richard's* suggestions as to weather conditions ten years hence can turn in the minds and hands of some into certainties, or at least serious predictions. With the weather, this rarely turns into a serious problem. With therapy, they do. For believing that something might well be a proper description of your disturbing emotional state is quite different than being certain it is. You may say it is up to the therapist to make this very distinction, but the codification of these connections into a very official sounding book called *DSM-IV*, together with the rules and regulations, often equally misleading, of the APA, make it quite difficult for all but the most self-assured therapists to do so.

Finally, I discovered a relatively small band of scientifically-trained academics and clinicians who are sympathetic to these concerns (Ken Gergen, Mary Gergen, Sheila McNamee, John Shotter, Tom Strong, Andy Lock, Lynn Hoffman, Harlene Anderson, Ian Parker, Erica Burman, and others), and I am encouraged to articulate my strong view that it is science (and hard-nosed philosophy of science) which stimulates the growth of post-modernism and not fuzzy-headed thinking by inebriated Frenchmen, à la Sokol.[7]

Were there no space constraints in this volume, I would lend some completion to this somewhat rambling chapter by unpacking the Sentence NAD (from p. 229): Within a performatory (as opposed to a cognitive) modality (community), we (social therapy/social therapists) seek to help create a pointless dialectical (a mixture of Plato's and Marx's) group

7. In *Beyond the Hoax: Science, Philosophy and Culture* (2008), Alan Sokol continues *ad infinitum* to do little but berate those poor hung-over Frenchmen.

conversation (a conversation oriented toward discovery/creation) in order to generate a new game (a Wittgensteinian game) which completes (in a Vygotskian sense) the thinking, and is itself (by magic, aka art) a performance (though more activity than an action).

I hope to do so in a subsequent article.

Acknowledgements

Many thanks to Dr Lois Holzman, my lifelong collaborator, for teaching me virtually all that I know about psychology.

Thanks to my Developmental Philosophy Class held every Saturday afternoon at the East Side Institute in New York City for their patience and assistance.

Thanks to Kim Svoboda and Jacqueline Salit for their assistance in reading and writing this chapter.

REFERENCES

Beck, A. T. (1979) *Cognitive Therapy and the Emotional Disorders,* New York: Penguin Press.

Davidson, D. (1980) 'Actions, reasons, and causes', in D. Davidson, *Essays on Actions and Events*, Oxford: Clarendon Press, pp. 3–19.

Davidson, D. and Quine, W. V. O. (1997) *In Conversation: Donald Davidson. The Quine Discussion*, London School of Economics: Philosophy International (PI) (video recording).

Gergen, K. J. (2006) *Therapeutic Realities: Collaboration, Oppression and Relational Flow*, Chagrin Falls, Ohio: Taos Institute Publications.

Hempel, C. G. (1942) 'The function of general laws in history', *Journal of Philosophy*, 39 (2): 35–48.

Holzman, L. and Mendez, R. (2003) *Psychological Investigations: A Clinician's Guide to Social Therapy,* New York and London: Brunner-Routledge.

Hood [Holzman], L. and Newman, F. (1979) *The Practice of Method: An Introduction to the Foundations of Social Therapy*, New York: Institute for Social Therapy and Research.

King, M. L. Jr. (1992) 'The role of the church in facing the nation's chief moral dilemma', in M. L. King, Jr., C. Carson, P. Holloran, R. Luker, and P. A. Russell, *The Papers of Martin Luther King, Jr.: Volume IV: Symbol of the Movement, January 1957–December 1958*, Berkeley: University of California Press, pp. 184–91; accessed in August 2008 at: www.stanford.edu/group/King/publications/papers/vol4/570425.002-The_Role_of_the_Church_in_Facing_the_Nations_Chief_Moral_Dilemma.htm.

Kuhn, T. S. (1970) *The Structure of Scientific Revolutions*, Chicago: University of Chicago Press.

Marx, K. (1845) 'XI Theses on Feuerbach', reprinted 1969, in *Marx/Engels Selected Works, Vol. One*, Moscow, USSR: Progressive Publishers, pp. 13–15.

Nagel, E. and Newman, J. R.; Hofstadter, D. R. (ed.) (2001) *Gödel's Proof,* New York: New York University Press.

Newman, F. (2003) 'Undecidable emotions (What is social therapy? And how is it revolutionary?)', *Journal of Constructivist Psychology*, 16 (3): 215–32.

Newman, F. and Gergen, K. (1999) 'Diagnosis: the human cost of the rage to order', in L. Holzman (ed.), *Performing Psychology: A Postmodern Culture of the Mind,* New York and London: Routledge, pp. 73–86.

Newman, F. and Holzman, L. (1993) *Lev Vygotsky: Revolutionary Scientist,* New York and London: Routledge.

Newman, F. and Holzman, L. (1997) *The End of Knowing: A New Developmental Way of Learning*, New York and London: Routledge.

Newman, F. and Holzman, L. (2006/1996) *Unscientific Psychology: A Cultural-performatory Approach to Understanding Human Life*, Lincoln, Neb.: iUniverse Inc. (originally published Westport, Conn.: Praeger).

Quine, W. V. O. (1951) 'Two dogmas of empiricism', *Philosophical Review*, 60: 20–43. Reprinted in W. V. O. Quine (1953) *From a Logical Point of View*, Cambridge, Mass.: Harvard University Press.

Ryle, G. (1949) *The Concept of Mind*, Chicago: University of Chicago Press.

Scriven, M. (1958) 'Definitions, explanations, and theories', in H. Feigl, G. Maxwell, and M. Scriven (eds), *Concepts, Theories, and the Mind–Body Problem: Minnesota Studies in the Philosophy of Science, Vol. 2*, Minneapolis: University of Minnesota Press, pp. 99–175.

Searle, J. R. (1992) *The Rediscovery of the Mind*, Cambridge, Mass.: MIT Press.

Searle, J. R. (1999) *Philosophy and the Habits of Critical Thinking*, Conversation with John R. Searle by Harry R. Kreisler; at: http://globetrotter.berkeley.edu/people/Searle/searle-con2.html, retrieved August 2008.

Searle, J. R. (2005) *Mind: A Brief Introduction*, New York: Oxford University Press.

Searle, J. R. (2006) *Freedom and Neurobiology: Reflections on Free Will, Language and Political Power*, New York: Columbia University Press.

Sokol, J. (2008) *Beyond the Hoax: Science, Philosophy and Culture*, New York: Oxford University Press.

Styers, R. (2004) *Making Magic: Religion, Magic, and Science*, New York: Oxford University Press.

Thorndike, L. (1941) *A History of Magic and Experimental Science*, New York: Columbia University Press.

Vygotsky, L. S. (1978) *Mind in Society*, Cambridge, Mass.: Harvard University Press.

Wittgenstein, L. (1921) 'Logisch-philosophische abhandlung', *Annalen der Naturphilosophische*, Vol. XIV, 3/4; first English publication (1922), *Tractatus logico-philosophicus*, London: Routledge & Kegan Paul.

Wittgenstein, L. (1953) *Philosophical Investigations*, Oxford: Blackwell.

CHAPTER 19

CBT'S INTEGRATION INTO SOCIETAL NETWORKS OF POWER

MICHAEL GUILFOYLE

Like any clinical practice, CBT participates in societal networks of power relations. This chapter explores one aspect of this, by posing the question of how its success and widespread recognition may be a function not of its effectiveness *per se*, but of its comfortable integration with existing cultural and institutional power arrangements. Our Enlightenment heritage calls for a rationalist ordering of the therapies, in accordance with narrow and pre-constructed values that correspond with those of society's most powerful institutions. It is argued that it is within this context that we should understand CBT's overwhelming emergence as the therapy of choice. The risk of its institutional success is the establishment and legitimization of a therapeutic hegemony, and the gradual diminishment of a once rich landscape of therapeutic possibilities.

CBT's complicity with contemporary power arrangements – in, for example, legal, educational, psychiatric, psychological, political, even common-sense institutions – is so blatant that the therapy critic might hardly know where to begin. What can I say about CBT, from the broadly critical psychological perspective that I typically adopt, that is not already open to view?

CBT's increasing domination of the therapeutic landscape is extraordinarily hard to challenge. It is worth dwelling on this for a moment, because it tells us much about what is happening in the therapeutic world. The difficulty in critiquing CBT lies not in its alleged scientifically proven status, which can easily be challenged (see the many relevant chapters in this volume): its selective use of scientific principles; its blurring of efficacy and effectiveness; its skewed research populations and simplistic categorical view of the person; its mechanistic and objectivist orientation to research, despite the availability of alternative models of science that might enable more nuanced accounts of persons (c.f. Clarkson, 2003); there is even much contradictory 'scientific' evidence. A considerable amount of research, for example, supports the notion that common factors contribute more to therapeutic change than specific factors associated with (for example) CBT (Andrews, 2000; Messer and Wampold, 2002; Bohart and House, this volume). But such critiques have little impact.

So we might focus instead on ethics, and argue that CBT focuses on problems instead of people, in its own language rather than that of the client, that it patronizes in its educative stance, and that it only works to the extent that the above-mentioned common factors are

---

An earlier version of this chapter appeared in the *European Journal of Psychotherapy and Counselling*, 10 (3), 2008, pp. 197–206.

actively put into practice (e.g. Castonguay et al., 1996). Indeed, CBT practitioners claim to be collaborative (e.g. Chadwick et al., 1996), but this only superficially addresses these ethical concerns. This self-labelling is perhaps, as Goldberg (2001) would have it, symptomatic of dishonesty in the therapeutic professions. But perhaps this is less a denial of power than a kind of blindness to it. To this effect, Proctor (2002) argues that the tendency in CBT to confuse collaboration with client compliance and docility effectively conceals power and what she considers to be the 'paternalism' of its practices (ibid.: 79). She notes that this paternalism is underscored by the educative style associated with the approach. Here, on the one hand we have the 'well-motivated intentions' (Allison, 1996: 156) of the therapist posing as a naïve guarantee of the practice's ethical standing, and on the other hand a client 'relegated to the role of the ignorant pupil' (Proctor, 2002: 77). Under such circumstances, one wonders how nuanced ethical questions concerning the subtleties of power operations and the constructive power of language can be appropriately addressed.

We might then examine CBT's collusion with psychiatric power structures, and the manner in which it has, in the process, summarily dismissed decades of meticulous attempts by psychologists and others to question these very systems. Well-known critiques of this power network – of which the CBT practitioner cannot in good conscience claim ignorance – include the concern that forms of subjectivity are imposed upon clients (and related 'labelling' critiques), that clinical categories can have self-fulfilling effects, that clinical interactions lean toward monologue rather than dialogue, and that social, cultural, and political issues (e.g. of gender and inequality) are at best ignored, or at worst reproduced (e.g. Kirk and Kutchins, 1997). Considering that CBT functions within this network, what more can be said on these issues? What benefits might accrue from a reiteration of such concerns, or from the production of new ones? Indeed, is there any real sense of compulsion within the CBT community to seriously engage with these challenges, and will such dialogue make any difference?

It seems that challenges against CBT on scientific, ethical, or political grounds are likely to be fruitless. This probable impotence is itself already an indication that something very significant has happened in the therapeutic world. It seems that the title of 'most important' therapy – or even more medically, the 'first line treatment of choice' (Wilson, 1996: 197) – can be awarded without any serious consideration of the numerous philosophical, ethical, and political formulations that have been designed to give us pause in how we think about therapy. Certainly, there is much support for CBT. We often hear about its 'evidence' base, which in today's rhetoric of science, of facts and final truths, carries significantly more weight than arguments about ethics, values, power, or epistemology. One wonders to what extent its practitioners recognize – as do scientists in the 'hard sciences' – that such philosophical issues matter; that empirical evidence cannot be properly evaluated without recourse to the frameworks these philosophies provide.

Our best objections and cautions, which include some of the issues already touched on – the awkward 'scientific' findings, our insights into the ethics of language use and the obfuscations of power, our deconstructions of psychiatric diagnoses – are more easily dismissed, out of hand, than ever before. They do not even have to be addressed. This did not matter so much when therapists were given space to practise in any number of ways, and toward a range of different ends; to make choices about how to work instead of having practices prescribed by professional bodies and other crystallizations of power. But it matters a great deal now, as many therapists find their approaches de-legitimized to the extent that they are not represented on centralized lists of approved therapies. Attention need not be given to the voice of the dissenting therapist, unless she or he can learn to speak in the prescribed language, act in accordance with pre-constructed and independently developed priorities, and measure his or her work using prescribed methods. The psychoanalyst's concerns about CBT's inattention to unconscious forces (see Milton's Chapter 9, this volume) need not be heard unless there is a specific sort of evidence to support his claims; the feminist therapist's questions about the role of subtle forms of gender discrimination in producing distress can be ignored if they are based only on case studies. It has become legitimate to dismiss critique that is not couched in the correct way. Thus, we might challenge CBT's narrow version of science, its complicity with psychiatry, and so on; but these critiques are, in any case, no longer on the agenda for dialogue over what shall be counted as a valid therapy.

I aim here to develop some ideas about how this agenda is constructed and maintained. In the process, I discuss CBT's institutionalization as the 'most important' therapy, and the marginalization of its competitors.

MANAGING THE THERAPEUTIC HORIZON

In order to understand CBT's political situation, it is useful to situate it briefly in relation to its strategic competitors: the full range of therapies aiming for recognition, circulation, and reproduction. This aggregate, comprising hundreds of approaches, can be seen as a therapeutic discursive horizon in that they constitute a kind of store of culturally available ideas and practices from which therapists are, in principle, able to draw. In what is sometimes described as a post-modern age (cf. Lyotard, 1984), in which difference and choice are celebrated (e.g. Sampson, 1993) and essentialism and grand narratives are treated with suspicion, one would expect to find in the therapeutic industry a proliferation of creative ideas and practices. Indeed, Safran and Messer (1997) noted precisely such a multiplication of therapeutic approaches in the second half of the twentieth century, broadly enabled by the pluralism and contextualism of post-modernism. In recent years, however, many Western societies have begun to aim once more, with renewed vigour, to fulfil a more convergent, consensually orientated, rationalist vision of the world that is our Enlightenment heritage (e.g. Habermas, 1972/1987; cf. Brazier's and Lees' Chapters 6 and 7 respectively, this volume), and from which we have been unable to escape. Correspondingly, Safran and Messer (1997) have noted in the therapeutic domain a recent move toward convergence (which they see approvingly as integrationism), as attempts are made to organize and manage this seemingly unwieldy therapeutic diversity.

Under the influence of this Enlightenment heritage, and perhaps out of a fear of the alterations of power that a truly inclusive, post-modern social system might bring, certain ideas, despite the avowed respect for difference and choice so intrinsic to the rhetoric of modern societies, have become entrenched as absolutes. All societies must adopt specific versions of democracy; consensus must overcome difference at a fundamental level; consensus is to be established around objective, absolute truths, and we should not be satisfied with diverse opinions/perspectives; science is the only proper means for knowing the truth, and scientists are the only valid truth tellers.

With such assumptions in place, a normative, closely regulated, and ultimately authoritarian society is created, held in place in part by a series of attenuated forms of government: from formal policy developers, to institutional policies and practices, to practitioners in the field. Governmental duties have been extended to include the scientist-practitioner – in our case, the therapeutic 'officer' (Hook, 2003) – who is deemed qualified, and is awarded the authority to guide us on what is in our best interests, and on how we should think, act, interact, and live our lives.

It is in such circumstances that the proliferation of therapeutic approaches seems to be grinding to a halt, and pulled into reverse. Under the influence of Enlightenment principles of rationalism and consensus, we feel the need to suppress this therapeutic variation in order to discover the objectively 'best' treatments. This, our Enlightenment principles inform us, is the most responsible and ethical thing to do. Exemplifying this stance, King and Ollendick (1998), for example, make the often-cited twin assertions that the identification of empirically validated treatments facilitates protection of clients and ensures the survival of the profession. And it was originally rationalized in the National Institute for Health and Clinical Excellence (NICE) system of guidelines as a way of overcoming the 'lottery' model of health-care provision. In these terms, the quest for the 'best' and most scientific therapy is easily constructed as a noble undertaking.

Thus, each approach must be evaluated according to absolute scientific methods and principles; and once those principles are in place, a kind of consensus can be generated. Under the influence of such consensus – and the positive *valuation* placed on consensus as opposed to difference – the critical therapist starts to doubt his or her own ideas, as the impression is created that 'right-thinking' practitioners recognize the importance of having therapeutic work monitored and legislated, of evidence-based practice, of meeting economic needs, insurance-company demands, and psychiatric and forensic requirements of clear diagnoses, categorical interventions, and unequivocal recommendations. Not all therapies satisfy these demands, and so the multitude of approaches – of *choices,* for clinician and client alike – that we might have expected begins to dwindle, as the therapeutic landscape is gradually overtaken by a few selected approaches, of which CBT is the most salient example. A therapeutic hegemony sets in.

What I have referred to as the therapeutic horizon has already begun to take on a new shape. It is being actively shaped by numerous forces inside and outside of the therapeutic industry itself. Consider the following: the American Psychological Association (APA) has drawn up lists of approved therapies, and is joined by insurance companies in expecting psychologist practitioners to use psychiatry-like diagnostic categories, and to match these up with their corresponding validated interventions. The APA is a world leader among psychological bodies, moreover, and so others are closely following suit. Training courses in the Western world, in clinical psychology in particular, are increasingly advocating the use of such 'evidence-based' practice, drawing from these lists to inform training and practice. Clearly, many therapies are not represented on such lists because they do not play the 'games of power' (Foucault, 1980: 298) at which CBT has proven itself so adept. Many therapies are simply not amenable to standardization, and they might conceptualize problems, measure change, and construct objectives in ways that do not suit the criteria laid out by the APA and other governing bodies. And yet their awkwardness in this regard may have the longer-term effect of their de-legitimization and eventual disqualification as reputable therapies. It is these approaches, adjudged to be unscientific and based on conjecture rather than fact, whose opinions can be ignored; whose concerns are increasingly absent from the agenda of the dialogue on valid therapies.

Under the force of such pressures, the apparently scientific selection of CBT has shaped the profession of clinical psychology to such an extent that some see the clinical psychologist, specifically, as a 'specialist in cognitive behaviour therapy' (Marzillier and Hall, 1992: 7). Further, CBT is now being prescribed from government level in the UK (see Pilgrim's Chapter 21, this volume). Economist and ex Prime Minister Tony Blair's former advisor Lord Richard Layard (2004) has called for the training of 10,000 CBT specialists for the UK health services. This call has received rapid support from diverse sources (e.g. the Body Dysmorphic Foundation [2006], and the 'We need to talk' document [see Sainsbury Centre for Mental Health, 2006]).

CBT is also recommended for numerous designated problem 'types' by NICE and the Department of Health in the British NHS. CBT – above all other approaches – is systematically being called forth as the Western world's therapy of choice, and this is beginning to give the therapeutic landscape a decidedly skewed appearance.

The therapeutic horizon, in other words, is managed, ostensibly in the name of truth, but more accurately in the service of prevailing power arrangements. Political and economic forces are dictating that only certain therapies will be allowed to remain in place; therapies that are, for instance, time-limited and scientific, but which more fundamentally speak into, rather than away from, the linguistic and practice contexts of relevant institutions. Therapies are to be arranged in terms of their capacity to meet the needs of societal systems of power. Thus, the plethora of available approaches is given an order, and each therapy assigned a place along a narrowly constructed continuum of proven effectiveness. This ordering is then advertised directly or indirectly by such bodies as NICE, the APA, and other psychological and therapeutic governing bodies, by Departments of Health and other interested government officials, by media talk-show hosts, and sometimes by those therapists who find their favoured approach catalogued on the approved therapies list, and who are thereby given permission – it seems one is merely telling the objective truths of science, after all – to express disapproval of other therapies in their writing, in their engagements with other professionals, and of course very persuasively (given the power imbalance) in sessions with clients. With all of this public activity, CBT now finds its name and its ideas entering into mainstream common-sense discourse.

THERAPEUTIC DOMINANCE AND POLITICAL SERVICEABILITY

In any society that values consensus and absolute truth, competition will inevitably involve a differentiated 'natural' selection of participants. At present, as I have argued, this is moving toward a situation of therapeutic hegemony and a reduction of available therapies. This may not be the final result, and we may not be witnessing an end to therapeutic history, since we cannot know what new developments might be ushered in by changes in politics (e.g. reduced intervention in the therapeutic industry), or in the 'science' of therapy (e.g. a growing respect for research into the so-called 'common factors', which might once more open up the field – see Bohart and House, Chapters 16 and 17, this volume). But at present, various forms of government – from public officials, to insurance and mental health industries, to therapy's governing bodies – seem to have converged to promote specific therapeutic practices (of which CBT is the exemplar) and to demote others. But then, we must ask: if CBT has been selected from the universe of therapeutic possibilities as 'the single most important... approach' (Salkovskis, 1996: xiii), what has it been selected to do?

If we consider the range of forces that have converged to establish a broad-based (though not universal) consensus on the issue, then we cannot simply assume that therapies are chosen on the basis of their scientific standing or their capacity to improve happiness, minimize distress, or even advance mental health. This is not to suggest that CBT practitioners do not strive at precisely these goals. Rather, my question concerns CBT's institutionalized selection as the best therapy; the hegemonic status it is gradually being granted by powerful bodies of public, economic, and professional governance. It is surely reasonable to suspect that there are likely factors involved in CBT's success which transcend those that therapists and clients tend to value the most. To take an obvious instance, Lord Layard advocates CBT in the UK at least in part because it will aid the economy: it will get people back to work more quickly than other therapies, and thereby reduce strain on the benefit system (cf. Pilgrim's Chapter 21, this volume). Of course, these are valid economic points, but this does not make them sound therapeutic ones. It would be naïve to believe that economists, governments, insurance companies, and so on – primary shapers of the therapeutic landscape – are more invested in the population's happiness than in its productivity and its maintenance of societal institutions.

We can briefly consider the question of CBT's serviceability to society's institutions by taking another example. If science is the defining criterion for a selected therapy, then what would happen if it emerged – scientifically – that the most effective therapies were those that challenged many of society's institutions: that proactively put on hold the drive for economic growth in order to prioritize psychological well-being; which challenged psychiatry's centrality in mental-health practice; or pointed toward unjust economic, educational, and foreign policies rather than cognitive distortions as key factors in maintaining distress? Would such a therapy be afforded the same advertising and promotion that we are witnessing in the case of CBT? As it is, such therapies (e.g. narrative, feminist, and some psychoanalytic approaches) do not, in any event, fit the shape of official society's desired therapies, although numerous efforts are under way to reshape them so that they lose their critical edge and become more serviceable to existing power arrangements (Guilfoyle, 2005).

Different therapies do different things, a fact that such bodies as NICE and the APA seem unwilling to acknowledge, and which some CBT practitioners might forget when they claim to have superior skills. Therapy is at risk of losing the range of contributions it is able to make to society. The suppression of its variation might mean that it becomes accomplished at a narrow range of *externally* determined practices. It is the significance of these external influences that we should question; more perhaps even than the fact that CBT is winning the competition. The more pertinent question is how the rules for competition are constructed, and which institutions stand to gain.

As therapists we must be mindful of being reduced to government agents, to agents of governance. CBT practitioners face this quandary immanently. It is not in our job description to reproduce existing power arrangements, to satisfy the needs of society's most powerful institutions. Yet the political reality is that therapies that perform such a reproductive function are useful institutional partners, and thereby more likely than others to become successful, popular, and recognized, and even to become part of common-sense discourse (which itself then enhances the likelihood of effectiveness).

All therapists risk becoming inadvertent agents of 'social control' (Hare-Mustin, 1994: 20), a position that we should surely resist. But CBT's popularity is such that it is being inundated with very tempting invitations to perform precisely such a function. One would like to think these invitations will be in some way refused. But that would involve undermining the very games of power to which CBT's technologies are so well suited.

REFERENCES

Allison, A. (1996) 'A framework for good practice: ethical issues in cognitive behavioural therapy', in S. Marshall & J. Turnbull (eds). *Cognitive behaviour therapy*, London: Balliere Tindall, pp. 155-180.

Andrews, H. B. (2000) 'The myth of the scientist-practitioner: a reply to R. King (1998) and N. King and Ollendick (1998)', *Australian Psychologist*, 35 (1): 60–3.

Body Dysmorphic Foundation (2006) 'Campaign for increasing access to cognitive behavioural therapy', http://www.thebddfoundation.org/campaignincreasing.htm; retrieved from world wide web, 16 October 2006.

Castonguay, L. G., Goldfried, M. R., Wiser, S., Raue, P .J., and Hayes, A. M. (1996) 'Predicting the effect of cognitive therapy for depression: a study of unique and common factors', *Journal of Consulting and Clinical Psychology*, 64 (3): 497–504.

Chadwick, P. D., Birchwood, M. J., and Trower, P. (1996) *Cognitive Therapy for Delusions, Voices and Paranoia*, Chichester, UK: Wiley.

Clarkson, P. (2003) *Citrinas* – therapy in a new paradigm world', in Y. Bates and R. House (eds), *Ethically Challenged Professions: Enabling Innovation and Diversity in Psychotherapy and Counselling*, Ross-on-Wye: PCCS Books, pp. 60–74.

Foucault, M. (1980) *Power/Knowledge: Selected Interviews and Other Writings 1971–1977* (C. Gordon, ed.), New York: Harvester Wheatsheaf.

Goldberg, C. (2001) 'Influence and moral agency in psychotherapy', *International Journal of Psychotherapy*, 6 (2): 107–15.

Guilfoyle, M. (2005) 'From therapeutic power to resistance? Therapy and cultural hegemony', *Theory & Psychology*, 15 (1): 101–24.

Habermas, J. (1972/1987) *Knowledge and Human Interests* (trans. J. Shapiro), Oxford: Polity Press.

Hare-Mustin, R. T. (1994) 'Discourses in the mirrored room: a postmodern analysis of therapy', *Family Process*, 33 (1): 19–35.

Hook, D. (2003) 'Analogues of power: reading psychotherapy through the sovereignty–discipline–government complex', *Theory & Psychology*, 13: 605–28.

Kirk, H. and Kutchins, S. (1997) *Making Us Crazy: DSM: The Psychiatric Bible and the Creation of Mental Disorders*, New York: Free Press.

King, N. J. and Ollendick, T. H. (1998) 'Empirically validated treatments in clinical psychology', *Australian Psychologist*, 33 (2): 89–95.

Layard, R. (2004) 'Mental health: Britain's biggest social problem?', http://www.strategy.gov.uk/downloads/files/mh_layard.pdf; retrieved from world wide web, 16 October 2006.

Lyotard, J. F. (1984) *The Postmodern Condition: A Report on Knowledge*, Minneapolis: University of Minnesota Press.

Marzillier, J. and Hall, J. (1992) *What Is Clinical Psychology?* (2nd edn), Oxford: Oxford University Press.

Messer, S. B. and Wampold, B. E. (2002) 'Let's face facts: common factors are more potent than specific therapy factors', *Clinical Psychology: Science and Practice*, 9 (1): 21–5.

Proctor, G. (2002) *The Dynamics of Power in Counselling and Psychotherapy: Ethics, Politics and Practice*, Ross-on-Wye: PCCS Books.

Safran, J. D. and Messer, S. B. (1997) 'Psychotherapy integration: a postmodern critique', *Clinical Psychology: Science and Practice*, 4 (2): 140–52.

Sainsbury Centre for Mental Health (2006) 'NHS failing to act on talking therapies clinical guidance', http://www.scmh.org.uk/80256FBD004F6342/vWeb/pcKHAL6V3FH7; retrieved from world wide web, 16 October 2006.

Salkovskis, P. M. (1996) 'Preface', in P. M. Salkovskis (ed.), *Frontiers of Cognitive Therapy*, London: Guilford Press.

Sampson, E. E. (1993) *Celebrating the Other: A Dialogic Account of Human Nature*, San Francisco: Westview Press.

Wilson, G. T. (1996) 'Treatment of bulimia nervosa: when CBT fails', *Behaviour Research and Therapy*, 34 (3): 197–212.

CHAPTER 20

CBT:
THE OBSCURING OF POWER IN THE NAME OF SCIENCE

GILLIAN PROCTOR

In this chapter I suggest that the most important factor that may determine whether or not the client deems a therapy relationship successful is the dynamics of power in this relationship. If therapists take control, and do not think carefully about how to avoid domination during therapy, how can we expect clients to walk away feeling more in control? In this chapter I explore how cognitive behaviour therapy (CBT) addresses the issue of power in therapy, and I suggest that there are some problems with the CBT model, which mean that CBT therapists need to give this issue some serious consideration.

POWERLESSNESS AND DISTRESS

I maintain that the experience of powerlessness is one of the most significant causal factors contributing to the experience of psychological distress (Proctor, 2002). There is much more evidence for environmental causes of distress than, for example, biological or genetic causes (for example, Bentall, 2004). Common factors associated with distress are poverty, deprivation, and abuse (cf. Pilgrim, 1997). I would argue that underlying all these factors is the experience of powerlessness.

The experience of abuse is a significant causal factor in all types of psychological distress, with the numbers of survivors of abuse being very high amongst survivors of the psychiatric system (for example, Williams and Watson [1994] suggest a figure of at least 50 per cent). Surviving experiences of abuse is likely to involve regaining power and control (Kelly, 1988). Power, control, and the experience of powerlessness are strongly associated with all kinds of psychological distress.

Clearly, the way to deal with difficulties that stem from abuse, deprivation, and powerlessness is not to impose further power and control. Yet the dynamics of power in therapy certainly make it easy for the therapist to have power over the client. As Dorothy Rowe points out in endorsing Proctor (2002), 'When we enter into therapy we give enormous power to the therapist because we want to see that person as someone who can take our pain away. Such power can be abused' (dust-jacket endorsement). The power that society affords us as therapists leaves us with a large burden of responsibility to do what we can to try and ensure that we do not abuse this position of power.

An earlier version of this chapter appeared in the *European Journal of Psychotherapy and Counselling*, 10 (3), 2008, pp. 231–45.

There are clear values in the foundation of the practice of therapy, the most obvious general aim being to help the client and help improve the client's quality of life. How each therapy model, and indeed each therapist, believes the client's life will be improved is a matter of ethics and value judgements. Given the association of distress with powerlessness, having a sense of agency or control over one's life is likely to be important to clients. How do therapists assist clients with this aim, given the power in the therapy relationship? Fish (1999: 67) cites Foucault (1980: 298), suggesting a way forward in dealing with relations of power:

> 'I do not think that a society could exist without power relations, if by that one means the strategies by which individuals try to direct and control the conduct of others. The problem, then, is not to try to dissolve them in the utopia of completely transparent communication but to acquire the rules of law, the management techniques, and also the morality, the *ethos*, the practice of the self, that will allow us to play these games of power with as little domination as possible.' (original emphasis)

ASPECTS OF POWER IN THERAPY

I identify three aspects of power in the therapy relationship (Proctor, 2002). The first is *role power*: the power inherent in the roles of therapist and client due to the authority given to the therapist to define the client's problem, and the power the therapist has in the organization and institutions of her/his work. The second aspect of power is *societal power*: the power due to the social structural positions of the therapist and client, with respect to aspects of identity such as gender, age, and so on. The final aspect of power in the therapy relationship is *historical power*: the power due to the personal histories of the therapist and client, and their experiences of power and powerlessness. These personal histories and experiences will affect, and to some extent determine, how individuals are in relationships, and how they behave, think, and feel with respect to the power in the relationship.

POWER IN THERAPY

Psychotherapy outcome research demonstrates that the most important key to successful therapy is the quality of the therapy relationship (Bozarth, 1998; Lambert and Ogles, 2004; Paley and Lawton, 2001). The most consistent relationship variables related to effectiveness are the therapeutic alliance, goal agreement, and empathy (Norcross, 2002). I suggest that each of these variables could perhaps better be explained by an over-arching variable, described by *the dynamics of power* in the therapy relationship. A therapy relationship characterized by empathy, goal agreement, and an effective alliance would be a relationship where the therapist is not taking power-over the client, and is encouraging the client's power-from-within, i.e. a mutual respectful relationship. In contrast, an unhelpful therapy relationship would be one in which the therapist uses power-over the client and diminishes the client's sense of power-from-within.

MODELS OF POWER

Much of the literature on power in therapy has taken a structural approach. This approach sees power as a possession wielded by a therapist over a client in a negative way. Writers such as Masson (1989) argue that therapists have authority, with which comes power which is necessarily negative and even abusive. Structural perspectives emphasize the importance of structures and roles, but leave little room for the agency of individuals. In contrast, post-structural ideas (in particular, those of Foucault) emphasize the individual in dynamic social relation to others, and also incorporate the notion of agency of individuals, which widen the scope of analysis from a radical environmental behaviourism to considering the internal life and histories of individuals and their relationships. There are long-standing debates about the primacy of structure or agency. More recently, various theorists have argued that both are important and irreducible to the other, and have proposed ways to investigate power whilst holding both in mind. More detail of structural and post-structural approaches to power can be found in Proctor (2002).

CBT AND POWER

APPEAL TO SCIENCE

Broadly speaking, cognitive behaviour therapy (CBT) is based on the claim that the cause of distress lies in the individual's maladaptive thinking, or cognitive processes. Recent adaptations of, or additions to, CBT theory (such as Compassionate Mind Therapy or Acceptance and Commitment Therapy) tend to consider emotions in more detail, whilst still focussing on the cognitive processes. At the same time as claims for CBT to be a collaborative endeavour with the client, the therapist has the knowledge about how to think in a more helpful way, and this knowledge is claimed to rest upon research evidence. Thus, the authority of the therapist rests on an appeal to science.

The whole basis of the model, then, is strongly founded on principles of modernism and the rationality of science, as described at some length in a number of chapters in this book. 'Knowledge' and research 'evidence' are not questioned, but are presented as fact, and the therapist is assumed to be in an objective position to present this knowledge. Thus, CBT is presented as a 'psychoeducational approach', albeit with the call for an active and involved student. However, more recent, so-called 'third-wave' departures from classic CBT theory, such as Compassionate Mind therapy (Gilbert, 2004) do focus more upon the importance of the therapy relationship. From a Foucaultian perspective, traditional CBT (e.g. Beck, 1976; Beck et al., 1979) is rife with 'regimes of truth', normalizing principles on which the 'right' or 'helpful' way to think are based. The focus on 'realism' can be used to discount or challenge the feelings or views of the client, who can then be accused of being prey to 'cognitive distortions'. Rationality is a clear value behind CBT, and what is defined as irrational is discounted or challenged.

THE OBJECTIVITY OF THE CBT THERAPIST

Along with the appeal to science to justify CBT principles comes the position of the therapist as objective. Together with the authority that comes with the role of the therapist, this expert stance and idea of objectivity brings with it a great deal of role power for the CBT therapist. Starhawk (1987: 147) suggests the dangers inherent in the therapist's authority:

> 'Healing that empowers and liberates springs from a mutual struggle with the forces that hurt us all. When we start believing we are "more together" than someone else, we use our healing power as another way to establish our own superiority.'

Within traditional CBT literature, there is some caution about the objectivity of the therapist. Marshall (1996), for example, points out that the therapist's authority leads to ethical implications that therapists have a duty to consider. She also emphasizes the importance of supervision to ensure ethical practice, and to ensure that the therapist's agenda does not impinge on the therapeutic relationship. She emphasizes the danger of the therapist using their power to fulfil their own needs in the therapy relationship, whereas the aim should be to use this power to help the client.

However, the assumption in the CBT model is that the therapist can be in an objective position to decide scientifically what is best for the client. Thus, the aim of supervision here is to ensure that the therapist is acting from this neutral position, rather than from a position in the therapy relationship from where the client could be used to fulfil the therapist's needs. Given the philosophy of the CBT model, however, it is not apparent how a focus on self-awareness in supervision could be accommodated (and it is certainly not theorized as being part of the model). This would be particularly so if supervision were a process by which the therapist and supervisor joined forces to decide what is in the best interests of the client.

The possibility of being in a neutral objective position is not problematized. It is clear that the concept of power referred to here is one in which the therapist is assumed to possess the power, and power is assumed to be unidirectional – characteristics of a structural model of power. However, unlike structural models of power, it is not assumed that this imbalance of power is necessarily negative. Instead, the power imbalance is justified and legitimized, again with the appeal to the rationality of science and the knowledge of the therapist.

Telford and Farrington (1996: 149) suggest that the therapist is not in a neutral position but is part of the therapy relationship: 'Cognitive behaviourists must wake up to the fact that the notion of the therapist as a neutral onlooker is no longer acceptable within therapy'. Here, there is some acknowledgement that 'objectivity' has been questioned, and that the possibility of a therapist being a neutral scientist whose values are not involved is dangerous. However, despite some focus on the importance of the therapy relationship, the full implications of this problematizing of objectivity are not explored with respect to the knowledge base of CBT as well as the therapist's position in the relationship. Inconsistencies remain in the questioning yet also the acceptance of the authority of the therapist.

The client's acceptance of the therapist's authority is seen as a necessary prerequisite for CBT, and when a client disagrees with the model or does not comply with requests, this is seen as a 'set-back' – or, indeed, an opportunity to challenge the client's thoughts and beliefs. There are many examples within the CBT literature of how therapists should handle a rupture in the alliance, a 'set-back', or a disagreement with the client. Most suggest using the opportunity for the therapist to correct the client's misunderstanding, for example Beck

(1995: 73) and Padesky and Greenberger (1995: 8–9). These examples again follow the idea of the CBT expert educating the client.

There are also clear examples of where a therapist persuades the client to agree with the therapist's perspective. Marcinko (2003), for example, discusses the 'problem' of clients not wanting to take medication, and dealing with this by saying:

> 'however if the patient wants the therapist to work on other goals with him or her or to help him or her pursue his or her values, the therapist would be more motivated to do so if the patient agreed to work on medications as well'.
>
> (ibid.: 328)

However, there are also examples where the therapist does take responsibility for their behaviour and how it has affected the client, and take on board the client's perception rather than challenge it (e.g. Padesky and Greenberger, 1995: 54–6). Stevens et al. (2003) point out the dangers in the traditional CBT approach, writing: 'When such significant ruptures in the alliance occur, the faith that cognitive behaviour therapists have in technique and the belief that ruptures in the alliance are roadblocks to be overcome can work to the detriment of treatment' (ibid.: 278). Instead, they suggest that at such points of disagreement, the therapist should focus on the alliance.

From the beginning, CBT is presented as the right way to think; and success is when the client thinks and behaves in accordance with the CBT model. The danger here is that if therapy fails, it is because the client has not followed the therapist's suggestions well enough; the responsibility is with the client. As Spinelli (1994: 244) explains, due to the therapist's unquestioning belief in the principles and assumptions underlying the CBT model, therapeutic failure can 'be blamed on... the client's misapplication of (or unwillingness to apply) the specified instructions presented by the therapist'.

SOCIAL CONTROL

Spinelli (ibid.) points out that the therapist makes judgements about what is rational or desirable, and that rather than this being a scientific appraisal, these judgements are culturally influenced. Furthermore, the appeal to the rationality of science itself is clearly a value held by mainstream culture. Spinelli explains that, 'In this way, the therapist becomes a broadly libertarian representative of the norms and codes of conduct of society in which both the therapist and client are members' (ibid.: 249). However, he points out that these cultural norms are not 'objective', and that in pretending to be objective, cognitive behaviour therapists 'run the risk of imposing a socially conformist ideology on the client' (ibid.). Pilgrim and Treacher (1992: 30) similarly explain that 'psychologists... could play out a highly political role in terms of the management of the population, whilst at the same time disowning such a role by pointing to their "disinterested" scientific training and credentials'.

Spinelli (1994: 248) discusses the notion of the 'objectivity' of the therapist, and casts doubt on the validity of this claim, even within science itself: 'The problem with this view, however, is that the notion of a truly scientific investigator, observer, or experimenter has been sufficiently cast into doubt by developments within science itself.' Spinelli's critique is from a structural framework of power (see Proctor, 2002). It is assumed that objectivity gives authority and power to the therapist, authority and power being synonymous, as though power were *a possession*. Power is seen to be unidirectional and oppressive.

His critique of science, however, fits in much more with a Foucaultian perspective on power. Foucault's analyses of the human sciences (1973), of the history of madness (1977a), and of the history of sexuality (1979) all provide an analysis of the context in which therapy takes place. He describes the idea of the 'confession' as a disciplinary technique, and questions the objectivity of 'madness' as a category entailing treatment. Foucault's analyses encourage us to investigate the way in which psychotherapy can be a context for surveillance and disciplinary techniques of the self, of normalization. He describes the ways in which power can be observed in the practices within psychiatry and psychotherapy which attempt to normalize individuals.

Foucault's notion of the stylization of the self is particularly relevant to issues of power in therapy, as therapy explicitly sets out to reconstitute the self, according to normalizing rules (particularly in CBT). However, Foucault does not place a value judgement on these practices of power, and also emphasizes the productive aspects of power (explained by Butler, 1990: 98 as 'the way in which regulative practices produce the subjects they come to subjugate'). He also emphasizes the resistances which will always be present wherever there is power.

Here, Foucault's ideas about the relationship between power and knowledge, and the role of normative rules in constituting subjects, are both relevant (see Proctor, 2002). It is clear that the explicit aim in CBT is to reconstitute the subjectivity of the client; to change the way the client thinks about the world. Thus, it seems that Foucault's 'practices of the self' are an integral part of what happens in therapy. Theory in CBT is a normalizing discourse. From Foucault's later work, this describes the dynamic nature of power, where individuals constitute themselves within the context of the normative rules, the disciplinary techniques of the self. These regulative practices are explicit within CBT, where the normative rules of how a client should reconstitute him/herself are spelt out. Beck (1995: 26), for example, explains that the goals of the initial session include 'socializing the patient into cognitive therapy'.

It is also clear from Foucault's consideration of the practices of the self that the client also has a role in resisting and constituting themselves within the context of these normative rules. However, as McNay (1992) points out in her critique of Foucault, by not prioritizing how much different techniques of the self are imposed to different levels, Foucault's notion of the subject's agency, and the idea of aesthetic stylization of the self, hides the force of cultural norms. There is an issue here concerning how much the therapist uses his/her authority to enforce the norms established by CBT, how much the client has a choice to constitute themselves in their own way, or whether the only choice is to take on the idea and norms of CBT wholeheartedly or leave therapy. Given also that clients will seek therapy when in a state of distress, their choices or resistance to the norms communicated by the therapist are likely to be very limited. Thus, it may be more realistic to talk about Foucault's concept of disciplinary power as he applied it to the human sciences, whilst also acknowledging a limited role for the client in terms of resistance.

THE 'COLLABORATIVE' RELATIONSHIP

The style of therapy is described as 'collaborative empiricism' (Beck et al., 1979). Beck (Beck at al., 1979; 1995: 221) explains: 'It is useful to conceive of the patient–therapist relationship as a joint effort.... The partnership concept helps the therapist obtain valuable "feedback" about the efficacy of therapeutic techniques and further detailed information about the patient's thoughts and feelings.' Kirk (in Hawton et al., 2005: 14) clarifies the nature of this 'collaboration', writing that: 'The collaborative nature of the therapeutic relationship should be discussed; the patient is expected to participate actively by collecting information, giving feedback on the effectiveness of techniques, and making suggestions about new strategies'.

The therapist is expected to structure sessions and use reinforcement selectively to encourage the patient to talk more about what the therapist considers most relevant and most likely to promote change. Therapists are to explain to their patients that talking about how problems are *now* is most useful, as CBT focuses on the immediate circumstances.

Thus it is clear that the 'collaborative' relationship emphasizes the therapist's expectations of the client, that the client will contribute to the therapist's ideas and plans for treatment (within the CBT model). Padesky and Greenberger (1995: 6) explain,

> 'Collaboration requires an active stance on the part of both therapist and client to work together as a team. Since many clients enter therapy expecting to play a more passive role ("Fix me"), the therapist often needs to socialise the client to expectations for mutual collaboration.'

What seems to be described here is more the expectation on the client to take responsibility for the therapy. Again, the danger here is that the client is made responsible if therapy does not work.

Whilst perhaps some matters are negotiable, there are clearly some aspects of CBT to which the patient must agree for the therapy to go ahead. It is clear that the therapist structures sessions and decides what is useful for the client to talk about. Thus, the idea of collaboration seems to be the demand that the client will conform to and welcome the therapist's approach, and agree to various forms of activity that the therapist suggests.

An often discussed example in the CBT literature to illustrate the notion of collaboration is the expectation of the client to complete homework. Tompkins (2003: 63) suggests that therapists reinforce homework compliance and 'similarly avoid reinforcing homework non-compliance'. Padesky and Greenberger (1995) discuss the expectation of clients to complete homework as part of the idea of collaboration. Here, the notion of collaboration is used interchangeably with 'compliance with assignments' (ibid.: 35). They suggest how a therapist may increase compliance/collaboration by saying, 'Clients who do assignments tend to get better faster. This explanation is often sufficient to increase compliance. It is best to provide a thorough rationale for active therapy participation along with or before the first assignment.' (ibid: p. 35).

Tompkins (2003: 63) describes further the nature of collaboration concerning homework, writing that

> 'clients usually understand more fully than the therapists do what is or is not a useful homework assignment and what difficulties may arise.... At times, a client may suggest a homework assignment that seems tangential to the focus of the therapy session. Rather than dismissing the assignment out of hand, therapists can explore the client's rationale for the assignment (be curious), perhaps soliciting the advantages and disadvantages of this assignment over another one the therapist might suggest.'

So the client may suggest homework tasks which seem unlikely to prove better than the therapist's suggestions (given their superior knowledge of CBT) and the idea of completing homework is a given.

'COLLABORATION' BUT DIFFERENT ROLES

Turnbull (1996: 20) suggests that this is not collaboration between equals:

> 'It is better to see the client and therapist occupying different roles but collaborating on a joint enterprise. The therapist's role in the relationship is to make decisions concerning therapy and the client's role is to take decisions about how this can be applied to his or her lifestyle. In order to work properly, this collaboration needs to be based on a mutual respect for each other's role.'

He cites Rogers' core conditions as key qualities of a therapist, which will help develop trust and encourage collaboration. He suggests that these conditions should be used to encourage compliance in the client. Here again, the notion of collaboration and compliance are used interchangeably. Turnbull also points out an aspect of the cognitive behaviour therapist's power with respect to the client, that of the therapist's authority and of their 'superior knowledge' (ibid.: 20). He contends that the client must accept the therapist's superior knowledge, although not to the extent where the client's ability to self-manage is compromised. How to achieve this balance is not explained any further. In short (ibid.), 'There are times when the authority of a therapist's knowledge must be exercised and accepted by the client'. Thus, for Turnbull it is important that the client accept the role of the cognitive behaviour therapist as the one with the knowledge and hence the role of decision-maker with regard to therapy. Here the connection between power and knowledge is explicit.

CRITIQUE OF NOTION OF 'COLLABORATION'

Lowe (1999) critiques the notion of 'collaboration' as an appeal to promote equality, which he argues is impossible in the context of therapy and the power embedded in the institutional role of the therapist. He explains (ibid.: 82):

> 'How collaborative can collaboration be ... if they are institutionalised within a particular mode of practice? It is one thing to offer clients a voice within a professional therapeutic discourse, but it might be quite another thing to allow them a discourse of their own.'

He further points to the effects of these discourses with respect to power, in fact to increase the power of the therapist, by concealing it (p. 83): "Though the declarative intent of these ideas may be to empower clients, the constitutive effects might be quite the opposite, being not so much disempowering but what Potter (1996) calls *mis*-empowering: adding new tools to the armoury of the already powerful.' Thus he demonstrates how the rhetoric of 'collaboration' can actually increase the power of the therapist and hide the power imbalance between therapist and client.

Telford and Farrington (1996) usefully point to the dangers within CBT of the rhetoric of 'collaboration' and 'equality' in the therapy relationship obscuring the power differential between client and therapist that does remain. They also suggest ways in which the therapeutic relationship can be used to help clients take more control over their own therapy. They give an example where the therapist avoids suggesting solutions to the client but instead 'guides' the client to find their own solutions. Similarly to the idea of the therapist reinforcing matters when the client talks about issues that the therapist believes are most relevant to change, this seems to reflect a one-dimensional understanding of power (as described by Lukes, 1974) – a level of the therapist's power is still being missed here. The therapist 'guiding' the client to what they believe will be a good solution means that the therapist is shaping the outcome of the client's decisions, and is using power-over the client described by Lukes' (1974) second dimension of power. Ultimately, it seems that the client is encouraged to take control over their own therapy as long as they do it following the therapist's model and ideas; almost a situation of 'you can make the decision, as long as you decide what I think is good for you'. At the same time, the therapist is encouraged to use their power to increase the client's compliance with CBT. Thus, the therapist's authority is not really questioned or problematized.

The notion of 'collaboration' seems to appeal to a notion of reducing power imbalances in therapy. However, the notion of power implied by this is a one-dimensional view of power. Collaboration is seen to have been achieved when the client agrees and complies with the therapist's world-view. The notion of collaboration seems to be very muddled with the idea of compliance in CBT. However, as Gramsci points out (Ransome, 1992), there is a distinction between coercive and consensual control, and power is still involved in consensual control.

There are further dimensions of power (as suggested by Lukes, 1974) which are missed from the account of collaboration. The extent to which the therapist determines what can be put on the agenda to talk about, or how much the client has been shaped to know what the therapist does not want to hear about, is not considered. It is also clear that the therapist is seen to have authority about what is best for the client, authority that is legitimized by the therapist's knowledge of science.

It would be more honest and accurate to refer to compliance instead of 'collaboration' and thus be explicit about the nature of the power relations involved.

AUTONOMY OR BENEFICENCE

Issues of power raise ethical questions, and values are an inescapable part of the consideration of power. In ethical guidelines for therapists (e.g. those of the British Association for Counselling and Psychotherapy – BACP, 2002), the traditional approach to ethics has been to consider the balance of the ethical principles, which together comprise the ethics of justice (see Keys and Proctor, 2007). These principles are doing good (beneficence), avoiding harm (non-maleficence), and respecting autonomy and justice. The balance between the ethical principles of doing good (beneficence) and respecting autonomy has been unclear and left to decisions by individual therapists, depending on their positioning toward the idea of the therapist as expert or the client as expert.

The main ethical principle which underlies the practice of CBT is beneficence. The therapist is believed to be in a better position to decide what the client needs than is the client; the authority of the therapist is justified by the principle of beneficence or paternalism. There has been little consideration given to the dangers of the power inherent in the beneficent CBT therapist's position. It is suggested that an aspect of CBT is to give the client the information about the model to enable self-understanding and autonomous decision-making. However, it is not clear at what point the client's autonomy is considered, particularly if the client does not agree with what the therapist believes to be best. Respecting the client's autonomy is directly opposed by the belief that the therapist has rationality and science on their side, and therefore knows what is best for the client, whatever they may believe.

Ultimately the client's views can be dismissed as 'irrational' with the model of the therapist being superior, with an appeal to science that could be difficult for a client to argue with, given the authority that science still has in this culture. Allison (1996: 160) does exercise a word of caution about therapists making these decisions with respect to the threat of the client's autonomy:

> 'Basing decisions on the foundation that you are exercising your judgement in order to bring about a better outcome for the client may well be a paternalistic way of working and may subjugate the client's autonomy to the therapist's power.'

However, there are no suggestions for how to avoid subjugating the client's autonomy in CBT.

PATERNALISM

Turnbull (1996) discusses in more detail paternalism in the therapy relationship in CBT. He supports the view that the therapy relationship can indeed display aspects of paternalism. He also agrees that CBT can be paternalistic in the early stages of a relationship where the therapist

> 'may sometimes need to coerce the client into carrying out actions which he or she will find unpleasant in order that progress can ultimately be made. This is something that may often be required early in therapy when the client may not be in a position to make choices.'
>
> (ibid.: 19)

Turnbull defends this type of coercion by stating that it should be based on the ethical principles of beneficence, but he does admit that this should be acknowledged as an example of paternalism. He does not explain why, at the start of therapy, a client may not be in a position to make choices, and does not seem to consider the alternative of providing the client with the necessary information to be able to make a choice. Compliance seems to be sought in preference to informed consent, and no comments are made about the dangers of the therapist justifying coercion by beneficence, or the possibility of the therapist being in a position to know the client's best interests. There seems to be no question that the therapist's knowledge of the model and the scientific principles behind CBT mean that this puts the therapist in a position to know what is best for the client.

PATERNALISM OR AUTONOMY?

Searle (1993) discusses ethical dilemmas in therapy and the competing values of paternalism or autonomy. She suggests that moral justification for the teleological principle of beneficence is sought from the outcome, arguing that this ethical principle is often used to defend paternalism. Beneficence is used to protect the client from autonomy when this could result in harm, or even just when the therapist does not agree with a client's decision and believes they know best. She describes the competing deontological principle of autonomy, which suggests that the therapist has a duty to respect the integrity and individuality of their client and must therefore respect autonomy. Searle asserts that the values of the therapist influence therapy in many ways, particularly because of the power difference in the therapy relationship. She suggests that it is essential that clients should make their own choices regarding values, and that being exposed to the therapist's value system should be an issue for informed consent.

In CBT, therapists are encouraged to express their values and belief in the cognitive model as the 'right' values and beliefs. Informed consent is often ignored in favour of coercion, and autonomy rejected in favour of beneficence, thus increasing the power of the therapist. The principle of beneficence also seems to be justified again by the belief that the outcome of a client changing their thinking in accordance with CBT principles is inevitably good and beneficial to the client. The risk of whether a particular client may not believe that the ends justify the means is not considered, again as a result of the appeal to research and science which then concludes that CBT is right for everybody, despite even the research demonstrating that CBT helps less than 100 per cent of clients. The whole approach of one way of thinking being the answer for everyone is in direct contradiction to respect for the autonomy of each individual client.

POWER-WITHIN OF THE CLIENT

The rhetoric of 'collaboration' in CBT seems to imply the importance of the increasing agency or 'power-within' of the client. Telford and Farrington (1996: 125) refer to the client's power, writing:

> 'if therapy is successful, it must help the client to assume his/her own power, in other words to become his/her own therapist. Thus if the client is to generalise his/her gains and self-maintain, the balance of perceived power must shift from being invested (by the client) in the therapist to being invested in the client him/herself.'

Here the concept of power used is implicitly one in which power is seen as a possession, ideally to be passed from the therapist to the client, although the power is always over the client's life. There seems to be a conflation of two models of power here; one about domination and power over someone ('power-over'), which the therapist initially has over the client. Then the client should take power from the therapist over their own lives. This seems to be an internal individual notion of power, or the feminist notion of 'power-within' (see Proctor, 2002). The idea of passing power from the therapist to the client also seems to suggest the notion of the therapist initially having power over the client, and gradually the client resisting this power, the goal of therapy being the abolition of the therapist's domination. It is not clear, however, how this resistance or process is supported or encouraged by the behaviour of the therapist. The goal of therapy to encourage the client's 'power-within' is not consistent with the means of the therapist's 'power-over' the client.

SELF-REGULATION

This concept of power assumes a behavioural, one-dimensional concept of power, visible only when the therapist dominates and controls the therapy by their instructions. Implicit in the writing about CBT is the notion that therapy is successful when the client takes on the CBT model and the world-view of the therapist; i.e. when the client begins to regulate and discipline themselves in line with how the therapist would do this. Thus, even when the client begins to make their own decisions and is seen to be taking her/his own power, it could be argued that this reflects the client's internalization of the norms suggested by the therapist, and the client has begun to regulate themselves with no further need for the therapist to encourage this. This idea is reminiscent of Foucault's reference to Bentham's Panopticon (Foucault, 1977b), when surveillance starts to be carried out individually by those being surveyed. Here, clients take over the therapist's role and become surveyors and regulators of their own thoughts. However, this does not remove the power in the norms internalized by the client, or the power of the therapist in communicating and encouraging these norms to be internalized.

POWER IN PERSONAL HISTORIES

It could be claimed that the intention behind CBT, to change the negative automatic thoughts and negative schemata of the client, could be to increase the internal feeling of 'power-from-within' in the client, and reduce the power of clients' personal histories of powerlessness. However, the means by which CBT attempts to achieve this is not consistent with the ends. It is difficult to argue that the aim of CBT is to increase the power of the client, by the therapist using 'power-over' or their authority.

STRUCTURAL SOCIAL POWER

CBT theory takes no account of issues of power due to social-structural positions. There is a danger that in challenging the 'realism' of a client's thoughts, the material realities of power are ignored and deemed 'unrealistic'. The focus in CBT is on changing the thinking of the individual, which entails the danger of ignoring the social-structural positions and the material realities of oppression and power in peoples' lives.

CONCLUSION

Very little attention is paid to the issue of power in most of the CBT literature. Yet CBT invests much authority in therapists who, according to the model, know what is best for their client. There are few considerations of the dangers of this position, or even a questioning of the assumptions underlying this position. A belief in the importance of cognitive processes does not have to lead to a belief in an authoritative CBT therapist who educates the client in the right way to live their life. I maintain that it is necessary for CBT to look realistically and honestly at the dynamics of power in therapy relationships. For without such an inquiry, CBT therapists are in danger of obscuring their power, and of not taking an ethical stance to avoid domination and abuse.

Given the association of distress with the experience of powerlessness, should the ultimate aim of therapy be to try to help clients take more control of their lives? If so, then CBT therapists surely need to consider carefully how their practice helps or hinders this aim, particularly with respect to the internal consistency of the means and the end. If therapists take control, and do not think carefully about how to avoid domination during therapy, how can we expect clients to walk away feeling more in control?

REFERENCES

Allison, A. (1996) 'A framework for good practice: ethical issues in cognitive behaviour therapy', in S. Marshall and J. Turnbull (eds), *Cognitive Behaviour Therapy*, London: Balliere Tindall, pp. 155–80.

Beck, A. T. (1976, 1991) *Cognitive Therapy and the Emotional Disorders*, London: Penguin.

Beck, A. T., Rush, A. T., Shaw, B. F., and Emery, G. (1979) *Cognitive Therapy of Depression*, New York: Guildford Press.

Beck, J. S. (1995) *Cognitive Therapy: Basics and Beyond*, London: Guilford Press.

Bentall, R. (2003) *Madness Explained: Psychosis and Human Nature*, London: Penguin.

Bozarth, J. (1998) *Person-Centered Therapy: A Revolutionary Paradigm*, Ross-on-Wye: PCCS Books.

British Association for Counselling and Psychotherapy (BACP) (2002) *Ethical Framework for Good Practice in Counselling and Psychotherapy*, Rugby.

Butler, J. (1990) 'Gender trouble, feminist theory, and psychoanalytic discourse', in L. J. Nicholson (ed.), *Feminism/Postmodernism*, London: Routledge, pp. 324–40.

Cousins, M. and Hussein, A. (1984) *Michel Foucault*, London: Macmillan Education.

Fish, V. (1999) 'Clementis's hat: Foucault and the politics of psychotherapy', in I. Parker (ed.), *Deconstructing Psychotherapy*, London: Sage, pp. 54–70.

Foucault, M. (1973) *The Order of Things: An Archaeology of the Human Sciences*, New York: Vintage Books.

Foucault, M. (1977a) *Madness and Civilisation*, London: Tavistock.

Foucault, M. (1977b) *Discipline and Punish*, London: Penguin Press.

Foucault, M. (1979) *The History of Sexuality, Volume 1: An Introduction*, London: Penguin Press.

Foucault, M. (1980) *Power/Knowledge: Selected Interviews and Other Writings 1972–1977*, Brighton, Sussex: Harvester Press.

Gilbert, P. (2004) 'Evolutionary approaches to psychopathology and cognitive therapy', in P. Gilbert (ed.), *Evolutionary Theory and Cognitive Therapy*, New York: Springer.

Hawton, K., Salkovskis, P., Kirk, J., and Clark, D. (2005) *Cognitive Behaviour Therapy for Psychiatric Problems*, Oxford: Oxford University Press.

Keys, S. and Proctor, G. (2007) 'Ethics in practice in person-centred therapy', in M. Cooper, M. O'Hara, P. Schmid, and G. Wyatt (eds), *The Handbook of Person-centred Psychotherapy and Counselling*, Basingstoke: Palgrave Macmillan, pp. 353–65.

Kirk, J. (2005) 'Cognitive-behavioural assessment', in K. Hawton, P. Salkovskis, J. Kirk, and D. M. Clark (eds), *Cognitive Behaviour Therapy for Psychiatric Problems*, Oxford: Oxford University Press, pp. 13–51.

Lambert, M. J. and Ogles, B. M. (2004) 'The efficacy and effectiveness of psychotherapy', in M. Lambert (ed.), *Handbook of Psychotherapy and Behavioural Change*, 5th edn, New York: John Wiley.

Lowe, R. (1999) 'Between the "No Longer" and the "Not Yet": postmodernism as a context for critical therapeutic work', in I. Parker (ed.), *Deconstructing Psychotherapy*, London: Sage, pp. 71–85.

Lukes, S. (1974) *Power: A Radical View*, London: Macmillan Press.

McNay, L. (1992) *Foucault and Feminism: Power, Gender and the Self*, Cambridge: Polity Press.

Marcinko, L. (2003) 'Medication compliance with difficult patients', in R. L. Leahy (ed.), *Roadblocks in CBT: Transforming Challenges into Opportunities to Change*, London: Guilford Press, pp. 318–40.

Marshall, S. (1996) 'The characteristics of cognitive behaviour therapy', in S. Marshall and J. Turnbull (eds), *Cognitive Behaviour Therapy*, London: Balliere Tindall, pp. 29–54.

Masson, J. M. (1989) *Against Therapy*, London: Fontana.

Norcross, J. C. (ed.) (2002) *Psychotherapy Relationships that Work: Therapists Contributions and Responsiveness to Patients*, New York: OUP.

Padesky, C. A. and Greenberger, D. (1995) *Clinician's Guide to Mind over Mood*, London: Guilford Press.

Paley, G. and Lawton, D. (2001) 'Evidence-based practice: accounting for the importance of the therapeutic relationship in UK National Health Service therapy provision', *Counselling and Psychotherapy Research*, 1 (1): 12–17.

Pilgrim, D. (1997) *Psychotherapy and Society*, London: Sage.

Pilgrim, D. and Treacher, A. (1992) *Clinical Psychology Observed*, London: Routledge.

Potter, J. (1996) *Representing Reality: Discourse, Rhetoric and Social Construction*, Sage: London.

Proctor, G. (2002a) *The Dynamics of Power in Counselling and Psychotherapy: Ethics, Politics and Practice*, Ross-on-Wye: PCCS Books.

Ransome, P. (1992) *Antonio Gramsci: A New Introduction*, London: Harvester Wheatsheaf.

Rowe, D. (1989) 'Foreword', in J. Masson, *Against Therapy*, London: Fontana.

Searle, Y. (1993) 'Ethical issues within the therapeutic relationship: autonomy or paternalism?', *Clinical Psychology Forum (BPS)*, 31–6.

Spinelli, E. (1994) *Demystifying Therapy*, London: Constable.

Starhawk (1987) *Truth or Dare: Encounters with Power, Authority, and Mystery*, San Francisco: Harper & Row.

Stevens C. L., Muran C., and Safran J. D. (2003) 'Obstacles or opportunities? A relational approach to negotiating alliance ruptures', in R. L. Leahy (ed.), *Roadblocks in CBT: Transforming Challenges into Opportunities to Change*, London: Guilford Press, pp. 274–94.

Telford, A. and Farrington, A. (1996) 'Handing over: generalisation and maintenance of self-management skills', in S. Marshall and J. Turnbull (eds), *Cognitive Behaviour Therapy*, London: Balliere Tindall, pp. 121–52.

Tompkins, M. A. (2003) 'Effective homework', in R. L. Leahy (ed.), *Roadblocks in CBT: Transforming Challenges into Opportunities to Change*, London: Guilford Press, pp. 49–68.
Turnbull, J. (1996) 'The context of therapy', in S. Marshall and J. Turnbull (eds), *Cognitive Behaviour Therapy*, London: Balliere Tindall, pp. 11–28.
Williams, J. and Watson, G. (1994) 'Mental health services that empower women: the challenge to clinical psychology', *Clinical Psychology Forum*, 64: 11–17.

CHAPTER 21

READING *'HAPPINESS'*:
CBT AND THE LAYARD THESIS

DAVID PILGRIM

'Money can't buy me love...'

(Lennon and McCartney, 1964)

INTRODUCTION: THE 'LAYARD THESIS' SUMMARIZED

In this chapter, I examine an important recent contribution from an economist, Richard Layard, to debates about the social and economic sources of mental distress and ways of responding to the latter. Layard's book *Happiness* is one of many contributions from him about these topics. It provides a persuasive case for 'upstream' causes of mental-health problems, which includes a critique of modern consumerism. A much less persuasive case is made, though, for therapeutic social engineering in response to psychological casualties of these socio-economic forces.

Layard's work has been a very useful stimulus for debates about mental health in society. Many of these have been around for a long time in disciplines outside of economics, and so it may be relevant that it has taken an economist to encourage discussion about mental health in the political class. It confirms one of Layard's key points that, currently, when measuring social progress, finance is privileged over the subjective lives of ordinary citizens.

Layard utilizes a range of evidence from genetics, neuroscience, medicine, philosophy, psychology, and sociology (as well as drawing heavily on his own discipline of Economics) to make his case. The latter starts with the claim that whilst absolute poverty certainly leads to misery, for those not in that state, happiness does not increase with more wealth. Setting out this stall in the opening paragraph of his first chapter of *Happiness* (Layard, 2005) is this clear enough statement: 'There is a paradox at the heart of our lives. Most people want income and strive for it. Yet as Western societies have got richer, their people have become no happier' (ibid.: 3).

Layard goes on to marshal evidence, not just to support this claim but also to suggest causal mechanisms and corrective interventions. To use a medical metaphor here, he provides us with a diagnosis and some thoughts on aetiology or pathogenesis, as well as a treatment plan. He goes beyond medical metaphor, though – he also literally accepts medical categories and authority.

An earlier version of this chapter appeared in the *European Journal of Psychotherapy and Counselling*, 10 (3), 2008, pp. 247–60.

Indeed, an academic feature of his book is that whilst Layard is highly logical and detailed in his curiosity about empirical claims from all the disciplines upon which he draws, he spends little time or interest in interrogating the concepts and theories favoured by them. The exception to this is that he does make small detours of conceptual clarification in response to philosophy and economics. Thus, for example, he challenges Kant with MRI scans to show that the philosopher was wrong to claim that doing the right thing should give no pleasure. Similarly, he shows that the reductionist emphasis of Hobbes on punishment to maintain moral order was flawed.

The broad sweep of Layard's thesis is very sound. In economies in which real income levels have risen steadily, the cultural expectation is to want more money. Consequently, there is an unending game of catch up – more money is given, but more is wanted. The gap between actual income and that deemed appropriate for happiness and need satisfaction inevitably leads to chronic dissatisfaction. Moreover, that restless and grasping focus on work and its riches has created economies fraught with other consequent problems of venal materialism and 'rampant individualism' (a warranted favoured phrase of Layard). At the heart of this dissatisfaction is 'The Hedonic Treadmill'. As he puts it succinctly,

> '... living standards are like alcohol and drugs. Once you have a new experience, you need to keep having more of it if you want to sustain your happiness... you have to keep running in order that your happiness stands still ....'
>
> (ibid.: 48)

The news gets worse, however. It is not merely that modern consumerism is a false god promising happiness but not delivering; the social and cultural arrangements around that idol bring pain and suffering to many. Most of us have a distressing work–life balance (especially in the USA and the UK). The idealization of the ultra-rich legitimizes large discrepancies in wealth and de-legitimizes re-distributive economic policies, such as high taxation. Not only have authoritarian socialist experiments in the East (rejected by Layard) been displaced by anarchic 'wild west' capitalism to the further detriment of its long-suffering citizens, but social democracy in northern Europe (highly favoured by Layard) has been in retreat. In Scandinavia, for example, the stable emergence of social democracy has now broken down, and further south it has been captured by neo-liberal economics and conservative social policies ('Blairism' in the UK exemplifies this point).

According to Layard, socio-economic arrangements that focus singularly on the pursuit of personal financial advantage divert us from understanding the factors that might illuminate a more important type of wealth. He argues that 'the aim of politics is to make the world a friendlier place not an assault course' (ibid.: 232). I presume that he means here that the aim of politics *ought* to be this, as clearly, by his own argument, it is currently failing.

Layard identifies seven main factors that create a synergy for happiness: good family relationships; enough money to avoid absolute poverty; enjoyable work; community engagement and friendships; good health; personal freedom; and a clear personal value system. By implication, people may lose the level of happiness achieved in life by any negative aspects of the seven factors. Thus, happiness and its opposite are shaped and maintained dynamically by an interaction of these factors in a person's life. By the end of the book, he lays out a range of policies to support this shift of emphasis to happiness, and away from the rat race of money-chasing.

By focusing on chasing more money, individualism in the capitalist economy creates life-styles at odds with this synergy for happiness. Family relationships are undermined; work becomes an obsessive vehicle for wealth and status; social bonds in the community and with friends are weakened by individualism; and health is affected negatively. Personal freedom is intrinsic to rampant individualism, but it is expressed at the cost of all the above when only expressed egotistically. As for personal value systems, these are individualized and secularized, so the advantages of collective political and religious meaning systems are lost. Layard talks of a 'moral vacuum' created by this collapse of mutuality and social solidarity.

Moreover, the aggregate loss of trust and respect for others arising from materialistic egotism brings with it high crime and suicide rates. The predictions of post-Second World War economists that increasing overall wealth in a society would bring lower crime rates has proved to be wrong, as is evident in Western Europe and North America.

Having summarized Layard's thesis and broadly endorsed it, I now want to offer what I consider to be some substantial shortcomings. Layard is an economist, not a psychologist or sociologist, and so he has either been brave and erudite, or unwise and arrogant, to take on such a huge topic about the nature of well-being in its social context. Human happiness is surely a huge topic by anyone's estimation. Poking around curiously with a stick in the arcane world of other disciplines will lead to some bits of uni-disciplinary knowledge emerging, but others remaining hidden. The point I am making here, then, is not *ad hominem* about Layard but a more general one about the challenge of inter-disciplinarity. The other general point I want to make, before critiquing Layard's *Happiness,* is that whatever Layard's personal take on his topic, all of us, but especially those in and around the therapy trade, need to reflect long and hard on the relationship between upstream causes and downstream solutions.

THE SELECTIVE USE OF EVIDENCE AND NAÏVE REALISM

Some of Layard's empirical claims about social differences in happiness are questionable. For example, he minimizes gender and age differences in happiness, arguing that the seven factors noted above generate degrees of well-being in all of us. However, there are clear differences in gender and age. Far more women than men present with 'common mental health problems', and medical sociologists have not resolved the reasons for this gender gap (Rogers and Pilgrim, 2005). As for age, a predictable inverted 'U'-shaped curve characterizes the life span in relation to misery. Basically, the young and the very old are disproportionately worse off (Rogers and Pilgrim, 2003).

As an economist, Layard is predictably stronger on the link between labour-market position and happiness. He points out, correctly, that unemployment and insecure employment impact negatively. However, he endorses the picture offered by Helliwell (2003) that unemployment has the greatest negative impact – a conclusion which is challengeable. Other studies indicate that global mental-health scores for the unemployed lie between secure employment and insecure employment, with the latter actually creating the greatest distress and existential uncertainty (Rogers and Pilgrim, 2003).

Taken overall, these are important points of academic hygiene, but they do not alter the validity of Layard's basic argument. The greater doubt arises not from his empirical claims, but that he approaches the academy and the clinic with all their relevant disciplines and associated vested interests with such enthusiastic and artless trust. The whole spirit of Layard's work is one of bullish empiricism, and the latter is naïve not critical (cf. Bhaskar, 1989).

This naïve realism in turn creates an uncritical trust in pre-existing bodies of knowledge. And because the latter are bound up with disciplinary interests, there is no interrogation of the power relationships they contain. These interests and quests for power from academic disciplines – and especially their applied wings, the professions – readily tip into rhetoric and strategies to gain the privileges of epistemological control, occupational autonomy, dominance over others, political influence, and improved income. The elaborate facts so favoured by Layard's style of argumentation are theory-laden, and they also reflect preferred concepts. Human science cannot proceed properly unless these are interrogated – it is not just a matter of methodological rigour about knowledge claims ('facts'), though this is still important.

This caution is not limited to Layard's work. A range of post-Popperian philosophers, such as Feyerabend, Lakatos, Bhaskar, Kuhn, and others have highlighted the argument that empirical claims need to be understood in relation to concepts and theories. And sociologists of science have reinforced this necessity when they have investigated the way in which scientific knowledge emerges, is contested, and changes. Layard's retained faith in a post-Enlightenment approach to all matters in the world, including the conventional wisdoms of modernist human science, is both a strength and a weakness. The advantage is that he has no post-modern doubts. Consequently, this faith in the contemporary scientific academy saves his readers the interminable intellectual fiddling on the spot of the post-structuralism that has infected social science in the last 20 years.

But between the modern and the post-modern, as the philosophers I list above indicate, there remains a serious case to 'check our facts'; not in the sense of their accuracy (an empirical question of methodology) but in relation to their pre-empirical or non-empirical character. There are two good reasons for this sort of cautious or critical inquiry. The first is that taken-for-granted *factualism*, as disciplinary knowledge prefers to present itself, could lead to mystification, not clarification. Experts, applied and academic, often present their currently preferred reality as superior to that of colleagues in the past and in other disciplines. But experts may be wrong in the way that they theorize the world, and they may generate misleading data and truth claims by testing those theories.

Second, *naïve empiricism* means that concepts preferred at a moment in time may be poor, so we need a method to check this possibility. Theories and concepts are pregnant with values and interests – they are not merely simple springboards for logical and empirical inquiry. Thus, pre-empirical critique is just as important as empirical inquiry in the human sciences.

Instead of exercising caution on these two fronts, Layard is simply seduced by the certainties of factualism and naïve empiricism. It is important to distinguish my line of caution and criticism of Layard's naïve realism here from that of post-modernists who argue that 'everything is socially constructed', so we can never make stable knowledge claims about reality. It is not reality which is socially constructed, but our *understanding* of reality. This is why we should approach knowledge claims in human science and their underpinning interests sceptically. Layard fails in this task; indeed he does not even make a start on it in his book.

THE TECHNICAL FIX OF CBT AND THE FAITH IN PSYCHIATRIC KNOWLEDGE

Most forms of psychological intervention to ameliorate distress are derived not from the academic discipline of psychology but from medicine. For example, medical practitioners, not psychologists, first championed psychoanalysis and existential analysis. Many of the early members of the British Psychological Society were medical practitioners, and significantly the first separate section of the Society was formed in 1919 – the Medical Section. The flow of 'shell-shock doctors' from the 'Great War' swelled its ranks (Stone, 1985).

When psychodynamic therapy was superseded in legitimacy by behavioural, and then cognitive behavioural, treatments in the late twentieth century, clinical problems were clearly the main 'pull from the front'. The morphing of behaviour therapy into the seemingly contradictory model of cognitive behaviour therapy had no coherent 'ism' as a 'push from behind' in the academy. Indeed, very few forms of therapy have emerged purely from academic psychology. Kelly's personal-construct therapy (PCT) is an exception here. But PCT was then quickly incorporated into 'cognitive-analytical therapy' by a pragmatic general medical practitioner (Ryle, 1990).

As for the bigger players in the cognitive-therapy field, these were pragmatic psychologists and psychiatrists in the clinic (Beck, 1976; Ellis, 1994). They were seeking accessible and efficient treatments, which avoided the time-consuming past–present focus of the psychodynamic tradition. Their primary interest was not about researching ordinary cognitive functioning (the norm in academic departments of psychology during the 1980s), but about altering dysfunctional conduct. Thus, 'cognitive therapy' in its various guises has been driven, by and large, not by academic psychology but by practical concerns in clinical settings.

The above historical reality testing is relevant, given that Layard makes much use of psychology in his book *Happiness* as a discipline that offers a corrective to the economic reductionism of his own profession. He also suggests that applied psychology today carries similar helpful wisdoms to that of ancient cosmologies like Buddhism. He is enamoured by what he calls the 'new psychology', and implies or assumes that it is a unitary body of knowledge waiting to be tapped for human betterment. However, in the light of the previous discussion, he focuses on clinical innovations, not academic psychology; and it is not clear from the text whether he is aware of conflating the syncretism of CBT with the 'new psychology'. He rejects the historical determinism of the old. Freud is mentioned episodically to demonstrate how daft you can get. He also rejects historical determinism of a different kind – Skinner's radical behaviourism. His love of the academic new is reflected in contestable comments like: 'fortunately psychology has returned to the study of feelings' (ibid.: 128).

However, there are problems with his infatuation with the new. For example – and this may reflect Layard's belief in scientific incrementalism – psychology has not progressed linear fashion, with outmoded models being cast aside. Instead, we find layers of approach co-existing, which wax and wane in fashion. For example, there are plenty of psychologists (academic and applied) who remain attached to both behaviourism and psychoanalysis. Moreover, Layard does not mention social constructionism. His academic psychology advisors, acknowledged generously at the end of the book, seem to have emphasized inner events rather than social representations and discursive practices. The latter are studied as often now by social psychologists as by sociologists, and they have particular points to make about therapy (McNamee and Gergen, 1992; Parker, 1999).

Moreover, there is no clear evidence that psychology has, by and large, returned to feelings *per se*, but it has (for now) accepted the need to study internal events. The latter in the main are represented in undergraduate courses in psychology not in their affective form, but in their *cognitive* form. Feeling states *are* studied, but less often than verbalized cognitions. Thinking is now studied systematically. We now have 'cognitive science', but 'affective science' is fairly well hidden.

Moreover, as has been noted, the interest by some applied (not academic) psychologists in the relationship between thought, action, and affect has not been driven by academic innovations, but by the interests of clinical psychiatrists. This may seem a trivial point, but it is not. Unless it is made, then a superficial reading is that psychological science has marched resolutely forward to advise clinical practitioners about how to conduct their work, state-of-the-science fashion. CBT may be the current orthodoxy in clinical psychology, but it is essentially a form of psychiatric treatment, the roots of which are not in cognitive science. Any resemblance to cognitivism, in cognitive therapy, is superficial; and when it occurs genuinely, it has been a *post hoc* cultivation.

Layard alludes to psychiatry – or more often its by-product, mental illness – much in his work. The term 'by-product' is used here to point up that Layard's naïve acceptance of psychiatric representation is at work. I do not mean that people are not frightened, or profoundly sad or crazy. What I am emphasizing, *contra* Layard, is that the medical codifications of 'anxiety disorders' or 'depression' or 'schizophrenia' add little or nothing to ordinary-language representations of misery and madness. Consequently, we need to understand the variety of interests which maintain categories which are scientifically dubious and are experienced often as stigmatizing and unhelpful by their recipients (Pilgrim, 2007).

Moreover, psychiatric diagnoses are not straightforward facts but representations that are conceptually weak and tautological. Symptoms are used to warrant a diagnosis, and the symptoms are explained by the diagnosis (Pilgrim, 2005):

Q: How do we know this patient is depressed?
A: Because they are low in mood and feel unable to face work.
Q: Why are they low in mood and cannot face their work?
A: Because they are suffering from depression.

Layard's confidence in psychiatric diagnosis and in the new suggests that he takes current expert claims at face value. This leads to his own version of tautology. For example, he asks, 'Which causes more misery: depression or poverty? The answer is depression... mental illness is probably the largest cause (*sic.*) of misery in Western society' (ibid.: 181). But depression *is* misery: the former is a medical codification of the latter. If we say that misery is the largest cause of misery, it is absurdly circular. So how can Layard use the same logic persuasively when substituting the word 'depression' at the start of the formula? The answer probably rests in his pre-empirical assumption offered to him by psychiatrists (and, by the way, many psychologists) that depression has a non-problematic facticity that separates it clearly from ordinary misery. Not only is this position empirically challengeable, but the social and political implications are also enormous.

Thus, for example, it means that depression-as-illness is located in individuals. Our whole focus risks shifting, in a blinkered fashion, to their medical problem, rather than the very upstream factors Layard is so keen to emphasize. It also assumes that discontinuous emotional states exist in nature. Whilst this is logically possible, where is the evidence? Everything we know about emotions is that misery is ubiquitous and fluctuating between and within individuals, and across time and place. People, over time, move up and down a *continuum* of misery and happiness. Indeed, Layard himself endorses this assumption when discussing Buddhism, which accepts suffering as a regular part of the emotional flux of living and dying. Moreover, the diagnosis of depression not only diverts us from socio-political relationships to the diseased person, it renders the latter a passive victim of their putative disease. It thereby risks robbing them of their agency and their opportunity for existential reflection.

Elsewhere, with colleagues I have explored this problem with psychiatric diagnosis in general (Pilgrim, 2007), and the diagnosis of depression in particular (Pilgrim and Bentall, 1999; Pilgrim and Dowrick, 2006). Here I will simply note that Layard compounds the epistemic fallacy common in psychiatric and other forms of expert knowledge – the confusion of the map with the territory. Because psychiatrists reify 'major depression', it becomes for them a real *natural* category rather than a point on an existential continuum. This claim of naturalism is premature, as philosophers interrogating psychiatric nomenclature have demonstrated (Cooper, 2004). The latter demonstrates how commercial and professional interests have shaped premature claims of psychiatric success about categorizing misery and madness.

Depression, like other functional psychiatric diagnoses, is not readily distinguished from normality. This is a crucial test of a diagnostic category because medicine operates the binary principle of present/absent. Nor is 'clinical depression' readily distinguished from other common distress, such as anxiety. Nor are the causes of depression definitely known (it lacks aetiological specificity). Nor is a medical treatment specified for it and not applied to other conditions (it lacks treatment specificity). When we take all of these shortcomings together, depression is a very poor medical concept, yet it has entered the vernacular. It has widespread legitimacy, but it is a mystification that obscures a range of necessary moral, political, and intellectual explorations implied by ordinary-language accounts of 'distress', 'misery', or 'unhappiness'.

Because Layard accepts the psychiatric reification of 'depression', he also accepts the currently preferred expert technical fix for the putative condition – CBT and anti-depressants. It should be emphasized, though, that Layard does not argue that the cure for misery can ever be a total technical fix. For example, early on he endorses both psychological and pharmacological successes, but asks sceptically, '…how much further can this process go in the relief of misery?' (ibid.: 9). His wider preference is for upstream prevention by the construction of social and economic policies implied by the seven factors he highlights (listed earlier).

Thus my criticism here is not one of Layard's wholesale psychological or psychiatric reductionism, as he makes a clear case for socio-economic determinism. Rather it is that he invests too much faith in the technical fix, and he implies that the mechanisms of extreme misery are being increasingly explicated by modern therapeutic technologies, when they are not. It is as though he cannot carry through the full implications of his own reasoning about upstream factors.

So despite his lack of crude reductionism, Layard still falls into the traps of the illusory technical fix and of psychiatric reification. Under the heading 'disorders of the mind', he argues, with typical enthusiasm for what is for him the factually obvious, that:

> 'What drug you need depends on what kind of problem you have. If we consider only serious mental problems, about a third of us will experience one of them some time in our life. They include schizophrenia (1% of us), depression (15%), manic-depression (1%)...' [*he goes on to list more psychiatric categories* – DP]
>
> (ibid.: 208)

In case the reader is in doubt about Layard's faith in medical categories, he goes on to describe the pros and cons of drugs for relief suffering to say this: 'We all become what we would call depressed at some time in our lives. But a major depression is something quite different.' (ibid. : 209)

In his enthusiasm for anti-depressants, Layard then goes further by accepting that depression is 'associated' with serotonin depletion, but he does not interrogate the uncertainty about the direction of causality. For example, is a headache caused by a lack of aspirin in the brain? (The answer is 'no'.) And could suffering a saddening loss or insult to the self lead to changes in the brain? (The answer, by Layard's own arguments earlier in his book, is 'yes'.) Moreover, the putative pharmacological rationale for the SSRIs is becoming weaker, as more and more randomized controlled trials (RCTs) show a narrowing gap of results in the drug and placebo arms (Dowrick, 2004; Moncrieff and Kirsch, 2005).

Layard does not limit his confidence in a therapeutic regime for depression to pharmacology. He advocates the optimal combined use of drugs and talk. By implication, we need more therapists, and more and better drugs. Music to the ears is consequently offered to his psychiatric colleagues:

> 'We should spend more on tackling the problem of mental illness. This is the greatest source of misery in the West, and the fortunate should ensure a better deal for those who suffer. Psychiatry should be a top branch of medicine, not one of the least prestigious.'
>
> (ibid.: 233)

This conclusion is well intentioned. Who can argue with wanting to ameliorate misery? But it is without reference to the contestation that surrounds psychiatry, and which has done for so long. Not only has that profession, in the main, opted for a categorical view of human functioning, which does not hold scientific water and has dehumanizing consequences, but it has been a source of recurring criticism from insiders and outsiders alike. The enlightened biopsychosocial model favoured by Layard is not typically applied in psychiatric practice (Pilgrim and Rogers, 2005), and it tends to default, in practice, to psychosomatic reasoning, thus ignoring and obscuring the social (Pilgrim et al., 2008).

Finally, Layard's commitment to the technical fix of CBT reinforces the view that the *model* of intervention to ameliorate human distress is all that matters. In fact, over 30 years of process–outcome research in psychotherapy tells us that it is the therapeutic alliance, not other variables (like the model utilized, therapist background, gender, age, etc.) that is the best predictor of success (Lambert, 2007; cf. many of the chapters in this volume). Thus, the seduction of technology diverts our attention from the centrality of relationality. Layard makes his particular contribution to this mystifying techno-centric discourse about how people change and how they might feel better about themselves and the world.

DISCUSSION

In the first part of *Happiness*, Layard lets us know that we are being short changed over happiness. He has got all of the upstream factors in place to make his case, except one. He emphasizes the general role of the family as a stable point of reference for mental health in the growing child. However, no mention is made of those attending psychiatric facilities having high rates of childhood sexual abuse. Also, physical abuse in childhood predicts both violence and re-victimization in adulthood. A consequent omission, then, is that an effective child-protection policy would be an important building block of a public policy aimed at raising the average level of happiness in the population. Thus, Layard is particularly weak in truly understanding the mediating factors about relationality, support, and attachment in the emergence and amelioration of mental-health problems (cf. Pilgrim et al., 2009, forthcoming).

Moreover, there is an implication here for the therapy trade. We know that a minority of therapists surveyed anonymously admit to boundary violations about sexual contact (Pilgrim and Guinan, 1999). We also know that this is a source of iatrogenic distress for clients, with some of them experiencing re-victimization. Layard flags the adverse effects of drug treatment but does not mention this risk from talking therapies (save that they might be offered ineffective forms). He writes as if therapy is always benign, when we know that bad therapists create deterioration effects, and that many clients gain no benefit while being exposed to its risks.

In line with his confidence in therapy, Layard believes there are now experts in misery. As we know, there is a counter-argument to this assumption, with some vociferously rejecting therapeutic expertise (Masson, 1989), or damning it with faint praise (Smail, 1996). Whatever stance we take on either side of these arguments, therapy has to be viewed as a problematic form of social engineering. It contains risks as well as potential benefits. It is not just a good news story.

THE WEAKNESSES OF CBT

I now want to return at this point to the weakness of CBT (liked by Layard) and the remaining strengths of the older traditions, such as psychoanalysis and existentialism (disliked by Layard).

CBT is a technology without a true theory. Moreover, it has taken much of its advocates in nursing and clinical psychology (which should know better) in a direction which reinforces the irrationalities of psychiatric diagnosis. The latter leads to a nomothetic rather than idiographic approach to therapeutic work, with patients being fitted into *a priori* categories, which are then 'treated' – hence we find CBT 'for' depression, GAD, schizophrenia, and so on (e.g. Tarrier et al., 1998).

The tendency for clinical psychologists to utilize rather than reject psychiatric categories has been evident since behaviour therapy, and then cognitive behaviour therapy, become medicalized. Behaviour therapy and CBT have become part of the psychiatric treatment armamentarium, taught to and delivered by nurses (cookbook-style). These clinical techniques have simply become forms of treatment for mental illness. The medicalization trend has been reflected in the work of Aaron Beck and his colleagues. Having no theoretical allegiance to behaviourism *per se*, but a desire to extend the applicability of behaviour therapy to inner events, Beck's a-theoretical psychiatric pragmatism prevailed. Hence, there was the eventual dominance of the current orthodoxy of cognitive behaviour therapy and its emphasis on treating diagnostic categories. Psychiatric knowledge and medical dominance were thereby left intact, neither scrutinized nor criticized. In his book, Layard simply accepts this inheritance and its epistemological assumptions.

But does any of this matter? After all, those on the outside of these professional concerns may understandably be left cold by the history and the arguments. I would argue that it *does* matter because of questions of reflexivity and comprehensiveness. Whatever we think of the behaviourists of the 1960s, they were trying to develop a general psychological frame of reference that could not just enable and test behavioural change, but be the basis of context-specific formulations. As such, it could be applied to the therapist themselves in accounting for their own current behaviour in relation to their peculiar reinforcement history, and it was linked to general psychological theorizing. But because of the medicalization of behaviour therapy and, subsequently, CBT, we are left in a paradoxical position, 40 years on. Some CBT practitioners now special-plead for formulation in the face of diagnostic imperialism (Bruch and Bond, 1998; Butler, 1999), but many others simply accept the advantages of the latter medical orthodoxy without question and at their peril (Pilgrim and Carey, 2009; Scott and Sembi, 2006).

In the latter regard, clinical psychologists in the thrall of CBT have now often become part of the problem rather than the solution. Under pressure to obtain research grants allocated by medical committees that are committed to DRGs (diagnostic-related groups), clinical-psychology research on, for example, 'CBT for schizophrenia' reinforces the idea that madness and misery are carved at the joints of nature, when they are not. Being a contested discipline with biology at one end and sociology at the other, we also find psychology containing bio-determinists, who can operate comfortably within a biomedical paradigm. The epistemic fallacy (confusing reality with what we call reality) and the ontic fallacy (naïvely limiting the immediate surface of what we see as reality) are reinforced then not by psychiatrists but by *psychologists* (Pilgrim, 2007).

If CBT has little to say theoretically about general human functioning, and reinforces questionable medical categories, what are the implications of Layard rejecting older and, in his view, outmoded psychological models? The first is that given his commitment to understanding the subjective elements of 'human nature' – both its rational and its non-rational character – Layard may be throwing the baby out with the bathwater. Although Eysenck was the first in the queue to attack the therapeutic effectiveness of psychoanalysis (Eysenck, 1952), when putting forward a bid for legitimacy for behaviour therapy, it should be remembered that the focus of his disdain was never primarily intended as a form of treatment for mental illness. Its main goal was to understand the unconscious – Freud did therapy out of the necessity to earn a living (Freud, 1959).

If judged by the standards of treatment effectiveness, psychoanalysis is indeed poor. It is, however, a reflexive theory (applicable to therapist and client alike) and is elaborately theoretical. Moreover, some variants of it have had useful hermeneutic potential in social science – a value that can also be found in existentialism. The latter is reflexive, and it enables us to understand people as agents in their social context. It thereby allows us to take the personal accounts of people seriously to illuminate both their context and their view of that context. This in turn allows us to listen to misery without necessarily turning its narrators into patients who 'suffer from depression' (Pilgrim and Dowrick, 2006). Ironically, Layard at points endorses the need for this existential sensibility (ibid.: 8) when citing Frankl (1985). Can we seriously imagine CBT illuminating and shaping investigations of such general importance to social science in ways that have flowed from psychoanalysis and existentialism? Theoretically confused and practically obsessed CBT has no such obvious prospects.

Thus both psychoanalysis and existentialism can give a voice to misery in social science without necessarily being co-opted narrowly as 'treatment methods'. This cannot be said for CBT or drug treatments. Accordingly, these socially mute technologies risk individualizing distress and disconnecting it from its biographical and social origins. This point about the older traditions being pathways into social understanding has another connection with Layard's thesis. He is keen to argue on moral grounds that the acceptance of suffering is wrong. He makes this response to those who have argued against the widespread utilization of drugs like Prozac: 'The most puritanical of them argue that misery is a part of human experience. We should accept misery rather than fight it. This view is simply immoral' (ibid.: 218).

The apocryphal graffiti, 'you are born, it's horrible and then you die' is rather nihilistic, but it is also true for many people. For example, try being poor, female, suffering sexual abuse in childhood, and being re-victimized in adulthood, and see how happy you can become by learning to reverse your 'faulty' thinking about these facts of your life. And Layard is content to endorse Buddhism, without conceding that it takes a version of the above graffiti seriously. However, it then offers forms of mental discipline and Stoicism to transcend the dire implications of ubiquitous suffering.

Some of this dispute I am constructing here with Layard may be semantic. Surely it is possible to accept that suffering is indeed intrinsic to the human condition, without being accused of being cruel or puritanical in response. Life really is tough and all of the dramas T. S. Eliot points to, surrounding 'birth and copulation and death', ensure their fair share of misery for many of us much of the time, however our society is organized. Layard himself argues that our consumerist culture ensures a high prevalence of misery. So why can we not raise political expectations in line with Layard's upstream arguments, and yet still accept that suffering is not necessarily pathology requiring treatment? The pathologization of individual victims risks diverting us from the upstream arguments Layard himself makes so very well

CONCLUSION

In this chapter I have outlined the case made by Richard Layard in his book *Happiness*, and offered a view about its strong and weak points. I was left supporting his upstream analysis and proposals, but I suggest that child protection should also be incorporated into this frame of reference. I was less convinced, though, about Layard's faith in the technical fix, when we try to pull struggling people out downstream. Yes, some are drowning, not waving. Others are just getting by, fairly browned off and not even waving. Should they all be assessed ('diagnosed') and offered therapy to turn them into patients? There is after all, as they say about human misery, 'a lot of it about'.

At the time of writing, there is a confluence of government interest in CBT by 'increasing access to psychological therapies' and its interest in the fiscal savings of using CBT to get people with mental-health problems back to work. That meeting of interests prompts a socio-economic analysis of the downstream response to unhappiness analogous to the one offered by Layard about its upstream causes. By naïvely endorsing the technical fix of therapy Layard has now become a target, rather than a source, of that type of socio-economic critique.

The latter invites us to think critically about the limits of forms of therapeutic social engineering. Instead of more CBT for the masses, we might imagine and seek to create other possibilities. These could include ordinary forms of social solidarity, mutual support for the survivors of childhood adversity, and political initiatives to reverse the effects in the UK of nearly 30 years of neo-liberal governance from parties of both political hues. The latter has atomized communities and encouraged the 'rampant individualism' Layard understandably laments.

REFERENCES

Beck, A. T. (1976) *Cognitive Therapy and the Emotional Disorders*, New York: Meridian.

Bhaskar, R. (1989) *Reclaiming Reality*, London: Verso.

Bruch, M. and Bond, F. W. (1998) *Beyond Diagnosis: Case Formulation Approaches in CBT*, Chichester: Wiley.

Butler, G. (1999) 'Clinical formulation', *Comprehensive Clinical Psychology*, 6: 1–24.

Cooper, R. (2004) 'What is wrong with DSM?', *History of Psychiatry*, 15 (1): 1–25.

Dowrick, C. (2004) *Beyond Depression: A New Approach to Understanding and Management*, Oxford: Oxford University Press.

Ellis, A. (1994) *Reason and Emotion in Psychotherapy* (revised and updated), New York: Birch Lane Press.

Eysenck, H. J. (1952) 'The effects of psychotherapy: an evaluation', *Journal of Consulting Psychology*, 16: 319–24.

Frankl, V. (1985) *Man's Search for Meaning*, New York: Basic Books.

Freud, S. (1959) 'The question of lay analysis', in *The Complete Works of Sigmund Freud*, London: Hogarth.

Helliwell, J. (2003) 'How's life? Combining individual variables to explain subjective well-being', *Economic Modelling*, 20: 331–60.

Lambert, M. (2007) 'What we have learned from a decade of research aimed at improving psychotherapy outcome in routine care', *Psychotherapy Research*, 17: 1–14.

Layard, R. (2005) *Happiness: Lessons from a New Science*, London: Penguin.

McNamee, S. and Gergen, K. (eds) (1992) *Therapy as Social Construction*, London: Sage.

Masson, J. M. (1989) *Against Therapy: Warning – Psychotherapy May be Hazardous to Your Mental Health*, London: HarperCollins.

Moncrieff, J. and Kirsch, I. (2005) 'Efficacy of antidepressants in adults', *British Medical Journal*, 331 (16 July): 155–7.

Parker, I. (ed.) (1999) *Deconstructing Psychotherapy*, London: Sage.

Pilgrim, D. (2007) 'The survival of psychiatric diagnosis', *Social Science and Medicine*, 65 (3): 536–44.

Pilgrim, D. (2005) 'Defining mental disorder: tautology in the service of sanity in British mental health legislation', *Journal of Mental Health*, 14 (5): 435–43.

Pilgrim, D. and Bentall, R. P. (1999) 'The medicalisation of misery: a critical realist analysis of the concept of depression', *Journal of Mental Health*, 8 (3): 261–74.

Pilgrim, D. and Carey, T. (2009/forthcoming) 'Contested professional rationales for the assessment of mental health problems: can social theories help?', *Social Theory and Health* (in press).

Pilgrim, D. and Dowrick, C. (2006) 'From a diagnostic-therapeutic to a social-existential response to "depression"', *Journal of Public Mental Health,* 5 (2): 6–12.

Pilgrim, D. and Guinan, P. (1999) 'From mitigation to culpability: rethinking the evidence about therapist sexual abuse', *European Journal of Counselling, Psychotherapy and Health*, 2 (2): 153–68.

Pilgrim, D., Kinderman, P., and Tai, S. (2008) 'Taking stock of the biopsychosocial model in "mental health care"', *Journal of Social and Psychological Sciences*, 1 (2): 1–39.

Pilgrim, D., Rogers, A., and Bentall, R. P. (2009) 'The centrality of personal relationships in the creation and amelioration of mental health problems: the current interdisciplinary case', *Health* (in press).

Rogers, A. and Pilgrim, D. (2003) *Mental Health and Inequality*, Basingstoke: Palgrave.

Rogers, A. and Pilgrim, D. (2005) *A Sociology of Mental Health and Illness* (3rd edn), Milton Keynes: Open University Press.

Ryle, A. (1990) *Cognitive-Analytic Therapy: Active Participation in Change*, London: Wiley.

Scott, M. J. and Sembi, S. (2006) 'Cognitive behaviour therapy treatment failures in practice: the neglected role of diagnostic inaccuracy', *Behavioural and Cognitive Psychotherapy*, 34: 491–5.

Smail, D. (1996) *Getting By Without Psychotherapy*, London: Constable.

Stone, M. (1985) 'Shellshock and the psychologists', in W. Bynum, M. Shepherd, and R. Porter (eds), *The Anatomy of Madness*, London: Tavistock.

Tarrier, N. Yusupoff, L., Kinner, C., McCarthy, A., Gladhill, G., Haddock, G., and Morris, J. (1998) 'A randomised control trial of intense cognitive behaviour therapy for chronic schizophrenia', *British Medical Journal*, 317: 303–7.

CHAPTER 22

L'ANTI-LIVRE NOIR DE LA PSYCHANALYSE: CBT IN FRENCH/LACANIAN PERSPECTIVE

ROBERT SNELL

INTRODUCTION

France is facing an Anglo-Saxon invasion – by 'les TCC', *les thérapies cognitivo-comportementales*, better known on Britain's shores as cognitive behaviour therapy (CBT). Developed out of the ideas of the American behaviourists J. B. Watson and B. F. Skinner, and cognitive psychologists from the USA and Canada such as Albert Ellis, Albert Bandura, and Aaron Beck, CBT/TCC has in fact been part of the therapeutic landscape in France for several decades – the *Association française de thérapie comportementale et cognitive* was founded as long ago as 1971, and there is a significant home-grown literature. What has been taking place over the last few years is, as Jacques-Alain Miller writes in his book *L'Anti-Livre noir de la psychanalyse* (Miller, 2006), a new marketing onslaught: TCC re-launched and presented to health administrators and insurance companies as 'a fully developed product, meeting European and international standards, and offering rapid and low-cost solutions to the majority of psychological problems'. In the process, psychoanalysis in France,'a school of irony, scepticism, and disrespect, definitively anti-modern', finds itself under new and fierce attack.

This attack comes from two main directions. On the one hand is a campaign launched in 2001 by INSERM – the *Institut national de la santé et de la recherche médicale*, the equivalent of the British NICE (the National Institute for Clinical Excellence). The report which INSERM published in February 2004 claimed to be a scientific evaluation of three approaches to psychotherapy, the psychoanalytic, the cognitive behavioural, and family and couples therapy. Its research aimed to ascertain the most up-to-date, 'effective', 'evidence-based' treatment for mental-health problems; the public, it proclaimed, had a right to nothing less. Psychoanalysis came out last (INSERM, 2004). The INSERM campaign was backed up on TV, on the internet (including, for a time, on a government website), and in the periodical and popular press, for example in the glossy magazine *Psychologies,* with its questionnaires and surveys, and its focus on 'life-style' and 'well-being'.

On the other hand is a book which appeared in September 2005. Barely registered in Britain (although it did receive a weary rebuttal, by a French psychoanalyst, in the *International Journal of Psychoanalysis*) (Kipman, 2006), *Le Livre noir de la psychanalyse* (Van Rillaer et al. 2005) was a publishing sensation in France. 'The Black Book of Psychoanalysis' – in English

An earlier version of this chapter appeared as a review article in the *European Journal of Psychotherapy and Counselling*, 9 (2), June 2007: 231–9.

the title sounds like something dreamt up by the late Ivor Cutler – is a compilation of often rehearsed anti-Freud arguments penned by some familiar enthusiasts (Borch-Jacobsen, Crews, Ellis, Sulloway, and Swales, amongst others); it was heavily promoted by the weekly news magazine *Le Nouvel Observateur,* and it seeks, in the process of debunking psychoanalysis, to advance the claims of 'les TCC'.

L'ANTI-LIVRE NOIR DE LA PSYCHANALYSE

Commentators sympathetic to psychoanalysis, such as the analyst and historian Elisabeth Roudinesco, were quick to point out the conspiracy-like feel of these various initiatives (Roudinesco, 2005). *L'Anti-Livre noir de la psychanalyse* is the most concerted counter-attack so far, mounted by the impassioned cohorts of Lacanian psychoanalysis and their allies, under the generalship of Lacan's son-in-law and leading heir, Jacques-Alain Miller. The *Anti-Livre noir* contains contributions by some 44 analysts and academics. In best Napoleonic tradition, it calls to its aid the spirits of the great national departed, from Cyrano de Bergerac to the poet Baudelaire and (to the delight of this writer) the flamboyant Théophile Gautier. One contributor cites Maréchal Foch, architect of the allied victory in Europe in 1918: 'My centre's collapsing, my right flank's retreating – excellent conditions! I shall attack!' As Miller states at the outset, the book is not a defence – against an 'enemy we did not even know we had... [and] a pot-pourri of complaints as booming as they are ineffectual'. The *Anti-Livre noir* is an attack, and it is a blistering one.

For where the British psychoanalytic establishment has, for the most part, been anxious to go along with the challenge to produce 'evidence' and demonstrate 'treatment efficacy', the francophone world – as represented in Miller's book, at least – will have none of it. In a detailed and tightly argued essay at the very heart of the book, Yves Cartuyvels, an eminent Belgian Professor of Law who has spent his professional life examining the nature of evidence, refutes the claims of cognitive behaviour therapy to be founded – 'objectively' and 'scientifically' – in solid evidence. Such claims are mere scientism; they rest on 'a superannuated conception of science as the measure of ultimate truth' and a naïve nineteenth-century scientific positivism:

> 'the epistemology of science might as well not have bothered underlining, as it has been doing for many years, the social construction of science, or describing the interplay of its actors, and the interests and values behind the practice of science...'

These claims also necessitate a refusal to accept that a patient might choose 'a rationality other than scientific rationality in response to psychic malaise'. In any case, what, Cartuyvels asks, is 'effective' in the field of mental health?

> 'The suppression of a symptom? Help with living with a symptom? Who fixes and defines the thresholds of effectiveness? Science? The therapist? The subject? Are these thresholds the same from one individual to another, from one kind of suffering to another?'

Cartuyvels brings his lawyer's eye to *Le Livre noir*'s methods of argumentation. In 1997 two science academics, A. Sokal and J. Bricmont, published a book called *Impostures intellectuelles*, which took various important thinkers to task, Derrida, Lacan, Baudrillard, and Deleuze, for example, for, the authors claimed, misappropriating scientific and mathematical concepts in order to lend cheap credibility to their theorizing. The *Livre noir*'s procedure is the same: attack the authors' good faith, the better to disqualify their works (the book's main thrust is that Freud and several generations of his followers, not least Jacques Lacan, perpetrated a money-making fraud). The result, however, does not even begin to refute an underlying philosophical position; what it does do is to combine a powerful impact in the media with an absence of in-depth discussion. Indeed, its media impact precisely depends on an absence of demanding, in-depth discussion. Such a project also allows for, or requires, misapprehensions of its own: Cartuyvels cites a work by one of the *Livre noir*'s lead contributors, Jacques van Rillaer, which writes off Lacan as 'an apostle of pleasure and egotism'. Such readings are, for Cartuyvels, merely evidence of breathtaking epistemological feebleness.

While Cartuyvels argues for a plurality of therapeutic approaches, for him 'the Freudian "tool-box" is, heuristically, incomparably richer than the terms of reference of a "scientific" psychology whose arguments are regularly linked to staggering truisms'. He has fun listing some of these: in cases of depression, it is better to have a family, and access to pleasant social activities; those with eating disorders should not have too much food in the house – and so on. If, as Cartuyvels writes, the cognitive-behaviourists' 'neo-positivist stance is, to the mind of a jurist… rather surreal', it also has more disturbing, political, and ethical implications. For 'behind the war of the "Psys" is a fundamentally political question': can one ever seriously attempt to separate – as these claimants to 'scientific objectivity' would have us do – psychic from social suffering? To break this conceptual link is to try to wave good-bye to questions of 'normality and deviance, exclusion and increasing inequality'.

Cartuyvels's conviction is that 'the human being is specifically a being of meanings and language… and psychic suffering calls to this dimension'. This is a conviction shared by all the contributors to *L'Anti-Livre noir de la psychanalyse*. The first of its four sections is entitled *Coups d'épingle:* the English 'pin-pricks' does not do justice to the sense of something over-inflated being spiked, or the voodoo-like quality of the pricking enacted in the 39 short essays which follow. Most were written by psychoanalyst members of Lacan's *École de la Cause freudienne*. Gérard Miller early on explodes the INSERM authors' claim that their report is a response to a public demand. The report cites two organizations representing patients and their families; the only demand Miller can discern is that these organizations were indeed founded in a demand, one of them 40 years ago, for a public voice. The INSERM experts, Miller discovered, had only the most cursory meetings with these organizations, in order to inform them, it seems, that their expert task was to read the extensive Anglo-Saxon CBT literature, since it was only this – they ignored the mass of French clinical writing, from all orientations, except some of their own – that they considered 'scientifically' based. The results of their exhausting endeavours, as the representatives of patients and families were not naïve enough to doubt, were a foregone conclusion.

The bitter wit of Gérard Miller is echoed in other brief contributions. So too is a dark sense of something very sinister unfolding. Jean-Claude Maleval explores another facet of INSERM's *expertise collective* ('collective assessment'), the researchers' commitment to

'Psychological Autopsy' (INSERM, 2005). This is a means of determining, in the most 'objective' possible way, that is, without the interfering presence of a living, if suicidal, person, the reasons and risk factors behind suicide. Maleval traces some of the historical antecedents for such thinking, in the nascent materialist psychiatry of the mid-nineteenth century in France, in the ideology of the early behaviour modifiers, with their electric shocks, in the First World War, in Watson and Rayner's notorious experiment with 'phobic' Little Albert in the 1920s, and in French publications of the1960s and 1970s: translations of Eysenck, and works by J. Wolpe and Jean Cottraux – who is an editor of the *Livre noir.* 'Les TCC', writes Maleval, 'are the avatar in the health domain of techniques of control and domination'.

What a godsend for neuro-biological psychiatry suicide is, ponders Pierre Sidon: 'Psychological Autopsy' allows full play to the quantifiable. With the requirement for the clinical interview out of the way, and thus 'disconnected from the Real, biological psychiatry can take to dreaming limitlessly', about (this is a quotation from the INSERM team) 'neurobiological determinants, independent of psychiatric pathologies'. Child and adolescent mental health is also well within the INSERM researchers' purview; they propose, as Sophie Bialek demonstrates, a national programme of tests and measures within the education and health systems. The particular report to which Bialek refers (*Troubles mentaux. Dépistage et prévention chez l'infant et l'adolescent,* 2001) is by a collective of unnamed experts. It fails to mention that three more relationally minded paediatricians from the original team had withdrawn, disquieted no doubt by a sense of where the work was going: one of the report's concluding recommendations is to 'develop animal models of developmental anomaly'.

Who indeed are the INSERM experts? They are, as Catherine Lazus-Matet shows, drawn from a small world of academic psychologists and therapeutic practitioners with more than a passing interest in the cognitive. They include a psychoanalyst, the president of the International Psychoanalytic Association, no less – Daniel Widlocher, who is also, hardly incidentally, a member of the AFTCC, the *Association française de thérapie comportementale et cognitive.* Ivy Blackburn (University of Newcastle) has written two books with Jean Cottraux on cognitive therapy for depression and personality disorder. David Servan-Schreiber is a cognitivist from the USA. Mardjane Teherani was a student of Widlocher's. Others are on the INSERM staff. And so on. The experts' collective claim to be 'independent' is unsustainable.

The 'psychoanalysis' of the INSERM research is a medicalized version, with aims consistent with those of the World Health Organization ('the promotion of well-being'), in other words psychoanalysis adapted so as to be measurable (thus it can be shown *objectively* not to perform very well). Jacques-Alain Miller, with whom Widlocher collaborated in 2004 on a book on the future of psychoanalysis, takes him to task later in the *Anti-Livre* for the particular manner in which he has 'cognivitized' psychoanalysis (unconscious 'drive' becomes domesticated 'instinct'). As Herbert Wachsberger points out, what the experts call psychoanalysis's 'ethic' is far removed from what Lacan meant when he spoke of the 'ethics of psychoanalysis', its ability to render the subject to himself. For 'les TCC' of course reject the unconscious in favour of 'maladaptive behaviour' (Hélène Deltombe). It is the genetically founded 'biosocial symptom' that is the 'keystone in the INSERM report's vault'. 'So-called mental health is the capacity to conform to the dominant values of the society'; this is neo-Darwinian pseudo-science, which, in Agnes Aflalo's analysis, points toward a racist *neo-hygiènisme,* a kind of born-again eugenics. Mental pathologies are defined in relation to religious and national norms; poverty, divorce, and immigration become factors in the definition of mental deviance.

The further tenet that the maladaptive symptom is something localized in the brain, rather than something that requires the therapist to listen to the patient, inexorably becomes a justification for psycho-surgery: Valérie Pera-Guillot examines this with respect to 'Obsessive Compulsive Disorder' (*le trouble obsessionel compulsif*) and the horrible circularity with which the diagnosis, made, like that of 'ADD', on the premiss that it is a cerebral, neuronal dysfunction, indicates the pharmaceutical or surgical nature of the cure. Hervé Castanet remarks on the slippage which occurs in the INSERM report between the words 'official' and 'scientific', fearing a utilitarian utopia based on a principle-free 'official science'. Philippe La Sagna likens the social vision of 'les TCC' to that of scientology, noting a shared language of 'scientific management' and 'biofeedback': both envisage a techno-totalitarianism in which man is reduced to machine.

For built into this techno-totalitarian vision, as François Leguil shows, is a 'premeditated suppression of the question of the subject'. To undergo cognitive behaviour treatment the patient must first tacitly submit to the paradigm of measure, and engage in self-evaluation. Henceforth, treatment success is guaranteed: the self-evaluative questionnaire is conceived so that everything that cannot be taken care of is excluded from the clinical field, since only that which can be measured can be taken care of. The measurable comes before the measure; a fantasy of universal curability and expert clinical mastery flourishes; the enigma of the subject – that which, according to Baudelaire, is loathed by lazy believers in progress – disappears.

What all this can mean in practice is illustrated in a collection of case studies, all published by TCC practitioners. There is Aline, a patient of Dr Jean Cottraux himself, whose treatment he published in a book in 2004 (Cottraux, 2004: 4, 216–20). The overriding aim seems to be to get the patient back to work. Aline, a bus driver in the deprived suburbs, threatened and abused by her passengers, is indeed helped back to work through the self-affirmations Cottraux teaches her: 'I am intact, I have survived', she intones, as Cottraux aids her to re-live her trauma by making the gesture of drawing a knife blade across his throat. Aline has a family history of alcoholism and violence, and was raped at knife-point aged 18; in Cottraux's expert view, these are predisposing life-events which make it difficult for her to manage her present working conditions. He draws attention to an additional aggravating factor: 'it is often hard to work if trauma has taken place in the work place itself'. Carole Dewambrechies-La Sagna, who gives us this account in a laudably dead-pan manner, notes in passing how the compulsion to repeat, a Freudian concept *par excellence*, is tacitly commandeered by Cottraux and emptied of meaning. Meanwhile, Aline, who has gone back to work several times in the course of a single year, is no doubt swelling the statistics which show the efficacy of 'les TCC'. Dewambrechies-La Sagna suggests Dr Cottraux might like to present his theses to the bus drivers' union next time they are on strike.

Roberta's treatment for the OCD with which she has been diagnosed consists in the substitution of one ritual for another: she is now condemned to write, for hours daily, about the terrible thoughts she has been struggling to keep at bay, involving awful accidents which might befall her little boy. Estela Solano-Suárez offers a rather more compelling psychoanalytic way of thinking about Roberta's difficulties, one which might indeed offer some eventual relief. Monique Amirault retells the story of a treatment by proxy, published in a specialist journal under the title 'Cognitive and behavioural management of a case of erotomania'; this has echoes of *Les Liaisons dangereuses.* A middle-aged male professor seeks therapy for a young female student with whom he has got sexually involved. The 'treatment' culminates in the therapist, who never meets the young woman, advising the professor to introduce her to a substitute. The abuse of civil and human rights inherent in this procedure is, as Amirault says, scandalous.

Another patient, Clara, attracted to violence, seeking rejection, finds a TCC therapist who, like a ferocious super-ego, tells her to think positively, and then abandons her, the treatment, in the therapist's terms, having been brought to a successful conclusion (Hélène Bonnaud). Two troubled children have become highly adept at 'speaking "TCC"' and self-therapizing. One responds to self-evaluating questionnaires in her nightmares: 'My dog bites the ears of the other dogs. I have to answer if I love him (1) in spite of this, (2) very much, (3) not at all...' (Véronique Mariage). The husband of an alcoholic woman is instructed by her therapist to practise paradoxical intention and encourage his wife to drink even more (Anne-Marie Lemercier).

By this point in the book, the reader may be experiencing symptoms of mild delirium. As if further to reinforce the feeling that we have stepped into a caricatural parallel universe, Jean-Pierre Klotz, and later Pierre Streliski and Jasmine Grasser, tease out links between B. F. Skinner's science fantasy novel of 1948, *Walden 2,* and dream of a 'scientific utopia' closer to the INSERM home page. Even closer to home is the pervasiveness of 'les TCC' on television, in particular in programmes like *Super Nanny*, a huge success in France (Catherine Lacaze-Paule, Marlène Belilos). The TCC model of child rearing, of 'normalized happiness, happiness by rote' – key words 'punishment, behaviour, distraction, order, participation, by-pass refusals, explanation, family meeting, objective, gain the attention...' – has its counter-parts in the world of relationships, work, and leisure (Rose-Paule Vinciguerra offers a reading of the magazine *Psychologies*), and in 'techno-scientific' sport, with its requirement for participants to engage in 'mental preparation, coaching, sophrology, neuro-linguistic programming, mental imaging, rational emotive therapy, cognitive and affective stress management...' (Françoise Labridy).

The apotheosis of TCC thinking on learning and education is the TEACCH programme (Treatment and Education of Autistic and Related Communication Handicapped Children, founded under psychoanalytic auspices at the University of North Carolina in 1960); Alexandre Stevens explores some wider implications of its 'brutal imperative: Communicate!':

> 'Autists must communicate. But does anyone wonder for an instant what there might be to say to them? No. It is enough to describe the way in which you would need to communicate if you did have something to say!... the cognitive behaviour approach denies the subjectivity and desire at work in the fact of communicating...'.

Similarly for Marga Mendelenko-Kars: while the TEACCH programme, founded in Skinner's 'operative conditioning' of the 1930s, aims at a reduction or elimination of disturbances supposedly caused by a faulty genetic set-up, the disappearance of the subject is anticipated too, as the INSERM report makes clear. Jean-Pierre Rouillon adds a further important and pregnant thought: '[in TEACCH] signal and conditioning take... the place of the Real, that which produces an encounter with autism in us all...'.

Six short essays spell out the different ways in which 'les TCC' have colonized Western European countries, Italy, Belgium, Greece, Spain, Great Britain, and France, each with their differing health legislation and institutions, and the extents of this colonization. What about the fertile breeding grounds which must surely be being provided by former Communist bloc members of the EEC? A third-from-last *coup d'épingle* reminds us of how Lacan demonstrated, in 1967 (*Seminar*, book XV), that the great Soviet scientist Ivan Petrovich Pavlov was in fact a Lacanian, in so far as Pavlov proved the theory according to which a signifier represents a subject for another signifier. In Pavlov's most famous experiment, writes Marie-Claude Sureau,

> 'the sound of the trumpet is the signifier which represents the subject Pavlov for another signifier, the gastric secretion produced by the dog at the sound of said trumpet... the dog... is conditioned to salivate not at the approach of the plate but at the sound of the trumpet' (i.e. Pavlov).

The experimenter, in Lacan's subtle and mischievous thesis, is fundamentally implicated in his experiment. Furthermore, unlike modern neuro-cognitivists and behaviourists, who are concerned only with the biological, real behaviourists like Pavlov are obliged to consider the centrality of the structure of language. Marie-Hélène Brousse argues, alongside Lacan, that psychoanalysis itself, with its recognition of the autonomy of the signifier and of human symbolic memory, is an authentically cognitive discipline, which behaviourist therapies are absolutely not. On the contrary, 'the expression "TCC" is a stolen label, a mendacious piece of advertising, a smoke screen for an attempt to eradicate the signifier in the human being'. The *coups d'épingle* cease with an imaginary dialogue (first published in the newspaper *Libération*) in which Jacques-Alain Miller takes up the theme with which *L'Anti-Livre noir de la psychanalyse* set out, that the TCC project is above all an exercise in marketing, 'merchandizing the mental'.

'What is at stake in society' (*L'Enjeu de société),* a topic already widely opened up by the pin-prickers, is the title of the next section, which contains Cartuyvels' seminal essay. A third section, *Ponctuations,* offers further pauses for thought. Alain Abelhauser, professor of psychopathology at the University of Rennes II, addresses an open letter ('Cette frase contient quatres ereurs'; 'This sentance contains for erors'. But there are only three. But that makes four, since the sentence is wrong. Is it three or is it four?) to the director of INSERM, in which he argues for the undecidable, against the reductionist certainties of the *expertise collective.* A clinical psychologist, Michel Normand, examines the sheer scale of 'les TCC''s ambition, to shape and embody national policy on mental health. Philippe La Sagna publishes an open letter to Philippe Pignarre, author of *La Sorcellerie capitaliste* (2005) (*Capitalist Witchcraft* – not in English translation to date), denouncing the dark witch of scientism. Eric Laurent, a Lacanian analyst who will be known to many in the UK as a speaker at analytic conferences, takes up in greater depth and detail Marie-Helene Brousse's theme: 'les TCC' are not part of the cognitive project.

A final section, 'Reflections of a Philosopher', offers two essays by Clotilde Leguil-Badal, philosopher and psychologist. The first, 'Être ou ne pas être?', pits Sartre against a neuroscientific view which claims to hold the key to the resolution of all our difficulties. Scanning techniques now mean we can see brain activity – what, though, of the voice of the brain's owner? There is what Leguil-Badal calls a 'new Empire' of cognitive neuroscience: its special domain, its object, is spirit, soul, subject. In the new 'biologization' of spirit, 'brain' becomes a kind of politically correct version of 'unconscious'. Neuroscience, with its seductive pull toward a theory of cerebral determinism, invites us to forget our freedom. Her second essay, 'On cognitivism', is a powerful argument for why an analytic cure cannot be a measurable thing. It speaks of Lacan's other use of mathematics, *le mathème*: his little fractions 'recount something of the logic of the illogical symptom... and the singularity of the subject... they are of a couple with poetry...'..

CONTEXTUALIZING DISCUSSION

It has felt important to try to summarize *L'Anti-Livre noir de la psychanalyse* in some detail, if only to convey an idea of the quality of its thinking to non-French readers. A concluding attempt to contextualize might also be helpful. While standing up for the inalienable right of the speaking subject to his and her idiosyncratic unconscious and unique subjectivity, psychoanalysis in France has also been more firmly established as part of a medical and health hegemony than has British psychoanalysis, which had probably lost any equivalent position by the late 1960s. This at least is the superficial impression one can have from this side of the Channel – it no doubt needs much refinement and qualification. Broadly speaking, psychoanalytic groupings within the UK seem either to want to regard themselves as part of an establishment (the BPC trainings, whose members are, incidentally, often very interested in neuroscience), or to relish a position on the oppositional margins (the 'College of Psychoanalysis', some UKCP trainings).

French psychoanalysis as a whole seems to manage to be both official *and* oppositional (particularly its Lacanian branch): this, together with the new, aggressively marketed profile of 'les TCC', needs to be appreciated if we are to understand how much the Lacanian practitioners represented in this book feel to be at stake, and the vehemence and the theoretical rigour and force of their collective and individual responses. Such has been the energy of the psychoanalytic response, and the official clout psychoanalysis still has in France, that in February 2005 the Minister of Health, Philippe Douste-Blazy, publicly declared psychic suffering to be 'neither measurable nor open to evaluation', and withdrew the INSERM report from his Ministry's website. A war of words continues to be waged on the net between analysts and affronted cognitive-behaviourists.

The struggle so eloquently dramatized in *L'Anti-Livre noir de la psychanalyse* is of course far from merely a local one. For example, CBT has made huge political advances in the UK in recent years. Meanwhile those of us who assert ourselves as psychoanalytic practitioners in the UK often tend to view CBT in a collegiate spirit, or else to see it as just part of the climate, to be lived with, made the most of, even, like the British weather, in spite of its unfriendliness. Historically, intellectual and ideological debates in France have been highly polarized, with few holds barred: think for example of the bloody wars between the Freudians and the Lacanians. One might wish that Jacques-Alain Miller and his colleagues had addressed, as a fair-minded British commentator might, patients' documented claims that CBT has helped them gain a sense of control and mastery over unmanageable feelings, and made daily life feel a bit more liveable. One might have wished their response could have been a little more nuanced and less political. But this would have been naïve; it might also have been to gloss over the sheer grotesqueness of some of the practices they report (students of French literature might be reminded of certain *Contes Cruels* by Villiers de l'Isle Adam). There is a political and ideological battle going on, in the UK as in France and elsewhere; in France, where the conflict has only recently flared into a full-scale battle, the lines are now starkly drawn. The *Anti-Livre noir* offers a breadth and vigour of argumentation that has to date – prior to the publication of this volume – been missing from debates in Britain. Psychoanalysts, and psychotherapists of whatever persuasion, if they are concerned to oppose the technologizing of the human spirit, need to take its arguments very seriously indeed – and to enjoy them.

Acknowledgements
All translations are by the author. With very special thanks for his help, linguistic and editorial, to George Craig.

REFERENCES

Cottraux, J. (2004) *Les Visiteurs du soi*, Paris: Odile Jacob.

INSERM (2004) 'Psychothérapie, trois approches evaluées'. Une Expertise Collective de l'Inserm. http://www.inserm.fr/fr/questionsdesante/mediatheque/expertises/att00001953/26fvrier2004.pdf. Also published in book form, Paris: Editions Inserm.

INSERM (2005) Retrieved at: http://ist.inserm.fr.basisrapports/suicide.html (March).

Kipman, S. D. (2006) In the *International Journal of Psychoanalysis*, 87 (5): 1425–8.

Miller, J-M. (ed.) (2006) *L'Anti-Livre noir de la psychanalyse*, Paris: Editions de Seuil.

Roudinesco, E. (2005) *Pourquoi tant de haine?* [Why so much hate?], Paris: Navarin.

Van Rillaer, J., Pleux, D., Cottraux, J., Borch-Jacobsen, M., and Meyer, C. (eds) (2005) *Le Livre noir de la psychanalyse: Vivre, penser et aller mieux sans Freud* [Living, thinking, and feeling better without Freud], Paris: Les Arènes.

CHAPTER 23

BECK NEVER LIVED IN BIRMINGHAM:
WHY COGNITIVE BEHAVIOUR THERAPY MAY BE A LESS HELPFUL TREATMENT FOR PSYCHOLOGICAL DISTRESS THAN IS OFTEN SUPPOSED

PAUL MOLONEY & PAUL KELLY

INTRODUCTION

In recent years, a growing number of central-government agencies and therapeutic psychologists have argued that cognitive-behavioural therapy (or CBT) should be the treatment of choice for mental-health practitioners, particularly for those working in the time-limited and pressured circumstances of primary-care services (Tarrier, 2002). The CBT approach is used across a diverse range of health, and educational training fields – including the treatment of anxiety and depression, the management of disruptive school children, and the rehabilitation of criminal offenders (Harber, 2005; Holmes, 2002; Mair, 2004). A key economic consultant to the UK Labour Government has recently proposed a huge expansion in the number of publicly funded CBT therapists, with the twin aims of returning back to work those who suffer from long-term depression and of helping to combat the social and personal malaise that seems to be afflicting us at record levels (Layard, 2005, 2006; cf. Pilgrim's Chapter 21, this volume).

Clearly, CBT enjoys a wide credibility: supported by claims that it is the most effective of all therapies, that it is well founded in clinical outcome research and in the findings of cognitive science, and that it is a uniquely collaborative approach, which enables people to master their own problems (e.g. Beck, 1995; Fenell, 1997). In this chapter – whilst acknowledging that recipients of CBT can often report that it is helpful – we nonetheless wish to question these claims. Instead, we suggest that the current popularity of CBT may at least equally reflect the needs and values of the mental-health professions, and of those political and social institutions that help to mould their aims and activities.

The chapter will begin with a brief discussion of the nature of CBT as practised within the NHS – the basis of most of our own clinical and professional experience – and will then move on to a critical examination of the approach from three perspectives. These include, first, a body of psychological research that casts doubt on some of the key ideas that underpin the CBT approach; secondly, that section of the psychotherapy outcome-research literature that bears on the effectiveness of CBT; and thirdly, the mental-health epidemiological literature – which points to the environmental origins of much of the distress encountered by CBT therapists

Earlier versions of this chapter appeared in the *Journal of Critical Psychology, Counselling and Psychotherapy*, 3 (4), 2003, pp. 214–28, and in *Clinical Psychology*, 34, 2004, pp. 4–10.

working in public services, and which indicates the need for therapeutic work that highlights social action over the exploration of the client's putative internal psychological world.

THE SCOPE AND NATURE OF CBT

In the UK, CBT has enjoyed a strong historical association with the profession of clinical psychology, particularly in NHS outpatient settings (Clegg, 1998; Pilgrim and Treacher, 1992). After a recent period of therapeutic eclecticism within clinical and counselling psychology, CBT may be returning as the preferred approach for most therapeutic psychologists working in the public health services, as supported by recent government planning for mental health care (Department of Health, 2001; Roth and Stirling, 2006).

Yet this seemingly straightforward picture becomes far muddier upon closer examination. To begin with, rather than being the discrete entity that it is taken to be, the term 'cognitive-behavioural therapy' in fact encompasses well over a dozen distinguishable approaches, in which the link between practice and theoretical foundations can vary widely (Chadwick et al., 1996). Indeed, some authors go so far as to suggest that 'CBT' cannot be distinguished from 'interpersonal therapy' (Tarrier, 2002). The origins of the approach – or family of approaches – are likewise multi-stranded, and include an (arguably) incompatible mixture of applied learning theory, the more accessible aspects of the psychodynamic tradition, selected elements of laboratory-based cognitive psychology, and pragmatic clinical experience (Beck and Weishaar, 1989; Hawton et al., 1989).

What cognitive-behavioural practitioners do seem to share is the view that personal problems are the product of the interacting elements of cognition, physiology, behaviour, emotion, and (often last of all) environmental influences, or 'maintainers'. In practice, treatment will usually focus upon enabling the client to change their 'unhelpful' beliefs by means of a series of structured exercises. This entails the assumption that the client's more accessible thoughts – and the deeper patterns or 'schemas' that are said to underlie them – are the key determinants of their reactions to events, and that these thoughts can be readily examined and then modified so as to yield therapeutic change (e.g. Davidson, 2000; Padesky, 1994; Trower and Casey, 1988).

CONCEPTUAL DIFFICULTIES WITH CBT

Perhaps one of the strongest arguments in favour of CBT is that the therapy is seen as being derived from a scientifically valid body of knowledge based within the discipline of cognitive science. However, this claim can be challenged on a number of levels.

As already noted, CBT is founded on the idea that our thoughts – or our 'cognitive processes' – are central to the origin, maintenance, and ultimate relief of our anguish (Beck, 1995; Beutler and Guest, 1989). And yet, as some reviewers have recognized, evidence for this idea is at best equivocal (Bracken, 2002; Cromby and Standen, 1999; Godsi, 2004). For example, although there are indications that depressed persons may make negative comments more frequently (or quickly) than non-depressed individuals, this may actually reveal little about any *causal* relationship between cognition and emotion. Such a process could easily reflect the way in which aversive environments have primed many individuals more readily to access pessimistic beliefs about themselves and their world. Likewise, the finding that successful completion of laboratory tasks by depressed individuals can elevate their mood may offer little support for the claim that this has been achieved by the direct falsification of the person's underlying negative beliefs (e.g. Beck, 1995). A more reasonable interpretation of this work may be that the person's basic belief repertoire includes positive dimensions that are activated by positive experiences, and vice versa. In other words, an individual's prevailing negativity may result much more from the negative experiences that they have been undergoing than from their depressive thinking style (see Fancher, 1995).

Similar arguments can be made in relation to the loss of meaning that is said to characterize the so-called post-traumatic stress reactions and the states of anxiety and fear that underlie many forms of phobia. These disturbing states may have a lot more to do with the disintegration of the sufferer's world and to the reality of external threat, respectively, than with the alleged breakdown of internal psychological structures (Bracken, 2002; Davidson, 2000; Smail, 1987).

An even more important flaw within most models of CBT may lie in the poor fit between the concepts of mind offered by most writers in the field, and those offered within other branches of psychology. For instance, historical and cross-cultural research suggests large variations in the way in which human beings have understood the causes of their thoughts and actions. The lesson is that currently accepted Western views on the nature of the self – especially within popular culture and the world of the psychotherapies – need have no special claim to validity (Crook, 1980; Martin and Barresi, 2006). In the context of clinical problems, there is evidence that the self-abnegating language commonly found among depressed Westerners seems to be much less common among distressed people from other cultural groups, including those who originate from many South East Asian and African communities. This is because such cultures seem less inclined to favour the kind of guilt- and responsibility-based explanations for personal unhappiness, that are associated with Western Christianity and the Protestant work ethic (Chan, 1990; Marsella, 1981; Sue and Sue, 1990).

Conversely, when seeking to account for the likely origins of their own experiences of ill-health, contemporary Westerners may have a propensity to discount the harmful effects of those social and material adversities with which they may be struggling, and instead attribute their problems to their own apparent lack of will power, or internal moral resolve (Blaxter, 1997; Cornwell, 1984; Ehrenreich, 2006). It is no accident that this culturally endorsed narrative fits rather well with the myth of the unfettered and autonomous individual that underpins consumer capitalism, most forms of psychotherapy, and perhaps especially CBT: all of which posit hidden reserves of insight and motivation, upon which we can supposedly draw in order to overcome our misfortunes (Cushman, 1995; Illouz, 2008; Smail, 2005).

Indeed, the practice and theory of CBT seems to be premissed upon the quintessentially Western idea – that we can easily scrutinize and then modify our own thinking, although it is sometimes unclear whether this Cartesian notion of an internal observer should be regarded as a metaphor or a reality (see Baars, 1997). However that may be, a wide variety of research suggests that the seemingly straightforward process of peering into the causes of our thoughts, feelings, and conduct may often be inaccurate and misleading; and to an extent that seldom seems to be recognized by advocates of the cognitive and behavioural therapies.

To begin with, the ability to report upon what is supposedly going on inside our heads is not some kind of quasi-perceptual talent, but is instead an ever-fallible capacity which we develop during childhood, in response to the promptings and ideas supplied by the adults and by the wider culture around us (Hulbert and Schwitzgebel, 2007; King-Spooner, 1990; Lyons, 1985). Thirty years of social-psychological research consistently support this picture. In a wide range of everyday situations – from consumer choice, to responding to persuasion, to helping others in distress – our degree of insight into the influences that help to shape our judgements and our actions can be surprisingly limited. Instead, it seems that we may habitually rely upon *a priori* folk theories to explain ourselves to ourselves, as much as to one another (Caldini, 1994; Doris, 2002; Nisbett and Ross, 1980; Wegner, 2002).

The seemingly unrelated field of clinical neurology tells a similar story. For example, the well-known experiments conducted with so called 'split-brain' patients have shown that the explanations offered by such individuals for the causes of their feelings and actions can be blatantly in error from the standpoint of an external observer, though completely compelling for the person concerned (Gazzaniga, 1990; Hilgard, 1986). There is every reason to think that these findings speak to those of us without neurological abnormalities. Indeed, similar results in other branches of neuropsychology confirm that there is no obligatory link between the parts of our brain that mediate our actions and those that generate explanations for the things that we do (Claxton, 1999; Dennett, 1991; Gazzaniga, 1990; Parfitt, 1987). Rather, neuroscientists are increasingly inclined to view the brain as a collection of massively parallel systems, which blend seamlessly with the networks of sensory information that come from the body and from the world in which it moves, and which give rise to the persistent illusion of an internal actor-observer, sitting somewhere inside of our heads (Claxton, 1999; Damasio, 1994, 2000; Norretranders, 1998).

In the context of the practice of CBT, all of this implies that there is no 'Cartesian Theatre' of the mind, in which our thoughts might be viewed and then manipulated in the way that most writers appear to suggest. The seemingly straightforward task of finding a 'cognition' that is supposed to give rise to other thoughts or feelings suddenly seems far from dependable; and the therapeutic narrative that places client insight and self-control as central to their recovery highly questionable. For many, this narrative may turn out to have little connection with the webs of social and material influence that are actually causing their distress, and that are helping to shape their experience and conduct (Bargh and Ferguson, 2000; Cromby and Standen, 1998; Smillensky, 2000).

CBT AND THE PSYCHOTHERAPEUTIC OUTCOME RESEARCH LITERATURE: A CRITIQUE

Despite the above difficulties with the theoretical bases of CBT, there is a growing consensus within the mental-health field that the effectiveness of this approach is well supported by clinical research (e.g. Department of Health, 2001; NHS Executive, 1996; Roth and Fonagy, 1996). This research appears to provide valid evidence based largely upon randomized controlled trials of the effectiveness of CBT in the treatment of many forms of distress. However, a thorough review of the literature reveals that this claim may lack firm support, for a number of reasons.

First of all, the field has long suffered from a bias toward the selective reporting *and* publication of those studies that show only the desired positive results (Boyle, 2002). Secondly, many research trials involving CBT share significant methodological problems. These flaws include an over-reliance upon selected and relatively privileged research populations, such as university students; the use of inadequate control groups for comparison purposes (such as individuals who remain on a waiting-list or receive less convincing forms of pseudo therapy), and an absence of adequate longer term follow-up of treated individuals. Where such follow-up extends beyond twelve months or more, the results are often less than encouraging (Epstein, 2006; James, 2007).

Other methodological problems associated with this research have included sample sizes that are too small to allow confident generalization to other clinical populations, and systematic participant selection and attrition effects that make results hard to interpret (Bolsover, 2002; Holmes, 2002; Mair, 1992). Statistically significant differences in outcome between participant groups may frequently conceal large numbers of people for whom treatment has been ineffective, or perhaps even harmful. Moreover, assessments of outcome have, for the most part, relied upon abstract numerical measurements that may be of questionable reliability, and have limited clinical or even personal meaning (Kline, 1988; see also Tolman, 1994).

This sceptical note seems to be further warranted by the tendency for the alleged superior performance of CBT (and indeed the overall potency of any form of psychological therapy) to diminish in the context of inner-city community-based clinical settings, where hard-pressed clinicians are likely to be serving populations that experience high levels of social and economic deprivation (cf. Hagan and Donnison, 1999; Richards, 1995). Here, comparisons of CBT with other psychological therapies have suggested that the former may offer little or no significant additional benefit in the treatment of such common problems as alcohol and drug abuse, depression, chronic anxiety, and behavioural and emotional disturbance (Dawes, 1994; Dineen, 1999; Elkin, 1994; Epstein, 1996; Hemmings, 2000; Leff et al., 2000; Sandell et al., 2000; Sanders and Tudor, 2001).

A further and highly significant challenge to the evidence base for the effectiveness of CBT consists in the large body of comparative clinical-outcome literature that has accumulated over the last half century. This has convincingly shown that for a wide range of clinical problems, psychotherapy effectiveness bears little relation to the therapist's clinical orientation or even to their qualifications and alleged expertise (Bergin and Garfield, 1994; Dawes, 1994; House, 2003; King-Spooner, 1995; Spinelli, 2001; cf. Bohart and House, Chapter 16, this volume)). These startling conclusions seem to have passed almost un-remarked in the professional training literature, which, especially in the field of the cognitive and behavioural therapies, seems to emphasize the acquisition of ever-more refined technical skills (see Proctor, 2002).

As if these problems were not enough, the CBT outcome literature shares with the more general psychotherapy outcome literature an even more pervasive difficulty, which is seldom acknowledged. We are referring to an almost exclusive reliance upon the reports of those who are most personally involved – including the client, the clinician, and workers from the agencies and institutions that support the therapeutic work – in the absence of any fully independent check upon the treated person's progress in the world beyond the consulting room. This is a serious issue in psychotherapy research, because of the powerful social and interpersonal influences that are likely to be in play, in what is in many ways a unique situation within our culture – part confessional, part healing ritual, and much else besides (Frank and Frank, 1991). This is perhaps especially so for practitioners of CBT, who appear to trade upon the alleged technical-scientific authority for what they do, and upon widely held beliefs in the magical healing power of self-affirmation (cf. Beck, 1995; see also Carrette and King [2004] and Ehrenreich [2006] for illuminating accounts of how these latter-day creeds increasingly saturate the worlds of business, politics, and education).

The general failure of the research literature to get to grips with these potentially powerful influences leaves open the strong possibility that the alleged benefits of CBT reflect little more than the way in which client reports of treatment are shaped by their own expectations and those of their therapist (Eisner, 2000; Epstein, 1996, 2006).

Finally, at the broader level of clinical ethics, a further question might be asked about what the overall social outcomes of CBT might turn out to be – even if it were as 'effective' as its supporters claim. If clinical outcomes are defined and evaluated individually – i.e. as the attainment of individual happiness in the world as it stands, then CBT may be argued to be 'effective'. However, if outcomes are defined and evaluated on a wider social plane, then the overall outcome of CBT may be to contribute to the protection of those in positions of power in society, by deflecting attention from the ways in which pervasive social inequalities and the widespread abuse of power result in the types of distress seen in clinical settings. Without implying any conscious intent on the part of the CBT therapist, an implicit aim of the approach may nonetheless be to generate conformity in clients as opposed to institutional change in society. In this respect, CBT is perhaps the most 'effective' form of individual 'treatment' (Prilleltensky, 1994; Smail, 1984; Willoughby, 2002).

AN ALTERNATIVE VIEW: SOCIAL INEQUALITIES (AND NOT COGNITIONS) AS THE FUNDAMENTAL DETERMINANTS OF PERSONAL DISTRESS

In contrast to this individualized view of how psychological pain comes about, many writers and researchers in the mental-health field have highlighted the way in which toxic environmental influences can lead to individual distress. Widespread social and economic inequalities mean that many people are likely to experience their world as an essentially coercive place, even though our culture may provide few opportunities for them to recognize – let alone articulate – this experience. Times of economic and political upheaval of the kind that we have witnessed in Britain over the last 25 years are likely to have a harmful impact upon the identity and self-confidence of wide swathes of the population, including many middle-class professionals, who have recently begun to taste the kinds of work-place insecurity that were once the almost exclusive lot of exploited manual workers (Mirowsky and Ross, 1989; Sennett, 1998; Smail, 1993; Vale et al., 1999). Though in the end, of course, these effects are likely to be harshest for those with the least financial, social, and material assets (Pilgrim, 1997; Stoppard, 2000; Wilkinson, 1996). When it comes to the practice of psychological therapy, we would suggest, any attempt to modify 'negative' thoughts is unlikely to have much impact upon the sufferer's long-term psychological state – beyond their ability to alter the landscape of social and material influences in which they are embedded.

CONCLUSION

As the title of this chapter suggests, our argument is that – although aspects of CBT may be helpful, particularly those parts that encourage the individual to confront the environmental causes of their malaise, *where this is possible* – the practice and theory of CBT can only be seen as effective if viewed from the standpoint of those in positions of social and economic privilege. For the vast majority of clients who are struggling with an intractably difficult world – which of course includes many of those seen by psychologists in areas of relative deprivation, such as large parts of post-industrial Birmingham, for instance – the emphasis of CBT on alleviating distress through challenging thoughts may be profoundly misleading for client and therapist alike. In the long run, this attempt to gaze into the client's 'cognitions' while downplaying the consequences of their world, their experience, and their history may have the effect of suggesting that oppression doesn't matter and that it's just the way in which you view it that counts. We wonder who benefits most from this message?

Acknowledgements

We would like to thank Guy Holmes, David Smail, and William Epstein for their helpful comments on early drafts of this chapter.

REFERENCES

Baars, B. (1997) *In the Theatre of Consciousness: The Workspace of the Mind*, London: Oxford University Press.

Bargh, J. A. and Ferguson, M. J. (2000) 'Beyond behaviourism: on the automaticity of higher mental processes', *Psychological Bulletin*, 126 (6): 925–45.

Beck, A. (1995) *Cognitive Therapy: Basics and Beyond*, New York: Guilford Press.

Beck, A. T. and Weishaar, A. T. (1989) 'Cognitive therapy', in A. Freeman, K. Simon, L. Beutler, and H. Arkowitz (eds), *Comprehensive Handbook of Cognitive Therapy*, New York: Plenum Press.

Bergin, A. E. and Garfield, S. L. (eds) (1994) *Handbook of Psychotherapy and Behaviour Change*, New York: John Wiley.

Beutler, L. and Guest, P. (1989) 'The role of cognitive change in psychotherapy', in A. Freeman, K. Simon, L. Beutler, and H. Arkowitz (eds), *Comprehensive Handbook of Cognitive Therapy*, New York: Plenum Press.

Blaxter, M. (1997) 'Who's fault is it? People's conceptions of the reasons for health inequalities', *Social Science and Medicine*, 44: 747–56.

Bolsover, N. (2002) 'Commentary: The "evidence" is weaker than claimed', *British Medical Journal*, 324 (February): 298–301.

Boyle, M. (2002) *Schizophrenia: A Scientific Delusion?* (2nd edn), London: Routledge.

Bracken, P. (2002) *Trauma: Culture, Meaning and Philosophy*, London and Philadelphia: Whurr.

Caldini, R. B. (1994) *Influence: The Psychology of Persuasion*, New York: Morrow.

Carrette, J. and King, R. (2004) *Selling Spirituality: The Silent Takeover of Religion*, London: Routledge.

Chadwick, P., Birchwood, M., and Trower, P. (1996) *Cognitive Therapy for Delusions, Voices and Paranoia*, Chichester: Wiley.

Chan, D. W. (1990) 'The meaning of depression: Chinese word associations', *Psychologia*, 33: 191–6.

Claxton, G. (1999). 'Whodunnit? Unpacking the "seems" of free will', *Journal of Consciousness Studies*, 6 (8–9): 99–113.

Clegg, J. (1998) *Critical Issues in Clinical Practice*, London: Sage.

Cornwell, P. (1984) *Hard Earned Lives*, London: Jonathon Cape.

Cromby, J. and Standen, P. (1999) 'Taking our selves seriously', in J. Cromby and D. J. Nightingale (eds), *Social Constructionist Psychology: A Critical Analysis of Theory and Practice*, Buckingham: Open University Press.

Crook, J. (1980) *The Evolution of Human Consciousness*, Oxford: Oxford University Press.

Cushman, P. (1995) *Constructing the Self, Constructing America*, San Francisco: Perseus.

Damasio, A. (1994) *Decartes' Error: Emotion, Reason, and the Human Brain*, New York: Putnam.

Damasio, A. (2000) *The Feeling of What Happens: Body, Emotion, and the Making of Consciousness*, New York: Vintage.

Davidson, K. (2000) *Cognitive Therapy for Personality Disorders*, Oxford: Butterworth Heinneman.

Dawes, R. (1994) *House of Cards: Psychology and Psychotherapy Built on Myth*, New York: Macmillan.

Dennett, D. (1991) *Consciousness Explained*, Harmondsworth: Penguin.

Department of Health (2001) *Treatment Choice in Psychological Therapies and Counselling*, London: HMSO.

Dineen, T. (1999) *Manufacturing Victims: What the Psychology Industry Is Doing to People*, London: Constable.

Doris, J. (2002) *Lack of Character: Personality and Moral Behaviour*, Cambridge: Cambridge University Press.

Eisner, D. (2000) *The Death of Psychotherapy: From Freud to Alien Abductions*, New York: Preager.

Ehrenreich, B. (2006) *Bait and Switch: The Futile Pursuit of the Corporate Dream*, London. Granta.

Elkin, I. (1994) 'The NUMH treatment of depression collaborative research programme; where we began and where are we?', in A. Bergin and S. Garfield (eds), *Handbook of Psychotherapy and Behaviour Change*, Chichester: Wiley, pp. 114–42.

Epstein, W. (1996) *The Illusion of Psychotherapy*, New York: Transaction Publishers.

Epstein, W. (2006) *Psychotherapy as Religion: The Civil Divine in America*, Reno: University of Nevada Press.

Fancher, R.T. (1995) *Cultures of Healing: Correcting the Image of American Mental Health Care*, San Francisco: W. H. Freeman.

Fennel, M. J. (1997) 'Low self esteem: a cognitive perspective', *Behavioural and Cognitive Psychotherapy*, 25 (1): 1–25.

Frank, J. D. and Frank, J. B. (1991) *Persuasion and Healing: Comparative Study of Psychotherapy*, 3rd revised edn, Baltimore: Johns Hopkins University Press.

Gazzaniga, M. (1990) *Mind Matters*, Boston: Houghton Mifflin.

Godsi, E. (2004) *Violence and Society: Making Sense of Madness and Badness*, Ross-on-Wye: PCCS Books.

Hagan, T. and Donnison, J. (1999) 'Social power: some implications for the theory and practice of cognitive behaviour therapy', *Journal of Community and Applied Social Psychology*, 9: 119–35.

Hansen, S., McHoul, A., and Rapley, M. (2003) *Beyond Help: A Consumer's Guide to Psychology*, Ross-on-Wye: PCCS Books.

Harber, C. (2005) *Schooling as Violence*, London: Routledge.

Hawton, K., Salkovskis, P. M., Kirk, J., and Clark, D. (1989) 'The development and principles of cognitive behavioural treatments', in K. Hawton, P. M. Salkovskis, J. Kirk, and D. Clark (eds), *Cognitive Behaviour Therapy for Psychiatric Problems: A Practical Guide*, Oxford: Oxford University Press.

Hemmings, A. (2000) 'Counselling in primary care: a review of the practice evidence', *British Journal of Guidance and Counselling*, 28: 233–52.

Hilgard, E. R. (1986) *Divided Consciousness: Multiple Controls in Human Thought and Action*, New York: Wiley.

Holmes, J. (2002) 'All you need is cognitive behaviour therapy?', *British Medical Journal*, 324 (February): 288–91.

House, R. (2003) *Therapy Beyond Modernity: Deconstructing and Transcending Profession-centred Therapy*, London: Karnac.

Hulbert, R. T. and Schwitzgebel, E. (2007) *Describing Inner Experience? Proponent Meets Skeptic*, Cambridge, Mass. and London: MIT Press.

Illouz, E. (2008) *Saving the Modern Soul: Therapy, Emotions, and the Culture of Self Help*, Berkeley and London: University of California Press.

James, O. (2007) *Affluenza*, London: Vermillion.

Johnstone, L. (2000) *Users and Abusers of Psychiatry*, London: Routledge.

King-Spooner, S. (1990) 'The fictional nature of introspection', *BPS Psychotherapy Section Newsletter*, 8: 19–29.

King-Spooner, S. (1995) 'Psychotherapy and the white dodo', *Changes*, 13: 45–51.

Kline, P. (1987) *Psychology Exposed: Or the Emperor's New Clothes*, London: Routledge.

Layard, R. (2005) *Happiness: Lessons from a New Science*, Harmondsworth: Penguin.

Layard, R. (2006) 'The case for Psychological Treatment Centres', retrieved 4 October 2006, from: http://cep.lse.ac.uk/layard/psych_treatment_centres.pdf.

Leff, J., Vernals, S., and Wolff, G. (2000) 'The London depression intervention trial: randomised controlled trial of anti-depressants versus couple therapy in the treatment and maintenance of people with depression living with a partner', *British Journal of Psychiatry*, 175: 95–100.

Lyons, W. (1985) *The Disappearance of Introspection*, Cambridge, Mass.: MIT Press.

Mair, G. (2004) 'Introduction: What works and what matters', in G. Mair (ed.), *What Matters in Probation*, Cullompton, Devon: Willan Publishing.

Mair, K. (1992) 'The myth of therapist expertise', in W. Dryden. and C. Feltham (eds), *Psychotherapy and its Discontents*, Buckingham: Open University Press, pp. 135–60; abridged in R. House and N. Totton (eds), *Implausible Professions*, Ross-on-Wye: PCCS Books, 1997, pp. 87–98.

Marsella, A. (1981) 'Depressive experience and disorder across cultures', in H. Triadus and J. Draguns (eds), *Handbook of Cross Cultural Psychology*, Boston: Allyn and Bacon.

Martin, R. and Barresi, J. (2006) *The Rise and Fall of Soul and Self: An Intellectual History of Personal Identity,* New York: Columbia University.

Mirowsky, J. and Ross, C. (1989) *The Social Causes of Psychological Distress*, New York: De Gruyter.

NHS Executive (1996) *Psychotherapy Services in England*, London: HMSO.

Nisbett, R. E. and Ross, L. (1980) *Human Inference: Strategies and Shortcomings of Social Judgement*, Englewood Cliffs, NJ: Prentice Hall.

Norretranders, T. (1998) *The User Illusion: Cutting Consciousness down to Size*, Harmondsworth: Penguin.

Padesky, C. A. (1994) 'Schema change processes in cognitive therapy', *Clinical Psychology and Psychotherapy*, 1 (5): 267–78.

Parfitt, I. (1987) 'Divided minds and the nature of persons', in C. Blakemore and S. Greenfield (eds), *Mindwaves: Thoughts on Intelligence, Identity and Consciousness*, New York: Basil Blackwell.

Pilgrim, D. (1997) *Psychotherapy and Society*, London. Sage.

Pilgrim, D. and Treacher, A. (1992) *Clinical Psychology Observed*, London: Routledge.

Prilleltensky, I. (1994) *Morals and Politics of Psychology: Psychological Discourse and the Status Quo*, Albany: State University of New York Press.

Proctor, G. (2002) *The Dynamics of Power in Counselling and Psychotherapy*, Ross on Wye: PCCS Books.

Richards, B. (1995) 'Psychotherapy and the hidden injuries of class', BPS Annual Conference Section, Brighton, 1994, *BPS Psychotherapy Section Newsletter*, 17: 21–35.

Roth, A. and Fonagy, P. (1996) *What Works for Whom? A Critical Review of Psychotherapy Research*, New York: Guilford Press.

Roth, A. and Stirling, P. (2006) 'Expanding the availability of psychological therapy', retrieved 12 February 2006 from: www.bps.org.uk/dcp/news/layard.cfm.

Sandell, R, Blomberg, J., Lazar, A., Carlsson, J., Broberg, J., and Schubert, J. (2000) 'Varieties of long term outcome among patients in psychoanalysis and long-term psychotherapy: a review of the findings in the Stockholm outcome of psychoanalysis and psychotherapy project (STOPP)', *International Journal of Psychoanalysis*, 81: 921–42.

Sanders, P. and Tudor, K. (2001) 'This is therapy: a person-centred critique of the contemporary psychiatric system', in C. Newnes, G. Holmes, and C. Dunne (eds), *This is Madness Too: Critical Perspectives on Mental Health Services*, Ross-on-Wye: PCCS Books.

Sennett, R. (1998) *The Corrosion of Character: The Consequences of Work in the New Capitalism*, New York: Norton.

Smail, D. (1984) *Illusion and Reality: The Meaning of Anxiety*, London: Dent.

Smail, D. (1987) *Taking Care: An Alternative to Therapy*, London: Dent.

Smail, D. (1993) *The Origins of Unhappiness: A New Understanding of Personal Distress*, London: Harper Collins.

Smillensky, S. (2000) *Free Will and Illusion*, Oxford: Clarendon Press.

Smith, M. and Glass, G. (1977) 'Meta analysis of psychotherapy outcome studies', *American Psychologist*, 32: 752–60.

Spinelli, E. (2001) *The Mirror and the Hammer: Challenges to Therapeutic Orthodoxy*, London: Macmillan.

Stoppard, J. M. (2000) *Understanding Depression: Feminist Social Constructionist Approaches*, London: Routledge.

Sue, D. and Sue, D. W. (1990) *Counselling the Culturally Different: Theory and Practice* (2nd edn), New York: Wiley.

Tarrier, N. (2002) 'Yes, cognitive behaviour therapy may be all that you need', *British Medical Journal*, 324 (February): 293–8.

Tolman, C. (1994) *Subjectivity and Society: An Introduction to German Critical Psychology*, London: Routledge.

Trower, P., Casey, A., and Dryden, W. (1992) *Cognitive Behavioural Counselling in Action*, London: Sage.

Vail, J., Wheelock, J., and Hill, M. (1998) *Insecure Times: Living with Insecurity in Contemporary Society*, London: Routledge.

Wegner, D. (2002) *The Illusion of Conscious Will*, Cambridge, Mass.: MIT Press.

Wilkinson, R. (1996) *Unhealthy Societies: The Afflictions of Inequality*, London: Routledge.

Willoughby, C. (2002) 'Do counsellors have an ethical duty to explore the environmental sources of their client's distress?' *Journal of Critical Psychology, Psychotherapy and Counselling*, 3 (2): 231–47.

Chapter 24

CONCLUSION

CONTESTING THERAPY PARADIGMS ABOUT WHAT IT MEANS TO BE HUMAN

Del Loewenthal & Richard House

Concluding a book such as this one is never an easy task; and with such a rich diversity of contributions from both proponents and sceptics around CBT, we will endeavour to be succinct, economical, and unavoidably selective in our summing-up.

The foremost issue we wish to address in this final chapter is the question of what any dialogue around CBT should be focussed upon. For us, it is essentially concerned with what it means to be human, and the questions of knowledge and method that arise from this. It is therefore these ontological, epistemological, and methodological concerns that are, for us, central to the debate about therapy paradigms which has periodically been raised in earlier chapters.

In recent years, the CBT field as whole, and its practitioners in particular, have certainly had to deal with the very complex task of holding and making sense of what are very divergent forces – on the one hand, arguably inappropriate over-idealization from government, policy-makers, and a populace all perhaps yearning for easy 'quick-fix' solutions to the challenges of living; and on the other, critical (cf. Chapters 5–23, above) and sometimes unfairly dismissive attention from within the therapy world itself.

To what extent do the criticisms levelled at CBT from within the therapy world, and hopefully represented in this book, have any substance; and, we wonder, are the differences alleged to divide CBT and the other therapy modalities more imagined and expedient for *both* 'sides', than is actually the case (assuming that it's *ever* possible to say or to know what is 'actually the case'...)?

To our knowledge, this book represents the first time that such a rich array of proponents and critics of CBT have entered into anything approaching public dialogue – which in itself is a somewhat sad commentary on our field's capacity to engage with difference, especially when there are issues of power, resources, and identity involved. There is also a view in some circles that any such associated profession-level turmoil is actually connected, at least in part, with what we cannot bear *in ourselves*, and which we therefore displace on to others, with inner-psychological conflict thereby being inappropriately externalized; a process which has perhaps been all too apparent in the psychological therapies which, as such, thereby become the very worst kind of advert for what these same therapies are aspiring to address.

We are hopeful that such questions as raised by our contributors can increasingly be faced and reflected upon by more psychological therapists – a process which surely needs to happen, and with some urgency, if the unpleasantness of current schisms in the field are to lose at least some of their divisiveness, and take us toward the kind of engaged and constructive, mutually respectful dialogue and tolerance of difference that we think all would agree are important values of our psychotherapeutic work.

It would certainly be possible to write a series of books on the theme of 'against and for…' for all of the various therapy modalities; indeed, this may be the first book in such a series. However, in the current book we have focussed on CBT because it has recently become *the* main modality supported by the state – a quite unprecedented development in modern political life, and one which throws up many questions about the legitimate place of the state – if any – in making legally enforced (and therefore necessarily limiting) decisions about the talking therapies in what is (allegedly?) a putatively open democracy. Moreover, state managerialism (Loewenthal, 2008) with its arguably disingenuous discourse of transparency etc. (e.g. House, 2008), can be understood as a means for creating insecurity and securing a state mechanism of control; and the CBT modality certainly fits this kind of managerialism better than any other. In marked contrast, it should be noted that it is by no means an inevitability that the state will necessarily embrace a managerialist, instrumentalist ideology – for as Snell points out (Chapter 22), 'in February 2005 the Minister of Health, Philippe Douste-Blazy, publicly declared psychic suffering to be "neither measurable nor open to evaluation", and withdrew the INSERM report from his Ministry's website'. So the resigned fatalism that seems to have overtaken parts of the British psychoanalytic establishment in the face of the NICE evidence-based juggernaut is perhaps at best premature, and at worst a chronic self-betrayal of psychoanalysis (see Parker and Revelli, 2008).

At least one of us (DL) doesn't have a problem with the view that CBT could be particularly helpful with some clients; however, what is at issue for many if not most of CBT's critics is when it becomes *the* dominant mode; for whilst it might arguably be appropriate sometimes to help people by taking their mind off the problem, if this approach becomes generalized to society at large, then a catastrophe is almost inevitable. There is also the concern that CBT can be more easily manualized than other approaches (cf. Bohart and House, Chapter 16), though these have been, and are still in the process of being, dumbed down, with extraordinary claims that even psychoanalysis can be manualized!

It is important to distinguish clearly between the state and policy-making uses to which CBT is being put, on the one hand, and on the other, the sincere good faith of many CBT practitioners on the ground, who have a genuine, principled, and thought-through commitment to their chosen modality, as represented in Chapters 2–4 of this book. There is indeed a rigorous debate unfolding within the CBT modality itself, and there are also many dissenting voices with regard to how CBT is being used by the government through Improving Access to Psychological Therapies (IAPT), and so on.

More generally, however, perhaps the main concerns that come through in this book are the underlying assumptions about what it means to be human, together with the nature of therapeutic change and psychotherapeutic knowledge itself. In terms of *ontological* questions, there are the assumptions of whether we see people as both good and evil, rational and irrational, free or determined; and it is in these realms where one of the great divides emerges between CBT and other therapy modalities. One way of understanding such a divide is between holistic and mechanistic approaches – whereby the former begins with the indissoluble human soul and its resources, whereas the latter looks consciously to manipulate human experience (most notably, via cognition), on the view that this latter route will necessarily enhance well-being. From existential, post-existential (see Loewenthal, Chapter

12), and post-modern (Loewenthal and Snell, 2003) perspectives, the great danger is that such interventions will have precisely the opposite effect of that intended, and will move human subjects even further away from what it means to be human than they are already.

There are, no doubt, many clients who would be very grateful not to have to think about that which is troubling them. For some, this requires a working through of that which they might dread, and for others, a more up-front reformulation is attempted. One might say that for most people, then, the sooner they can stop worrying about what is troubling them, the better. But there is also the argument that we all get through life by the successful repression of unthinkable anxieties. One set of methods would seem to bring to this kind of problem an immediate helping hand; whereas an alternative approach encourages thoughts that are troubling one to be uncovered, in the hope that as a result of this 'working through', the client will in future be able to allow thoughts to come to him or her. In some ways, both approaches aspire for the client to be freed up from that which previously constricted them, and there are probably circumstances in which both will have their place.

With regard to *epistemological* questions, a major issue is the place of what Polyani calls 'tacit knowledge' (cf. House and Bohart, Chapter 17), which may account for why it would appear that the relationship in therapy (and elsewhere) is of vital importance. Thus, the learning that can take place in therapy through the relationship can never be fully described by a set of competencies. Much of what we are discussing was expressed as a parody in the film 'Dead Poet's Society' (1989), where a comparison is made with a teaching relationship that is to do with the heart, and all its ecstasies and dangers, as opposed to a deadening one that relies upon technique.

More clearly than other approaches, CBT seems to be saying that methods will change as new evidence becomes available (cf. Mansell, Chapter 2). Initially, this is a very attractive argument; but besides the possible detrimental effect on client and therapist of personal therapy for the therapist not being a training requirement, there is a major difficulty with regard to what is accepted as legitimate research. And this is in turn part of a cultural trend in which, for example, one might see doctoral theses in universities having an increasingly important quantitative component. Yet this quantification is often a positivistic technique and, at best, poor science.

SOME UNRESOLVED EDITORS' QUESTIONS

Having read our own book closely, we are left with some lingering questions raised by several of the contributors. First, in Chapter 2 and Chapter 4 respectively, both Mansell and Hemmings claim (and other contributors argue similarly) that CBT is not 'a single, knowable entity'. Such a claim is all very well, but if this is the case, then why is the term 'CBT' even used by practitioners who allegedly practise 'it'? – and certainly in such an arguably casual and uncritical way across modern culture. This strikes us as rather similar to the unfalsifiability critique of so-called '*post-hoc* justification' propounded by philosopher of science, Karl Popper (Popper, 1963), in which he convincingly lambasted those theories which insulated themselves from any kind of sustained criticism or refutation, simply by changing one aspect of the theory every time it was undermined ('third-wave' CBT perhaps being a case in point), thereby leaving the main body of the theory untouched *and effectively immune from refutation.*

In other words, the chameleon-like nature of CBT allows its proponents to insulate it from any criticism that might stick, because it can always be claimed that *somewhere* in the diverse CBT stable, 'it's not being done like that'.... So in this way, then, 'CBT' becomes little more than an expedient branding label which conceals far more than it reveals, and is used much more for its *political* effects than it is accurately to represent and correspond to the actual content of the approach.

This seems to us to be a potentially devastating critique; however, it is one that has also previously been levelled at, for example, psychoanalysis, where it has been argued that proponents of this modality put forward the concept of 'defence mechanisms' whenever criticisms have been laid at it. Also, CBT is probably wrongly suffering from that which has happened in the past – in that when a modality becomes popular, many others jump on to the band wagon of trying quickly to change their approach in an attempt to get in under the wire. Nonetheless, it is perhaps doubly ironic that the very argument adduced by Popper to challenge the scientificity of Freudian psychoanalysis is now eminently quotable against what claims to be the crowning-glory of modern 'scientific' therapy practice – evidence-based CBT. In David Pilgrim's words (Chapter 21), 'CBT is a technology without a true theory' – and, moreover, 'theoretically confused and practically-obsessed'.

A related criticism is that 'third wave' forms of CBT are (Hemmings, Chapter 4) 'rapidly integrating [or is it *colonizing*? - eds] other theoretical models into their practice', such as Gestalt and object relations in Schema therapy, Buddhist mindfulness techniques in mindfulness CBT, Relational Frame Theory in ACT, and the dialogic approach described by Strong et al. in Chapter 13. This apparent eclecticism would appear to have little if anything to do with theoretical authenticity; and there is the danger of falling into opportunistic exploitation of other approaches which are effectively 'bolted on' as soon as any of the core assumptions of CBT are exposed to concerted challenge. The difficulty for CBT is that it can then be accused of adopting an unscientific approach when it is a modality that makes such a strong claim to relatively pure scientific credentials. As Winter asks in his final paragraph (Chapter 11), one has every right to ask just when such therapies can no longer be legitimately deemed to be 'cognitive-behavioural'. And as Tudor points out (Chapter 10), 'as all therapists work with cognition and behaviour, in this sense we *are* all cognitive and behavioural therapists'; and he continues, 'this is an argument in favour of sharing conceptual and clinical space rather than claiming territory'.

Mansell (Chapter 2) also claims that 'while it is appropriate to allow certain evidence-based psychotherapies, like CBT, to be accredited by the health system, we need space for innovators who adapt and devise their own approaches from a firm cultural and scientific foundation'. Such a view could be seen to raise as many questions as it answers. Thus, the term 'evidence-based' is used quite uncritically, and assumes that what constitutes valid evidence is an unproblematic given, when clearly it is not (cf. Winter, Chapter 11). Moreover, it is perhaps a naïve view that claims that in the face of the State's uncritical anointing of CBT as *the* therapy of choice, that there will then be any space left at all in this brave new therapeutic world for new innovation – for the whole history of the way innovation works and flourishes suggests otherwise. Paying lip-service to the virtue of innovation is all very well, but if one supports an approach which a government latches on to in an uncritical totalizing way, then such lip-service is just that – and at worst, empty aspirations.

There is also the issue raised by Lees (Chapter 7) and Brazier (Chapter 6), that we need to locate therapy practices within the evolution of human consciousness. In the case of CBT, it seems clear that no matter how it is dressed up in what some would see as a *post-hoc* justificatory way (cf. earlier), it universally privileges *thinking and cognition* over other ways of being – yet who says that this is invariably, or even remotely, the most fully realized way of being human? As Bracken and Thomas put it (Chapter 8), 'the 'acceptance of cognitivism, and of computer models of mind and thinking, cannot be explained by the empirical success of these approaches alone. Instead, it appears to be driven by other cultural aspirations and ideals as well.'

Having trained in the 1990s as holistic body psychotherapist, I (RH) have worked with many clients over the years who, in my judgement, have demonstrably suffered chronically from *a surfeit* of thinking, and who have learnt to use thinking as a kind of comforting 'dependency object' that can never in principle succeed in '(re)solving' the problems that are demanded of it (cf. Winnicott's notion of the 'mind object', where children, from a developmental standpoint, prematurely develop a precocious mind at far too early an age because of a failure of the early nurturing environment – see Corrigan and Gordon, 1995). In such cases, RH's clinical view is that the introduction of yet more of an emphasis on thinking is *the very last thing* that such clients need on their healing journey – and all his therapy experience has confirmed this. *Yet the kinds of symptoms that are exhibited by such clients are the very ones for which the NICE guidelines would recommend CBT!* – i.e. yet more emphasis on the cognitive, at the expense of the rest of the client's being. As Bracken and Thomas put it (Chapter 8), 'CT is not independent of the "cognitive theory of mind". Therefore, the therapist is effectively training the patient to accept this particular model of mind.' We have never seen any reference in the CBT literature that shows any awareness of what should surely be a key therapeutic issue, i.e. an informed consideration of the possibly iatrogenic nature of a CBT-type 'intervention' with clients for whom more thinking will merely exacerbate their difficulties.

However, both editors consider that the issues of thinking, thoughtfulness, and 'the cognitive' are not at all straightforward – for there are great subtleties and distinctions here that need very careful specification and thinking through in a psychotherapeutic context. Thus, for example, we could in some circumstances be equally critical of humanistic approaches which uncritically privilege the emotional over the cognitive; and there might be a substantial, even a decisive difference between thinking, on the one hand, and allowing thoughts to come to one, on the other

In Chapter 4, Hemmings suggests that, 'as a profession we move away from potential paradigm zealotry to a more pan theoretical model of therapy'. He continues, 'if we can maintain a continued dialogue with the formulationist wing of CBT this could be a possibility. By doing this we could, as a profession, examine how different paradigms of psychological therapy can integrate into a broader more complex and viable alternative to medication'.... Some of the otherwise critical chapters in the book are in fact already endeavouring to find some kind of rapprochement with CBT – see, for example, the chapters by Strong et al., Tudor, and Newman. However, there is the concern that such moves could be a kind of procedural expediency that places the desire to avoid conflict and schism above paradigmatic authenticity and internal consistency.

Pilgrim's concern with the epistemic fallacy (i.e. confusing reality with *what we call* reality) appears to be a strong argument, as is his scepticism about the functions served by diagnostic labelling (with which CBT commonly colludes), for 'we need to understand the variety of interests which maintain categories which are scientifically dubious and are experienced often as stigmatizing and unhelpful by their recipients' (Pilgrim, Chapter 21; cf. Parker et al., 1995). Thus, for Pilgrim a diagnosis of depression 'not only diverts us from socio-political relationships to the diseased person, it renders the latter a passive victim of their putative disease. It thereby risks robbing them of their agency and their opportunity for existential reflection.' He continues, 'This claim of naturalism is premature, as philosophers interrogating psychiatric nomenclature have demonstrated' (cf. Bracken and Thomas, Chapter 8). For Pilgrim, it is *commercial and professional interests* 'that have shaped premature claims of psychiatric success about categorizing misery and madness' – which fits all too cosily with Layard's 'invest[ing] too much faith in the technical fix,... impl[ying] that the mechanisms of extreme misery are being increasingly explicated by modern therapeutic technologies, when they are not'.

We are most interested in Michael Guilfoyle's position, where he argues (in Chapter 19) that 'CBT participates in societal networks of power relations', thence suggesting that CBT's 'success and widespread recognition may be a function not of its effectiveness *per se*, but of its comfortable integration with existing cultural and institutional power arrangements'. For Guilfoyle, a 'rationalist ordering of the therapies in accordance with narrow and pre-constructed values that correspond with those of society's most powerful institutions' is in great danger of precipitating 'the gradual diminishment of a once rich landscape of therapeutic possibilities'.

From her psychoanalytic perspective, Jane Milton (Chapter 9) refers illuminatingly to 'how great the conceptual differences sometimes are between practitioners of the two treatments [i.e. CBT and psychoanalysis], which can lead to major difficulties in communication'. For Milton, 'the cognitive clinical paradigm remains fundamentally different from the psychoanalytic one, and... true rapprochement is more apparent than real' – and she proceeds to offer an examination of the way in which modern CBT therapists tend to modify their technique. Thus, for Milton, any possibility of a common-ground paradigmatic rapprochement between CBT and psychoanalysis seems very remote. At the level of research, Milton maintains that 'We are dealing with a complex interpersonal process involving multiple variables. Controls may become impossible to achieve and randomization is a questionable activity in comparative trials where patients show marked preferences or aptitudes for different ways of working.' We cite Milton's view here just to make the point that claims that a pan-theoretical, trans-paradigmatic common ground between CBT and other approaches certainly cannot be assumed.

Strong et al. (Chapter 13) usefully raise the issue of the self from a Foucaultian perspective. For them, there is a problem with the term 'self', as CBT can effectively involve 'taking on CBT in apprenticing oneself to its practices of "self-subjectification", and policing or disciplining oneself accordingly. Said another way, *this is how one learns to be a person on CBT's terms.*' (emphasis added). For Strong et al., then, 'ideology can creep into CBT in insidious ways, [and] the practices and philosophy of certain approaches to CBT, applied as a personal technology for self-conduct, can be seen as a kind of ideology.' This is of especial concern when clients 'are instructed to disattend to certain features of their realities that can't be remedied with thought modification (e.g. poverty) or in forms of "self-monitoring" and "self-control" that preclude other avenues to happiness and contentment'.

Finally, we are somewhat surprised by two apparent omissions in this book, hardly referred to by our contributors. The first concerns what many see as the need for personal therapy in the training of psychological therapists, which is not a training requirement for CBT practitioners, thus appearing to make CBT more cost effective – but only when the accounting system adopted is at the individual level rather than at the level of society as a whole. Thus, with CBT's 'technological' approach, the 'person of the therapist' is not seen as a central 'measuring instrument' of the work, and CBT therapists therefore need to be far less concerned than other practitioners about whether what they are saying is truly *for* the client, or is more about their own issues. Many if not most therapy approaches would view lack of such therapist awareness as preventing the therapist from really hearing the client, thereby inhibiting the client from being able to speak of what is really troubling them. This in turn may cause ill-health in both the client *and* the therapist, and further prevents, perhaps intentionally, our culture from facing up to underlying societal problems, which, if tackled, could reduce the need for therapy, whatever its label.

The second surpising omission is that nowhere in the book is there any discussion of the implicit (and sometimes explicit) *theory of change* and its mechanics, as advocated in CBT. Thus, CBT practice is based on the assumption that cognition and ideation somehow precede, *and can therefore unproblematically be invoked to control,* emotion; yet on the basis of careful psychological research, this assumption is called into significant question – for as Zajonc (1980) has quite unambiguously shown, it seems far more likely that *emotions precede thoughts, rather than the other way around.* Thus, Zajonc found that by no means all feelings (or preferences) are based on cognitive processes, but often *precede* them; and affect certainly doesn't appear to require extensive cognitive processing to occur. Given this finding, combined with Damasio's work on holistic perspectives on the brain, thinking, and emotion (e.g. Damasio, 1994, 2000), it may seem something of a surprise that CBT has managed to continue to maintain its legitimacy, notwithstanding the argument that its theoretical basis for change may be at best challenged, and at worst fundamentally flawed. All this could be seen to confirm the arguments of Guilfoyle (Chapter 19) and others that CBT's cultural ascendancy has far more to do with its implication and maneuverings within regimes of power and influence, than it is to do with any demonstrable *scientific* legitimacy. And it further suggests that CBT's attempt to control emotion via thought may well sometimes perpetrate an even greater 'violence' on human being than many of us previously intuitively felt to be the case.

In a book that is very far from being replete with data analysis, we end with a tell-tale statistical observation. Preliminary data from the two 'demonstration' IAPT sites in Newham, London (Newham IAPT, 2007) and Doncaster, England (Richards and Suckling, 2007) appear to bring into question whether the 'success rates' arising from introducing CBT-informed high- and low-intensity therapeutic services are any more effective than either previous or current NHS mental-health provision. Moreover, it is also very far from clear from this preliminary data whether the hoped-for resulting return to employment (cf. Pilgrim's Chapter 21) will actually occur. Those who are sceptical about the ubiquity and uncritical enthusiasm with which CBT is being embraced as a socio-economic 'engineering tool' will certainly be watching this unfolding statistical story with great interest. Note, also, the term '*demonstration* site', above – this being the 'official' language used by the NHS and IAPT. There once was a time when the cautious language of '*pilot*' rather than '*demonstration*' site would no doubt have been used; and such language is perhaps symptomatic of the extent to which state research on CBT is being pursued to prove and legitimize decisions that have *already* been taken, rather than being a genuinely open inquiry into the efficacy or othererwise of CBT in relation to chosen efficacy criteria.

A FINAL REFLECTION

This concluding chapter has selectively focused upon certain lacunae in the CBT story which particularly strike us, based on ontological, epistemological, and methodological concerns. Other writers would no doubt have homed in on different dimensions of the CBT phenomenon, with its various inconsistencies, and its alleged weaknesses and strengths. We hope that each reader who manages to have reached this far in the book will make their own list of the strengths and weaknesses of the criticisms of CBT, and that the book's diverse contributions will help them to reach a more informed decision about where the balance of argument lies in the story that we have called 'against and for CBT'.

Whatever the shortcomings of this book – and there will undoubtedly be many – we hope that it will make a significant contribution to the emerging debate about the place of CBT within modern therapy culture – and the extent to which CBT's current position of cultural and political ascendancy is based more on science, or upon ideology.

REFERENCES

Corrigan, E. G. and Gordon, P-E. (eds) (1995) *The Mind Object: Precocity and Pathology of Self-sufficiency*, New York: Jason Aronson.

Damasio, A. R. (1994) *Descartes' Error: Emotion, Reason, and the Human Brain*, New York: Putnam.

Damasio, A. R. (2000) *The Feeling of What Happens: Body, Emotion, and the Making of Consciousness*, New York: Vintage.

House, R. (2008) 'The dance of psychotherapy and politics', *Psychotherapy and Politics International*, 6 (2): 98–109.

Loewenthal, D. (2008) 'Regulation or ethics as the basis of psychoanalytic training', in I. Parker and S. Revelli (eds) *Psychoanalytic Practice and State Regulation*, London: Karnac Books, pp. 85–93.

Loewenthal, D. and Snell, R. (2003) *Postmodernism for Psychotherapists*, London: Routledge.

Newham IAPT (2007) *Newham Improved Access to Psychological Therapies (IAPT): The First Year, Draft 3*, Mental Health Matters; NHS Newham Primary Care Trust; London Borough of Newham, 21 September.

Parker, I. and Revelli, S. (eds) (2008) *Psychoanalytic Practice and State Regulation*, London: Karnac Books.

Parker, I., Georgaca, E., Harper, D., and McLaughlin, T. (1995) *Deconstructing Psychopathology*, London: Sage.

Popper, K. R. (1963) *Conjectures and Refutations*, London: Routledge & Kegan Paul.

Richards, D. and Suckling, R. (2007) *Doncaster Improved Access to Psychological Therapies (IAPT) Demonstration Site: Annual Report*, Doncaster: University of York and IAPT Doncaster, September.

Zajonc, R. B. (1980) 'Feelings and thinking: preferences need no inferences', *American Psychologist*, 35 (2): 151–75.

CONTRIBUTORS

ARTHUR C. BOHART Ph.D. is currently affiliated with Saybrook Graduate School and Research Center and is also professor emeritus at California State University, Dominguez Hills. Art is the author of a number of articles and chapters on person-centred psychotherapy, empathy, and the client as active self-healer, including *How Clients Make Therapy Work: The Process of Active Self-healing* (co-author, Karen Tallman, American Psychological Association, 1999).

PAT BRACKEN works with the West Cork Mental Health Service, where he is a Consultant Psychiatrist and Clinical Director. He co-edited the book *Rethinking the Trauma of War* with Dr Celia Petty, published in 1998 by Free Association Books. His own book *Trauma: Culture, Meaning and Philosophy* was published by Whurr in 2002. With his colleague Professor Phil Thomas, he published the book *Postpsychiatry: A New Direction for Mental Health* (Oxford University Press, 2005).

DAVID BRAZIER is a spiritual teacher, Buddhist priest, head of the Amida Order; man of letters – author, poet, critic; doctor of philosophy; psychotherapist; educator; social innovator; traveller; father; husband; woodsman. His next book, *Love and Its Disappointment: The Meaning of Life, Therapy and Art*, is in press for 2009.

CHRISTY BRYCELAND completed her Ph.D. in Clinical Psychology at the University of Calgary in 2006 under the supervision of Henderikus J. Stam. Her doctoral dissertation explored the impacts on Alberta psychologists of increasing professional regulation in the face of eroding professional identity. She currently lives and works in British Columbia, Canada. Her clinical practice focusses on the assessment and diagnosis of children and youth with developmental disabilities.

ISABEL CLARKE is an NHS consultant clinical psychologist and psychological therapies lead at Woodhaven, psychiatric inpatient hospital for the New Forest. Here she is pioneering a 'Third Wave' CBT approach to therapy for inpatients, featured in the following publication: Clarke, I. and Wilson, H. (eds) (2008) *Cognitive Behaviour Therapy for Acute Inpatient Mental Health Units: Working with Clients, Staff and the Milieu*, London: Routledge. Other publications and talks can be found on her website: www.isabelclarke.org

MICHAEL GUILFOYLE is Lecturer in Clinical Psychology at Trinity College Dublin, Ireland. His work has focussed on the power dynamics of the therapeutic relationship, and the relationship between clinical practices and societal power systems. He is also currently exploring the applicability of various discourse-orientated theories to understanding the therapist's experiences and other relational possibilities in narrative therapeutic practice.

DR ADRIAN HEMMINGS is a Chartered Psychologist and a UKCP-registered psychotherapist. He has many years experience working as a clinician in the NHS and third-sector organizations. Until recently he was Professional Head of Psychology for a primary care trust. Adrian also worked for twelve years as a Research Fellow, University of Sussex, with a particular interest in the use of psychological interventions in primary care. He integrates a cognitive behaviour approach into his clinical work.

RICHARD HOUSE Ph.D. is Senior Lecturer in Psychotherapy and Counselling, Research Centre for Therapeutic Education, Roehampton University. His books include *Therapy Beyond Modernity* (Karnac, 2003), co-editing *Implausible Professions* (1997) and *Ethically Challenged Professions* (2003 - both PCCS Books). Richard is Theory Editor, *European Journal for Psychotherapy and Counselling*, and helped to found the Independent Practitioners Network. He co-orchestrated the two *Daily Telegraph* Open Letters on 'toxic childhood' and 'play' in 2006 and 2007. Correspondence: r.house@roehampton.ac.uk

JOHN D. KAYE Ph.D. is an academic and a clinical psychotherapist in private practice. As a Critical and Postfoundationalist psychologist, he regrets the limits placed on psychological inquiry and practice by the logico-positivist paradigm's continuing dominance, with the scientist-practitioner model's rhetorical reliance on the chimera of 'evidence-based practice'. As a Discursive psychologist, John is heartened and amused by the rise of 'third wave' language-based therapies such as ACT and Mindfulness, sheltering under the CBT banner.

PAUL KELLY trained as a clinical psychologist in Birmingham. He was involved in setting up the West Midlands Community and Critical Psychology Interest Group and the Midlands Psychology Group. He was also active in the Irish Mental Health Forum. Since returning to live in Ireland in 2004, he has been working as a psychologist in the Student Health Centre at University College Dublin and is involved in the Irish Critical Psychology Network.

JOHN LEES is a registered counselling practitioner and is responsible for developing curricula and research at the University of Leeds. He is also Co-ordinator of Quality Assurance, Learning and Research at Crossfields Institute: Education, Training and Research inspired by Anthroposophy. He has written various articles on such themes as anthroposophy, practitioner research, and clinical practice in the field of counselling and psychotherapy.

DEL LOEWENTHAL has a chair at Roehampton University, directs its Research Centre for Therapeutic Education, and practises as an existential-analytic psychotherapist. Publications include *Post-modernism for Psychotherapists* (co-author, Robert Snell, Routledge, 2003), *What is Psychotherapeutic Research* (co-editor, David Winter, Karnac, 2006), and *Case Studies in Relational Research* (Palgrave Macmillan, 2007). Del is founding editor of the *European Journal of Psychotherapy and Counselling*, and guest editor of a special issue of *Philosophical Practice* on post-existentialism (both from Routledge).

MISHKA LYSACK Ph.D. RSW RMFT is an assistant professor in the Faculty of Social Work and an adjunct assistant professor in the Department of Psychiatry in the Faculty of Medicine at the University of Calgary, teaching social work practice, environmental issues, and family therapy. Mishka is a *Clinical Member* and *Approved Supervisor* of AAMFT (American Association for Marriage and Family Therapy) and a *Clinical Teaching Member* of AFTA (American Academy of Family Therapy).

DR WARREN MANSELL is Senior Lecturer at the University of Manchester and a Chartered Clinical Psychologist within primary and secondary care. He co-chairs the scientific committee for the British Association of Behavioural and Cognitive Psychotherapies annual conference. He has authored over 40 publications, and is currently evaluating a cognitive model of bipolar disorder, exploring the utility and validity of a transdiagnostic CBT approach, and uses Perceptual Control Theory as an integrative self-regulatory framework.

JANE MILTON studied medicine at Cambridge University and at the London Hospital Medical College. Her psychiatric training was in Bristol, Oxford, and the Maudsley Hospital, and she was a consultant psychiatrist in psychotherapy, first at King's College Hospital and then at the Tavistock Clinic. A training analyst at the Institute of Psychoanalysis, she is now in full-time psychoanalytic practice. Jane is also involved in psychoanalytic development in eastern Europe.

PAUL MOLONEY is a counselling psychologist working in an adult learning disability service in Telford, UK. His critical perspective upon Psychology as a discipline has been strongly informed by his experiences of growing up and working within inner-city communities – particularly in Birmingham.

FRED NEWMAN is co-founder of the East Side Institute for Group and Short Term Psychotherapy, a psychotherapist, playwright, and director. He received his Ph.D. in analytic philosophy and the foundations of mathematics from Stanford University, and his writings on psychotherapy, politics, culture, and social change are philosophically informed (e.g. *Performance of a Lifetime: A Practical-Philosophical Guide to the Joyous Life* and, with Lois Holzman, *Unscientific Psychology* and *The End of Knowing*.

PROFESSOR STEPHEN PALMER Ph.D. is Founder Director of the Centre for Stress Management. He is Honorary Professor of Psychology at City University, and Consultant Director of the New Zealand Centre for Cognitive Behavioural Therapy. He is a Chartered Psychologist, UKCP-registered psychotherapist (CBT and REBT), Albert Ellis Institute Certified Supervisor of REBT, and Fellow of the British Association for Counselling and Psychotherapy. His books include *Brief Cognitive Behaviour Therapy* (with Curwen and Ruddell, Sage, 2000).

DAVID PILGRIM Ph.D. is Professor of Mental Health Policy at the University of Central Lancashire. With a background in both clinical psychology and medical sociology, he has published widely on mental-health matters. His recent books include *Key Concepts in Mental Health* (Sage, 2005) and *A Sociology of Mental Health and Illness* (Open University Press, 2005), written with Anne Rogers, which won the BMA medical book of the year award for 2006.

GILLIAN PROCTOR (D. Clin. Psych.) is a Clinical Psychologist with Bradford and Airedale teaching PCT mental-health team, and an honorary research fellow at the Centre for Citizenship and Community Mental Health, University of Bradford. Ethics, politics, and power are Gillian's special interests, and her publications include *The Dynamics of Power in Counselling and Psychotherapy* (author; PCCS Books, 2002), and *Politicising the Person-centred Approach: An Agenda for Social Change* (co-editor; PCCS Books, 2006).

FRANK C. RICHARDSON is professor of educational psychology at the University of Texas. He has authored numerous articles and books in the areas of psychotherapy theory and the philosophy of social science, including *Stress, Sanity, and Survival*, *Re-envisioning Psychology*, and *Critical Thinking About Psychology*, and has recently served as president of Division 24 (Theoretical and Philosophical Psychology) of the American Psychological Association.

ANDREW SAMUELS is Professor of Analytical Psychology, University of Essex, holding visiting chairs at New York, London, and Roehampton Universities. An early UKCP Honorary Fellow and co-founder of PCSR, he works in clinical practice with a blend of post-Jungian, relational psychoanalytic, and humanistic approaches, and internationally as a political consultant. Andrew was an 'Expert Reader' of the draft National Occupational Standards for Psychoanalytic/Psychodynamic Psychotherapy. Translated into 19 languages, his books include the recent award-winning *Politics on the Couch* (Karnac).

ROBERT SNELL is an analytic psychotherapist in private practice, an Honorary Senior Research Fellow at Roehampton University, School of Psychology and Therapeutic Studies, and a group and individual therapist in Psychological and Counselling Services at the University of Sussex. He is the author of *Théophile Gautier: A Romantic Critic of the Visual Arts* (Oxford University Press, 1982), and co-author, with Del Loewenthal, of *Postmodernism for Psychotherapists: A Critical Reader* (Routledge, 2003).

HENDERIKUS J. STAM is a Professor of Psychology at the University of Calgary, Alberta, Canada. Among positions he has held, he is a former President of the Society for Theoretical and Philosophical Psychology (Division 24) of the American Psychological Association. The editor of *Theory & Psychology*, he has written numerous papers on foundational and conceptual issues in psychology as well as topics in the history of psychology.

TOM STRONG is a psychologist and counsellor-educator with the Division of Applied Psychology, University of Calgary. His research focuses on the collaborative, critical, and practical potentials afforded by discursive approaches to psychotherapy. Co-editor (with David Paré) of *Furthering Talk* (Kluwer Academic/Plenum), and co-author (with Andy Lock) of the forthcoming *Social Constructionism: Sources and Stirrings in Theory and Practice* (Cambridge University Press). More information on Tom's work can be found on his website at: http://www.acs.ucalgary.ca/~strongt

OLGA SUTHERLAND is a psychologist and is working as a post-doctoral fellow in the Couple and Family Therapy Program at the University of Guelph in Canada. She is using conversation analysis to examine psychotherapy processes and outcomes. Olga's doctoral research focussed on collaboration in the therapeutic relationship.

PHILIP THOMAS is Professor of Philosophy, Diversity, & Mental Health, University of Central Lancashire. He is also chair of Sharing Voices Bradford, a community-development project working with the city's Black and Minority Ethnic communities in the field of mental health. Phil worked for over 20 years as a consultant psychiatrist, and is well known for his writings with Pat Bracken on 'Postpsychiatry'. He is also a founder-member and co-chair of the Critical Psychiatry Network.

KEITH TUDOR is a registered psychotherapist practising in Sheffield, where he is a founding Director of Temenos (www.temenos.ac.uk) which runs a course offering a critical engagement and dialogue between person-centred therapy and cognitive behaviour therapy. Keith is a widely published author/editor, including five books on the person-centred approach, its psychology and therapy. He is series editor of 'Advancing Theory in Therapy' (Routledge), and is Honorary Fellow in the School of Health, Liverpool John Moores University.

DAVID A. WINTER is Professor of Clinical Psychology and Programme Director of the Doctorate in Clinical Psychology at the University of Hertfordshire; and Head of Barnet Clinical Psychology Services in Barnet, Enfield, and Haringey Mental Health NHS Trust. He has published extensively on personal-construct psychology and psychotherapy research. David is a Fellow of the British Psychological Society, and has chaired its Psychotherapy Section, as well as the Experiential Constructivist Section and Research Committee of the UKCP.

ROBERT L. WOOLFOLK – professor of psychology and philosophy, Rutgers University and visiting professor of psychology, Princeton University. With numerous papers and several books on psychotherapy, psychopathology, and psychology's philosophical foundations, and over thirty years' clinical practice, Rob has sought to integrate the scientific and humanistic psychotherapy traditions. He previously edited the *Journal of Theoretical and Philosophical Psychology*, authored *The Cure of Souls*, and co-authored *Stress, Sanity, and Survival* and *Treating Somatization: A Cognitive-Behavioral Approach*.

INDEX